CW00727667

POETRY AND ECOLOGY
IN THE AGE OF MILTON AND MARVELL

Literary and Scientific Cultures
of Early Modernity

Series editors:

Mary Thomas Crane, Department of English, Boston College, USA
Henry Turner, Department of English, University of Wisconsin-Madison, USA

This series provides a forum for groundbreaking work on the relations between literary and scientific discourses in Europe, during a period when both fields were in a crucial moment of historical formation. We welcome proposals for books that address the many overlaps between modes of imaginative writing typical of the sixteenth and seventeenth centuries – poetics, rhetoric, prose narrative, dramatic production, utopia – and the vocabularies, conceptual models, and intellectual methods of newly emergent "scientific" fields such as medicine, astronomy, astrology, alchemy, psychology, mapping, mathematics, or natural history. In order to reflect the nature of intellectual inquiry during the period, the series is interdisciplinary in orientation and publishes monographs, edited collections, and selected critical editions of primary texts relevant to an understanding of the mutual implication of literary and scientific epistemologies.

Other titles in the series:

Francis Bacon and the Refiguring of Early Modern Thought
Essays to Commemorate The Advancement of Learning *(1605–2005)*
Edited by Julie Robin Solomon and Catherine Gimelli Martin

Ways of Knowing in Early Modern Germany
Johannes Praetorius as a Witness to his Time
Gerhild Scholz Williams

Food in Shakespeare
Early Modern Dietaries and the Plays
Joan Fitzpatrick

Science, Literature and Rhetoric in Early Modern England
Edited by Juliet Cummins and David Burchell

Robert Greene's Planetomachia *(1585)*
Nandini Das

Poetry and Ecology
in the Age of Milton and Marvell

DIANE KELSEY McCOLLEY
Rutgers University, USA

ASHGATE

© Diane Kelsey McColley 2007

All rights reserved. No part of this publication may be reproduced, stored in a retrieval system or transmitted in any form or by any means, electronic, mechanical, photocopying, recording or otherwise without the prior permission of the publisher.

Diane Kelsey McColley has asserted her moral right under the Copyright, Designs and Patents Act, 1988, to be identified as the author of this work.

Published by
Ashgate Publishing Limited
Gower House
Croft Road
Aldershot
Hampshire GU11 3HR
England

Ashgate Publishing Company
Suite 420
101 Cherry Street
Burlington, VT 05401-4405
USA

Ashgate website: http://www.ashgate.com

British Library Cataloguing in Publication Data
McColley, Diane Kelsey, 1934-
Poetry and ecology in the age of Milton and Marvell. – (Literary and scientific cultures of early modernity)
    1. English poetry – Early modern, 1500-1700 – History and criticism 2. Nature in literature
    3. Ecology in literature 4. Science in literature 5. Technology in literature
    I. Title
    821.4'0936

Library of Congress Cataloging-in-Publication Data
McColley, Diane Kelsey, 1934-
    Poetry and ecology in the age of Milton and Marvell / by Diane Kelsey McColley.
    p. cm.
    Includes bibliographical references.
    ISBN-13: 978-0-7546-6048-4 (alk. paper)
    1. English poetry—Early modern, 1500-1700—History and criticism. 2. Literature and science—Great Britain—History—17th century. 3. Great Britain—Intellectual life—17th century. 4. Marvell, Andrew, 1621-1678—Knowledge—Natural history. 5. Milton, John, 1608-1674—Knowledge—Natural history. 6. Philosophy of nature in literature. 7. Ecology in literature. 8. Nature in literature. 9. Environmental policy in literature. I. Title.

  PR545.S33M33 2007
  821'.70936—dc22

2007003761

ISBN: 978-0-7546-6048-4

Printed and bound in Great Britain by Antony Rowe Ltd, Chippenham, Wiltshire.

In memory of Fay Porter Nowell

*to June and Alan in the shared love of poetry
and "Trees, flowers & herbs; birds, beasts & stones"*

and for

*Joschka,
Kelsey and Katie,
Max and Stuart
Lauren and Isabelle
Jae, Rowan, and Sachaa
Eden Fe, Peter, Eli, and Lucy Jean
Cassandra and Amalia,
Ian and Genevieve Joy,
Zhenya, Jacob, Julia, Clara, and Svetlana*

Contents

List of Plates

Note on Editions and Orthography

For the most frequently quoted poets I have used the following editions: for Milton, primarily John Leonard's gently modernized *Milton: The Complete Poems*, which retains older spellings and puctuation when needed for wordplay or prosody, supplemented by Merritt Hughes's and Roy Flannagan's editions; for Marvell, Elizabeth Donno's *Andrew Marvell: The Complete Poems*, with occasional changes in punctuation from Nigel Smith's recent *The Poems of Andrew Marvell*, which provides a plenitude of information, both historical and poetic; for Vaughan, Alan Rudrum's *Henry Vaughan: The Complete Poems* (revised edition, 1983); for Margaret Cavendish, *Poems and Fancies*, London, 1653. Other modern editions used may be found in the bibliography.

Much of the less-known poetry and early modern prose is from seventeenth-century editions. I have kept quotations in the original spelling, but for the sake of correspondences of eye and ear have conformed certain letters such as *u* and *v* or *I* and *J* to modern fonts. Italics, abundant in texts whose writers habitually underscored nouns in general, have been preserved only when used to indicate quotations or special emphasis. I have silently corrected typographical errors, but, unlike Mr. Bentley, only obvious ones.

Preface

This book was supported by a Research Fellowship at the Huntington Library from the Mellon Foundation, an external leave grant from Rutgers, the State University of New Jersey, and a short-term fellowship from the William Andrews Clark Memorial Library and Center for Seventeenth-and Eighteenth-Century Studies. I am grateful to the staffs of these libraries, especially Robert Ritchie, Susi Krasnoo, Romaine Ahlstrom, Christopher Adde, Mona Noureldin, David Zeidberg, and Aaron Greenlee.

Friends for whose conversational support of this project I am grateful include, alphabetically, Cheryl Clark, Olivann and John Hobbie, Carolyn A. McColley, Sherwood Parker, Elaine and Michael Zickler, and innumerable colleagues, among them Joan Blythe, Gardener Campbell, Richard DuRocher, Karen Edwards, Wendy Furman-Adams, Ann Gulden, Ken Hiltner, Al Labriola, John Leonard, Barbara Lewalski, Stella Revard, Alan Rudrum, John Tanner, Jeffrey Theis, William Shullenberger, June Sturrock, and others included in the Bibliography. Huntington Library fellows and readers provided lively discussions, including Kevis Goodman, Barbara Donegon, Jesse Matz, Christine Krueger, Al Brownmuller, Ted Miller, Richard Kaeuper, John Demaray, and John M. Steadman. Carolyn Parker helped with library errands at Rutgers. Also, in memoriam, I thank Arthur E. Barker, Anita Parker Purves, Florence Morris Thornberry, and Lydia Vandivere Kelsey.

In the midst of writing this book I took time off for brain surgery, which provided a personal perspective on the relation or unity of body and mind. I would like to thank Dr. James P. Chandler of the Department of Neurosurgery at Northwestern Memorial Hospital for his skill and kindness. As my daughter Margaret marvelled, "He had my mother's brain in his hands." Thanks too for many comforts and joys then and now to Susanna McColley and Russell Brown, Margaret McColley, Teresa McColley and Dennis Haydon, Rebecca and David Wilk, Carolyn and Mark Bruguera, Rob McColley and Heather Winters.

Diane Kelsey McColley

Acknowledgments

I wish to thank the Huntington Library in San Marino, California, for the use of its extraordinary rare books library and for permission to include nine of the ten illustrations in this book. For permission to include the tenth, "Orpheus Playing to the Animals," my thanks to the Rijksmuseum, Amsterdam. I am also grateful to the publishers for permission to include excerpts from the following publications: "Ecology and Empire," in *Milton and the Imperial Vision*, edited by Balachandra Rajan and Elizabeth Sauer: Pittsburgh, Duquesne University Press, 1999; "'All in All': The Individuality of Creatures in *Paradise Lost*," in *'All in All': Unity, Diversity, and the Miltonic Perspective*, edited by Charles W. Durham and Kristin A. Pruitt: Selinsgrove: Susquehanna University Press and London: Associated University Presses, 1999; "Milton's Environmental Epic: Creature Kinship and the Language of *Paradise Lost*," in *Beyond Nature Writing: Expanding the Boundaries of Ecocriticism*, edited by Karla Armbruster and Kathleen R. Wallace: Charlottesville and London: University Press of Virginia, 2001; and "Water, Wood, and Stone: The Living Earth in Poems of Vaughan and Milton," in *Of Paradise and Light: Essays on Henry Vaughan and John Milton in Honor of Alan Rudrum*, edited by Donald R. Dickson and Holly Faith Nelson: Newark, Delaware: University of Delaware Press, 2004.

Introduction

The State of Nature and the Problem of Language

a single raindrop irrigates the tongue

Derek Walcott, *Origins*

In seventeenth-century England the beginnings of empirical science and an awareness of what we now call "ecological" issues coincided with so remarkable a flowering of poetry that it is often called the golden age of English verse. At the same time, the language of natural history and philosophy began to be separated from poetry and other kinds of speech in order to banish what Francis Bacon called "The idols and false notions that are now in possession of the human understanding."[1] The resulting disciplines made possible the relief from human suffering and the prolongation of life provided by medical science, along with innumerable other benefits, and also the unrestrained technology and commerce that eventually produced the current environmental predicament.

The poets discussed here both embraced new knowledge of nature and recognized the costs of power over nature intemperately used. Reading their works alongside those of seventeenth-century writers we might now call proto-scientists, developers, and conservationists, one is struck by insights that went unheeded and language that is still vital and sometimes prophetic: seeing nature as habitats and watersheds, rich in connected lives and vulnerable to misuse; regarding plants and animals not only as providers of human sustenance, pleasure, and wisdom, but also as fellow creatures whose lives belong to themselves; weaving the fabric of language in ways that enable the mind and the senses to perceive the wovenness of the natural world. By close reading of poems within the contexts of early modern natural history, philosophy, and theology, I hope to show the importance of this dimension of early modern studies and to persuade those who think that pre-Romantic and pre-Darwinian poetry, especially if it is monotheistically religious, is intrinsically unecological, or that "ecocriticism" of it is intrinsically anachronistic, to reconsider.

The modern term *ecology* describes the work of these poets better than the classical and early modern *economy*. Both come from the Greek *oikos,* or household, but economy's other root is *nomos,* law, while ecology's is *logos,* word, knowledge, reason, or the expression of thought. Xenophon's *Oeconomicus* concerns rules for the efficient management of an estate; "ecology" suggests that our use of knowledge needs to be good for the whole household of living things.

---

1   Bacon, *Aphorisms* I: XXXVIII, in *The New Organon*, ed. Anderson, 47.

John Milton, Andrew Marvell, Henry Vaughan, Margaret Cavendish, Thomas Traherne, Anne Finch, and other early modern poets shared an impulse to give responsible attention to the earth and to non-human creatures. They were in various ways vitalists, or animist (as opposed to mechanist) materialists, monists rather dualists, who held matter and spirit to be inseparable, at a time when the old polarities of God and nature, matter and spirit, and body and soul were intensely debated. Among modes of thought that wedged these dyads apart were uses of allegory that detach types from particulars; aspects of neo-Platonism that place truth in a transcendent realm; theology (much disputed) that regards other creatures as servants of the human body and soul; the kinds of natural philosophy that treated animate beings as mindless mechanisms; and the kinds of experiment and classification that separated non-human creatures from each other and from human empathy.

In bringing together these monistic poems, I hope to show that ecological wisdom was already present and is still valuably operative in them and to illustrate ways that their language not only expresses thought and perception but can help form and integrate our capacities to perceive, consider, and speak of the natural world.

The state of nature in early modern England

Seventeenth-century England had the same "environmental" problems we have today, some age-old, others produced by new technology: deforestation, air pollution, confinement of rivers and streams, draining of wetlands, overbuilding, toxic mining, maltreatment of animals, uses of land that destroy habitats and dispossess the poor. Human beings and other beings have always manipulated nature, but these problems were accelerated by increased power over nature without a sufficient ethic or polity to temper this power. John Evelyn wrote in 1661, shortly after the restoration of Charles II, that "it will become our Senators . . . that they will consult as well the State of the Natural, as the Politick Body of this Great Nation . . . since, without their mutual harmony, and well-being, there can nothing prosper, or arrive at its desired perfection."[2] This advice has gone largely unheeded.

Many seventeenth-century poets did heed the "Natural Body" of the nation and the world. Most of those included here have close links to natural history and philosophy: Henry Vaughan was a medical doctor and his brother Thomas an experimental hermeticist; Margaret Cavendish knew Descartes and Hobbes and spoke to the Royal Society; Milton corresponded with Bacon's admirer Henry Oldenburg, probably met Galileo and certainly regretted his confinement and censoring, and as Karen Edwards and others have shown, had detailed knowledge of natural history.[3] These poets both embraced advances in the knowledge of nature and warned against intemperate applications of it.

---

2   Evelyn, *Fumifugium: Or, The Inconveniency of the Smoake of London dissipated* (1661), 23.

3   Edwards, "Milton's Reformed Animals," 128; see also Edwards' *Milton and the Natural World*, which I have reviewed with other books in "Milton and Nature: Greener Readings."

The chief argument for experimental knowledge was the hope of relieving human suffering and prolonging life. The poets in this study wrote at a time when, Louis Schwartz tells us, "an upper-class married woman stood approximately a one-in-four chance of dying in childbed during her fertile years,"[4] and many of them wrote poems on death in childbirth and the deaths of children. In his earliest-written published English lyric poem, "On the Death of a Fair Infant Dying of a Cough," seventeen-year-old John Milton addresses his sister's dead child:

> O fairest flower no sooner blown but blasted,
> Soft silken primrose fading timelessly,
> Summer's chief honour if thou hadst outlasted
> Bleak Winter's force that made thy blossom dry. . . .

Soon followed "An Epitaph on the Marchioness of Winchester," who lived "Summers three times eight save one" and died along with her stillborn child. Milton experienced the deaths following childbirth of two of his own wives (one of them the "late espoused saint" of Sonnet XIX) and their newborn children, and also of his only son. Lycidas and Epitaphium Damonis mourn the deaths of young friends. Among the many seventeenth-century poems about the frequency and pain of early death are Ben Jonson's epigrams on the deaths of his first two children; Anne Bradstreet's memorial poem to her year-and-a-half old grandchild; and Donne's Anniversaries, "Nocturnal upon St. Lucy's Day," "Since she whom I loved," and other obsequies.[5] Marvell in "The Picture of Little T. C. in a Prospect of Flowers" exhorts the child to whose beauty "every verdant thing" responds, to "Gather the flowers, but spare the buds" lest Flora "Nip in the blossom all our hopes and thee." When in "Misery" Henry Vaughan writes "I am Earth," he is miserable. Such experiences make nature difficult to idealize or sentimentalize. These poets acknowledge feelingly that the life of the body can be painful and brief and the workings of nature can be negligent, malign, cruel, discordant, and insufficient.

The theological explanation of such suffering was that nature is tragically damaged, as Milton writes in "At a Solemn Musick," since

> disproportioned sin
> Jarred against Nature's chime, and with harsh din
> Broke the fair music that all creatures made
> To their great Lord, whose love their motion swayed
> In perfect diapason, whilst they stood
> In first obedience, and their state of good.
>
> O may we soon again renew that song,
> And keep in tune with Heav'n. . . . [6]

---

4 Schwartz, "'Scarce-well-lighted flame,'" 200.

5 Louis Schwartz in "'Conscious Terrors'" recounts the dangers of seventeenth-century obstetrics and argues that Milton's experience as a witness of suffering and death associated with childbirth profoundly affected his epic's wrestling with the ways of God.

6 Milton, "On the Death of a Fair Infant"; Jonson, *Epigrams* XXII and XLV, "On My First Daughter" and "On My First Son"; Vaughan, "Misery"; Milton, "At a Solemn Music" ll. 19–26.

The reparations of the state of nature that fuller knowledge might be able to provide depend in part on the reparation of the moral state of man.

In *The New Organon* (1620), having noted the powerful influence of the recent discoveries of "printing, gunpowder, and the magnet," Francis Bacon distinguishes three "grades of ambition in mankind":

> The first is of those who desire to extend their own power in their native country, a vulgar and degenerate kind. The second is of those who labor to extend the power and dominion of their country among men. This certainly has more dignity, though not less covetousness. But if a man endeavor to establish and extend the power and dominion of the human race itself over the universe, his ambition (if ambition it can be called) is without doubt a more wholesome thing and a more noble than the other two. Now the empire of man over things depends wholly on the arts and sciences. For we cannot command nature except by obeying her.

To those who object to the possible "debasement of arts and sciences to purposes of wickedness, luxury, and the like" he replies that the same may be said of any good thing: "Only let the human race recover that right over nature which belongs to it by divine bequest, and let power be given it; the exercise thereof will be governed by sound reason and true religion."[7] Bacon's acknowledgment of the need to obey nature somewhat mitigates his imperial language, but the "empire of man" has not notably been guided by "sound reason and true religion," the definitions of which would be hard to agree upon both then and now.

The Baconian program of empirical science required a rational, explicit, unambiguous language. John Wilkins, in *An Essay towards a Real Character and a Philosophical Language,* intended to restore the univocality lost in the Tower of Babel.[8] He hoped that his "real character," a non-alphabetical system of signs, and his system of classification would give commerce, evangelism, and experimental science a global language free of the vagaries of geographic origin, change, metaphor, and grammatical irregularity. His "philosophical language" provides "[t]he reducing of all things and notions, to such kind of Tables as . . . would prove the shortest and plainest way for the attainment of real Knowledge, that hath been yet offered to the World." Wilkins' "Real Knowledge" depends on a supposition that visible things, and even the nature of God, constitute a body of ascertainable facts capable of translation into unchanging and unambiguous language. His "Tables" divide living creatures into "things" by, for example, number of legs, method of reproduction, and kinds of usefulness to human beings.[9]

---

7   Bacon, *Aphorisms* I:CXXIX, *The New Organon*, 118–19. Descartes's *Discourse on Method* (1641; ed. Robinet, 97) states similarly that if we knew the elements and substances around us well we could become as masters and possessors of nature for infinite uses, but principally for human health.

8   Wilkins, *An Essay* (1668), b verso, b3, 162–8.

9   Potentially, Keith Thomas argues, classification would provide "more details, more objectivity," and become "less man-centered" (*Man and the Natural World*, 52). But Bacon's stated motive is not only empirical but imperial.

When John Milton exposes the demonic potentialities of an ambition to subjugate the earth, the speakers are Satan and Mammon. Rational science itself is not the problem; an aim of conquest and control does not make good science, and Milton and many other poets value reason and accurate knowledge of nature. The problem is the ambition to control the elements and turn earth, water, plants, and animals into resources without respect for natural processes and for beings other than human.[10] "[D]ominion of the human race itself over the universe" to be achieved with the aid of a static taxonomy is the reverse of the relation of ecology and poetry.

World pictures: Allegory, mechanism, and entering in

Among the "idols" of the past was a hierarchical and emblematic cosmos, discussed for example by Arthur O. Lovejoy in *The Great Chain of Being*, C. S. Lewis in *The Discarded Image*, and E. M. W. Tillyard in *The Elizabethan World Picture*. This idea of a beautiful and instructive natural order, with correspondences among all levels of being—even after Copernicus had cast human perceptions in doubt—provided poetry with infinite richness of image and analogy and also underwrote hierarchical attitudes toward plants and animals, men and women, and political and religious structures.[11] It is easy to apply those supposed essences unjustly. Using living things as metaphors can reduce their reality in the minds of readers: lions are not lions, but courage or wrath, and roses lose their particular faces to become emblems of perishability that exhort us to seize the day. The poets discussed here often retained emblematic, allegorical, and typological[12] connotations, but increasingly subordinated figurative meanings to observation, questioned or discarded oppressive hierarchal assumptions, and expressed specific and affinitive perception of actual animals, plants, elements, and processes. Even overtly emblematic poems like Vaughan's "Cock-Crowing" or Herbert's "The Flower" give empathetic attention to the living bird or blossom.

Literary critics have often invoked dualistic allegorical oppositions, supposing for example that Milton opposed man, reason, and heaven to woman, passion, and earth. This habit has gradually been reformed. John M. Steadman writes that Milton's epics "attempt (as far as possible) to depict the ideals of earthly and celestial happiness literally." Mindele Anne Treip expands the definition of allegory while freeing it from simple dualisms and automatic applications, and finds that Milton's Edenic

---

10 Writers who have traced the history of human dominion over nature include Clarence Glacken in *Traces on the Rhodian Shore*; William Leiss in *The Domination of Nature*; Keith Thomas in *Man and the Natural World*; and Richard H. Grove in *Green Imperialism*.

11 Gordon Teskey studies uses of allegory to support the power of the state in *Allegory and Violence*. On Milton's mitigation of marital hierarchy, see McColley, *Milton's Eve*, and Pruitt, *Gender and the Power of Relationship*.

12 Typology applies people and events from the Hebrew Bible to future ones, primarily to the life of Christ but also to others including the reader or viewer. Mindele Anne Treip writes that in Milton's typology the Edenic episodes are "inspired amplification of parts of the Bible" corresponding to the "inclusive concept of allegorism" of Protestants such as Luther and Calvin (*Allegorical Poetics and the Epic*, 225).

episodes "represent an imaginative, semi-fictive entering into the quality and texture of the invoked biblical experience" that is not a matter of multi-leveled "simultaneous readings" but is "experiential." Catherine Gimelli Martin finds Milton dismantling and reconstituting allegory by disrupting the ancient dualisms dividing matter and spirit, the rational and the mystical, empirical observation and divine revelation; instead, these common oppositions monistically coalesce.[13]

These coalescences and enterings-in, I would add, apply to vitalist poets' representations of nature; allegorical associations are subordinated to mimesis, informed by empirical observation. In Milton's Garden the elephant entertaining Adam and Eve (4. 346) may still suggest temperance and piety but "make[s] them mirth" by being himself. When Milton describes the migratory flight of "the prudent Crane" (7. 429–31), his sounds and rhythms let us share the cranes' sensations and hear the sound of wings. While the emblem of prudence remains, the allegory thins, and we see what the crane sees and join its purposeful attention.

In contrast to "the Elizabethan world picture," however, seventeenth-century natural philosophers developed the mathematical conception of the universe that E. J. Dijksterhuis calls "the mechanization of the world picture," and that made modern science and technology possible. Numerical descriptions of the cosmos from ancient times are best known in the Pythagorean tradition of the literal harmony of the spheres,[14] a conception compatible with the system of cosmic correspondences. But in the seventeenth century, mathematical formulations, culminating in Newton's *Principia* (1687), emerged as the basis of the physical sciences—"the whole science of inanimate nature, chemistry and astronomy as well as physics"[15]—and infinitely advanced the possibilities of human power over the physical world, for better and for worse.[16] The liberation of physical knowledge from the bonds of speculation and superstition gave us the beginnings of modern physics, chemistry, and biology. At the same time, the idea of a mechanical order that can only be expressed mathematically is, as Clarence Glacken says, "far removed from the bright and colorful beauties of external nature."[17] And when the mechanical description is applied to animate life, the relation between human beings and other beings becomes, even less than in an emblematic cosmos, a relation of love.

These "world pictures" need not be polarized in interpreting poems. But for vitalists, who objected to the separation of matter and spirit in natural philosophy and theology, "inanimate nature" is a fiction; all matter is living and, most explicitly

---

13 Steadman, *Milton and the Renaissance Hero*, 186; Triep, *Allegorical Poetics and the Epic*, 225; Martin, *The Ruins of Allegory*.

14 This tradition and its effects in poetry are elegantly set forth by S. K. Heninger, Jr., in *Touches of Sweet Harmony: Pythagorean Cosmology and Renaissance Poetics*.

15 Dijksterhuis, 4–5.

16 Carolyn Merchant contends that "the mechanistic worldview . . . replaced the Renaissance worldview of nature as a living organism with a nurturing earth at its center" so that "[t]he parts of matter, like the parts of machines, were dead, passive, and inert" (*Radical Ecology*, 49).

17 Glacken, 391.

in Milton's theology, derived from the substance of God,[18] and cannot be rightly known when we break "the fair music that all creatures made."

The plan of the book

Each chapter contains close readings of seventeenth-century poems in their historical contexts of natural philosophy, proto-science, developments in technology and their effects, and ethical and theological thought about the use, care, and enjoyment of the natural world. I begin with Marvell's "Upon Appleton House" because the poem concerns habitats, not just a well-managed estate; because Marvell treats nature both emblematically and literally; because he constantly jostles assumptions of hierarchy and enriches, renovates, and startles our ideas and perceptions of nature; and because, like David Abram and other ecological philosophers, Marvell notes that while we are perceiving other kinds of beings, they are perceiving us. The two ensuing chapters concern habitats and their destruction, show how the language of technology began to change the way people spoke and thought about the earth, and discuss poets' responses to the exploitation and pollution of earth, woods, water, and air. Chapters 4, 5, and 6 concern the poetry of plants and animals in the contexts of natural history, philosophy, theology, and ethics. The final chapter discusses Milton's epics as prophetic for his time and ours of "ecological" sensibilities and responsibilities. Each of these chapters shows how the language of poems promotes perception of nature and a sense of connection within it and argues implicitly for the value of literary studies in an increasingly technological world. The poets considered in them, not by denying figurative meanings but by insisting on the actualities of their origins in the natural world, united matter and spirit in their poems.[19] They welcomed empirical investigation for its accuracy of perception but opposed the pursuit of conquest and absolute control. Their poems combine empathy for living things and a sense of what Glacken calls "organic interrelations on the earth"[20] with perceptive observation and organic language—that is, language responsive, in sound and form as well as image and thought, to the lives of plants, animals, elements, and places—which can help the way we speak and the earth we care for heal each other.

The dilemma of language

A few years ago, I attended a conference on Literature and the Environment at which a conferee protested that human beings cannot talk about nature without laying claim to it. Language always separates us from what we give names to. It always appropriates. We were left speechless. The term "environment" is an example; it puts

---

18 Studies of seventeenth-century monism, vitalism, or animist materialism include Rumrich, *Matter of Glory* and "Milton's God and the Matter of Chaos"; Fallon, *Milton among the Philosophers*; Rogers, *The Matter of Revolution*; Cummins, "Milton's God and the Matter of Creation."

19 I am indebted, as ever, to Arthur E. Barker, for planting the seed of this insight.

20 Glacken, 393.

us in the center and sets us apart. How can words put us into right relation with the natural world?

June Sturrock ponders the problem in "Like Swallows":

Swallow,
I read
"Like swallows,"
And forgetting
Word, image, construct,
Remembered how last summer,
Living bird,
You swooped and soared
All day at the hunt,
All the air full

Of the bright arcs
Of your tracings, skimmer,
Skater through summer,
Singing your frantic song
Up, up on the high wire.

Airborn, air feeds you;
Light rules your matings,
Comings, goings,
Only in death
The dark earth holds you.

Real bird, departed bird,
Maker of flight from frail
Bone and feather,
Own end,
Liver, dier,

Words undo you
Cage you in quotation marks.
"Like swallows."[21]

Readers sometimes speak of "capturing" things in words, and that is a problem this poem voices and avoids; it expresses delight in the remembered rhythms of the swallow's flight with a sense of kindred vitality, creativity, vulnerability, and mortality. But one may not cage the poem in these abstractions any more than the poem cages the free bird, which is its "Own end" as we are ours.

One way we can learn to speak without appropriation is by listening to poets' ever-fresh particularity and responsive form. A living earth needs a living language. For the French philosopher of perception Maurice Merleau-Ponty, the inability to create new language is a form of aphasia: "[S]peech puts up a new sense, if it is

---

21 Sturrock, by permission of the author.

authentic speech."[22] His renunciation of a mechanist theory of language, and his advocacy of expression arising spontaneously from the perceptual experience of the body in the world, has much in common with the practice of vitalist poets. Language that represents connected beings in responsive and connected words is the kind of language I call "ecological." Poetry also has its musical or mathematical beauties, the forms, meters, and rhythms Milton called his "numbers," which correspond with the images and motions of living things and can open our minds and senses to the lives described and enter the ways we speak of them.

The poets considered here developed a practice of attentive empathy that counters allegorical, mechanical, instrumental, and commercial appropriation. But "empathy" raises the problem of imposing human emotions and intentions on other species.[23] Careful poets draw a careful line between sympathetic affinity and the falsification of identity.

Empathy and the pathetic fallacy

John Ruskin's phrase "pathetic fallacy" has entered the language of criticism as a critique of the imposition of human emotions on non-human nature, but is often used without its philosophical context or the distinctions its coiner was making.

"Of the Pathetic Fallacy"[24] opens with an attack on "the use of the most objectionable words that were ever coined by the troublesomeness of metaphysicians,—namely, 'Objective,' and 'subjective.' " Ruskin proposes to dispose of the notion that certain "qualities of things . . . depend upon our perception of them" and are subjective, while others are intrinsic and objective.

> From these ingenious views the step is very easy to a farther opinion, that it does not much matter what things are in themselves, but only what they are to us; and that the only real truth of them is their appearance to, or effect upon, us. Such impertinence, carried to a Berkeleyan extreme, produces the solipsism that things only exist because we perceive or think them.

To counter this egotism Ruskin asserts that for example "the word 'Blue' does not mean the sensation caused by a gentian on the human eye, but it means the power of producing that sensation; and this power is always there, in the thing, whether we are there to experience it or not, and would remain there though there were not left a man on the face of the earth." The ecological part of Ruskin's idea is the principle of always-thereness, the independent being of the not-human things that we may misperceive solipsistically and so be wantonly disposed to destroy.

---

22 Merleau-Ponty, *Phenomenology of Perception*, 194.

23 Lawrence Buell warns that "facile empathy with the misery of the beast or the human . . . may be frustrated" and "simple affinity" false, and that we need to get "past such ethical rubrics as anthropocentric and ecocentric" in *Writing for an Endangered World*, 233 and 225.

24 Ruskin, *Modern Painters* (1856), in *The Works of John Ruskin* 5:201–20. "Pathetic" comes from the Greek παηγοορ, sensitive, from παηγορ, liable to suffer. Ruskin is not rejecting pathos but distinguishing between appropriate and inappropriate literary uses of it.

For nature poetry, Ruskin's tests of truth are partly accuracy of observation—flowers may in fact droop, whether in sympathy with human feelings or not; partly fitness to the occasion; and partly the appropriateness of form to image. Swiftness should be stated swiftly. Poetry for Ruskin is weak if it resorts to falsifications of nature; the strong poet can express passion in images that are true in themselves. Thus Homer of Castor and Pollux (Iliad 3. 243): "'But them, already, the life-giving earth possessed there in Lacedaemon, in the dear fatherland.' . . . The poet has to speak of the earth in sadness, but he will not let that sadness affect or change his thoughts of it. No; though Castor and Pollux be dead, yet the earth is our mother still, fruitful, life-giving." The earth is not required to bear our emotions because the dead return to her soil, yet we may, if we wish, see her repossessing her children, or grieving at the loss of the life she has given. Homer has committed no fallacy, and the pathos is left for us to feel.

In great and passionate poetry, Ruskin allows, "all feverish and wild fancy becomes just and true. Thus the destruction of Assyria cannot be contemplated firmly by a prophet of Israel. . . . 'Yea, the fir-trees rejoice at thee, and the cedars of Lebanon' . . . So, still more, the thought of the presence of Deity cannot be borne without this great astonishment. 'The mountains and the hills shall break forth before you into singing, and all the trees of the field shall clap their hands.' Isaiah 14.8 and 55.12." But such expressions must have sufficient cause, and "the dominion of Truth is entire, over this, as over every other natural and just state of the human mind."[25]

The careless use of the phrase "pathetic fallacy" misses Ruskin's philosophical point about "subjectivity" and "objectivity," which points beyond poetics. When we perceive something well, it both becomes part of us and remains itself. To divide the two is to reject the gift of consciousness or distance the "object" and so withhold our love.

Similarly, the language of poetry, the language of responsible science, and the language of moral and political philosophy are all necessary parts of public discourse. In *The Hedgehog, the Fox, and Magister's Pox: Mending the Gap between Science and the Humanities,* evolutionary paleontologist Stephen Jay Gould writes of science and the humanities,

> These two great endeavors of our soul and intellect work in different ways and cannot be morphed into one simple coherence . . . . But the two enterprises can lead us onward together, ineluctably yoked if we wish to maintain any hope for arrival at all, toward the common goal of human wisdom, achieved through the union of natural knowledge and creative art, two different but nonconflicting truths that, on this planet at least, only human beings can forge and nurture.[26]

---

25 Compare Arne Naess's conception of the ecological self, whose maturity is in the ability to identify intuitively with more and more kinds of life. ("Self-Realization" in Sessions, *Deep Ecology*, 225–39.)

26 Gould, 6. In Consilience: The Unity of Knowledge, evolutionary sociobiologist E.O. Wilson writes, "The greatest enterprise of the mind has always been and always will be the attempted linkage of the sciences and humanities. . . . Only fluencies across the boundaries will provide a clear view of the world as it really is, not as seen through the lens of ideologies and religious dogmas or commanded by myopic response to immediate need" (8, 13).

Scientists, whose unbiased findings a self-interested body politic too often ignores, and poets, nature's scribes, who resist imperial language and enrich our own, and the rest of us, whose daily speech expresses and affects our perception and use of the natural world, belong to a planetary conversation concerning the state of "the Natural" as well as "the Politick Body" of the nation of earth.

However, Wendell Berry argues that Wilson's belief "in the ultimate empirical explainability of everything" is a kind of scientific imperialism (*Life Is a Miracle*, 30–31).

Chapter 1

Perceiving Habitats
Marvell and the Language of
Sensuous Reciprocity

Andrew Marvell's *Upon Appleton House* is a good starting place because it is, for a start, about a place; because it carries ecological and political concerns we still share; because it gathers and transforms traditional topics or "places" of poetic invention—metaphorical, allegorical, emblematic, and typological, the latter largely from the Book of Genesis; because it weaves these together with observation of the actual place and its inhabitants; and because Marvell's playful language is serious, lightsome, resonant, witty, unsettling, and ever fresh. In this chapter, I offer a close reading of a poem that unsettles and richly reseeds language to enable new perceptions, and through the multiplicity of its connections invites the reader's mind to engage in ways of thinking and perceiving that are less linear than radial and resemble habitats and watersheds more than roads and rooms.

In the seventeenth century, thanks in part to the development of the lens, representations of nature changed. Astronomers recognized that the heavenly bodies are material things, and micrographers described the minute perfections of insects and plants; visual artists, preceded by such lovingly meticulous ones as Albrecht Dürer and Joris Hoefnagel,[1] grew increasingly exact; poets became more attentive to the actual lives of plants and animals, and some expressed a desire—impelled in England by deforestation, mining, the engineering of waterways and wetlands, and the ruination of fields, woods, and men by the Civil Wars—to restore the land after the patterns of Vergil's *Georgics* and the Garden of Eden.

At the same time, the glimmerings of a sense of habitat began to dawn, partly in response to global exploration. Samuel Purchas in 1614 explains the distribution of animals: "God hath appointed to every Creature his peculiar nature, and a natural instinct, to live in places most agreeing to his nature."[2] Poets began to see what John Ray called the Terraqueous Globe[3] as the living household of living things, providing not only sustenance but wisdom and enjoyment gained from their inherent qualities.

---

1   Hoefnagel (1542–?1601) was commissioned by Emperor Rudolf II to illustrated the work of Georg Bocskay, secretary and calligrapher to Ferdinand I, and provided detailed miniatures of fruits, flowers, insects, worms, and small animals for the *Mira calligraphiae monumenta*.

2   Purchas, *Pvrchas his Pilgrimage*, 727.

3   Ray, *Three Physico-Theological Discourses* (1693).

Andrew Marvell and John Milton were, in part, poets of habitat. Their poems harbor a rich variety and activity of other kinds of lives. John Rodman speaks of ecological consciousness as including "a style of coinhabitation that involves the knowledgeable, respectful, and restrained use of nature" and the conception that "one ought not to treat with disrespect or use as a mere means anything that has a *telos* or end of its own."[4] All living things need nourishment; the ethical question is how human beings can protect the valuable achievements of human culture while letting or helping the rest of nature unfold towards its own *telos*. This chapter concerns Andrew Marvell's contribution to the perception and language of an unfolding world. In *Upon Appleton House*, written in the wake of the civil wars, Marvell, who shunned dogmatic ideas and cannot be pinned down to a static political position, presents the good government of an estate he hyperbolizes as "paradise's only map," offering a balance of order and freedom for the land and the body politic and a model for the reparation of a postlapsarian natural world.

Georgic poetry is traditionally about cultivation, language, and ethics, with Vergil's *Georgics* as its model. The georgic ideal developed in seventeenth-century Britain as a moral and spiritual as well as an agricultural revival.[5] Marvell went further than most in perceiving the non-human occupants of a cultivated habitat as deserving to live for their own sakes and offering abundant perceptual experience that enlarges the human continuum of body, mind, and spirit. In *Upon Appleton House,* as in *Paradise Lost*, the Edenic model incorporates the georgic. Both concern the preservation of nature and the work of restoring the shattered land, in which part of the poet's work is awakening and reintegrating human perceptions. Marvell makes the estates of the Lord General Thomas Fairfax, who had led the victorious parliamentary army in the war that resulted in the temporary abolition of the monarchy, a republic of animate nature. Milton, supporter of civil and religious liberty, depicts God's garden, epitome of nature, as the domain of a human race whose calling was to dress and keep its pristine abundance—to care for and preserve it according to its nature, a vocation practiced in *Paradise Lost* as in no other version of the Genesis story, and practiced well but not for long.

Both Milton and Marvell recognized that not only do we perceive habitats and their inhabitants; other species perceive and respond to us. Like current poets such as Pattiann Rogers, W.S. Merwin, and Wendell Berry, they represent the earth as an *oikos*, a house for all species. Their poems create, through multiple connections, an ecological way of thinking. For both, habitat includes and is temperately managed by human beings, minimally in Milton's pristine Eden and at several levels at Marvell's Nunappleton, ranging from complete control to nearly wild freedom. Both use to some extent the language of vitalism, which John Rogers defines as "in its tamest manifestation the inseparability of body and soul and, in its boldest, the infusion of

---

4   Rodman, "Four Forms of Ecological Consciousness Reconsidered," in Sessions, ed., *Deep Ecology*, 126.

5   Anthony Low in *The Georgic Revolution* and essays collected by Michael Leslie and Timothy Raylor in *Culture and Cultivation in Early Modern England* trace this development.

all material substance with the power of reason and self-motion."[6] Both resist the doctrine that nature is made only for human use and teach temperance in the uses we make of it apart from the nurturing of perception and understanding.

Other poets, such as Abraham Cowley and Edmund Waller, produced poems with more managerial attitudes. It would be tempting but wrong to divide these viewpoints politically between royalists, like Cowley and Waller, and supporters of Parliament, like Milton and Marvell, who became Milton's assistant in the office of Secretary of Foreign Tongues for the Commonwealth government. Some poets allegiant to the monarchy, notably Henry Vaughan and Margaret Cavendish, were animists. John Evelyn, an early hero of conservation, devoted to the royal cause and a member of the Royal Society, wrote the first tract on air pollution and a comprehensive manual of reforestation and suggested numerous measures that current conservationists support.

The topological or estate poem, also called the country house poem, brings together considerations of power, politics, social control, and land management.[7] The purpose of this genre is usually to express the values of a family and a society. For Ben Jonson, writer of court masques and courtly poems, Penshurst, the country seat of Sir Robert Sidney, sets forth the orderly hierarchical views of its line of possessors, from which Sir Philip Sidney sprang. *To Penshurst* compliments a well-ordered family and society, affirms man's dominion over nature by beginning and ending with hunting scenes (one of the hunters to whom the house is hospitable being the king), and describes ordered rows of fruitful trees, well-fed and well-trained servants, and carp and pheasant eager to be eaten. For Aemilia Lanyer, contrarily, the manor of Cookeham expresses the grief of friendship lost because of hierarchically stratified social relations, with nature rather than architecture or practices of cultivation carrying most of the expression.

In *Upon Appleton House*, Marvell expresses the values of an *oikos*, not as a symbolic backdrop or a model of hospitable wealth but as the place itself, interacting with a human mind to show how nature and perception affect each other. Like *To Penshurst*, *Upon Appleton House* is about wise cultivation, but it counts the cost—the bird accidentally killed by the stroke of a scythe is not eager to be trussed up and roasted—and it tempers human mastery over nature, both by drawing attention to creatures not under human control and by repairing for contemplative repose not to the ordered grove but to the old-growth woods. The estate, in the poem at least, fits into nature unarrogantly, like animals' dens and nests and like the "sober frame" of the house itself.

Marvell is presumed to have written *Upon Appleton House* during his residence as tutor to Mary Fairfax at Nunappleton in the early 1650's, while the spiritual use of a garden or woodland was still a respectable topic in scientific circles such as Samuel Hartlib's,[8] but joined with exact observation of nature. With the help of a

---

6   Rogers, *The Matter of Revolution*, 1.

7   For the development of Marvell's genre see Alastair Fowler, "The Beginnings of English Georgic," in *Renaissance Genres*, ed. Barbara Kiefer Lewalski, 105–25.

8   For more on Hartlib see Leslie and Raylor, eds, *Culture and Cultivation*; Barbara Kiefer Lewalski, "Milton and the Hartlib Circle"; and Richard DuRocher, *Milton Among the Romans*.

microscope, Sir Thomas Pope Blount could still say in 1693 that "every flower of the field, every fiber of a plant, every particle of an insect, carries with it the impress of its maker." But this impress was not stamped on Nature's Book as a license to read as we choose, "For the works of God are not like the compositions of fancy . . . that will not bear a clear light or strict scrutiny; but their exactness receives advantage from the severest inspection."[9]

Marvell's composition of fancy does bear scrutiny. He represents a natural world filled with other beings to be responded to on their own terms and takes a fresh look at nature not only as pictorial and metaphorical, though he retains those modes, but as organic and processive. He does so, as Asheley Griffiths has shown,[10] with accurate observation of the actual flora and fauna of Yorkshire. Although he shares with georgic revivalists such as Hartlib, John Evelyn, and John Beale an interest in describing an agricultural Eden, he also regards the natural world as the habitat of diverse creatures who are valuable not only as commodities and sources of spiritual wisdom, but also in themselves and their activations of the mind. While I agree with Alastair Fowler that estate poems are "rich tissues of . . . emblems," in the case of this one I find more "common interest between man and animals" than most such poems allow.[11]

These perceptions need a flexible and polysemous language in which, like the house at Nunappleton, "Things greater are in less contained" (1.44). In contrast to John Wilkins, who invented a categorical language of single significations,[12] Marvell sought a kind of multiply connective language that is "ecological" rather than "economical"—though its riches are highly compressed. John Beale wrote to Samuel Hartlib in 1659, treating spiritual experience with an openness of mind toward phenomena that was to become the earmark of scientific truth for the Royal Society, of "those strange Providences that lead mee, & opened my Spirite to inquire amongst them all Candidly and impartially for the best evidences of liquid truth."[13] Milton says in *Areopagitica*, "Truth is compar'd in Scripture to a streaming fountain; if her waters flow not in a perpetuall progression, they sick'n into a muddy pool of conformity and tradition."[14] Marvell's language is fluidly responsive to the liquidity of truth. Both organic nature and the perceiving spirit need to be free for this kind of truth to be known, and the liquidity of Marvell's language in *Upon Appleton House* overflows expected forms to carry new perceptions. One is the perception of land as a habitat supporting connected lives. Another is that while we are perceiving these diverse beings, they are perceiving us. A third is that the abundance of interactive perceptions nature offers is the birthright and nest egg of the human self.[15]

Several critical constructs have been applied to Marvell's poem that obscure these renovations. One is that like other country house poems, *Upon Appleton*

---

9   Blount, *A Natural History*, Preface, in Grant McColley, *Literature and Science*, 111.

10   Griffiths, "The Instructive Creatures of *Appleton House*." Paper presented at MLA 1995.

11   Fowler, "Country House Poems: The Politics of a Genre," 8 and 9.

12   Wilkins, *An Essay towards a Real Character and a Philosophical Language*.

13   Beale, quoted by Michael Leslie in "The Spiritual Husbandry of John Beale," in Leslie and Raylor, eds, *Culture and Cultivation*, 167.

14   Milton, *Complete Prose Works* 2:543.

15   Some of these perceptions are forerunners of ecophilosophy and the philosophy of perception in the late twentieth-century work of Maurice Merleau-Ponty, David Abram, and Arne Naess.

House is about an ideal society in an ideal natural setting, but that by Marvell's time neither of these ideals was tenable, so that Marvell produces an uncomfortable nostalgia. Another is that his treatment of nature is picturesque and emblematic, but that the hieroglyphs fail to master nature in masterful language, recording a regretful sense of loss of dominion over nature and over language. A third is that Marvell is distressed by the new science that questions old tenets about the stability of nature and the reliability of rational human perceptions. I think these notions have got hold of the wrong end of the stick.

Looking at the poem as part of a genre that tries to conserve a traditional way of life, George Parfitt finds it "stranger and more disturbing" than other country-house poems because "little is as it seems, little stays still under the observer's eye"; we have difficulty finding "what is praised," the picture of Fairfax is ambivalent, and despite the assertion that the microcosm of Nunappleton is "'heaven's centre, Nature's lap, / And paradise's only map' . . . the whole feeling of the poem is that paradise is elsewhere. . . . For Marvell Appleton, at best, can only remind us of what the ideal may once have been. Jonson focuses upon a particular place and gives it solidarity, but when Marvell contemplates such a place it insists on shifting with 'engines strange.'"[16]

I suggest that the poem itself is deliberately such an engine. Marvell can celebrate the shifting interactions of scene and eye because his poem is not about power. The way it unsettles conventional binary, categorical, idealizing, and mastering ways of seeing and valuing is exactly what makes it paradisal, for paradise—not the royal enclosure of its etymology, but the generative epitome of creation in its fullness— is copious, polysemous, and surprising. *Upon Appleton House* discovers new experiences for the senses and the mind through the very process that Parfitt finds disturbing: "little stays still under the observer's eye." It questions human dominion over nature along with other hierarchies and makes the act of perceiving produce value from nature quite apart from its value as either economic or emblematic commodity. It contemplates the lives of other creatures empathetically and receives delight, sorrow, and new kinds of instruction from them. When he addresses the woods, streams, gardens, and meads of a comparatively modest estate in Yorkshire as "paradise's only map," Marvell offers a corrective to human predation through images and emblems that unsettle hierarchical assumptions, both political and biological.

Holy mathematics

Marvell's estate poem is structured by the habitats through which the perceiver passes.[17] The survey begins with human habitations: the house, which conforms to nature in its fit proportions, and the ruined nunnery (represented in this protestant

---

16 Parfitt, *English Poetry of the Seventeenth Century*, 76–8. David Norbrook says reasonably "[T]he poem is cast in such a way as to resist any easy nostalgia for an old rural order" in *Writing the English Republic*, 289.

17 For information on the house and contemporary architectural fashions, see Nigel Smith's notes in *The Poems of Andrew Marvell*.

poem as artificial and dissolute before its dissolution) whose stones became its quarry. Next, it moves to the thoroughly managed garden, a work of artifice with the post-war program of converting artillery to flowers; and proceeds through the habitats of the estate from the most to the least controlled: meadow, river, and woods.[18] The poem touches on matters controversial in Marvell's time and ours: expansive construction, deforestation, the enclosure of public land, and the lives of animals.

Marvell's opening stanzas address the ruinous excesses of overbuilding. One cannot make a house, or a cathedral, or an orchestra, without digging and felling, but one can make choices. When Ben Jonson begins

> Thou art not, Penshurst, built to envious show,
> Of touch, or marble; nor canst boast a row
> Of polished pillars, or a roof of gold

he makes readers aware of the human or social costs of showy importations, while Marvell, also chiding human pride, begins with the costs to nature.

> Within this sober frame expect
> Work of no foreign architect,
> That unto caves the quarries drew,
> And forests did to pastures hew.

The stones of Appleton House were reclaimed from the ruined nunnery and the wood culled from a forest long-sustained. The arrogance of excessive construction contrasts with animal, avian, and reptilian decorum—

> Why should of all things man unruled
> Such unproportioned dwellings build?
> The beasts are by their dens expressed:
> And birds contrive an equal nest;
> The low-roofed tortoises do dwell
> In cases fit of tortoise shell;
> No creature loves an empty space;
> Their bodies measure out their place.

—and Marvell's economical stanza form fits the case he is making.

Edward Topsell had described the "Chelophagi" who "live by eating of Tortoises, and with their shells they cover their houses, make all their vessels, row in them upon the water, as men use to row in boats, and make them likewise serve for many other uses."[19] But for Marvell the proper occupants of tortoise shells are tortoises, who teach those who do not, like the Chelophagi, live in a subsistence culture to live more proportionally to their needs. Marvell's adroit diction brings to mind as well the "cases," adornments, inlays, and curious objects made of tortoise shell to

---

18 John Dixon Hunt in "Gard'ning Can Speak Proper English" (Leslie and Raylor 195–222) points out that this order corresponds with Cicero's three natures in *De Natura Deorum* (197).

19 Topsell, *The History of Four-footed Beasts and Serpents* (1658; first edition 1607), 796.

decorate the bodies and houses of the wealthy. From birds, beasts, and tortoises we should learn to express ourselves in "cases fit," and the compact form of the stanzas provides cases fit for the case Marvell is making. By such economical means, he fits his stanzas to the topic of unfitting construction.

It would be misleading to think of Appleton House as a humble abode; it is simply not a showy "trophy house" using stylish designs and rare materials and does not strive like them, Marvell says hyperbolically, to cover the earth and unite the world by breadth as the builders of the Tower of Babel, the types of arrogance, attempted to do by height.

> But [man], superfluously spread,
> Demands more room alive than dead.
> . . . .
> What need of all this marble crust
> T'impark the wanton mote of dust,
> That thinks by breadth the world t'unite
> Though the first builders failed in height?

Samuel Purchas remarks of the builders of Babel that God gave man two privileges, reason and speech; but by presumptuous building "this benefit of God in Nature was turned into a conspiracie against God and Nature . . . . in stead of thankefulnesse to god, and honouring his name, they would winne themselves a name and honour . . . . Babel or confusion is alway the attendant of Pride."[20] Marvell continues,

> Humility alone designs
> Those short but admirable lines,
> By which, ungirt and unconstrained,
> Things greater are in less contained.
> Let others vainly strive t'immure
> The circle in the quadrature!
> These holy mathematics can
> In every figure equal man.

The inner space that occupies a Fairfax or a Vere (one of whom Fairfax married) is larger than the outer space he or she occupies, and has richer furniture. The "den" by which an animal is suitably "expressed" is visually "Eden" writ smaller, and these human Edenic minds build small—as noble estates go—and contain the cosmos.

In manuscript, Marvell's stanzas (Italian for "rooms") could be aligned to form visual quadratures, but even in print they are conceptually square, having eight lines of eight syllables each. Numerically (and visibly if they are justified, in the printer's sense) the lines form a quadrant, like "the quadrant stones of Solomon's building" (I Kings 6–7).[21] (Could Marvell be parodying the ambition of the Foundation called Solomon's House in Bacon's *New Atlantis* to achieve "the enlarging of the bounds

---

20 *Pvrchas his Pilgrimage*, 45.
21 *Oxford English Dictionary*, quoted from Bp. W. Barlow, Defense, 1601.

of Human Empire, to the effecting of all things possible"?[22]) The number eight represents the visible cosmos—the seven known planets and the constellated stars of the zodiac—and the octave represents cosmic harmony. Symbolically a quadrature represents the earth in Renaissance numerology, earth having four elements, four seasons, four winds, and four "corners," with the corollary of heaven represented by threes. Earth, or humus, is alluded to in the etymology of "Humility," which a few stanzas later is the architect of "short, but admirable lines," like the poem's, "By which, ungirt and unconstrained, / Things greater are in less contained"—like the poem. Yet the things contained within the lines of the house and the poem are "ungirt and unconstrained" because they hold infinite valuable things, in the minds and conduct of the occupants and in the words of the poem.

"Things greater are in less contained" also describes the short but admirable lines of Marvell's stanzas; he packs endless resonance into his modest octaves. Although he writes in controlled couplets, the words are wild, and keep meaning more things. Look up the etymology of any arresting word in this poem and you are likely to find a chord of consonances. To be girt is to be girdled (like the mapped globe); belted and braced, as in "gird up your loins" (Fairfax is now ungirded of his sword); or besieged, as in war. It can also mean "enclosed," a loaded connotation in a poem about the land, enclosure of once-common lands being a matter of contention. The *Oxford English Dictionary* adds with regard to *gird* as a verb: "See GIRTH, GARTH; some scholars connect also Gothic gard-s, house, corresponding to GARTH, yard." The resonances of a well-chosen word are like the web of life: the land, the house, the householder, the war from which these are recovering, and the destabilizing of political constraints are all touched by the word "ungirt" in a small stanza about plenitude.

Often these multiplicities are problematic, setting the mind to work. Part of the owners' praise is that

> A stately frontispiece of poor
> Adorns without the open door.
> Nor less the rooms within commends
> Daily new furniture of friends.
> The house was built upon the place
> Only as a mark of grace;
> And for an inn to entertain
> Its Lord a while, but not remain.

Frontispieces of contemporary books were often framed by the engraved columns and pediment of a neoclassical doorway. Two oddities are left ajar: it is not the architecture that is stately, but the poor; yet unlike the "Friends" in the rooms, they remain "without" the door. They adorn the house because, better than expensive ornaments, they show forth the liberality of the family. Why do they come? Jonson says that both farmer and "clown" come to "salute" the Lord and Lady of Penshurst "though they have no suit," or legal case, to bring; instead they bring gifts. Marvell's

---

22 *New Atlantis*, in *Francis Bacon: A Critical Edition of the Major Works*, ed. Brian Vickers, 480.

stately "poor," a term absent from "To Penshurst," raises questions about the commonwealth state that Jonson does not raise about the monarchy; poverty had been exacerbated by the civil wars and by the deforestation, drainage, and enclosure of common lands that went on under both administrations.

As the poor commend, however ambiguously, the house, the "new furniture of friends," not the ornaments of wealth, commends the rooms. The house is "a mark of grace" and "an inn to entertain / Its Lord a while, but not remain," reminding the reader of a Lord who brought grace but found no place in the inn, and could not remain long in the inn of the world. Fairfax walks lightly on the earth, if you can say that of a man who has four houses: "Him Bishop's Hill or Denton may, / Or Bilbrough, better hold than they"—"they" presumably referring to the rooms.

Although in the house "all things are composéd here / Like Nature, orderly and near" (stanza 4) Nature is not constrained in its environs.

> But Nature here hath been so free
> As if she said, "Leave this to me."
> Art would more neatly have defaced
> What she had laid so sweetly waste,
> In fragrant gardens, shady woods,
> Deep meadows, and transparent floods.

Free—both unhampered and liberal—compared with what? A classic of estate management, Xenophon's *Oeconomicus*, stresses prudence, order, good management, and good government. For Xenophon laying "sweetly waste" would be an oxymoron.[23] In the dialogue Critobalus says to Socrates, "If the king dooth as you say: hee taketh as much heed to husbandry as he dooth to war" (a point applicable to Fairfax); garrisons exist to keep the peace for farmers, and the good farmer rides through the land and honors those who tend it well, but punishes those who leave lands uncultivated and underpopulated; the speaker regards nature (and woman) as entirely for the use of man. In the famous story of the Garden of Cyrus, the good king is himself a good gardener in a geometrically managerial mode:

> When Lisander began to marvail at it, because the trees were so fair and egally set, and the orders of the trees lay straight on against the other, and made goodly angles & corners wel proporcioned, and many sweet & plesant savours cam to their noses when they were walking, he wondering thereupon said thus. Forsooth Cirus the great beautifulness of these things is a great marvail to me, but I wonder much more of thim that hath measured and set them thus in order. Then Cyrus when he hard this did rejoyce and say, All these that ye see, I have mesured them and set them in order, and I can shew you some trees that I have set with mine owne hands.

The emphasis on order extends to women, slaves (who must be well treated so they won't try to escape), and animals; husbandry is joined to farming for sacrifices, food, and hunting. One of the dialogists, Ischomachus, is eloquent on the training of wives to self-control, good order, and profit. The speaker lectures his wife, not yet

---

23 For Milton on Xenophon see *Apology Against a Pamphlet*, in *Complete Prose Works* 1:891.

15: "There is nothing (good sweet wife) so profitable and so goodly among men, as is order in everything."[24]

So far Xenophon's ideal husbandman is autocratic, and everything prospers best under the master's eye. But later Isomachus explains that nature itself teaches the husbandman "how to order it best." The vine by climbing trees shows that it needs to be supported, and spreads leaves over the tender grapes to show their need for shade in summer. "And when it is time for the Grapes to wax ripe & sweet, the which is caused onely by heate of the Sun; it letteth the leaves fall to teach the husbandman, that it would be lightned and eased, that the frute may the better wax ripe." Nature also teaches the work ethic: Xenophon's Socrates asks why, if farming is easy to learn, some farmers prosper and others remain poor, and gets the answer that the earth, by being a good teacher, shows who is wicked and lazy. "They that doo for it and have care for it, it rewardeth them with farre much more."[25]

Xenophon provides classical authority for Bacon's aphorism, "For we cannot command nature except by obeying her,"[26] and for the early modern conviction, supported by the biblical concept of dominion as it was read by Calvinist instrumentalists, that leaving land uncultivated is not only wasteful but immoral. In the *Oeconomicus* nature is perceived as resources from which a farmer who reads nature's ways and cooperates with them can reap profit. The agricultural improvers of the seventeenth century also had laudable purposes, not only profit but also sustenance for the poor and for the spirit, and their discoveries brought immeasurable benefits. But they did not think of the land as habitat, or incorporate creatures other than human among the beneficiaries, or enjoy the presence of wild ones as do Marvell's speaker or Milton's Adam and Eve.[27]

The garden

The first part of the estate the speaker enters beyond Appleton House itself, however, is as managed as a garden can be, planted and clipped in the form of a fort. Gardens symbolically shaped were not unusual, but a military garden seems at odds with a place where "Nature" is "left . . . free." Freedom from an imperious monarch, though, is what the Parliamentary Army that Fairfax led was fighting for. Symbolically this garden turns swords into plowshares and restores England's "nursery of all things green" while elsewhere "war all this doth overgrow; / We ordnance plant and powder

---

24 Sarah Pomeroy's modern translation renders this section: "[A]ll things somehow appear more beautiful when they are in a regular arrangement. Each of them looks like a chorus of equipment, and the interval between them looks beautiful when each item is kept clear of it, just as a chorus of dancers moving in a circle is not only a beautiful sight in itself, but the interval between them seems pure and beautiful, too" (125).

25 *Xenophons treatise of Householde*, trans. Hervet (1573), folios 15–17, 23, 30, 57. See also Marchant's version (1853), 363.

26 Bacon, *Novum Organon, Aphorism* CXXIX, ed. Anderson, 119.

27 Compare Berry, *Home Economics: Fourteen Essays* (1987).

sow."[28] Fairfax has done his part in the Parliamentary cause and when offered more political and military power has preferred like Cincinnatus to cultivate his own garden. Whether the narrator applauds this relinquishing of power and responsibility is not clear, but the metaphor that immures it, Fairfax's flower-fortress, sprays floral fireworks in honor of armistice and a return to the primary calling of dressing and keeping the earth; the metaphorical garden "laid out . . . in sport / in the just figure of a fort" is a counterattack to the ordnance we plant when we turn gardens into actual forts and human beings into poppies that grow in Flanders' fields. Perhaps, as Abraham Cowley wrote of the philosophical husbandman, Fairfax's retreat to his estate was "but a Retreat from the world, as it is man's; into the world, as it is Gods."[29] The fortress-garden is militarily managed, commemorating a military revolution by defusing imperial militarism, and prefaces a lament for the Garden of England in that kind of war ironically called "civil."

> Oh thou, that dear and happy isle
> The garden of the world ere while. . . .
> What luckless apple did we taste,
> To make us mortal, and thee waste?

What might regenerate England's Eden is the kind of consciousness of creation for which the Genesis Garden is the primal metaphor, and the kind of conscience embodied in the gardener Fairfax, whose name means well-doing:

> For he did, with his utmost skill,
> Ambition weed, but conscience till—
> Conscience, that heaven-nursFd plant,
> Which most our earthly gardens want.

This moly or haemony of a prickly-leafed but golden-flowering conscience is the first requisite for the gardeners of a republic.

In keeping with the theme of aiding rather than enslaving nature, the garden is a transition to a series of increasingly less artificial habitats, presented in order of their degree of freedom and the diversity of their population: the georgic meadow, the seasonally manipulated river, and the old growth forest so full of creatures that it is "a yet green, yet growing ark": rather than, or in addition to, the usual typology of Noah's Ark as the church, Marvell literalizes it as a fulfillment of the type of the preservation of the animals. Of these habitats the speaker more convincingly alleges that Nature has been left freer than on other estates and has in turn been liberal. Therefore, says the speaking "I," this estate deserves to be surveyed "with slow eyes."

In this action of the eyes, Marvell retains older views of nature as representing the divine and moral states of man, but he does not retain the convention that relates

---

28 A World War I poster encouraging people to plant Victory Gardens and "Write to the National War Garden Commission" had as its motto "Every Garden a Munition Plant."

29 Quoted by Douglas Chambers in " 'Wild Pastorall Encounter'," in Leslie and Raylor, eds, *Culture and Cultivation*, 185.

dominion over the creatures to dominion over the beasts within us. He keeps a temperate version of the georgic view of nature as useful to human civilization, but he does not promote the views, popular with agricultural projectors such as John Norden, that it is man's duty to "convert every place to his fittest fruite," replacing diversified farming with regional monoculture, or that every foot of soil should be cultivated for the market, "be it never so wilde, boggy, clay, or sandy."[30] And Marvell adds a revised perception of nature as valuable to the mind, which in *The Garden* he calls "that ocean where each kind / Does straight its own resemblance find." Here innate ideas of "kinds" or species (in contrast to a *tabula rasa*) are presented not as a hierarchical scale of Platonic forms or a set of Aristotelian categories but as an "ocean" of fluid understandings and capacities for changed perspectives that keep the mind receptive, productive, and fully entertained by its kinship with "each kind."

The meadow

Entering the next and tamest of the estate's habitats, the speaker says so sibilantly that we hear the grass swishing against his body as he goes,

> And now to the abyss I pass
> Of that unfathomable grass,
> Where men like grasshoppers appear,
> But grasshoppers are giants there:
> They, in their squeaking laugh, contemn
> Us as we walk more low than them:
> And, from the precipices tall
> Of the green spires, to us do call.

This jest is one of Marvell's inversions of highness and lowness, pride and humility, that question hierarchies by sudden shifts of perspective. Christopher Fitter calls the "sleight-of-perspective" in the stanzas on grasshoppers and cattle

> disarranged vision . . . that seeks to enact an epistemological disorientation . . . . The hyperbolic distortions of the grasshopper passage, alarmed hallucinations immediate from the physical sensation of sinking into depths of "unfathomable grass," are in a sense confirmed by the scientific laws of optical relativism.[31]

What is alarming, beyond a surprising footfall, or hallucinatory? The grass cannot be measured in fathoms (six feet each), nor understood by being measured; one is enveloped by its richness and loses the sense of command over nature, the managerial attitude that, Fitter elsewhere argues, we need to discard. The speaker may literally see the grasshoppers on blade points above his head calling down—I have walked in such meadows myself. The mocking grasshoppers are not superior, they are merely

---

30 John Norden, *Surveiors Dialogue*, quoted by Andrew McRae, "Husbandry Manuals and the Language of Agrarian Improvement" in Leslie and Raylor 51.

31 Fitter, *Poetry, Space, Landscape: Toward a New Theory*, 286.

higher: hierarchy is doubly and amusingly undermined. Marvell mocks ideas of dominion in his political poems too; rank and power squirm under his pen.[32]

Marvell's inversion of hierarchy has charming classical precedents. In "The Grasshopper," a paraphrase from Anacreon, Abraham Cowley humorously compares the title character to Jove and other kings.

> Happy Insect, what can bee
> In happiness compared to Thee?
> Fed with nourishment divine,
> The dewy Morning's gentle Wine!
> Nature waits upon thee still,
> And thy verdant Cup does fill;
> 'Tis fill'd wherever thou dost tread,
> Nature's selfe's thy Ganymede.
> Thou dost drink, and dance, and sing;
> Happier than the happiest King!

All the fields and plants he sees are his kingdom, and man his servant:

> Man for thee does sow and plough;
> Farmer He, and Land-Lord thou!
> Nor doth Luxury destroy;
> The shepherd gladly heareth thee,
> More Harmonious then He.

The hinds gladly hear his prophecy of harvest. (Coexistence, without pesticides, gives pleasures.) He is then "Voluptuous, and Wise withal, / Epicurean Animal!" because his life does not outlast his mirth.[33]

The grasshopper observed by micrographer Henry Power, with whom Cowley shared enthusiasm for experimental biology, was not so lucky. Having "taken the Cornea or outward Film of the Eye quite off, and cleansed it so from all the pulpous matter which lay within it" he could "plainly see it foraminulous as before." And if you lift the "Corslet . . . with a pin, you may see their heart play, and beat very orderly for a long time."[34] Power, like Marvell, was especially interested in ways of seeing, but from a more mechanical point of view.

Whether Cowley's grasshopper mocks monarchs—the first king Cowley supported died early too, but lost his mirth—the anacreontic eschews the usual moral contrasting the grasshopper with more provident insects. Marvell contributes a new

---

32 John Creaser finds Marvell's metrics less mimetic and republican than Milton's "asymmetrical and expansive forms" because, while like Milton he is committed to liberty, Marvell seeks balance and stability in more regular verse that "leaves the reader feeling safe amid all the metamorphoses; metrically, we know where we are." "Prosodic Style and Conceptions of Liberty in Milton and Marvell," *Milton Quarterly* 34 (March, 2000), 1–13. See also Creaser's "Prosody and Liberty in Milton and Marvell" in Graham Parry and Joad Raymond, eds., *Milton and the Terms of Liberty* (Cambridge, UK: D.S. Brewer, 2002), 37–55.

33 Cowley, *Anacreontics*, from *Miscellanies*, 1656, in *Complete Works* 1:149.

34 Power, *Experimental Philosophy* (1664), 24. Foramina are perforations (*Oxford English Dictionary*).

perspective, that of perspective itself, which undermines luxurious hierarchies, for the republican poet an instability to be desired. Luxury and tyranny waste lives.

Marvell's meadow is also winter fodder. Enter the mowers, "Who seem like Israelites to be, / Walking on foot through a green sea . . . . With whistling scythe, and elbow strong, / These massacre the grass along." The allusion to the Red Sea passage invokes liberation, while massacres of people deemed heretical—like those in Milton's sonnet "On the Late Massacre in Piedmont"—were too frequent for the word not to startle, and the *Massacre of the Innocents* too often painted for that image not to be aroused. To continue the violence,

> . . . one, unknowing, carves the rail,
> whose yet unfeathered quills her fail.
> The edge all bloody from its breast
> He draws, and does his stroke detest,
> Fearing the flesh untimely mowed
> To him a fate as black forebode.

The bird (Plate 1) is snatched up by "bloody Thestylis" who supplies the mowers' dinner and who intends to truss the rail, but the reaper who has accidentally carved it is aghast, in contrast to the practitioners of unscrupulous dissection or husbandry who cause needless suffering because they have been freed from scruples by mechanist zoology. The mower "does his stroke detest," fearing that what has happened to the rail will eventually happen to him.

The mower's idea that what we do to nature predicts our own future is not just superstition. Our moral nature is by our dens expressed, and our *oikos*, our house, is the biosphere that we share with other beings whose fate is connected to ours. When the poet laments that building low—the humility he had, in the beginning, commended in the "sober frame" of Appleton House—has brought no safety to the rail, he rubs out the boundaries between humankind and the rest of the animal world while empathetically addressing the rail:

> Unhappy birds! What does it boot
> To build below the grass's root;
> When lowness is unsafe as height,
> And chance o'ertakes, what 'scapeth spite?

The rail's "orphan parents' call / Sounds your untimely funeral"; the species must either "sooner hatch or higher build." Marvell puts himself in their place, at the grass roots, and mourns with them. His language is monistic and vitalistic in its reflections upon the similarities his mind finds with "each kind."

The meadow section concludes with another exercise in perspective after the reapers have leveled the meadow.

> This scene again withdrawing brings
> A new and empty face of things,
> A leveled space, as smooth and plain
> As cloths for Lely stretched to stain.
> The world when first created sure
> Was such a table rase and pure.

The *tabula rasa*, a clean or erased writing tablet, was later applied to the mind as a principle of John Locke's *Essay Concerning Human Understanding* (1690), which erased ideas of a sovereign language for those who agreed that there are no innate ideas and words are voluntary signs: "Words, in their primary or immediate signification, stand for nothing but the ideas in the mind of him that uses them"; otherwise all human beings would speak the same language.[35] Locke warns of the fallacy of thinking that abstract names can supply knowledge of essential being.

> Were I to talk with any one of a sort of birds I lately saw in St. James's Park, about three or four feet high, with a covering of something between feathers and hair, of a dark brown colour, without wings, but in the place thereof two or three little branches coming down like sprigs of Spanish broom, long great legs, with feet only of three claws, and without a tail; I must make this description of it, and so may make others understand me. But when I am told that the name of it is cassuaris, I may then use the word to stand in discourse for all my complex idea mentioned in that description; though by that word, which is now become a specific name, I know no more of the real essence or constitution of that sort of animals than I did before; and knew probably as much of the nature of that species of birds before I learned the name, as many Englishmen do of swans or herons.[36]

John Wilkins and other catalogers addressed the deficiency of commonly understood names and supplied just such descriptions of size and form as Locke does, but neither name nor description can convey "the real essence or constitution of that sort of animals." Long before Darwin, Locke began to erase the dividing lines between animal species, on the grounds that what may be said of species cannot be applied to individuals: "Nothing I have is essential to me. An accident or disease may very much alter my colour or shape; a fever or fall may take away my reason or memory, or both; and an apoplexy leave neither sense, nor understanding, no, nor life." Further, "There are creatures in the world that have shapes like ours, but are hairy, and want language and reason. There are naturals among us that have perfectly our shape, but want reason, and some of them language too."

Marvell, too, seems to be making his poem a table "rase and pure," like a mown field, on which to rewrite ways of perceiving nature. If nature is always in flux, and human cultivation or culture needs to be responsive to it, then perception and language need to be flexible too, and the "ocean of the mind" a habitat of well perceived, not Platonically formulated, forms. There are no inflexible ideas, innate or not, governing Marvell's imagination; his thoughts fluctuate freely in a gestural language responsive to the flux of perception. He finds like Locke that naming is not enough, and demonstrates Merleau-Ponty's theory of authentic speech as a gestural response by his perpetual originality.

So, it turns out, Marvell's meadow is not, after all, a *tabula rasa*—we are not to dwell on one idea as if it were sovereign—for the stanza shifts to a different simile:

> Or rather such as the *toril*
> Ere the bulls enter at Madril.

---

35 Locke, *An Essay Concerning Human Understanding* (1894), 2:9.
36 Locke, 85, 58, 73.

When the "table" changes to a bull ring we see not violence to bulls but perhaps a political party locking horns with the monarchy.

> For to this naked equal flat,
> Which Levellers take pattern at,
> The villagers in common chase
> Their cattle, which it closer rase;
> And what below the scythe increased
> Is pinched yet nearer by the beast.
> Such, in the painted world, appeared
> D'Avenant with th' universal herd.

The Lord General Fairfax does not exclude common grazing, at least on the seasonal stubble, by enclosure. Levellers, the radical proponents of equality, were especially concerned with the preservation of common lands, including the fens or wetlands, also called the Levels, which were being drained and enclosed, of six eastern counties including Yorkshire and the Hatfield Level near Marvell's native Hull. Marvell's comparison of "the naked equal flat" of Fairfax's meadows with political platforms is more than metaphorical.

Though mention of Sir William D'Avenant may be a pleasantry, it appears oddly enough alongside the Levellers, and in Marvell's kind of poem, to deserve comment. D'Avenant was a court dramatist, succeeded Ben Jonson as poet laureate, and was knighted for valor in the civil war. As a royalist in exile, he was a companion, in Paris, of the Duke and Duchess [Margaret Cavendish] of Newcastle and of Thomas Hobbes. *Gondibert* was preceded by *The Author's Preface to his Much Honor'd Friend, M[r]. Hobbes* who had "done me the honour to allow this Poem a daylie examination as it was writing," to which Hobbes returned *The Answer of Mr. Hobbes to Sir. Will. D'Avenant's Preface Before Gondibert.* The paired essays are considered a landmark in neoclassical criticism, contain royalist assumptions, and so again destabilize Marvell's political landscape. D'Avenant cites, for example, how "unapt for obedience (in the condition of Beasts whose appetite is Liberty, and their Liberty a license of Lust) the People have often been" and blames the clergy for "mistaken lenity"; he means "to show how much their Christian meeknesse hath deceav'd them in taming this wilde Monster the People; and a little to rebuke them for neglecting the assistance of Poets." Hobbes states a triple analogy:

> As Philosophers have divided the Universe (their subject) into three Regions, Caelestiall, Adrial, and Terrestriall; so the Poets . . . have lodg'd themselves in the three Regions of mankind, Court, Citty, and Country, correspondent in some proportion, to those three regions of the World. For there is in Princes, and men of conspicuous power (anciently called *Heroes*) a lustre and influence upon the rest of men, resembling that of the Heavens; and an insincerenesse, inconstancy, and troublesome humor of those that dwell in populous Citties, like the mobility, blustring, and impurity of the Aire; and a plainesse, and (though dull) yet a nutritive faculty in rurall people, that endures a comparison with the Earth they

labour. From hence have proceeded three sorts of Poesy, *Heroique, Scomatique* [satirical], and *Pastorall*.[37]

So much for the Levellers and Marvell's "stately frontispiece of poor."

However, D'Avenant's poem is appealingly sympathetic to the actual "condition of Beasts" in the stanzas on the stag hunt (Book I, Canto II) and on the Creation painting (Book II, Canto VI) to which Marvell alludes. Hunting was a royal and aristocratic activity, for which England had large forest preserves, but D'Avenant's sympathy is entirely with the stag. One supposes that, as in Sir John Denham's *Cooper's Hill*, the stag is in part an allegory of Charles I. Yet the story of the noble stag and "the Monarch Murderer . . . Destructive Man!" can also be read as sympathetic to animal victims, like *The Hunting of the Hare* by his friend Margaret Cavendish. The painting, which in D'Avenant's description is as animated as Achilles' shield, has some affinity with Marvell's poem. On the fourth day of creation,

> Then to those Woods the next quick Fiat brings
> The Feather'd kinde; where merrily they fed,
> As if their Hearts were lighter then their Wings;
> For yet no Cage was fram'd, nor Net was spread.

On the sixth, before the creation of the species that was to appropriate them after man's first disobedience,

> Then strait an universal Herd appears;
> First gazing on each other in the shade;
> Wondring with levell'd Eies, and lifted Ears,
> Then play, whilst yet their Tyrant is unmade.[38]

By this allusion the Fairfax family, not being or supporting tyrants, receive approval of their husbandry and an example of the way the poem compliments the house and themselves: "Things greater [the creation] are in less [the painting and the poem] contained."

Back at Nunappleton, the meadow is now "ungirt," and so is the perceiver's imagination. The cows appear as small in the wide distance as unfocussed fleas appear large in "multiplying glasses"[39] and move as slowly as constellations; they are insects and stars, very small and very large things in a universe recently made more seeable:

> They seem within the polished grass
> A landskip drawn in looking-glass,
> And shrunk in the huge pasture show

---

37 *Gondibert*, ed. David F. Gladish, 30 and 45. The prefaces were published in Paris in 1650 and again with the poem in 1651.

38 *Gondibert*, 75 and 166.

39 Donno's gloss, 252 n. to ll. 461–2: "such as fleas appear in microscopes not yet brought into focus; this is the obverse of James Howell's statement (*Epistolae Ho-Elianae*, 1650), 'such [multiplying] glasses can make a flea look like a cow' (Leishman p. 222 n.)."

As spots, so shaped, or faces do—
Such fleas, ere they approach the eye,
In multiplying glasses lie.
They feed so wide, so slowly move,
As constellations do above.

In *Micrographia*,[40] published in 1665, Robert Hooke commends his "helps for the eye" because it is our business to rectify the effects of the Fall, beginning with "a watchfulness over the failings and an inlargement of the dominion of the Senses." Looking through his instrument, Hooke finds beauty in minute creatures usually thought detestable vermin, including the flea: "The strength and beauty of this small creature, had it no other relation at all to man, would deserve a description"; his "six legges he clitches up altogether, and when he leaps, springs them all out, and thereby exerts his whole strength at once . . . the Microscope manifests it to be all over adorn'd with a curiously polish'd suit of sabel Armour, neatly jointed, and beset with multitudes of sharp pinns . . . the head is on either side beautify'd with a quick and round black eye." This flea is beautiful, an armored hero. Marvell too, and presumably earlier, finds things worth description and admiration that others think useless to man. He inspects nature though the multiplying glass of his mind and renovates the act of seeing itself. To see, says Dante, is to love. But Hooke's love of insects does not delay his carving them up alive.

In contrast with Hooke, another post-Marvellian writer, Richard Bentley, imagining what unlimited perceiving would be like, *does* suffer the "alarmed hallucinations" Fitter attributes to Marvell. In 1692 Bentley preached eight sermons "for proving the Christian Religion against notorious Infidels," an annual series founded by the bequest of the natural historian Robert Boyle. Bentley's relentlessly dualist sermons help one see why he found it necessary to rewrite large patches of *Paradise Lost* in the notes to his edition in order to make it more conventional. Milton thought matter derived from the substance of God. Bentley thinks it wholly distinct from soul or spirit.

The passage on the limits of perception comes in Sermon III, in a consideration of the human body as proof of God's wisdom and beneficence. Considering the many parts of a finger, say, down to its "Myriads of little Fibres and Filaments, not discoverable by the naked Eye," and how small a part of the body a finger is and the whole body's "Fitness, and Use, and Subserviencey to infinite Functions," the religious man cannot think of it "otherwise than as the Effect of Contrivance and Skill, and consequently the Workmanship of a most intelligent and beneficent Being." Atheists (presumably such as Lucretius) agree about fitness and usefulness but attribute them to "dead senseless Matter" itself and "vehemently oppose, and horribly dread the Thought" that they "arise from Wisdom and Design." Bentley undertakes to answer atheistic objections, one of which is that an infinite and beneficent power would have given us more senses, and more perfect ones. He argues that a perfect God could set bounds to the capacities of matter, and that "our Senses have that Degree of Perfection, which is most fit and suitable to our Estate

40 Hooke, *Micrographia*, 210.

and Condition." If human beings had wings, for example (here Bentley manifests a Hobbesian sense of human depravity that might well call divine benevolence into question), either the world would clip them or we would be extinct by now, "nothing upon that Supposition being safe from Murder and Rapine."

As to the senses,

> if the eye were so acute as to rival the finest Microscopes, and to discern the hair on the Leg of a Gnat, it would be a Curse and not a Blessing to us; it would make all Things appear rugged and deformed; the most finely polished Chrystal would be uneven and rough; the Sight of our own selves would affright us; the smoothest Skin would be beset all over with rugged Scales, and bristly Hairs: And besides, we could not see at one View above what is now the space of an Inch, and it would take a considerable Time to survey the then mountainous Bulk of our own Bodies.

This disproportion would be "little better than Blindness"; God gave us the "Invention and Industry" to invent the optical glass instead. If our hearing were more acute we could have no secrets and would be tormented by noise. More acute touch would make burdensome even the pressure of our clothes, and the "whole Body would have the Tenderness of a Wound."[41] In this sermon Bentley tidies up theology the way he tidies up Milton's poem. He likes theological "polished Chrystal" and "smoothest Skin," not ruggedness and bristles. Marvell's flea-sized cows and cow-sized fleas, in contrast, exercise an acuteness and relativity of perception that breaks down such dogmatic categories.

As Marvell's "engine" changes the scene again, the sluices of Denton open to flood the water meadow and make "the meadow truly be / (What it but seemed before) a sea. . . . The river in itself is drown'd, / And isles the astonished cattle round." This new play on being and seeming takes us from the Garden to the Flood, not (yet) in Genesis but in, appropriately, the first book of Ovid's *Metamorphoses*. But while in Ovid the exhausted animals perish, in Marvell the livestock are merely astonished. Instead of destroying them, the flood throws land and river creatures together in a watery ark.

The woodlands

The chief ark in the poem, though, is the wood in which the speaker, taking "sanctuary" from the flood, chooses punningly to "embark." In this very wood Noah might have found "Fit timber"—the root meaning of *timber* is "build"—but this whole old-growth forest is an ever "green" and a "yet growing" ark that may be selectively used but will not, the speaker believes, ever be clear cut; its ancient stocks "Nature's cradle decked" and "Will in green age her hearse expect." Here "All creatures" (at least indigenous ones) in abundance have a living sanctuary, including the speaker as he retreats from the flooding of the water-meadows.

---

41 Bentley, in *A Defense of Natural and Revealed Religion* 1:24–5. My thanks to Kevis Goodman for this reference.

But I, retiring from the flood,
Take sanctuary in the wood;
And, while it lasts, my self imbark
In this yet green, yet growing ark,
Where the first carpenter might best
Fit timber for his keel have prest.
And where all creatures might have shares,
Although in armies, not in paires.

Like Noah's ark, which is a type of the church, this grove is a temple and has "wingèd choirs." Marvell's description of the nightingale, often an emblem of poets, is ecological and political.

The nightingale does here make choice
To sing the trials of her voice.
Low shrubs she sits in, and adorns
With music high the squatted thorns.
But highest oaks stoop down to hear,
And list'ning elders prick the ear.
The thorn, lest it should hurt her, draws
Within the skin its shrunken claws.

Marvell puts the nightingale in her chosen habitat, "here" in the woods, and her chosen lowly position among thorns—reminding us of Philomela's metamorphosis into a nightingale who sings out of pain caused by a tyrant.[42] But the message is not that the bird needs pain to sing; on the contrary, oaks, elders, and thorns listen to and protect her. Birds and poets need freedom to sing where they "make choice," and kings or governors, represented by oaks, and councils or senators, represented by elders, should "stoop down" and "prick the ear" to hear those in lowly places able, partly because of the lowliness of a well-tuned spirit, to make "music high." "Stoop" returns us to the modest proportions of Appleton House and the greater men in stanza 4 who in more temperate times "did stoop / To enter at a narrow loop" like the strait gate "which leadeth unto life" (Matthew 14). "Prick the ear" resonates with thorn, but this remarkable thornbush (though its relative provided a torment for the suffering Christ) treats the nightingale as the elders should treat birds and poets.

But the nightingale, like the rail, chooses a lowly position to her peril. The *Ornithology* of John Ray and Francis Willoughby (1678) does not stoop to listen to poets when it instructs those trying to find and capture a nest of nightingales to "put meal-worms on a thorn and see where the cock carries them." Further, "To take old nightingales, make a Trap-cage or Net-trap baited with worms or maggots. Tie the tips of his wings with some brown thread, not straining it too hard, that he may not have strength to beat himself against the top and wires of the Cage."[43] Caged nightingales, the beauty and virtuosity of whose songs Ray praises at length, presumably were not among the "furniture of friends" at Appleton House.

---

42 The story of Philomela and Tereus is told in Ovid's *Metamorphoses*, Book 6.
43 Ray, *Ornithology*, 223.

Like the meadow, the wood has its transgressions. The speaker treads on strawberries, those emblems of righteousness, and the heron (who sometimes builds flimsy nests) drops its firstborn from "the ash's top" as a distressing instance of child sacrifice. The figurative meaning does not mitigate the reality; nature's ways feed the mind with more than comfits and shock us out of complacency even about the ways of Providence. The mindless or instinctual violence of nature should disturb, but it shows us that the deliberate violence of men in their uncivil wars and their incivility to fellow creatures should disturb more.

The hero of Marvell's wood is not the nightingale or the connubial stock-dove whose melancholy song he loves, but a bird less emblematically familiar, the hewel, or hew-hole.

> But most the hewel's wonders are,
> Who here has the holtfester's care.
> He walks still upright from the root,
> Measuring the timber with his foot,
> And all the way, to keep it clean,
> Doth from the bark the woodmoths glean.
> He, with his beak, examines well
> Which fit to stand and which to fall.

John Ray's *Ornithology* gives a detailed description of the "green Woodpecker, or Woodspite, called also the Rain-fowl, High-hoe, and Hew-hole" and its expertise at building and at using its long tongue "ending in a sharp, stiff, bony thorne . . . to stab and draw out Insects lurking" in trees.[44] But Ray does not make them arborists. A hundred and fifty years after Marvell wrote, however, the American ornithologist Alexander Wilson would observe that, contrary to the prejudice of foresters who shot woodpeckers in the belief that they demolished trees, the bird's "exertions . . . contribute most powerfully to the protection of our timber" by extracting the insect larvae that are the real culprits. "And yet ignorance and prejudice stubbornly persist in directing their indignation against . . . the constant and mortal enemy of these very vermin, as if . . . the thief-catcher should be confounded with the thief."[45] Marvell already understood that the woodpecker is a good forester. He chooses tainted trees to build in and feeds his young the "traitor-worm." Like Fairfax, he cleans the mortal worm from Eden's map. It is only where his tapping finds "the hollow oak to speak, / That for his building he designs" that "through the tainted side he mines," healthily hastening the dying tree's demise. And the political message is one of strength in weakness:

> Who could have thought the tallest oak
> Should fall by such a feeble stroke!

---

44 Ray, 134.
45 Wilson, *American Ornithology*, in *The Norton Book of Nature Writing*, 79.

Marvell's "easy philosopher," contemplating the birds and plants, learns their *own* language (not the ornithologists' and botanists') and has nearly the means to become a bird or a plant himself:

> Thus I, easie philosopher,
> Among the birds and trees confer:
> And little now to make me, wants
> Or of the fowles, or of the plants.
> Give me but wings as they, and I
> Straight floating on the air shall fly:
> Or turn me but, and you shall see
> I was but an inverted tree.

The speaker confers with the birds and trees, and enters their kind of being. "Little now to make me wants / Or of the fowls, or of the plants" means that little is lacking to make him into a bird or a tree, but also that the birds and plants provide almost enough stuff to make the speaker himself. With another witty bit of inverted syntax, he literalizes the common emblem of man as an upside-down tree; he is not only nearly metamorphosed into a tree, but suggests that he "was" one all along. This shifting from nature as object of our gaze to ourselves as nature disputes attempts to separate and objectify it. And man as tree can provide still-standing timber for the yet-growing ark of poetry.

The speaker learns the birds' languages:

> Already I begin to call
> In their most learn'd original:
> And where I language want, my signs
> The bird upon the bough divines;
> And more attentive there doth sit
> Than if she were with lime-twigs knit.

The bird not only sees the speaker's gestures but "divines" their meaning, more attentive to his communications than if she were trapped by being glued to the twig— another allusion to human cruelty. The lines intimate the kind of mutual perception that David Abram draws from Merleau-Ponty: "to see the world is also, at the same time, to experience oneself as visible, to feel oneself *seen*."[46] This conception might once have been thought the fancy of an ego- and anthropocentric poet; but twentieth-century developments in zoology, anthropology, and ecological philosophy and ethics urge the recognition, which Marvell anticipates, of a seeing, knowing, feeling world of other species responsive to us.

In return, the speaker's own attention is so complete that he knows each leaf individually.

> No leaf does tremble in the wind
> Which I, returning, cannot find.

---

46 Abram, 68.

But he also reads them prophetically:

> Out of these scatter'd sibyl's leaves
> Strange prophecies my fancy weaves:
> And in one history consumes,
> Like Mexique paintings, all the plumes.

Like Aeneas's golden bough, which admits him to the underworld, the leaves unlock prophecies from which fancy weaves "one history"; while leaves and plumes are the poet's tools as he writes on the one with the other. But Marvell's simile "like Mexique paintings" makes an ecological point. In *Sylva Sylvarum* Bacon commends "The Pictures of Indian Feathers" as comfortable and pleasant to behold."[47] The ornamental and commercial use of hummingbirds' brilliant plumes nearly extinguished them.

The prophetic metaphor makes the leaves metonymies of nature in which one can find the wisdom of the three seminal cultures from which his, and his poem, spring:

> What Rome, Greece, Palestine, ere said
> I in this light mosaic read.
> Thrice happy he who, not mistook,
> Hath read in Nature's mystic book.

Nature's book was generally recognized as God's "second" book, the Bible his first. Marvell admonishes us that nature's writing too is "mystic," full of divine allegories and mysteries that can too easily be "mistook" if read impiously. In fact, he finds the wisdom of not only Greece, the cradle of western philosophy, and Rome, the empire Aeneas was on his way to found when he visited the Sybil, but even the biblical wisdom of Palestine in the "light mosaic" of each trembling leaf and the changing light between them. The phrase itself is a mosaic pattern of movable parts: "light mosaic" because a mosaic of leaves makes a mosaic of light; "light" because this mosaic is made of leaves and light instead of stone; light-giving, because through it shines the light of three founding cultures, and one of these received the Mosaic law as recounted in the "Books of Moses" whose author led his people in the Exodus from slavery in Egypt, an event that was read as the type of all liberation.[48]

Immersed in nature and reading her "mystic book," the speaker comes upon a masque.

> And see how Chance's better wit
> Could with a mask my studies hit!

---

47 Bacon, *Sylva Sylvarum* (1664), 211.

48 In his letter to Can Grande, Dante uses this story and Ps. 114 (AV), *In exitu Israel de Aegypto*, to explain the levels of allegory in the *Commedia*, where the spirits in the Ship of Souls sing it (*Purgatorio* 2.46–7). The figure of rowing pilgrims in Marvell's *Bermudas* have some kinship with these. See also Ken Hiltner's *Milton and Ecology* on Satan's tempting the Son to adopt Roman, Greek, and "exalted Judaic thinking and culture" (89); conceivably Marvell's "not mistook" suggests that nature can sometimes be a better teacher than dominating cultures.

> The oak leaves me embroider all,
> Between which caterpillars crawl:
> And ivy, with familiar trails,
> Me licks, and clasps, and curls, and hales.
> Under this antic cope I move
> Like some great prelate of the grove.

The leaves and light are his costumer, together embroidering him with the shapes of oak leaves—the Sybil's tree, but also the trees that "stoop down to hear" the nightingale. Caterpillars, lascivious ivy, and not just a priest but a bishop of a sacred grove are an odd list of dramatis personae: animal, vegetable, and presiding humanity. But this is a mask and masque of the whole sentient world. It also lightly draws in family and religion: "familiar trails" are the ivy's licking, clasping, curling, trailing vines, but by connecting them to the prelate we are brought back to the nunnery from which Appleton House was built and that was "no religious house till now" that it houses a religiously reformed family.

All of these, caterpillars that produce oak moths, ivy with its snares, prelates (but of sacred groves), have potentially sinister connotations. But here they constitute a habitat of plant, animal, and human visitor. The "I" moves under the forest's "antic cope"—both ancient and playful, both canopy and vault, its shadows an embroidery of oak leaves and caterpillars punningly turned to a prelate's robe. The caterpillars—enemy to oaks, but food to hewels—are traitors metamorphosed and transubstantiated by the balance of a natural world in which the speaker has "encamped," he says, "my mind." Resting on "pallet's swoll'n of velvet moss" and cooled by the wind, he thanks them: "Thanks for my rest, ye mossy banks; / And unto you, cool zephyrs, thanks." His mind encamped among the trees, he adds, has been safe from temptations and political and military volleys,

> Where the world no certain shot
> Can make, or me it toucheth not.
> But I on it securely play,
> And gall its horsemen all the day.

He asks woodbines, brambles, and "courteous briars" to chain and nail him there in terms that remind us of the captivity of love, and even the crown of thorns and the cross of supernal love. Although it is full of emblems, we cannot reductively emblematize this natural world; all creatures great and small have their instructive but animated and interwoven places in the ecology of both the estate and the ocean of the mind. Thus Marvell galls the horsemen (both apocalyptic and worldly) who would use this green, yet-growing ark of the natural world only as their hunting grounds.

To camp, however, is not to dwell. The speaker comes out of the woods still speaking the language of man, but with an enlarged vocabulary. The river has now receded, and he emerges, like Gonzalo in *The Tempest*, to find the meadows "fresher dyed," the grass "as green silks but newly washed." The river, Nunappleton's "only snake," holds the meadow in "wanton harmless folds" and in its mirror "all things gaze themselves, and doubt / If they be in it, or without." This double perspective reflects the speaker's experience of entering into the lives of birds and oaks, rivers and grass, yet also belonging to a human and political world.

Only if one reads the poem as nostalgia for changeless tidiness in nature and society is one perturbed by the shifting scenes that worry Parfitt or the "scenic incongruities" in which Fitter finds that "Disturbance invades meaning as well as order." If one likes vitality, the suggestive oddities Fitter finds epistemologically disturbing—the "hatching throstle's shining eye" viewing the passerby and the caterpillars crawling between the oak leaves of the contemplative's "cope"—revitalize perception. Fitter's discomfort derives from his assumption that nature is "inescapably dualistic within a Christian tradition," holding "opposing aspects" of "postlapsarian instability and menace" and "refuge from such tensions of dominion: in the amnesia of sensual glut, and intimations of transcendence."[49] As we shall see in subsequent chapters, the theology of nature held by Marvell and Milton among others was not dualistic but monistic, and divinity not transcendent but immanent. While Marvell's responses can be both sensuous and transcendent, he also shows that one can live in monistic unity with nature and its creative flux if dominion over nature is not one's dominant intention. If one looks at nature in the spirit of the Voice from the Whirlwind in the Book of Job, nature's dynamic unexpectedness can explode moral simplicities and activate poetic imagination.[50] The choice is not between "menace" and either "sensual glut" or "transcendence" but between a desire for stasis and a recognition that the untamable energies of nature are the stuff of creation.

This choice is political as well as practical and illustrates the differences between "Economy" or the management of nature's house and "Ecology," or a knowledge of it that for Marvell includes delight, gratitude, the interplay of the untamable energies of nature, imagination, and language. But what about human responsibility for nature's well-being, apart from leaving nature somewhat free? Enter Fairfax's young daughter and Marvell's pupil, Maria Fairfax.

Tilling conscience

We have glimpsed human work on the estate before: the military gardeners, the mowers and reapers, Thestylis who despite her pastoral name trusses the rail. But the welfare of the estate belongs ultimately not to the georgic figures but to the virgin Maria, neither a worker nor an empress over nature, who presides by her presence.[51] This precedence is not a matter of Maria's perception of nature, but of nature's perception of her. Marvell tells his pupil that nature responds not just to our industry but to our inner being, the harmony of body and soul by which we "conscience till."

See how loose Nature, in respect
To her, itself doth recollect.

---

49 Fitter, *Poetry, Space, and Landscape*, 289–90.

50 On God's poetry in Job see Robert Alter, *The Art of Biblical Poetry*, chapter IV.

51 Donald M. Friedman discusses this topos in "The Lady in the Garden," *Milton Studies* 35 (1997), 114–33.

Even "The sun himself, of her aware, / Seems to descend with greater care." Nature's awareness of and responsiveness to Maria epitomize Marvell's sense of sensuous and moral interchange between human beings and the rest of nature. Hyperbolic praise of a young girl, like Donne's in the *Anniversaries*, makes her the soul of the world. But rather than using this metaphor, or allusions to innocent Eve, Marvell compares Maria strangely and beautifully to a native bird, the "modest halcyon" or kingfisher, to whose coming the speaker animistically attributes the calm of evening that coincides with its arrival.

> So when the shadows laid asleep
> From underneath these banks do creep,
> And on the river as it flows
> With ebon shuts begin to close;
> The modest halcyon comes in sight,
> Flying betwixt the day and night;
> And such an horror calm and dumb,
> Admiring Nature does benumb.

"Horror" still bears its etymology of trembling or shuddering and its meaning, used until the early nineteenth century, of "A feeling of awe or reverent fear" (*Oxford English Dictionary* 4). But it includes the kind of multiple meanings that jostle together in early modern English words and give them such perplexing richness. This concept of an "evening" includes the aweful and avoids sentimentalizing its tranquillity.

The evening takes its color from the kingfisher:

> The viscous air, wheres'e'er she fly,
> Follows and sucks her azure dye;

the water thickens and plots to make the bird, or her shadow, stay, and the stunned fish are encrystalled in the gelid stream; even men are stilled.

> The jellying stream compacts below,
> If it might fix her shadow so;
> The stupid fishes hang, as plain
> As flies in crystal overta'en;
> And men the silent scene assist,
> Charmed with the sapphire-wingèd mist.

And now comes a timely perplexity: the simile appears to attribute the effects of the even-ing of the light to the halcyon and the suspended clarity of nature to Mary Fairfax. Both are individual intensifications of nature's state, compacting our perceptions so that all else becomes individual and intensified and hangs in suspense like the stunned fish.

> Maria such, and so doth hush
> The world, and through the evening rush.
> No new-born comet such a train
> Draws through the sky, nor star new-slain.

For straight those giddy rockets fail,
Which from the putrid earth exhale,
But by her flames, in heaven tried,
Nature is wholly vitrified.

The inclusion of slain star and rotting earth keeps us in the world of mortality, but for a moment nature's processes, which usually elude us by their swiftness and subtlety, halt at the arrival of their epitome, and we can see more clearly. Maria is like a comet rushing through the evening, but comets and falling stars pass quickly and she, having been "tried" in heaven, becomes a furnace in which nature is turned to glass. What can this sudden de-animation of nature mean?

Such hushed crystallization is a trope of praise in which all things are calmed and clarified by reverence for the goddess-giftgiver that Maria represents, or of the reverence of nature for the image of God in her, or of Nature's recognition of Maria as her own epitome. Elizabeth Donno notes that "A lady's power over a landscape was a standard topos."[52] Yet Marvell's use of it is more than compliment. I think that the passage subtly comments on ways that human beings, in the biblical phrase, subdue the earth. If nature is responsive to us, our moral state affects it. Even if it were not, our moral choices preserve or destroy it. Maria does not "subdue the earth" in the ways that phrase is usually interpreted. She does not personally subject or exploit it, but gives it her own qualities of beauty, straightness, sweetness, and purity, which it receives and returns. This pattern of giving, receiving, and returning is represented in Renaissance art by the Three Graces, incorporated in Maria. Thus nature is "vitrified" as a looking-glass in which human beings can see their own natures in the effects they have on it.

Maria's mirror contrasts to the looking-glasses of the vain because only she— only the inner beauty and virtue of humanity—can keep Nature fair and pure.

'Tis she that to these gardens gave
That wondrous beauty that they have;
She straightness on the woods bestows;
To her the meadow sweetness owes;
Nothing could make the river be
So crystal pure but only she;
She yet more pure, sweet, straight, and fair,
Than gardens, woods, meads, rivers are.

Thus "what first she on them spent, / They gratefully again present" in meadow carpets, garden garlands, "the limpid brook" where she may see her own beauties, and a screen of woods because "she would not have them seen," because she would prefer to be found wise than fair.

For she, to higher beauties raised,
Disdains to be for lesser praised.
She counts her beauty to converse
In all the languages as hers;

---

52 Donno, 254 n.

Nor yet in those herself employs
But for the wisdom, not the noise;
Nor yet that wisdom would affect,
But as 'tis heaven's dialect.

The "woods, gardens, and meads" of Nunappleton far exceed "Thessalian Tempe's seat" and "the dead's Elysian Fields" (stanza 95) just as, John Beale would write to Samuel Hartlib in 1658, English husbandry can be "like the Worke or Garden of God" and "exceede the best phansys of old Poets. Their Elysian fields their Thessalian Tempe, their Peneian Groves."[53]

Marvell acknowledges that the georgic ideal is far from realized in most of the world—except Nunappleton.

'Tis not, what once it was, the world,
But a rude heap together hurled,
All negligently overthrown,
Gulfs, deserts, precipices, stone.
Your lesser world contains the same,
But in more decent order tame,
You, heaven's centre, Nature's lap,
And paradise's only map.

At first glance, this stanza seems to undo the relation of cultivated and wild nature the speaker has been enjoying. "Tame" suggests something more domitable than the "yet green, yet growing ark" of a free and accommodating habitat. But the "world" that is not tame here is the infertile disarray into which the creation has been "negligently overthrown" by "man unruled," and the "decent order tame" of Nunappleton is that of Nature's fertile "lap," both in being not fearful to man and in being "not fearful of man."[54] Its order is decent, like the first abundant garden, because the human inhabitants have "conscience tilled."

To say that Nunappleton is "Paradise's only map" is to say that this actual garden is the best guide for the restoration of post-war England to the nearest resemblance to Eden that can be achieved. I don't propose that the poet claims that human predation can be cured by temperate agriculture or that nature, wounded by the first gardeners of Eden, is not perplexing, dangerous, and sometimes cruel. The river is, in fact, not the only snake. The poem is full of punning allusions to the recent wars and other violences, not only human ones: the stork and the heron sacrifice their firstborn (stanza 67) as warring nations do.[55] But these very perplexities challenge the Baconian program of conquest and control. What can amend human predation is "Conscience, that heaven-nurs'd plant, / Which most our earthly gardens want." Maria is nursed in a "domestic heaven," and this poem is one of her nurses. Conscience gets many prods, from the problematic "stately frontispiece of poor" to the spurious innocence of the desecrated nunnery to the death of the rail to the death-mask of the vain ladies

---

53 Quoted by Michael Leslie in "The Spiritual Husbandry of John Beale," in Leslie and Raylor 155–6.

54 Tame: *New Shorter Oxford English Dictionary*.

55 Nature's perplexities in Marvell's poems are further considered in Chapter 4.

in contrast to Maria Fairfax's inner knowledge and virtue. Even more, it is prodded awake by the detailed, polysemous responsiveness of Marvell's elegant craft, which releases such a burst of possibilities as to alter the chemistry of our thoughts: whatever mental traps we might be caught in are swept away by the proliferation of choices and connections. The poet goes hand in hand with nature, as Sidney says, but here in ways homologous with the evolving processes of a natural world that is ever changing and yet, astrophysicists tell us, consistent in properties revealed by harmonic analysis.[56]

In the habitat of the poem, paradise is not leisured affluence or an ideal order but this liquid activity of mind responding to the organic processes of a place worth caring for because it really lives. This place has room for wild as well as cultivated nature, and its fish twang unharmed at Marvell's "quills" like piscatorial virginal-players and like readers feeding on the baits of his pen without getting hooked on dogmatic lines.[57] In an early stanza we hear that "the tortoises do dwell / In cases fit of tortoise shell"; and we recall that the tortoise's dwelling is often made into vain commodities. In the end, we come back to the tortoise and to "cases fit" in an image that may remind us of Topsell's "Chelophagi" who eat tortoises and "row in them upon the water"[58]; but the similitude is between men and tortoises, and the coracle is only a metaphorical shell.

> But now the salmon-fishers moist
> Their leathern boats begin to hoist,
> And like Antipodes in shoes,
> Have shod their heads in their canoes.
> How tortoise-like, but not so slow,
> These rational amphibii go!
> Let's in: for the dark hemisphere
> Does now like one of them appear.

The macrocosm that hemispheres Nunappleton matches the microcosm of a fisherman with a coracle shoe on his head, and this image of amphibious man, denizen of both natural and spiritual habitats, shows us upside down, our own antipodes, to stand us right side up. We are inverted with respect to the world until we become rational enough to fit our habitats as tortoises fit their shells. One does not need to be a Lord General to gaze and graze on the common of nature and to care for it well within one's purview. By its way of seeing much in little, its radiant play of mind and matter, and its language in which "Things greater are in less contained," the poem itself in which we have dwelt becomes an oikos-system, a map for all houses, yet sends us forth into the rich habitation of responsive nature well perceived, to which *oikos*, as well as Appleton House itself, Marvell says, "Let's in."

---

56 See Stephen Landy, "Mapping the Universe."

57 Wyman Herendeen finds that "Marvell explores the power of the individual intellect to embrace nature and to be in accord with it. Marvell's is basically a Senecan, stoic ideal in which the individual's knowledge of and rapport with nature enables a self-realization which results in a transcendence beyond the self, and an integration in the natural order." From *Landscape to Literature*, 335.

58 Topsell, see n. 19 above.

Chapter 2

Earth, Mining, Monotheism, and Mountain Theology

The nurturing earth is pregnant.

Vergil, *Georgics*

In Ovid's myth of Phaeton, Phoebus Apollo, who drives the sun's chariot daily across the sky, gives one wish to Phaeton, his mortal son, who asks to drive the chariot, the craft of Vulcan, god of technology. Phoebus, dismayed but obliged to keep his word, orders his golden chariot brought forth and hitched to the fiery steeds with many admonitions: "Forget the whip, / But hold the reins with all your strength; these horses/ Race at their will." But the boy cannot control them; they race and plunge, the dry earth splits, grain fields turn to ashes, cities perish, forests burn, the poles grow hot, springs dry up, mountains lose their snow, sea mammals die, and "Ancient Earth, child-bearer of all things," cries out to Zeus: "Is this your will? Have I earned this for my / Fertility? For me who wear the scars / Of plough and spade?"[1] And Zeus blasts Phaeton out of the sky. Can Phoebus Apollo, god of reason and of poetry, regain control of Vulcan's chariot?

Ovid's word for Earth is *Tellus*, the active mother of living things, the genetrix, the nurturer. In Genesis, earth actively brings forth all plants and animals in response to God's voice. For Lucretius, they are "earthborn, / And truly earth deserves her title *Mother*"; she feeds them through "Channels from which a kind of milk-like juice / Would issue, as a woman's breasts are filled / With the sweet milk after her child is born."[2] In classical tradition, the Golden Age left nature undefiled; only in the Brazen was earth's womb invaded for the means of wealth and war.

George Sandys' translation of Ovid's *Metamorphoses* recounts that in the golden age "The yet-free Earth did of her own accord / (Untorne with ploughs) all sorts of fruit afford." During the Silver Age (providentially, to keep human beings from sinful sloth, according to Vergil's *Georgics*) Saturn's rebellious son Jove split the year into seasons: "Then, first was corne into long furrowes throwne: / And Oxen Under heavy yokes did growne." In the Iron Age came "Force, Treason, and the wicked love of gayne," forests were felled for ships, and "The Ground, as common earst as Light, or Aire" was cut up into private properties; "Nor with rich Earth's just nourishments content, / For treasure [men] her secret entrailes rent; . . . Curst Steele,

---

1 Ovid, *Metamorphoses*, Book II, trans. Horace Gregory.

2 Lucretius, *De Rerum Natura,* trans. Rolfe Humfries, 5:795–6, 812–14. Richard DuRocher discusses the "animist Roman view" (25) and Milton's use of it *Milton among the Romans*.

more cursed Gold, she now forth brought: / And bloody-handed Warre, who with both fought."[3]

Rifling the bowels of Mother Earth

As seventeeenth-century agricultural and mining technology changed, the language that had from antiquity characterized earth as the living mother of life began to change as well. One can follow these changes through the metaphor of earth's womb or inward parts, and through the career of a mining engineer and disciple of Francis Bacon named Thomas Bushell, who to some extent was a conservationist and a humanitarian as well as a promoter of Vulcan's craft.

In 1636, shortly after the publication of Sandy's Ovid and the performance of John Milton's *Maske at Ludlow*, Bushell presented a rock masque, together with the rock, to Henrietta Maria, Queen of England. The rock was a feature of his estate of Road Enstone near Woodstock in Oxfordshire, where he had discovered a "desolate Cell of Natures rarities" and turned it into a grotto with a banqueting room and "contemplative Groves and Walkes, as well as artificial thunder and lightning, raine, haile showres, drums beating, organs playing, birds singing, waters murmuring, the dead arising, lights moving, rainbowes reflecting f[r]om the same fountain." The queen accepted this tribute and commanded that it be called by her name. Music for the masque was written by Symon Ive, a composer of considerable skill and reputation, and the verse by Bushell himself.[4] His courtly use of the "pathetic fallacy" is an entirely different matter from the affinitive appreciation of contemporaries whose poems I nominate as proto-ecological. He writes,

> Harke, harke, how the stones in the Rocke
> Strive their tongues to unlock,
>   And would show,
>   What they know,
> Of the Joy here hath beene
> Since the King and the Queene
>   Deign to say
>   They would pay
> A visit to this cell:
> But all tongues cannot tell;
>   Nor language expresse
>   Our full thankfulnesse.

The birds and streams also devote themselves to the praise of the royal visitors, though the larks and thrushes and musical waters may be artificial.

In Milton's *Mask at Ludlow*, by contrast, the villain Comus attempts to tempt the Lady, scion of the governing class, with the luxurious living of the Caroline court

---

3   Sandys, trans., *Metamorphosis*, 3–4; compare Vergil's *Georgics* 1. Milton's sonnet "To Sir Henry Vane the Younger" calls iron and gold war's "two main nerves."

4   Bushell, *Severall Speeches and Songs*. Bushell's "improvements" were not commercial, but thanks to two royal visits he did profit in influence.

and a desire to subject all of nature to human delectation. He argues that nature pours forth her bounty "to please, and sate the curious taste" and "in her own loins / She hutched th'all-worshipped or, and precious gems / To store her children with." If subterranean treasures were not mined,

> th'unsought diamonds
> Would so emblaze the forehead of the deep,
> And so bestud with stars, that they below
> Would grow inured to light, and come at last
> To gaze upon the sun with shameless brows.   [731–5]

John Leonard succinctly glosses, "Gems were thought to grow and shine under the earth, so unsought gems would eventually illumine Hell."[5] George Sandys reverses Comus's conception: "Men through the wounded Earth inforce their way; / And shew the under Shades an unknowne Day."[6]

Mining lore suggests a further reading. Bushell reports Bacon's opinion that "subterranean Spirits hindered the perfect discoveries of the richest Mines . . . by the mischievous gambols they plaid there, as by raising Damps, extinguishing the Miners lights, firing the sulphurous matter of the Mine, and scorching the greedy and faithless Workmen. For not only *Socrates*, *Plato*, and *Aristotle*" believed that "multitudes of Evil Spirits" inhabited air, water, and "the hollow Concaverns of the Earth; but divers of our more modern learned Writers and Theologians are of the same perswasion." Among the moderns are Thomas Aquinas and Augustine, "who conceive that God hath permitted their temporal habitations therein" to test or punish human beings, like the legion of demons Jesus casts out in Mark 5.[7] Comus tells the Lady that by becoming inured to light, these subterranean spirits could enlarge their scope for mischief, and that she should deprive these imps of the lights in the ceiling of earth's womb by having them mined and wearing them. The Lady retorts that Nature,

> good cateress,
> Means her provision only to the good
> That live according to her sober laws,
> And holy dictate of spare Temperance.   [764–7]

Bacon's proposals go well beyond "spare Temperance" in *Sylva Sylvarum*, where he recommends, alluding to sympathetic magic, the wearing of precious jewels, for "Stones have in them fine Spirits, as appeareth by their Splendour: And therefore they may work by consent upon the Spirits of Men, to comfort and exhilarate them." He adds that other colorful possessions, like paintings made of hummingbird feathers, also cheer the (human) spirits.[8] Milton's masque parodies such promotions of luxury; Comus's notion of removing the jewels from the ceiling of the underworld

---

5   Leonard, ed., *John Milton: The Complete Poems*, note to ll. 732–6, 768.

6   Sandys, *A Paraphrase vpon Iob*, 34. Many of his lines are reminiscent of the *Mask*, published shortly before.

7   Bushell, *Mr. Bushell's Abridgment*, 10.

8   Bacon, *Sylva Sylvarum* (1664), 211.

to keep malicious Spirits underground parodies the doctrine of human responsibility for nature and aligns him with projectors who, however well-intentioned, would ransack Earth's inner parts for "th'all-worshipped ore." His advice to invade the earth matches his intent to invade the Lady, herself a *figura* of virgin nature.[9] For him, Earth's loins, and hers, are storehouses of pleasures to be rifled.

Turning an interesting rock formation into a mechanical grotto illustrates the reluctance of Western man to leave anything unaltered. But in the matter of mining, Bushell, though he may agree with Comus that unsought riches go to waste, was to some extent a conservationist. He proposed to accomplish Bacon's plan of rehabilitating drowned mines in England and Wales by closing vertical airshafts, boring lower down on mountainsides for access and drainage, and using bellows for ventilation. He argued that by providing local lead and silver to be coined at local mints, this program would relieve England of the necessity of importing minerals from the Americas, mined by slaves and profiting the Spaniards; give petty felons work suitable for mollifying stony hearts, but less cruel than death or deportation; save the expense of transporting unrefined ores; and replenish the King's coffers with silver coin without oppressive taxation. He regarded this task as a public service for which he risked financial ruin.[10]

However, Bushell's conservation program never considers the convenience of any creature not human, and the emerging concept of landscape does not touch him.[11] He calls mineable mountains "barren," perhaps to assure local communities that his plans will not damage agricultural or grazing land. He revered the principles of Solomon's House in Bacon's *New Atlantis* and wished to found an institute modelled on them. Both King James and Francis Bacon had been called "England's Solomon," James for his peacemaking and Bacon after the Hebrew king's reputation as a naturalist from 1 Kings 4.33: "And he spake of trees, from the cedar tree that is in Lebanon even unto the hyssop that springeth out of the wall: he spake also of beasts, and of fowl, and of creeping things, and of fishes." Bushell proposes to God in a "Miner's Prayer" that "Solomon beautified thine own Temple which he built with his far sought Mineral Treasure, and I would gladly erect a house to the honor of his name."[12]

---

9   Joan S. Bennett, in "Virgin Nature in *Comus*," compares the Lady with Natura in Alain of Lille's *Complaint of Nature*: Natura laments that humanity "disregards the restraints of temperance, breaks to pieces the seals of my chastity, pays no heed to the graciousness of my bounty," 27; trans. Douglas M. Moffat, 62.

10   Bushell mentions Bacon's address to Parliament about recovering drowned mines and employing felons in a biographical "Post-Script to the Judicious Reader" (3) following the *New Atlantis* in *Abridgment*.

11   Richard Francaviglia in *Hard Places* shows that modern open-pit mining and placer mining using dredges and hydraulic hoses are more devastating to the land than underground or "hard rock" mining (127–9).

12   Bushell, "The Miners contemplative Prayer in his solitary Delves . . . that the Reader may know, his heart implores providence for his Mineral increase, aswel as petitions liberty from men to dig for treasure in their barren Mountains,'" 12, in *Abridgment* just before the *New Atlantis*.

As Wallace Stegner's epic American novel *Angle of Repose* reminds us, promoters of technology are often public-spirited and even heroic, and we see by hindsight how their works grow out of control. Many such "projectors" as Bushell proposed conservation of land, provision of employment, and reparative technology for such mistakes as inefficient mining, unsustainable farming, and especially deforestation because of industrial charcoal-burning, and early modern proponents of coal mining justified their projects as ways of stopping the devastating deforestation of previous centuries. They included marketing and cost-effectiveness estimates and often what might now be called environmental impact statements. Bushell and Bacon were aware of mercury poisoning and other kinds of pollution from mining: "[T]hose that deal much in Refining, or other works about Metalls and Minerals, have their Brains hurt and stupefi'd by the Metalline Vapours . . . . the Spirits of Quick-silver ever flie to the Skull, Teeth, or Bones . . . . There are certain Lakes and Pits, such as that of Avernus, that poison Birds (as is said) which flie over them, or Men that stay too long about them."[13] But promoters of mining did not consider what it did to people and animals downstream.[14]

Literary tradition connects underground treasure with death, often personified as Hades, Pluto, or Mammon. Gold is rarely beloved of poets for reasons made manifest in the myth of Midas; desire for wealth disables the spirit. *Beowulf* shows heroes honored by gifts of gold, but the dragon's hoard acknowledges its perils. Chaucer, More, and Spenser see it as a divider of nations and a corrupter of souls, as Chaucer's Pardoner self-underminingly illustrates. More's Utopians mock the Anemolian Ambassadors for wearing gold and jewels; Utopians make slaves and criminals wear them as signs of disgrace or give them to children as toys. Sir Guyon in Spenser's *Faerie Queene*, after escaping with honor from the unnatural garden of erotic delectation, faints in the Cave of Mammon.

In Bushell one sees an alliance of desire for profit with hopes for public benefit that I think it useful to believe sincere; the road to ecological disaster is often paved with good but short-sighted intentions. However, Bacon's proposals in the *New Atlantis* go far beyond human necessity or the remedy of disease, and his pupil Bushell underestimates the service of mining to human vanity and lust for power.

Bushell's social conscience matched his conservationism. Though a royalist allied to the program that led to the establishment of the Royal Society, Bushell adjusted to Cromwell's Protectorate and went beyond even Milton's libertarianism, becoming "so sensible of other mens suffering restraint for conscience sake, as I procured the liberty of many Jesuit Priests, Anabaptists, Brownists, Familists of love, Adamites, and one of the Rosie Crucian." He learned from Bacon not to "punish any offender by the superior Officer, but as shall be judged by a Jury of penitential soules of their own Tribe," and "severity should never force a builder of his *Solomon's house*, since it is barbarous for a Christian to behold the Image of God used like a Dog." He fell short of Montaigne, who thought it barbarous to misuse animals as well. He taught that work should be for the Glory of God and the relief of the poor and promised

---

13   Bacon, *Sylva Sylvarum* (1664), 202.

14   At present mercury still poisons streams, hydraulic mining still depletes aquifers, mining rubble spoils lands of the Shoshone and Laguna nations among others.

(not disinterestedly) to help at his own expense the poor of any parish where laborers find minerals while ploughing and ditching. Prospectors should "come to no mans ground" without notice, pay "double trespass," and appeal to the Justice of the Peace if refused. No one should covet riches or perform wicked acts, "for the Mistery of divine Phylosophy will not admit of any of those to have a sheare in such a blessing."[15] But improvements in mining brought with them a language that made the earth, once the sentient mother of life, an object to be penetrated and blasted.

Simon Sturtevant, who argued that coal mining could reduce deforestation, was in 1612 already proposing a mineralogical language free of such metaphors as Earth's womb. "*Heuretica* is the Art of invention; *Metallica* is of two sorts, *Ignemetallica*, which worketh with fire and hearth, or *Inignemetallica*, which useth not the meanes of fire" and so forth.[16]

Other mining tracts retain the personification of the pregnant earth, but their metaphors are increasingly appropriative and eventually dead. Bushell called on James I, "our Christian Solomon," to bring "conceiled Treasures . . . into use by the industry of converted Penitents, whose wretched Carcases the impartial Laws have or shall dedicate as untimely feasts to the worms of the earth, in whose womb those deserted Mineral riches must ever lie buried as lost abortments, unless those be made the active Midwives to deliver them." A correspondent tells him, "Me thinks those Mountains are as so many pregnant Wombs, and now in labour call for your fortunate hands to deliver them, to the honor of your Royall Master, and perpetuated glory of the Nation."[17] Gabriel Plattes in 1639 extolled mining by lamenting the "number of Treasure and riches which lyeth hidden in the belly of the Earth, and doth no good." These minerals will be found in mountains, not valleys, "for the wombe of such earth is not apt for such a generation."[18]

John Milton protests these conceptions of Earth's womb as a factory of human commodities. In *Paradise Lost* mining is an activity of the Satanic party, in both the War in Heaven and the building of Pandemonium. Milton shows some knowledge of mining handbooks like Plattes's in his description of a hill the demons mine, "whose grisly top / Belched fire and rolling smoke; the rest entire / Shone with a glossy scurf, undoubted sign / That in his womb was hid metallic ore, / The work of sulfur" (ll. 670–74). The oddity of "his womb" may be the common use of "his" as "its,"[19] but also compares, without conflating, the womb of the generative Earth with the inward parts of Hell. Milton tells us that the demonic engineers are led by "Mammon, the least erected Spirit that fell / From Heav'n" (ll. 679–80);

> by him first
> Men also, and by his suggestion taught,
> Ransacked the centre, and with impious hands
> Rifled the bowels of their mother Earth

---

15   *Abridgment*, final treatise, 12 and 13.

16   Sturtevant, *Metallica* (1612), 33–4.

17   Bushell, "Post-Script to the Judicious Reader," in *Abridgment*, 4.

18   Plattes, preface "To the Reader," in *A Discovery of Subterranean Treasure* (1639), sig. C3v.

19   See Leonard, ed., *Complete Poems*, 726 n. 673.

For treasures better hid. Soon had his crew
Opened into the hill a spacious wound
And digged out ribs of gold. Let none admire
That riches grow in Hell; that soil may best
Deserve the precious bane.   [684–92]

Satanic mining is not limited to Hell; during the War in Heaven, Satan invents cannons and gunpowder from the underground source of "plant, fruit, flow'r ambrosial, gems, and gold," noting—not without aesthetic delight—that they grow from minerals

Deep underground, materials dark and crude,
Of spiritous and fiery spume, till touched
With Heav'n's ray, and tempered they shoot forth
So beauteous, op'ning to the ambient light.   [6.478–81]

These same materials, cast and touched with fire, will shoot forth destruction.

What are we to draw from the typically Miltonic perplexity that heaven should have such soil, or Satan should retain remnants of a heavenly mind? First, I think, Milton's materialism: all things are made from one first matter, and Heaven, Raphael says, may be more like to earth than we suppose. Second, Milton's commitment to free will and ethical choice: that heaven's flowers should shoot forth from ignitable minerals corresponds with the principle of *Areopagitica* that the *matter* of sin and virtue are the same[20]; the dark materials of Earth's womb bring forth fruits and flowers, or the dragon's hoard, depending on human (or angelic) choices.

Mining inevitably raises disputes over property rights, and earth's womb was disputed property. Moses Stringer, a more absolute royalist than Bushell, argued in *Opera Mineralis Explicata* (1713) that mineral wealth should belong absolutely to those holding patents from the crown. He recounts that Elizabeth I in 1565 had granted durable "Letters Patents" to a society of patentees giving them and "their Heirs and Assigns for ever, full, free and absolute Power and Authority to search, open, mine, dig and try in all Earths, Grounds, Soils and Places in her Realm of England, and other her Majesty's Dominions, and the Territories . . . and also in the Kingdom of Ireland, &c. to mine, dig and get all . . . Earths, Metals or Minerals whatsoever, to them and their Heirs for ever." James I in 1609 "Incorporated the said Society with the then Sir Francis Bacon . . . and other chief Ministers of State" in grants often ratified since. Among the members of the Corporation in 1713 was "Her Majesty's Chymist and Mineral Master General Moses Stringer." Stringer had no sympathy with the "late Rebellion" which usurped "all the Rights of the Crown"; people did as they pleased with the crown lands, gave grants opposing the Corporation's, and attempted to "destroy any Tools, Engins, Mills, Edifices, or Instruments made or form'd in prejudice to their works, whereby the Crown is oblig'd to defend this Corporation."[21] When the battle lines were drawn between protectors of private or

---

20   Milton, *Areopagitica*, in *Complete Prose Works* 2:527. Milton's point is that one cannot "remove sin by removing the matter of sin" because the same matter—whether it be nature, culture, or our own passions—is also the stuff of virtue.

21   Stringer, *Opera Mineralis Explicata* (London, 1713), iv–x.

common property and crown or corporate rights to do whatever they pleased with any land whatsoever, respect for mother earth herself was not a consideration.

Writers promoting technological progress often used biblical justifications. Simon Sturtevant concludes his preface with a prayer "beseeching the Lord, who by his holy spirit inspired *Bezaleel, Aholiab* and *Hiram*, with the light of Mechannicall Inventions, *and in all manner of workmanship*" to bless his enterprise (Exodus 31and 2 Chron. 2) and claims it apparent from scripture "that all Mechanic Arts and Inventions, as well as the graces of salvation, are the peculiar works, and gifts of Gods holy spirit in man." Stringer writes that since "God hath been pleased to furnish Man with a Soul capable of making large Improvements in all useful Arts and Sciences, and to submit his Works (which bear the Stamp of Divine Wisdom and Contrivance) to his Knowledge and Use; and indeed his giving us a Capacity to Philosophize on the Luminaries of Heaven . . . and a Knowledge of what is on the Earth, or in the Seas, does not seem a more gracious Act of Indulgence than his Revealing to us the hidden Treasures contained in the Bowels of the Earth, which are no less surprising than the rest of his Works."[22]

Reading this mixture of technology and religion one can see why many ecological critics assume that early modern literature could have no environmental ethic. In the classic essay of Lynn White, Jr., Western Christianity is "the most anthropocentric religion that the world has seen" because in contrast to paganism and most Asian religions, Christianity "established a dualism of man over nature for his proper ends." We must all, like St. Francis, "reject the Christian axiom that nature has no reason for existence save to serve man."[23]

However, seventeenth-century Christian poets often, and a few natural historians and philosophers sometimes, did reject that idea. While Aristotelian, Platonic, Thomistic, Calvinist, and Cartesian dualisms and the Baconian program of empire over nature held, to varying extents, that the non-human world had was created for the use of the rational and immortal human soul, these poets were proto-ecological in their opposition to these views.[24] Their philosophy is monistic and vitalistic, and their sense of the sacred encompasses the whole creation. They populate their poems with other-than-human beings whom they treat as worthy to live their lives in their own way, and they acknowledge the damage to both the natural world and the human spirit of penetrating and overexploiting the body of Mother Earth. They look at nature in part empirically, like the new philosophers, but as a fabric of lives, not a list of utilities. They complicate and delight our sense of connections by the woven processes of language they lead us through. They, too, mix talk of nature with talk of God, but that is because for them nature and spirit are indivisible.

---

22   Sturtevant, 55; Stringer, 7.

23   White, "The Historical Roots of Our Ecological Crisis," reprinted in *The Ecocriticism Reader*, Glotfelty and Fromm, eds, 9–10, 14.

24   Hobbes, however, states that: "although Sense and Memory of things, which are common to man and all living creatures, be knowledge, yet because they are given us immediately by nature, and not gotten by ratiocination, they are not philosophy" (*The English Works* 1:3).

Human vanity and the generative planet

The early modern topos of earth as sentient and nurturing mother promotes human spiritual and moral consciousness, but it is also concerned with the well-being of earth and her other offspring and with the rapes and degradations inflicted on her. It draws from the myth of Gaia but is primarily warranted by the conception in Genesis of earth's response to God's words, "Let the earth bring forth," in which "Mother Earth" is God's feminine partner in the work of generating all living things. In the mid-seventeenth century this topos was also supported by Biblical interpretation, theological monism, and poetic vitalism.

George Sandys, a voyager to Europe, the Middle East, and the New World, who translated Ovid in Virginia and on the high seas and collected accounts of global travelers, was also a member of the Caroline court, whose lavishness Milton's masque opposes. Yet Sandys's critique of the misuse of land and water is consonant with the outrage of native American activists like Carrie Dann or writers like Leslie Marmon Silko and Simon J. Ortiz for whom the homelands being wounded for gold and uranium—for wealth and war—contain irreplaceable sacred wisdom. In Sandys's expanded *Paraphrase vpon Iob* (1638), published shortly after both Milton's and Bushell's masques, mining epitomizes the exploitation of the "fostering earth" for wealth that destroys the spirit:

> Men through the wounded Earth inforce their way;
> And shew the under Shades and unknowne Day:
> While from her bowels they her Treasure teare;
> And to their avarice subject their feare.

The followers of Mammon suppress their fear of God's wrath as well as underground hazards to tear wealth from Earth's entrails. They tamper further by hydraulic engineering:

> There they with Subterranean Waters meet;
> And Currents, never touch't by humane feet:
> These, by their bold endeavors, are made dry;
> And from the industry of Mortals flye.

Though earth's brows are attired in grain, "her Jawes exhale imbosom'd fires" in places devoid of life, where "Torne Rocks" unfold precious jewels and gold as men's "restlesse Labors cleave the living Stone," tear up "Cloud-touching Mountaines," create new streams, dam rivers, view "the Magazines of Nature," and "what in Darknesse lurkt, to Light expose." But Wisdom cannot be found among the trophies of world conquest, such as topaz "sent from scorched Meroë or "Pearles presented by the Indian Sea," and her palace cannot be found in some yet "undiscover'd Land."[25]

Sandys's diatribe strikes at the roots of processes that Bushell and Stringer wished to justify and reform, and against a colonial acquisitiveness typified by Ralegh's advertisement to obtain the patronage of Elizabeth I for the colonization of Guiana:

---

25 Sandys, *Paraphrase vpon Iob*, 34–5.

The common soldier shall here fight for gold, and pay himself instead of pence, with plates of half a foot broad . . . . Those commanders and Chieftains that shoot at honour, and abundance, shall find there more rich and beautiful cities, more temples adorned with golden Images, more sepulchres filled with treasure, than either *Cortez* found in Mexico, or *Pizarro* in *Peru* : and the shining glory of this conquest will eclipse all those so far extended beams of the Spanish nation.

Ralegh personifies Guiana as a virgin to be raped, plundered, and possessed:

. . . *Guiana* is a country that hath yet her Maidenhead, never sacked, turned, nor wrought, the face of the earth hath not been torn, nor the virtue and salt of the soil spent by manurance, the graves have not been opened for gold, the mines not broken with sledges, nor their Images pulled down out of their temples. It hath never been entered by any army of strength, and never conquered by any Christian prince.

Ralegh's ethical argument is that if the English did not take Guiana, the native population would suffer under Spanish rule; and his commercial one is that England could acquire Guiana's many riches, though "Where there is store of gold, it is in effect needless to remember other commodities for trade."[26] But his enticements to invest and colonize do not suggest preservation of either nature or culture.

Tudor and Stuart monarchs, unlike More's Utopians, displayed power and the myth of prosperity by wearing abundant gold and jewels. The attitude at court toward the acquisition of underground treasures is expressed in a madrigal from *The Triumphs of Oriana* (to which collection John Milton Senior contributed), commissioned around 1600 by Thomas Morley in honor of the much-bejeweled Queen Elizabeth, which begins "The Lady Oriana / Was dight in all the treasures of Guiana." Michael Drayton's ode "To the Virginian Voyage" of 1606 exhorts idle Britons in imperial language "To get the pearl and gold, / And ours to hold, / Virginia, / Earth's only paradise" and then to "Let cannons roar, / Frighting the wide heaven" in celebration, "And plant our name."[27]

On the other hand, the apostrophe to gold in Joshua Sylvestre's translation of Du Bartas's *Devine Weekes and Workes* (1611) exclaims

O odious poyson! for the which we dive
To *Pluto's* dark Den: for the which we rive
Our Mother Earth; and, not contented with
Th'abundant gifts she outward offereth,
With sacrilegious Tools we rudely rend-her,
And ransak deeply in her bosom tender,
While under ground wee live in hourly fear
When the frail Mines shall over-whelm vs there. [133–4][28]

---

26   Ralegh, *The discovery of the large, rich, and beautiful Empire of Guiana* (1595) in *Selected Writings*, 118–19.

27   Milton expresses disdain for such projects in *Ad Patrem*, lines 93–4.

28   On Du Bartas and Milton see Grant McColley, *Paradise Lost: An Account of its Growth and Major Origins.*

Abraham Cowley, Milton's early rival and a supporter of the Restoration, joins the chorus against gold brought back from the Americas, which he mordantly represents as the revenge of the native American Nations by means of its corruption of Europe. In "America: Phoebus Speaks,"[29] contained in his Latin verse treatise *Of Plants*, Cowley tells the Incas that the gold Europe has stolen is good riddance and is now destroying their conquerors:

> That Gold which *Europe* ravish'd from your Coast,
> O'er *Europe,* now a Tyrant's Pow'r does boast.
> Already has more Mischiefs brought on *Spain*
> Than from insulting *Spaniards* you sustain.
> Where'er it comes all Laws are straight dissolv'd,
> In gen'ral Ruin all Things are involv'd:
> No land can breed a more destructive pest.
> Grieve not that of your Bane you're dispossest
> Call in more *Spaniards* to remove the rest.

The translator, Nahum Tate, may be remembering Milton's description of gold as a "precious bane." For Cowley gold is Helen and the Erinnys; "Fire, Sword, and Slaughter on her Footsteps wait," destroying whole empires. But the Americans have learned many things, some questionable:

> To live by wholesome Laws you now begin,
> Buildings to raise and fence you Cities in;
> To plow the earth, to plow the very Main,
> And traffic with the Universe maintain;
> Defensive Arms and Ornaments of Dress,
> To you the Arts of War and Peace are known,
> And whole *Minerva* is become your own. . . .
> Incas already have Historians been,
> And Inca-Poets shall e're long be seen.

Phoebus foresees that when Europe has been debauched with Inca gold, while "foreign and domestick War / At once shall her distracted Bosom tear" and the American natives have risen to glory with "Wit, Learning, Virtue, Discipline of War," Europe will bring back "Your native Gold": "O, should that fatal Prize return once more,/ 'Twill hurt your Country, as it did before." He also fears the corruption of the Americas through profits of commercial "traffick," and wishes them a better kind of glory,

> Whose Pomp no Crowds of Slaves, a needless Train,
> Nor Gold (the Rabble's Idol) shall support,
> Like *Motezum's*, or *Guanapaci's* Court;
> But such true Grandeur as old *Rome* maintain'd,
> Where Fortune was a Slave, and Virtue reign'd.

---

29 Cowley, *Poemata Latina* (1668), trans. Tate, in *Complete Works*, ed. Grosart, 2:278–9.

Cowley could not have foreseen the disasters to indigenous American nations when European settlers found gold in the North American West, but his prediction that the return of the "fatal Prize" would hurt their land has proven apt.

Western literature (among others) has largely held the acquisition of riches to be a morally degrading occupation; seventeenth-century poets gave increased attention to degradation of earth herself. In *Vanitie* (I) George Herbert assails the arrogance and emptiness of those who seek to penetrate mother earth or mother nature for profit or intellectual possession: the astronomer who surveys the planets as if he meant to buy or seduce one; the pearl diver who risks his life to profit from the vanity of a woman; and the alchemist or chemist whose invasiveness he describes as an illicit liaison. Each stanza investigates human work driven by pride, the production of luxury, or presumptuous experiment.

In the first stanza Herbert uses three metaphors to describe the work of the cosmos-traveling astronomer.

> The fleet Astronomer can bore,
> And thred the spheres with his quick-piercing minde:
> He views their stations, walks from doore to doore,
>   Surveys, as if he had design'd
> To make a purchase there: he sees their dances,
>   And knoweth long before,
> Both their full-ey'd aspects, and secret glances.

The astronomer's piercing mind bores and threads the spheres like a string of pearls; he views them proprietarily, like a potential purchaser of real estate; and he predicts their "aspects"—both facial expressions and the relative positions of the celestial bodies—like a knowing, illicit lover.

In stanza two, as the astronomer mentally pierces the skies, the diver bodily pierces the seas:

> The nimble Diver with his side
> Cuts through the working waves, that he may fetch
> His dear-earnéd pearl, which God did hide
>   On purpose from the ventrous wretch;
> That he might save his life, and also hers,
>   Who with excessive pride
> Her own destruction and his danger wears.

Whether God hid precious substances underground or underwater as wealth to be discovered or as "treasures better hid," risky to acquire and dangerous to the soul, was a topic of controversy. Herbert takes the view that God hid the pearl to save both the diver's life, if he were not so avaricious, and the moral well-being of the woman who "Her own destruction and his danger wears." Luxuries cost workers' lives and possessors' souls.

Having displayed appropriations of the skies and seas, Herbert comes to that of the generative earth by the chemist or alchemist who "can strip the creature naked."

> The subtil Chymick can devest
> And strip the creature naked, till he finde
> The callow principles within their nest:
>   There he imparts to them his minde,
> Admitted to their bed-chamber, before
>   They appeare trim and drest
> To ordinarie suitours at the doore.

"The creature" is the earthly creation, personified as a woman whom the chemist strips in order to find her unfledged (the literal meaning of "callow") inner workings. Their "nest" then becomes a bedchamber with the sexual analogy of an importunate suitor who does not wait for the desired bride to appear in her chosen clothing, but ransacks her inner parts by *droit de seigneur*. In doing so, he not only uncovers the "callow principles" but "imparts to them his minde"—intellectually appropriates them, projects his reasoning into their being, makes them the property of his intentions.[30]

The final stanza claims that the true buried treasure, which God plants in us, can be readily found in our own bosoms:

> What hath not man sought out and found,
> But his deare God? who yet his glorious law
> Embosomes in us, mellowing the ground
>   With showres and frosts, with love & aw,
> So that we need not say, Where's this command?
>   Poore man, thou searchest round
> To find out *death*, but missest *life* at hand.

The poem ends with pity for a materially obsessive, spiritually impoverished race who, like Chaucer's gold-seekers, find death. Possibly, *Vanity* (I) may also have been Herbert's response to Bacon's program of human empire over nature.

Thomas Traherne, who likens earth to heaven and finds an Eden in his native countryside, opposes the acquisition of subterranean treasures and allies himself to the generative earth by urging enjoyment of nature's riches without possession, which for him is the real loss of innocence: if we did not desire to own bits of the natural world, we would each possess the whole of God's earthly house. Gold and silver are dross, and Nature's free beauties the true jewels. In *Eden*, and in the Eden of his childhood, "Hard silver and dry gold / As yet lay underground." In *Adam*, the first man "Being full of wonder and felicity" had only thankfully "to meditate / Upon the throne in which he sate"—the earth.

> No gold, nor trade, nor silver there,
>   Nor clothes, nor coin, nor houses were,
> No gaudy coaches, feasts, or palaces,
> Nor vain inventions newly made to please;
> But native truth, and virgin-purity,
>   An uncorrupt simplicity.

---

30   See also Alan Rudrum, "The Problem of Sexual Reference in George Herbert's Verse."

Adam praised the world "Wherof himself was made supreme," but his angelic intuition makes him worthy of his supremacy:

> He had an angel's eye to see the price
> Of every creature; that made Paradise.
> He had a tongue, yea more, a cherub's sense
>   To feel its worth and excellence.

And in *Right Apprehension*, "A globe of earth is better far / Than if it were a globe of gold . . . A globe of gold must barren be." But "The earth's rare ductile soil, / Which duly yields unto the ploughman's toil / Its fertile nature, gives offence" to fallen men, because it rebukes "men's harden'd hearts" where "no fruit grows." Since man is "like his loved gold, / Stiff, barren, hard, impenetrable," he cannot know true felicity, and "His gold and he / Do well agree," both outwardly bright, but unfruitful.

Though he can also praise construction and trade, as in *Thanksgiving for the Body*, Traherne's praise of the creation is a critique of the commodification that debases nature and diminishes each human soul. In Milton's Eden, where marriage is the "sole propriety," there is no possession; for Traherne too non-ownership is part of innocence and the ground of delight. Possession diminishes not only others' but the possessor's capacity for enjoyment:

> Your Enjoyment of the World is never right, till you so Esteem it that evry thing in it, is more your Treasure, then a King's Exchequer full of Gold and Silver . . . . I remember the Time, when the Dust of the Streets were as precious as Gold to my Infant Eys, and now they are more precious to the Ey of Reason.[31]

And Henry Vaughan writes in "The Seed Growing Secretly":

> If this world's friends might see but once
> What some poor man may often feel,
> Glory, and gold, and crowns, and throne
> They would soon quit and learn to kneel.[32]

Milton's Satan, who refuses to kneel, sits on a throne that outshines "the wealth of Ormus and of Ind, / Or where the gorgeous East with richest hand / Show'rs on her kings barbaric pearl and gold" (2.1–4). Among the countries Adam may have seen "in Spirit" from the Hill of Paradise, Milton's narrator speculates, are

> Rich *Mexico* the seat of *Montezume*,
> And *Cusco* in Peru, the richer seat
> Of *Atabilpa*, and yet unspoil'd

---

31 Traherne, *Centuries, Poems, and Thanksgivings: First Century*, Meditation 25, 80. Graham Parry remarks that "it was Traherne's immense good fortune to be born in Paradise, to lose it once and yet regain it in his maturity," in *Seventeenth-Century Poetry: The Social Context*, 117. Barbara Kiefer Lewalski states, "Traherne finds in present experience, when transmuted by spiritual understanding, not only the adumbration but the substance of heavenly bliss" (*Protestant Poetics*, 357).

32 Vaughan, in Rudrum, ed., *Complete Poems*, 276.

Guiana, whose great City *Geryon*'s Sons
Call *El Dorado*.   [ll. 406–11]

Geryon is the symbol of fraud in Dante;[33] Geryon's Sons are the Spaniards who began the spoilage of the New World; "Yet unspoil'd *Guiana*" echoes Ralegh: "Guiana is a country that hath yet her maidenhead, never sacked, turned, nor wrought, the face of the earth hath not been torn," an unspoiledness which Ralegh had urged England's Virgin Queen to exploit.[34]

Earth's wounds and vitalist philosophy

To the literary entwining of respect for Mother Earth with true felicity, some poets added radical questioning of the mechanist principle that matter is separate from spirit. Milton proffers a key text: at the beginning of creation the Spirit of God "vital virtue infused, and vital warmth / Throughout the fluid mass" (7.236–7), and that self-activating inner potency remains in the forms differentiated during the subsequent days of creation. Thomas Vaughan, brother of the poet Henry Vaughan, chides the followers of Aristotle who "look on God, as they do on carpenters, who build with stone and timber, without any infusion of life. But the world, which is God's building, is full of spirit, quick, and living."[35] Since vitalists recognize the otherness of other beings as well as their kinship with us, their poetry rejects the fallacy that only human perceptions matter, and vitalist ideas were incompatible with a doctrine of nature's instrumentality that extracts the "dominion" passage from the Genesis creation poem and ignores its vitalism.

Margaret Cavendish, Duchess of Newcastle, who conversed with Hobbes and Descartes, wrote poems deploring human cruelty from the points of view of animals and Earth herself. In "Earth's Complaint" she gives Earth a speaking voice to lament the wounds of plow and mine.

> O *Nature, Nature*, hearken to my *Cry*,
> Each *Minute* wounded am, but cannot dye.
> My *Children* which I from my *Womb* did beare,
> Do dig my *Sides*, and all my *Bowels* teare:
> Do plow deep *Furroughs* in my very *Face*,
> From *Torment*, I have neither time, nor place.
> No other *Element* is so abus'd,
> Nor by *Man-kind* so cruelly is us'd.

Her thought is traceable to Hesiod, Vergil, and Ovid; plowing and mining had long inspired a kind of dread of tearing the face and inward parts of the Mother. But Cavendish speaks at a time when agricultural "projectors" taught that human beings have a duty to cultivate as much land as possible. Walter Blith, in *The English*

---

33   Dante, *Inferno*, Canto 17.
34   See Chapter 3.
35   Thomas Vaughan, *Anthroposophia Theomagica*, sig. B3v. Quoted in Rudrum, ed., *Henry Vaughan: The Complete Poems*, 557, n. to ll. 5–6.

Improover, in Joan Thirsk's words "wrote the very best farming book of the mid-seventeenth century."[36] The prefatory poem by P.W. promises prosperity: "Go tell the World of Wealth that's got with ease, / Of certaine Profit (gaine most men doth please)." In his preface, Blith promises to show how every kind of land can bring up to twenty- or even forty-fold more profit by his methods, which include straightening water courses to save land and keep cattle from falling in, irrigation, draining of boggy land, soil improvement such as composting and "plowing and planting" coarse pasture land "as not to Impoverish it," planting diverse woods so that "in two years, they shall rise more than in forty years naturally," and "such a Method of Enclosure, as shall provide for Poore," without depopulating the land. As to "the felling and destroying of the gallant Timber of the Kingdome," Blith suggests that "where any falleth Timber, hee might be commanded to Plant again twice or thrice so much, and nourish it, and maintaine it till it come to such growth as that it might defend it selfe."

Like promoters of mining, personifying the body of earth without apparent consciousness of animism, Blith lists lack of a thorough "searching of the bowels of the Earth": "all our Mines of Lead, Tinne, Iron, Coales, and silver Mines in Wales, were they not once hid? . . . and what should hinder but that in many places else the like may be discovered?" He urges searching both the kingdom and the world, and argues that his plan would benefit the kingdom, increase employment, and relieve the starving: "The Poore cry for it." He concludes, "Legislation encouraging improvement, or protecting against its hindering, would much conduce to the Public Welfare of the Kingdome."

Blith's acknowledges both Genesis and the classical tradition as he declares the fundamentals of agriculture: "God the Great Husbandman made all Creatures," plants "for the food of Man and Beast," and "all the creatures subservient to man, and man to husbandize the fruits of the earth, and dresse, and keep them for the use of the Creature. . . . All other callings proceeding hence, the Earth being the very wombe that beares all, and the Mother that must nourish and maintain all."[37]

Lynn White, Jr., records the history of deep plowing—Cavendish's "deep Furroughs"— and aligns it with the objectification of nature in the Christian era. Yet for Christian poets who did not adopt Thomist or Calvinist doctrines, or projectors' human-centered utilitarianism, nature was all alive and responsive, her bounty sacred and not to be acquisitively ripped from her body.

Henry Vaughan's vitalism makes all creatures, even stones, living witnesses. In "The Stone" Vaughan remembers Joshua's words to the people, "Behold, this stone shall be a witness unto us; for it hath heard all the words of the Lord which he spake unto us" (Joshua 24.27). The casting of lots, as George Eliot reminds us in *Silas Marner*, made a lottery of justice in some sects long after the scientific revolutionary war on superstition. Rather than denounce this Biblical practice, Vaughan subsumes it by extending percipience to all of nature. The "dark designs" which men and women may be bribed to conceal cannot be hidden from other creatures: "Hedges have ears, said the old sooth, / And every bush is something's booth." We forget "That busy commerce kept between / God and his Creatures, though unseen." All

---

36 Thirsk, "Making a Fresh Start," 27.
37 Blith, sigs. A2–A4 and p. 3.

creatures "hear, see, speak, / And into loud discoveries break, / As loud as blood." Nature witnesses and rocks can talk. God does not condemn men outright but seeks the testament of the creatures, even stones: "Hence sand and dust / Are shaked for witnesses, and stones, / Which some think dead, shall all at once / With one attesting voice detect / Those secret sins we least suspect." Everything in nature "turns Scribe and Register." I am not supposing that Vaughan means we can repeal the rules of evidence, but that we need only look about us to see nature witnessing to our moral condition.

David Abram defines magic as "the experience of existing in a world made up of multiple intelligences."[38] For Vaughan, devout Anglican and brother of the vitalist hermeticist Thomas Vaughan, all of nature is "quick"—aware and alive. In "The Morning Watch" the dew of evening and of grace that fell all night "*bloods*, / And spirits all my earth," which is to say his body, while his soul "breaks, and buds."

> In what rings,
> And *hymning circulations* the quick world
> Awakes, and sings;
> The rising winds,
> And falling springs,
> Birds, beasts, all things
> Adore him in their kinds.
> Thus all is hurled
> In sacred *hymns*, and *order*, the great *chime*
> And *symphony* of nature.

The idea that the world is made of music and hymns its maker is one of the cultural threads that encourage a sense of the connectedness of all creatures. Milton's "At a Solemn Music" holds that unharmonious "disproportioned sin / Jarred against Nature's chime, and with harsh din / Broke the fair music that all creatures made," and pleads "O may we soon renew that song / And keep in tune with Heav'n."

Can it be an accident that the words "blood" and "circulation" appear together in a poem published a year after the vitalist William Harvey published his revolutionary work on the circulation of the blood? And this work, though Harvey was the King's physician and, like Vaughan, loyal to the crown, challenged habitual discursive analogies between natural processes and political hierarchies. As John Rogers explains, Harvey attributed a "vitalist agancy to the blood" that "necessitates a reconfiguration of the whole map of bodily organization": rather than being the center of power "the heart is impelled by the blood, the other organs, and the bodily extremities."[39] For Vaughan, all the earth is as "quick" with life as his own body's vital circulation.

Mother Nature, who shares that title with Mother Earth, is sometimes represented as a nurse with flowing breasts. On the title-page to the *Exoticorum Libri Decem* of Charles Clusius (Plate 2), she squeezes out milk onto the globe of earth in her lap, which simultaneously suggests a pregnant womb. In "The Tempest," on rain after drought, Vaughan, instead, makes earth the wet-nurse of Nature.

---

38 Abram, *The Spell of the Sensuous*, 9.
39 Harvey, *De Circulatione Sanguinis*, 16–49; John Rogers, *Matter of Revolution*, 20–24.

> When nature on her bosom saw
>   Her infants die,
> And all her flowers withered to straw,
>   Her breasts grown dry;
> She made the earth their nurse, & tomb,
>   Sigh to the sky,
> 'Til to those sighs fetched from her womb,
>   Rain did reply,
> So in the midst of all her fears
>   And faint requests,
> Her earnest sighs procured her tears
>   And filled her breasts.

However allegorical, the poem keeps connected to actual processes of weather as the work of a living and life-giving Earth suckling nature's progeny. Instead of urging us to rise above nature, Vaughan presents everything in nature striving to rise and beckoning man to do the same: waterfalls "Chide, and fly up," mists mount, plants "Strive upwards still, and point him the way home." He does not uproot the emblematic plant from earth: each part adheres to one of the four elements, "complying"—cooperating, but also folded together—with their habitats, life-producing, starlike in their multiplicity, allied with the sun:

> *Plants* in the *root* with earth do most comply,
>   Their *leaves* with water, and humidity,
>   The *flowers* to air draw near, and subtlety,
> And *seeds* a kindred fire have with the sky.

Milton, both monist and vitalist in his poetic language, also presents Earth as generative and wounded Mother, carrying the lyric poets' sympathetic personifications to epic proportions. Milton's God does not create matter from nothing but, apparently, out of his own substance, from which he has withdrawn his ordering will; the result is Chaos, which becomes the turbulent storehouse of the materials from which self-motivating creatures can be made. The agent of creation is the Son, the Omnific Word, accompanied by the Spirit, who drives the chariot of Paternal Glory "Far into *Chaos*" and taking golden compasses "in his hand" circumscribes the universe from its materials, still "Matter unform'd and void."[40] After the Son has brought peace to these noisy and lively materials, the accompanying androgynous Spirit acts:

---

40   Whether chaos is evil, neutral, or a dynamic source of creativity is much disputed; see Regina Schwartz, *Remembering and Repeating*); Mary Norton, "Chaos Theory and *Paradise Lost* "; John Leonard, "Milton, Lucretius, and 'the Void Profound of Unessential Night'"; and John Rumrich in "Of Chaos and Nightingales." Leonard and Rumrich take opposing views in Pruitt and Durham, *Living Texts*. Juliet Lucy Cummins in "Milton's Gods and the Matter of Creation," argues that "Milton portrays the Spirit of God's virtue and warmth as masculine, formative, and vitalizing forces originating in God and operating upon prime matter to cause it to develop into the created world. God's masculine self converges with his feminine material identity at Creation when he literally 'put[s] . . . forth [his]goodness' (7.171) . . . . The result is a world that is positioned between two poles of a material spectrum, which are both divine: the base prime matter from which things are created and the holy light to which they proceed" (91–2).

> Darkness profound
> Cover'd th'Abyss: but on the wat'ry calm
> His brooding wings the Spirit of God outspread,
> And vital virtue infus'd, and vital warmth
> Throughout the fluid Mass, but downward purg'd
> The black tartareous cold Infernal dregs
> Adverse to life: then founded, then conglob'd
> Like things to like, the rest to several place
> Disparted, and between spun out on Air,
> And Earth self-balanced on her Centre hung. [7.233–42]

"Vital virtue" and "vital warmth," infused throughout the "fluid Mass" that constitutes the stuff of creation, implies potent activity throughout everything that is not "adverse to life."[41] Earth is not merely balanced but "self-balanced," and this principle of self-balancing applies to each creature and results from that "vital virtue" infused throughout the creation that the falls of Adam and Eve will wound.

After the creation of Light Raphael continues,

> The Earth was form'd, but in the Womb as yet
> Of Waters, Embryon, immature, involv'd
> Appear'd not: over all the face of Earth,
> Main Ocean flow'd, not idle, but with warm
> Prolific humor soft'ning all her Globe,
> Fermented the great Mother to conceive,
> Satiate with genial moisture, when God said,
> Be gather'd now ye Waters under Heav'n[42]
> And let dry land appear. [7.276–84]

What follows is the activity of Earth herself, expressed in active verbs and onomatopoetic prosody. Mountains upheave their backs, valleys sink, waters haste "with glad precipitance," rivers "draw their humid train," and the waters congregate in seas. Earth covers "Her Universal Face with pleasant green" and makes gay her sweet-smelling bosom with herbs and flowers, "That Earth now / Seem'd like to Heav'n," where Gods might "love to haunt / Her sacred shades" (285–308).

Milton's vitalist monist materialism does not pertain only to earthly nature. The same principles operate in Heaven and Hell, whether spiritually or corporeally— Raphael leaves that matter open when he agrees to narrate the War in Heaven:

> and what surmounts the reach
> of human sense, I shall delineate so
> By lik'ning spiritual to corporeal forms,
> As may express them best, though what if earth
> Be but the shadow of Heav'n, and things therein
> Each to other like, more than on earth is thought? [5.572–6]

---

41 John Rogers interestingly discusses this passage in *Matter of Revolution*, 132–3.

42 The "Waters under Heav'n" are distinguished from the circumfluous waters above the firmament. Rogers interprets this passage as Earth giving birth to herself in *Matter of Revolution*, 115.

If Earth is like heaven only in an allegorical sense, Raphael will provide fit likenings; but Earth may be essentially the same. In Raphael's account of the creation, God says he will create 'another world' and another race

> there to dwell,
> Not here, till by degrees of merit raised
> They open to themselves at length the way
> Up hither, under long obedience tried,
> And earth be changed to Heav'n, and Heav'n to earth,
> One Kingdom, joy and union without end.   [7.156–61]

An earth capable of union with heaven—a union dependent on human choice—is more like heaven already, and heaven more like earth, "Each to other like, than on earth is thought," especially by dualists and materialists who think matter separate from spirit, and therefore dead.

How did this poetry of a living earth come into an age of revolutionary natural history, in which the river of science and the river of poetry might seem to have diverged? It is clear that Milton, Vaughan, and Cavendish, and surely also Herbert and Traherne—both clergymen, university men, one a public orator and member of parliament, the other a habitual entwiner of nature and religious meditation—were not ignorant of the Baconian program but also were not merely personifying the natural world for the sake of allegorical lessons. They confront the new philosophy and technology in language that asserts the life of nature and promotes the life of words that are rooted in the natural world as well as the human community. To understand how they could do so in an age of religious conviction that many critics define as the enemy of ecology, we need to turn to a discipline rarely considered its friend: theology. I'll begin with a dispute about mountains and close with the debate over the immortality of all creatures.

Mountain theology

Many cultures regard mountains as sacred places or sites of prophetic revelation. But in seventeenth-century England the question of their godliness was disputed. Some writers, who imagined that a harmonious design must be without irregularities, and that symmetry and utility must be intrinsic features of God's work, thought them unnatural. Gabriel Plattes, on the grounds that God makes everything for man's convenience, states,

> Some have thought that the mighty Creator made the vast, deformed, and craggy Rocks and Mountaines in the beginning, but this appeareth to be an Opinion, whereby great dishonour may reflect upon the Creator, who besides his Omnipotent power, doth continually make use of his admirable Wisdome, and exquisite Artifice in all his Workes, and made nothing deformed or unfit for the use of which it was created: Now the Earth being ordained to beare Fruits for the use of Men, and Rocks are not fit for that purpose, it plainely appeareth that they came by accident.

Others think them produced over time "even as Warts, Tumours, Wenns, and Excrescences are engendered in the superficies of mens bodies." But Plattes has found by experiment that probably "Bituminous and Sulphurious substances [are] kindled in the bowells of the Earth," metals are "engendred in the cracks and crannies" of mountains, and water, whether Noah's flood or the motion of the seas, washed away looser soil and left rocks exposed.[43]

Plattes' tract is a handbook on finding, extracting, and refining minerals, including gold, with much use of quicksilver and no warning about its known toxicity. His theology of mountains as accidental excrescences abets untrammeled mining partly by removing them from the tradition with which Milton begins his epic, in which mountains are places of sacred revelation: "Sing, Heav'nly Muse, that on the secret top / Of Oreb, or of Sinai, didst inspire / That shepherd who first taught the chosen seed . . . or if Sion hill Delight the more, . . . I thence / Invoke thy aid to my adventrous song, / That with no middle flight intends to soar / Above th'Aonian mount."

Bill McKibben states in *The End of Nature*, "as Paul Brooks points out in *Speaking for Nature*, much of literature had regarded wilderness as ugly and crude until the Romantic movement of the late eighteenth century. Andrew Marvell, for instance, referred to mountains as ill-designed excrescences."[44] Writing after a war against tyranny in "Upon the Hill and Grove at Bilbrough," Marvell contrasts a gently rising hill to overweening monarchs.

> Here learn, ye mountains more unjust,
> Which to abrupter greatness thrust,
> That do with your hook-shouldered height
> The earth deform and heaven fright,
> For whose excrescence, ill-designed,
> Nature must a new centre find,
> Learn here those humble steps to tread,
> Which to securer glory lead.

Earth's center shifts when measured from excrescences, so that "Nature must a new centre find"—Marvell's metrics lose themselves too. Marvell uses language from Plattes as a metaphor of unjust kings (mountains cannot learn to tread humbly), to commend political moderation. His commendations of moderation anticipate McKibben's own thesis that our material immoderation may already have changed the earth irretrievably. This particular hill on the estate at Bilborough of the Lord General Fairfax—who had defeated the forces of an overweening monarch while protecting the churches in York from the window-smashing and sculpture-slashing of the more extreme radicals and then retired to his country properties—is a symmetrical symbol of Fairfax's moderation. In the "grove" part of the poem, Marvell speaks of trees as percipient beings, and also as emblems of Fairfax: they are both sentient and wise, and once grown "no further strive to shoot, / Contented if they fix their root."

---

43 Plattes, Gabriel, *A Discovery of Subterraneall Treasure* (1639), 5.

44 McKibben 51. I am not sure why McKibben describes his sense of loss as having nothing left to conquer.

Distrust of wild mountains may have come partly from the dangers lurking in them, both wild and human. John Evelyn, an ardent royalist, conservationist, gardener, and lover of the arts, preferred safety and symmetry to mountain crags. While traveling abroad to escape the turmoils of the British civil wars, Evelyn, on the way to Fontainebleau in March of 1644, passed

> through a forest so prodigiously encompassed with hideous rocks of whitish hard stone heaped one on another in mountainous heights, that I think the like is nowhere to be found more horrid and solitary. It abounds with stags, wolves, boars, and not long after a lynx, or ounce, was killed amongst them, which had devoured some passengers. On the summit of these gloomy precipices, intermingled with trees and shrubs, the stones hanging over, and menacing ruin, is built an hermitage. In these solitudes, rogues frequently lurk and do mischief (and for whom we were all well appointed with our carabines); but we arrived safe.

Of Fontainebleau Evelyn remarks "The Palace is nothing so stately and uniform as Hampton Court."[45] Safety aside, the preference for order and symmetry over wildness extends in Evelyn's age to neoclassical poetry and architecture and to royalist allegiances as well as geology and theology. The desire for civic order that led to the monarchical politics of Thomas Hobbes is an analogue of the dislike of obstreperous landforms.

Milton's vitalist creation story energetically refutes Plattes's assumption that God did not make mountains. God says "let dry land appear" and "Immediately the mountains huge appear / Emergent, and their broad bare backs upheave / Into the clouds" (7.284–7). The responsive activity of earth also produces each inhabitant from its habitat—waters generate, shores and fens hatch brood, earth brings forth— and each responds actively. And, to clinch the case for mountains, God the Father exalts the Son on his "holy hill" (45.604). Paradise is a mountain that "God had thrown . . . as his garden mould high raised" (4.226), and heaven too has varied landforms, "For earth hath this variety from Heav'n / Of pleasure situate in hill and dale." During the War in Heaven the loyal angels return the rebels' cannon fire by flinging mountains, promontories, and hills, which they "plucked . . . with all their load, / Rocks, waters, woods, and by the shaggy tops / Uplifting bore them in their hands" (6.644–6). When God sends the Son to stop this "Wild work" (697) the "uprooted hills" hear his voice and retire "each to his place" (781–3).

By the end of the seventeenth century, the attitudes of natural philosophers towards earth's irregularities were beginning to change. Thomas Burnet was a proponent of natural philosophy on the grounds that "Divine Providence . . . should not be willing that Mankind should be finally ignorant of that part of Nature, and of the Universe, which is properly their Task and Province to manage and understand. We are the Inhabitants of the Earth, and the Lords and Masters of it; and we are endowed with Reason and Understanding, doth it not then properly belong to us to examine and understand the works of God in this part of the Universe, which is fallen to our lot, which is our heritage and habitation?" He retains the language of mastery but turns it toward understanding and responsibility. Burnet thought that "the parts of the Earth

---

45   Evelyn *Diary*, 88–9.

outward and inward, hath something irregular and unnatural in it, and manifestly shows us the markes or footsteps of some kind of ruin and dissolution," nominating the Flood as the disrupter of an originally smooth and symmetrical globe. But later he adds,

> [T]here is nothing that I look upon with more pleasure than the wide Seas and the Mountains of the Earth. There is something august and stately in the Air of these things that inspires the mind with great thoughts and passions; We do naturally upon such occasions think of God and his Greatness and whatsoever hath but the shadow and appearance of the INFINITE, as all things have that are too great for our comprehension, they fill and over-bear the mind with their Excess and cast it into a pleasing kind of stupor and admiration .... [T]hese Mountains we are speaking of, to confess the truth, are nothing but great ruines; but such as show a certain magnificancy in Nature."[46]

More wholeheartedly, the pioneering biologist John Ray regarded mountains as proof of God's wisdom. He adheres to, but modifies, the view that all things were made for human use, and he also likes mountains, in a human-centered way, as landscapes and places of recreation. Alluding to views like Plattes's, he acknowledges rather testily:

> [I]t may be objected, that the present Earth looks like a heap of Rubbish and Ruines; And that there are no greater examples of confusion in nature than Mountains singly or jointly considered; and that there appear not the least footsteps of any Art or Counsel either in the Figure and Shape, or Order and Disposition of Mountains and Rocks. Wherefore it is not likely they came so out of God's hands, who by the Ancient Philosophers is said . . . to make all things in number, weight and measure.

Ray's attribution of preference for seemly geometrical form to ancient philosophers, rather than scripture—in a work dedicated to the Archbishop of Canterbury—leads to his rebuttal, beginning with his enjoyment of geological diversity.

> To which I answer, That the present face of the Earth, with all its Mountains and Hills, its Promontories and Rocks, as rude and deformed as they appear, seems to me a very beautiful and pleasant object, and with all that variety of Hills, and Valleys, and Inequalities far more grateful to behold, than a perfectly level Country without any rising or protuberancy, to terminate the sight.

Mountains are also useful, Ray points out, as places of human habitation, screens against adverse winds, reflectors of sunbeams, and providers of drainage. And like Samuel Purchas, Ray extends God's providence to others than us: diversity of landforms is "convenient for the entertainment of the various sorts of Animals, which God hath created, some whereof delight in cold, some in hot, some in moist and watery, some in dry and upland places," and Alpine birds and beasts could find their "proper food" in no other regions. Mountains also put forth "the greatest variety, and most luxuriant sorts of Vegetables," for the animals there, for medicines, and for the "exercise and delight" of collectors. As to utility, they can be used for grazing,

---

46 Burnet, *Sacred Theory of the Earth,* 8, 31, 139–40.

and mining would be impossible without the drainage their slopes provide. Most important, they are necessary for "the Generation and Maintenance of Rivers and Fountains," which proceed, he offers as a hypothesis, from rainwater; otherwise we would have mostly stagnant pools, if it is possible to have rain without mountains at all. Ray quotes Dr. [Edmond] Halley's opinion in "his Discourse concerning the original of Springs and Rivers" that ridges are "'Alembicks to distil fresh water for the use of Man and Beast'" and give gentle descent to streams.[47]

In short, some early modern natural philosophers thought wild mountains unnatural, but some major ones did not, and Romantic poets too had mixed reactions. When Percy Bysshe Shelley went to Chamonix in 1816 to admire Mont Blanc, he was dismayed: "how hideously / Its shapes are heaped around! rude, bare, and high, / Gastly, scarred, and riven," with the glacier crushing flowers in its path. For Shelley, Robert Ryan argues, by raising doubts about the existence of a wise God the mountain has "a voice . . . to repeal / Large codes of fraud and woe."[48] John Muir (1838–1914), geologist and glaciologist, who carried *Paradise Lost* in his pocket on a thousand mile hike[49] and later tramped joyfully across the highest peaks with a cheerful attitude toward God, exulted in glaciers as the creators of fertile habitats for delicate and abundant life: "Laboring harmoniously in united strength they crushed and ground and wore away these rocks in their march, making vast beds of soil, and at the same time developed and fashioned the landscapes into the delightful variety of hill and dale and lordly mountain that mortals call beauty."[50]

In *Paradise Lost*, well before Burnet and Ray, God plants his Garden on a "shaggy hill": "For God had thrown / That mountain as his garden mould high raised" and its elevated fountain nourishes the Garden (4.225–30). At the creation of the earth, the rising up of mountains and "Tumid hills" provides beds and channels for the waters necessary to life, which pour "with torrent rapture" or "Soft-ebbing" or "With serpent error wand'ring" (7.285–302). The vocabulary of this variety, which waters the earth and, as in Genesis, generates lives, also tests readers' responses: "tumid" can mean turgid or teeming; torrent rapture suggests violent seizure or swift-flowing bliss; "ebbing" suggests either decay or rhythmically varied flow; "serpent error" can mean noxious wrongness or winding wandering. These interpretive choices foretell and keep open the choices of Adam and Eve and exercise perceptual ones; some see geological processes as inimical, others as life-giving—as Milton also does: oceans generate "spawn abundant, living soul" (7.388) and brooks "R[u]n nectar, visiting each plant" (4.240). The alternative interpretations suggest that nature can become dangerous if dangerously employed.

---

47 Ray, John. *Three Physico-Theological Discourses* (1693), 35–42. *Pvrchas his Pilgrimage*, (727) is quoted on the first page of Ray's work.

48 *Shelley, Poetry and Prose*, 91–3. Robert Ryan sees this description as a rejection of human abuse, by grinding repressions, of the Law given to Moses on Mount Sinai, in *The Romantic Reformation*, 196–202.

49 Gifford, introduction in Muir, *The Eight Wilderness Discovery Books*.

50 Muir, *The Mountains of California*, 13.

Natural heresies: Deep ecology and monotheism

Deep ecologists hold that all forms of life, not just species but individuals, exist for their own sakes and that earth, water, and air should not be invaded by human beings for reasons that go beyond basic needs.[51] Some ecological critics assume that post-pagan but pre-Darwinian Western literature can express no environmental ethic, or that "Judeo-Christian" literature is always dualistic, favors transcendence, and must be held largely responsible for environmental devastation.[52] The hyphenation "Judeo-Christian" kneads together diverse groups who have sometimes died for their differences. Biblical texts of both testaments teach temperance and stewardship, rejoice in the beauty of the creation, and relate human moral reponsibility to the welfare of nature While some forms of monotheism may spurn this world, it seems to me that polarizing ecology and religion dismisses people and works of art valuable to the development of an ecological culture. Many religious poets have been monist materialists who opposed dualism and the desire for transcendence. We cannot read their work justly, or benefit from their biopoetic wisdom, without observing that they oppose earth-spurning thought in their theology.

Incarnation (from Latin *caro*, flesh), the distinguishing doctrine of Christianity, declares not only a relation but a fusion of flesh and God. This doctrine, countering the atheist materialism of Lucretius, required Christian theologians to grapple with the problem of the relation of matter and spirit in the created world. Cartesian dualists, in defense of experimental science, insisted on the separation of the two, arguing that God is untainted by corruptible matter and the immortal human soul is separable from it, but that animals have no souls and can be treated mechanistically. When Richard Bentley, later an editor of Milton,[53] chose atheist materialism as his target in fulfillment of the prescription for a series of sermons established by Robert Boyle "For the preservation of the Christian religion,"[54] he asserted that atomism is not a threat if you believe that matter is separate from the spirit of God that orders it and that the fleshly body is separate from the soul that animates it. This dualistic theology, with roots in Calvin and Thomas Aquinas, was at odds with the radically incarnational Christianity of Milton and other vitalist poets for whom God is immanent in all things.

At the same time, the Aristotelian theory of the three souls was breaking down. Aristotle distinguished among the vegetative soul, which can only grow and reproduce; the sensitive soul of non-human animals, which can also move and feel; and the rational souls of human beings, which incorporate the others, but also have reason and moral choice and, for Christian interpreters, share the divine image and the immortality of the soul. Natural historians were beginning to breach these boundaries. Sir Thomas Browne in a letter to Henry Power of 8 June 1659 writes:

---

51 See essays by George Sessions in *Deep Ecology for the Twenty-First Century*.

52 For example, Gary Snyder—a deeply spiritual poet—*A Place in Space*, 53; Lynn White, Jr., "The Historical Roots of Our Ecological Crisis"; and George Sessions, "Ecocentrism and the Anthropocentric Detour."

53 Bentley, ed., *Milton's Paradise Lost. A New Edition* (1732).

54 *A Defense of Natural and Revealed Religion*, vol. 1, Sermons 2–3.

"That there is a naturall sensation in plants as Dr. Harvey hath discoursed seemes verie allowable, & besides some other reasons, from the experiment of the sensible plant, w[hi]ch is also to bee found in minor degree in some others as Jacea, Scabious, Thistles & such as Borellus observed & publishes some yeares agoe, & might bee observed in others." Gabriel Harvey's and Martin Lister's discourses on sensation in plants broke through the wall between the vegetative and the sensitive soul and gave empirical evidence for Nehemiah Grew's assertion that plants are more like animals, and therefore like us, than natural philosophers had thought. Similarly, signs of animal intelligence observed by John Ray and others weakened the boundary between the sensitive and the rational souls.[55] These natural historians and the monistic vitalist poets are forerunners, in their sense of creature kinship, of Darwin, DNA studies, and the Human Genome Project. But the boundary between matter and spirit was for others inviolable, partly because it kept the soul uncontaminated by corruptible matter (though it could be corrupted itself by responding to temptations of both flesh and spirit) and that boundary allowed every kind of matter—including sentient bodies of non-human beings—to be the subject of objective experiment without ethical restraints.

Seventeenth-century poets fostered, to differing degrees, three anti-dualistic principles often deemed heretical: monism, vitalism, and the conservation of entities; and a fourth that I shall call philosophical justice. Monism is the belief that all creatures derive from one first matter that is inseparable from spirit. For John Milton, all things derive from the substance of God, who has within himself the power of heterogeneity. All creatures are therefore kindred, though gradiated, and participate to some degree in divinity, though rational ones—angels and men—may choose to depart from or draw nearer it.[56] Vitalism, which is implied in monism, asserts that nature is alive in all her parts. The conservation of entities applies the biblical promise of a new heaven and earth to all creation, denying the supposition that only angels and human beings would populate eternity and thereby questioning the Cartesian assumption that animals have no souls. Philosophical justice or magnanimity teaches, in the words of Montaigne, that "there [is] a kinde of respect, and a general duty of humanity, which tieth us not only unto brute beasts that have life and sense, but even unto trees and plants," to whom we owe "grace and benignity."[57] Poets who subscribe to some or all of these principles value other species for their own sakes, as implied in Genesis—with its refrains "and God blessed them" and "God saw that it was good"—and expect their inclusion in the apocalyptic renewal of heaven and earth.

---

55 Browne, *Works*, ed. Keynes, 4:270. Grew, Ray, and Lister also discuss this phenomenon, Lister in "A further Account concerning the Existence of Veins in all kind of Plants . . . and of some Acts in Plants resembling those of Sense," *Philosophical Transactions* 7–8.90:5131–7. For Grew, see Chapter 4.

56 For more on Milton's monism see Chapter 7. The fullest account is Steven M. Fallon's in *Milton among the Philosophers*, passim. For important distinctions see also Philip J. Donnelly, "Matter versus Body: The Character of Milton's Monism" and D. Bentley Hart, "Matter, Monism, and Narrative."

57 Montaigne, *Of Crueltie*, The Second Booke, Chapter XI, in *The Essays of Montaigne*, trans. John Florio (1603), ed. Henley, 126.

To an extent, the English liturgy mitigates dualism by drawing heaven and earth together, though it did not prevent Calvinists within the English church, or churchmen like Wilkins and Bentley, from segregating body and soul. In the seventeenth century, university students heard the liturgy of the Book of Common Prayer in daily chapel services, and others from king to plowman and including women and children heard it in church and in family gatherings. The communion service declares that both "heaven and earth are full of thy glory" and the communicants partake of the divine through grape and grain to preserve both "body and soul into everlasting life."[58] All the Psalms, with their pastoral and wilderness imagery, were said or sung through each month and many people sang metrical versions at home. Thomas Carew's translation of Psalm 104 for private use, set by Milton's collaborator Henry Lawes, renders verse 13 "When on [Earth's] Womb thy Dew is shed / The pregnant Earth is brought to bed / And with a fruitful Birth encreast / Yeilds Herbs and Grasse for Man and Beast."[59]

Among the canticles, the Benedicite calls "all the works of the Lord" from angels to elements to fish, fowl, beasts, and the children of men to bless their creator. William Byrd set a Christmas antiphon from the Latin liturgy that exclaims "O magnam mysterium et admirabile sacramentum, ut animalia viderent Dominum natum, jacentem in praesipio" [O great mystery and amazing sign, that animals should see the Lord born and laid in a manger][60] An Advent introit implores, "Drop down, ye heavens, from above, and let the skies pour down righteousness: let the earth open, and let them bring forth salvation" (Isa. 45.8)[61] This prayer, preceding the feast of the Incarnation, is haunted by ancient creation myths of the fertile mating of Uranus and Gaia, with earth as a metonymy of Mary's womb, and expresses the copula of heaven and earth, or righteousness and a life-giving soil.

Monism and the redemption of the creatures

John Milton's monist materialism—his refusal to divide matter from spirit, in disagreement with Plato, Athanasius, Aquinas, Calvin, Descartes, Boyle, Bentley, and innumerable others—is expressed throughout Paradise Lost and summed up in

---

58 Book of Common Prayer: preface to the communion and administration of the sacraments (1559 and after).

59 Carew, *Select Psalmes of a New Translation* (22 November 1655). From the Bridgewater collection, Huntington Library shelfmark RB131907. Words only. For description see Scott Nixon, "Henry Lawes's Hand in the Bridgewater Collection" and for CD performance see Henry Lawes in my bibliography.

60 Settings for recusant Catholics were allowed by the English prayerbook where Latin was the common language. Settings by Tomás Luis de Victoria, François Poulenc, Peter Maxwell-Davies, and Morten Lauridsen are also available on CD.

61 "Rorate coeli desuper," for the Votive Mass of the First Sunday in Advent by William Byrd and performed by the William Byrd Choir, dir. Gavin Turner, on *Byrd Gradualia: The Marian Masses*, vol. 1. Hyperion CDA66451. The Latin version ends "aperiatur terra et germinet salvatorem."

Raphael's figure of "one first matter" as a fruit-bearing tree (5.469–90)[62] Because all created beings, from angels to ants to subterranean stones, are diversified from the same living material, all are both different and kindred. The difference is of "degrees of substance"; beings nearer to God are "more refined, more spiritous, more pure," and species are "in their active spheres assigned, / Till body up to spirit work, in bounds / Proportioned to each kind." All species are not equal, and the relation of body and spirit in animated beings is one of degrees of refinement, but all "proceed [from God] and up to him return, / If not depraved from good." Milton's animist materialism also opposed the mechanist belief that matter is distinct from the animating soul. The "vital virtue" that the Spirit of God infused at the beginning (7.236) "in things that live" remains in and refines these differentiated forms.

The compilation of biblical interpretation in Milton's Christian Doctrine[63] holds that the world was not created out of nothing, but out of God. Since matter cannot have existed independently from God, it must have originated in God. Foreseeing objections to any doubt of God's unity that might slip into polytheism, the tractate states,

> [I]t is a demonstration of supreme power and supreme goodness that such heterogeneous, multiform and inexhaustible virtue should exist in God, and exist substantially . . . [and] that he should not shut up this heterogeneous and substantial virtue within himself, but should disperse, propagate, and extend it as far as, and in whatever way, he wills.

And how can the substance of God can become corruptible nature? "[M]atter, like the form and nature of the angels, came from God in an incorruptible state, and even since the fall it is still incorruptible, so far as its essence is concerned." But "When matter or form has gone out from God and become the property of another, . . . it is now in a mutable state." God transmits the power to act to heterogeneous forms but grants them identity and diversity; those endowed with reason, human or angelic (and animals, God says in *Paradise Lost* 8.374, "reason not contemptibly") have the opportunity to exercise it freely, with its risks, so that they may be growing, diversifying, self-activated individuals. A corollary is that "since all things come not only from God but out of God, no created thing can be utterly annihilated." Nor are body and soul separated in death; the whole person dies and the whole person will be renewed in the general resurrection.[64]

Insofar as the tractate uses separate terms for the parts of a human self, they are not dual but triune. "Man is always said to be made up of body, spirit, and soul . . . . So I will first prove that the whole man dies, and then that each separate part dies." Since it is chiefly the soul or spirit that sins, why should "the body, which was just as

---

62   This passage is discussed in Chapter 4.

63   Milton's authorship of parts of *Christian Doctrine* has been disputed by William Hunter, defended by Barbara Kiefer Lewalski and others, stylometrically analyzed by Thomas Corns et al., and textually analyzed by Michael Lieb. The sections of it to which I refer are consistent with the theology of his poems.

64   Milton, *Christian Doctrine*, Book I, Chapter VII, "Of the Creation," in *Complete Prose Works* 4:307–10.

immortal as the soul before sin brought death into the world . . . alone pay the penalty for sin by dying, although it had no part in the sin?"[65]

The statement is radical in comparison with the Christian humanist John Colet's explanation of the three parts of the redeemed self as body, soul, and the indwelling Spirit of God, which forms a new alliance of the soul "as matter, and the embracing spirit, as the formative principle." Since "the spirit excels the soul formed by it, far more than the soul excels the body which it forms," soul and spirit become "more truly one" than body and soul, since "the soul makes less resistance to its union with the spirit, than the body does to its connexion with the soul." Colet speculates that this aversion occurs because the body's dimensions "seem most adverse to unity."[66] This attitude toward the body resembles the idea that mountains are unsightly protrusions on the spherical earth.

Unlike other believers that God is in all things, Milton provides for the liberty of all creatures. According to the occult physician Robert Fludd, "God operateth all in all. He vivifieth all things. He filleth all things. His incorruptible Spirit is in all things." If God bestowed singular virtues so that "the creature can act of it self by a free will," God's virtue could be separated from his essence, whereas the "true essence of the Deitie is individuall [indivisible]."[67] By denying creatures' personal freedom of action, Fludd approaches voluntarism, the doctrine that God's will is sovereign and inscrutable, which was held by royalists to justify the divine right of kings to be sovereign and inscrutable also.

Fludd's logic is hard to gainsay: if a creature is filled with the Spirit of God, how can it have a will of its own? But for Milton, the Spirit that prefers above all temples "th'upright heart and pure" (1.18) is not a tyrant. He argues in *Areopagitica* that God gives freedom to rational creatures and that governments should do the same. An implication of monism in *Paradise Lost* is that although other animals, while sentient and intelligent, possess a lower degree of reason than human beings do, yet good moral government before the Fall allows them to live their lives freely. In *Paradise Lost*, after the apocalypse the faithful will be received "into bliss, / Whether in Heav'n or earth, for then the Earth / Shall be all Paradise" (12.462–4). Both Milton and Henry Vaughan believe in the resurrection of the creatures after the apocalyptic union of heaven with a purged and renewed earth. This doctrine opposed Aristotelian, Calvinist, and Cartesian instrumentality based on the supposition that only human souls are immortal.

Just as body works up to spirit, rather than being opposed to it, so after the apocalyptic judgment and purgation, "Earth [will] be chang'd to Heav'n, and Heav'n to Earth" (7.157–60). That Earth would be changed was orthodox; that Heaven

---

65 *Complete Prose Works* 4:400–401. Perhaps the aspersion about the lack of clear boundaries jibes at dualists like William Perkins, who argues that "the spirit signifies the minde," or understanding, and the soul "the will and affections," so that both are faculties of the soul: *An Exposition to the Creede, Workes* 1:152, quoted in n. 9 to Milton, *Christian Doctrine, Complete Prose Works* 4:401.

66 Colet, from a Latin lecture at the University of Oxford in 1497, in *An Exposition of St. Paul's Epistle to the Romans*, 28–9.

67 Fludd, in *Mosaicall Philosophy*, A2, 15–16.

would reciprocally change "to Earth" is an unorthodox assertion of the immortality of all creatures. By analogy with Eden, the creatures would delight the mind and senses and nourish human affections and wisdom simply by being themselves and living their lives.

Lovers of wildness will wonder how potential predators and raptors could be themselves in a country without death. How can an osprey who does not clasp fish with that thrilling swoop be truly an osprey, or a wolf who does not hunt hares be a wolf, or a hare not pursued be fully a hare? Perhaps the imagination of Milton's God could foresee employments for talents and talons, just as he has given his angels opportunities for unchronicled "acts of zeal and love" before Satan's rebellion (5.593). But in Paradise, to disguise himself for spying, Satan usurps the lion's potential "fiery glare" and the tiger's stealth (4.401–5); and the serpent, while still innocent ("to thee / Not noxious," 7.497–8) sports "brazen eyes / And hairy mane terrific" (7.496–8). Wildness without bloodshed is part of Edenic vitality.

In addition to the Sermon on the Mount, two passages in the Christian testament witness to the belief that the non-human creation was holy and everlasting. In Romans 8.19, "For the earnest expectation of the creature waiteth for the manifestation of the sons of God," and in Revelation 5.13 "every creature which is in heaven, and on the earth, and under the earth, and such as are in the sea, and all that are in them" worship the Lamb together.

According to the Authorized Version (1611) of Romans 8,

> 19. For the earnest expectation of the creature waiteth for the manifestation of the sons of God.

> 20. For the creature was made subject to vanity, not willingly, but by reason of him who hath subjected the same in hope,

> 21. Because the creature itself also shall be delivered from the bondage of corruption into the glorious liberty of the children of God.

> 22. For we know that that the whole creation groaneth and travaileth in pain together until now.

> 23. And not only they, but ourselves also, which have the firstfruits of the Spirit, we ourselves groan within ourselves, waiting for the adoption, to wit, the redemption of our body.

Many glosses interpret these passages as concerning only the elect. John Locke's *Paraphrase* of Romans edits out other creatures and subordinates other races when he renders verse 19 "For the whole race of mankinde . . . waiteth in hope" and adds "creature . . . signifies mankind especially the gentile world as the far greater part of the creation" (2.557).[68] In order to conclude that only mankind, perhaps with the

---

68 Locke is being traditional; Colet's *Exposition* is orthodox in reading Romans 8.14, translated in both 1650 and 1611, as "For as many as are led by the Spirit of God, they are the sons of God" exclusively to mean "Christians; *sons and heirs of God, and joint heirs with Christ*" (26). He makes no mention of the "creature" awaiting this manifestation.

elements and celestial bodies, awaits the resurrection, neo-Calvinists had to ignore or reduce both the "they" in verse 23 of the 1611 version and the translation and gloss of the Geneva Bible, published at the center of Calvinism for English Protestant readers in 1550, which reads quite differently:

22. For we know that everie creature groneth with vs also, and travaileth in paine together unto this present.

23. And not only the creature, but we also which have the first frutes of the Spirit, even the redemption of our bodie.

The marginal gloss makes even clearer the plurality of creatures by logically excluding the human species from the creatures that groan "with us" in verse 22:

The creatures shal not be restored before that Gods children be broght to their perfection: in the meane season they wait. [They are subject to vanity]: That is, to destruction, because of mans sinne. [By "everie creature"] He meaneth not the Angels, nether devils nor men.

Of "our bodie" it adds "Which shalbe in the resurrection when we shalbe made conformable to our head Christ." The body will share in the resurrection because Christ has become incarnate, and—according to the reading shared by at least Milton and Vaughan—the rest of the corporeal creation will be included.

Controversy over the meaning of this passage erupted between literal readers and doctrinal glossers who were reluctant to allow an inclusive reading of "the whole creation." The root of the problem seems to be that, as Alan Rudrum explains in a pioneering article, the Hebrew word for "creature" in Genesis is (transliterated) *nephesh*, "living creature," or everything that moves or breathes, while the Greek of Romans is *ktisis*, translated "the creature" (Vulgate *creatura*), which may mean the immutable cosmos without including living things. Rudrum traces the exclusionist attitude in patristic and neo-Calvinist commentary, and produces some advocates, who were deemed heretical, of the resurrection of the creatures, and attributes the neo-Calvinist attitude to a change in Theodore Beza's Latin translation of the word *ktisis* from *es creatae*, created things, to *mundus conditus*, the established world or the (supposed) immutable spheres beyond the moon.[69]

Why, then, did many seventeenth-century Christians insist that all things were made for human use and would not be encompassed by the general resurrection? Apparently, the combination of dualism in natural philosophy, experimentalism in natural history, Aristotelianism, Calvinism, and Royalism worked together against ethical and spiritual compassion for fellow sentient beings.

The Calvinist and Royalist commentator Andrew Willet gathers a range of opinion, but concludes that it is "against nature to constitute anything . . .which should be altogether idle" and therefore in Heaven "there shall be no use of these creatures, which now serve for the use of man." According to Willet

---

69 Rudrum, "Henry Vaughan, the Liberation of the Creatures, and Seventeenth-Century English Calvinism."

The most generall and received interpretation is, by the creature to understand corporalia
& irrationalia, things corporall and unreasonable, comprehending the heavens and stars,
with the earth, together with living creatures of all sorts, trees, and plants.

But he finds it most probable that

the bruit creatures which now onely serve for our necessarie use, shall not be partakers
of the glorie of the Sonnes of God; [since] there shall then be no use of them, . . . it is
probable, that they shall be abolished. . . . we understand here by the creature, onely
inanimata insensata, the things without life and sense, as the heavens and elements, and
the earth with the things therein. . . Pareus seemeth also to include the bruit beasts, yet
he thinketh they shall be abolished . . . . the onely doubt is, because afterward, v. 22, the
Apostle addeth a particle of universalitie, every creature, and so it should seeme, that the
Apostle excludeth no creatures at all.

Nevertheless, it is "most probable," Willet continues, that after the Last Judgment
"the heaven and earth shall both be the seate of the blessed; that there shall be an
entercourse betweene heaven and earth [and] the Saintes shall pass to and fro, from
heaven to earth" and that the heavens will be adorned with "things without life and
sense," sun, moon, stars and the earth with plants and trees. But it is also probable,
though not certain, "that the unreasonable creatures, as foules, beasts, fishes,
shall then cease" and not be "restored to any such glorie," for these creatures are
"appointed onely for the necessities of this life, for the foode, cloathing, and other
services of man, which then shall be at ende." Willet agrees with Peter Martyr's
opinion that "no kind of creatures shall remaine, . . . unlesse they shall have some
service or worke: for it is against nature to constitute anything . . .which should be
altogether idle, &c. then seeing there shall be no use of these creatures, which now
serve for the use of man, as for his profite in feeding, clothing, carrying, labouring,
or for his pleasure, it followeth, that they shall not be at all." However, this matter
may not be determined "as a point of faith."[70]

Vitalists and, increasingly, botanists questioned the idea that plants are "without
life and sense"; natural philosophers and historians such as Henry More and John
Ray questioned the idea that animals are utterly without reason and that they were
made only for the use of man; and poets, especially Henry Vaughan and John Milton,
objected to the exclusion of Earth and her progeny from eternity.

Henry Vaughan writes of Romans 8.19 in a poem steeped in the theology of
the liberation of the creatures. As Rudrum has pointed out, Vaughan chooses as his
epigraph Theodore Beza's first Latin translation of this Greek verse in which not
"the creature" but "created things" await the final revelation, before Beza had altered
"created things" to *mundus conditus*, or things such as celestial bodies that were
deemed immutable.[71]

---

70 Andrew Willet, *Hexapla: . . . A Six-Fold Commentarie upon . . . Romanes*, 367–73.
71 Rudrum, "For the the Earth shall be all Paradise: Milton, Vaughan, and the neo-
Calvinists on the Ecology of the Hereafter," 51–2.

"And do they so?"

Romans viii 19
Etenim res creatae exerto capite observantes expectant
revelationem Filiorum Dei

1

And do they so? have they a sense
    Of ought but influence?
Can they their heads lift, and expect,
    and groan too? why the elect
Can do no more: my volumes said
    They were all dull and dead,
They judged them senseless, and their state
    Wholly inanimate.
Go, go; seal up thy looks,
    And burn thy books.

Vaughan's "volumes" may include Aristotle and the mechanist philosophers who did not attribute life to matter or soul to creatures other than man. "Influence" may mean astrological effects or chains of merely mechanical motions; "wholly inanimate" means without soul, the mechanist view.[72] But in Vaughan's reading, every created thing—plants, animals, even stones, for "[t]he stones will cry out" (Luke 19.40)—expects the revelation; and, as an inconstant, mutable participant in human sinfulness, he wishes that, like them, he were "tied to one sure state," awaiting the revelation to "the elect." Rather than being excluded from the apocalyptic new creation, the non-human creatures are surer than he is of liberation from the throes they share with fallen humanity:

2

I would I were a stone, or tree,
    Or flower by pedigree,
Or some poor high-way herb, or spring
    To flow, or bird to sing!
Then should I (tied to one sure state,)
    All day expect my date;
But I am sadly loose, and stray
    A giddy blast each way;
Oh let me not thus range!
        Thou canst not change.

The exemplum of the steadfastness of the creatures has a drawback; scientists such as Wilkins and Ray to believe that species, whether considered as Platonic forms or as the creations of a providential God, could never become extinct. Hence Milton

---

72 For a brief but strong statement on the ravages of mechanism, see Carolyn Merchant, *Radical Ecology*, 48–59.

Milton introduces the idea that human beings need to take care of the species—"their seed preserve" (11.873)—expressing his sense of humanity's responsibility to care for the creation, a major theme of his epic. Vaughan's emphasis is on the longing of the creatures for the liberation from the throes they share because of human wrongdoing. (We might compare the beginning of Sophocles' *Oedipus Rex* where the land and the cattle suffer because of hidden crimes.) The Hebrew prophets also give expression to this conception; because of human sinfulness, "Therefore shall the land mourn, and every one that dwelleth therein shall languish, with the beasts of the fields, and with the fowls of heaven; yea, the fishes of the sea also shall be taken away" (Hosea 4.3).

Vaughan confesses that he tarries only briefly with God, while other creatures seek and signify him all the time. Those who "cannot quit the womb" or live buried lives, like the worms that live literally in tombs—or, following the logic of the first stanza, the very stones, who cannot quit the rifled womb of Earth—even they "groan" for freedom in God at the resurrection of all things. By including stones, Vaughan agrees with radical vitalists like Lady Anne Conway and Margaret Cavendish who attributed vital and eternal life to all beings.

3

> Sometimes I sit with thee, and tarry
>   An hour, or so, then vary.
> Thy other creatures in this scene
>   Thee only aim and mean;
>   Some rise to seek thee, and with heads
>   Erect peep from their beds;
> Others, whose birth is in the tomb,
>   And cannot quit the womb,
>   Sigh there, and groan for thee,
>   Their liberty.

The idea that other creatures "watch"—stay awake and aware—while "I sleep, or play" (like Donne's sonnet "Why are we by all creatures waited on?") attributes innocence to them; only man is morally corruptible. As a man, the speaker acknowledges the offering of Christ's blood and asks, like Donne in "Batter my heart," for sterner measures towards this errant "sheep."

4

> O let not me do less! shall they
>   Watch, while I sleep, or play?
> Shall I thy mercies still abuse
>   With fancies, friends, or news?
> O brook it not! thy blood is mine,
>   And my soul should be thine;
> O brook it not! why wilt thou stop
>   After whole showers one drop?
> Sure, thou wilt joy to see
>   Thy sheep with thee.

"The Book" too reaffirms the resurrection of all creatures, asking God that "when / Thou shalt restore trees, beasts and men" he, who sought God in his works, will have a place among them. "Palm-Sunday" confirms the startling faith that all things will participate in the resurrection, even stones—and so presumably earth herself:

> Trees, flowers & herbs; birds, beasts & stones,
> That since man fell, expect with groans
> To see the lamb, which all atones,
> Lift up your heads, and leave your moans!
> > For here comes he
> > Whose death will be
> Man's life, and your full liberty.

Christ atones for the whole creation, not only the human part. That wholeness is a consequence, too, of Milton's "one first matter" issuing from God and returning at the end in its splendidly differentiated heterogeneous forms, and of the work of the mediatory Son as both creator and redeemer.

A second scriptural warrant for belief in the salvation of all creatures is the vision of Heaven in Revelation 5, where "every creature which is in heaven, and on the earth, and under the earth, and such as are in the sea, and all that are in them" (Rev. 5.13) praise their redeemer together. This verse went curiously unglossed by the Geneva Bible and unnoticed by Bible illustrators, who rarely included animals in their Apocalypse series apart from the symbolic beasts of John's vision on Patmos. A medieval exception is the late thirteenth-century Trinity College Apocalypse. The commentary reads "Par tute creature sunt solement entendu les esluz" (By every creature only the elect are meant). But the illustration charmingly depicts men, women, land animals, birds, water birds, and fish with suggestions of their habitats. Perhaps Milton, a scrupulous literal reader of the Bible's problematic texts, had this verse in mind when dictating Michael's prophecies that after the Last Judgment the faithful will be received into bliss "Whether in Heav'n or earth, for then the earth / Shall all be Paradise" (12.463–5).

The supposition that the animals were made only for human use in the present life was held by Calvinist Bible commentators, but not by monist poets, who found cause for ethical consideration of animals in the callings of Adam and Eve to care for the creation and of Noah to save it, in the Hebrew psalmists and prophets, and in the doctrine of the incarnation. Religion has much to answer for, but it was not primarily theology but mechanist natural philosophy that implemented the kind of "dominion over all the earth" of which we see the ecologically devastating outcome.

Arne Naess comments, "The richness of reality is becoming even richer through our specific human endowments; we are the first kind of living things we know of which have the potentialities of living in community with all other living beings."[73] In this he agrees with poets who included the living stones of a living earth in their definition of living things, and with Milton's Adam when he exclaims at the vision of Noah's Ark (11.871–3):

---

73 Naess, "Self-Realization," in Sessions, ed., *Deep Ecology*, 234 and 239.SW.

                        I revive
    At this last sight, assured that man shall live
    With all the creatures, and their seed preserve.

Chapter 3

Air, Water, Woods

Of states in such moral gloom every seer of old predicted the physical gloom, saying, "The light shall be darkened in the heavens thereof, and the stars shall withdraw their shining [Joel 2.10]."

John Ruskin

Seventeenth-century English poetry is deeply and allusively concerned with what is actually happening to the natural world: not only the classic matters of mining and agriculture, but also accelerated air pollution, deforestation, damming of rivers, and draining of wetlands. These activities connect both to politics, causing land disputes and especially affecting the poor, and to religion, especially for those who believe that, as Milton's Michael says to Adam, "[God's] omnipresence fills / Land, sea, and air, and every kind that lives, / Fomented by his virtual power and warmed" (11.336–8).

Among the results of transforming the idea of earth from a nurturing mother to a body of extractable minerals was air pollution. In 1661, after finding the King's palace at Whitehall so filled with London's smoke that "Men could hardly discerne one another for the Clowd," John Evelyn in *Fumifugium* appealed for legislative action. Outraged that the "sordid and accursed Avarice of some few Particular Persons, should be suffered to prejudice the health and felicity of so many," and that "men whose very Being is Aer, should not breath it freely when they may," he made his plea that "our Senators . . . will consult as well the State of the Natural, as the Politick Body of this Great Nation . . . since, without their mutual harmony, and well-being, there can nothing prosper, or arrive to its desired perfection."[1]

Nearly 30 years earlier the Attendant Spirit, descending to earth in Milton's *Mask at Ludlow*, complained of "the smoke and stir of this dim spot." Eldred Revett in 1657 recommended flight to the country: "Come, let us down, / Bloat with this smoky town, / And broiled in heat / Of a tumultuous sweat."[2] In 1659 John Beale proposed to Evelyn, Graham Parry points out, "the idea of perfuming the whole region around his great garden by plantations of eglantine, lilac and woodbine, so that the air may be purified and restored, adding that London might benefit from such a 'sweet and easy remedy' of its pollution.' "[3] *Fumifugium* suggests "all the woodbinds" among the cures of London's noxious fumes. In *Paradise Lost* Eve suggests to Adam,

---

1 Evelyn, *Fumifugium*, sig. a verso and 23.

2 Fowler, *Seventeenth-Century Verse*, 706.

3 Parry, "John Evelyn as Hortulan Saint," in Leslie and Raylor, eds, *Culture and Cultivation*, 141.

> Let us divide our labors, thou where choice
> Leads thee, or where most needs, whether to wind
> The Woodbine round this Arbor, or direct
> The clasping Ivy where to climb, while I
> In yonder Spring of Roses intermixt
> With Myrtle, find what to redress till Noon.   [9.214–19]

and the type of the vocation of their descendants, in John Donne's words, "to conserve this world" and to keep the world in reparation, and leave it as well as we found it."[4] Though some would argue that Eve should have been more "clasping," her suggestion, though made in an unpolluted paradise, fits among Evelyn's plans for purifying London's poisonous air and Marvell's desire to repair England, the "garden of the world ere while."

Scholarship collected by Michael Leslie and Timothy Raylor on the Hartlib circle and the Georgical Committee of the Royal Society discloses a horticultural program for restoring the land after the civil wars that its promoters hoped would also restore health of body and soul and the moral integrity of England. For many, it constituted a preparation for the new heaven and earth prophesied in Revelation or the regained paradise of the millennium.[5] John Evelyn wrote to Sir Thomas Browne in 1660, Parry reports, that gardens "do influence the soule and spirits of man, and prepare them for converse with good Angells," and in 1659 proposed to Robert Boyle a hortulan saintly community, a modest and nonviolent alternative to Bacon's or Cowley's proposed academies, combining gardening and vegetable experiment with a simple, devout, and cultured life.[6] Such a life is the practice of Milton's Adam and Eve.

If the soil is earth's womb and water her circulatory system, air is her breath, and everything is benefited by air-cleansing plants, including plants themselves, which also live by respiration. The preface to Robert Boyle's *The General History of Air* states that "The continual use of the Air is so absolutely necessary to our Life," its quality so important to health, and its presence and the "powerful Pressure of it" a participant in so many phenomena, "that among mere Bodies there are perhaps few Subjects that more deserve our Curiosity, whether as we are Animals, or as we are Naturalists."[7] Boyle's experiments with Robert Hooke's air pump investigated it. Milton's Adam considers air as habitat when he speaks of "other creatures that possess / Earth, air, and sea" (4.431–2). So does his God: "is not the earth / With various living creatures, and the air / Replenished?" (8.370–71).

Air is also the stuff, the actual material, of speech and music. In the Garden of Eden air and song are conflated to one substance:

> The birds their choir supply; airs, vernal airs,
> Breathing the smell of field and grove, attune

---

4   Donne, *Essayes in Divinity*, 70.
5   Leslie and Raylor, eds., *Culture and Cultivation in Early Modern England*. See also Catherine Gimelli Martin, "The Enclosed Garden and the Apocalypse."
6   Parry, "John Evelyn as Hortulan Saint," Culture and Cultivation, 135, 132–3.
7   Boyle, *The General History of the Air* (1692), ix.

The trembling leaves, while universal Pan
Knit with the Graces and the Hours in dance
Led on th' eternal spring.   [4.264–8]

As Stephen Fallon observes, "The airs that are at once the breath of birds, their songs, and songs of spring meet the airs 'breathed' by the landscape."[8]

Air, Evelyn points out in *Fumifugium*, was considered by the Philosophers to be "the Vehicle of the Soul, as well as that of the earth, and this frail Vessell of ours which contains it"; we need it not only for respiration but for the spirits and humors that connect soul and body, so that its quality affects our tempers, even our politics, and works more quickly and continually even than food or drink;

> as the Lucid and noble Aer clarifies the Blood, subtilizes and excites it, cheering the Spirits and promoting digestion; so the dark, and grosse (on the Contrary) perturbs the Body, prohibits necessary Transpiration for resolution and dissipation of ill Vapours, even to disturbance of the very Rational faculties, which the purer Aer does so far illuminate, as to have rendred some Men healthy and wise even to a Miracle. And therefore the Empoysoning of Aer, was ever esteem'd no   lesse fatal then the poysoning of Water or Meate itself, and forborn even amongst Barbarians; since (as is said) such Infections become more apt to insinuate themselves and betray the very Spirits, to which they have so neer a cognition.[9]

What Londoners have to breathe, Evelyn continues, is "that Hellish and dismall Cloud of SEA-COAL," a "thick Mist accompanied with a fuliginous and filthy vapour, which renders them obnoxious to a thousand inconveniences, corrupting the Lungs, and disordering the entire habits of their Bodies; so that Catharrs, Phthsicks, Coughs and Consumptions rage more in this one City than in the whole Earth besides." The cause is immoderate use of mineral coal by brewers, dyers, lime-burners, salt- and soap-boilers, and others whose trades "infect the Aer more, then all the Chimneys of London put together," and "whilst these are belching it forth their sooty jaws, the City of London resembles the face rather of Mount Aetna, the Court of Vulcan, Stromboli, or the Suburbs of Hell, then an Assembly of Rational Creatures, and the Imperial seat of our incomparable Monarch." A "sooty Crust or furr" damages churches and palaces, spoils furniture and clothing, tarnishes silver, corrodes iron and stone, besoots leaves, water, and skin, is "an Avernus to Fowl," kills bees and flowers, and imparts "an ungrateful and bitter taste" to the few fruits that bud, but never ripen, so that "like the Apples of Sodome" they "fall even to dust."

Proof that air pollution damages plants, Evelyn continues, was provided when Newcastle was besieged by the recent war so that coal could not be delivered to "those fumous Works": gardens and orchards within London throve as never before or since. As Paracelsus says, "Aer only could be truly affirmed to have Life, seeing to all things it gave life."[10] Evelyn continues with much medical detail about the

---

8   Fallon, *Milton among the Philosophers*, 200.
9   As Clarence Glacken relates in *Traces on the Rhodian Shore*, Greek philosophers connected the bodily humors and the elements in which they subsist.
10 Evelyn, *Fumifugium*, 1–7.

diseases, depression, coughing and spitting, and loss of immunity to infections caused by coal-polluted air.

Many ecological mistakes result from trying to mend previous ones, in this case deforestation. Simon Sturtevant in *Metallica* (1612) writes of his inventions and royal privilege for

> the working, melting, and effecting of Iron, Steele, and other Mettles with Sea-coale, or Pit-coale. . . . that the Woods and Timber of our country might be saved, maintained and preserved from the great consumption and waste of our common Furnaces and Iron-Milnes, which as they are now ordinarily built and framed, can burne, spend, and consume no other fewell but Char coale.

Like other projectors, he claims cost-efficiency: Britain has eight hundred iron mills "each spending 500. pound a year in charcoal, which in pit-coale will be done with the charges of 30. or 40. pounds, or fifty if transported far."[11] What he did not foresee was the centuries of air pollution that the use of mineral coal ["Sea-coale, or Pit-coale"] would cause.

In parts II and III of *Fumifugium*, Evelyn urges dispersing coal-burning industries outside the city and considers remedies for unemployment (fewer jobs for chimney-sweepers but more for bargemen) and higher cost: brewers, for example, would have the expense of transportation but also cleaner water and less competition from imported beer and ale. Abandoned industrial properties could be turned into dwellings, and fires would be reduced, as would complaints from France that English smoke is ruining their vineyards.

Evelyn finds a precedent for legislation in an act from the seventh year of James I against burning moors out of season, for reasons that read like a prescient epitome of slash-and-burn land clearing, global warming, and El Niño effects: burning in spring and summer causes destruction of wildfowl and a "multitude of grosse vapours" that cause unseasonable storms, so crops either fail to ripen or are consumed by wind-driven fires. This offense was punishable by a month in jail without bail and a fine of twenty farthings. "Care was taken," Evelyn points out, "for the Fowl and the Game, as well as for the Fruites, Corn, and Grasse, which were universally incommoded by these unwholsome vapours that distempered the Aer, to the very raising of Storms and Tempests, upon which a Philosopher might amply discourse."[12]

Milton attributes air pollution suitably to Satan, the "Prince of the Air," who invents it during the War in Heaven. Satan's cannons belch smoke that obscures Heaven's heavens, and their roar

> Embowelled with outrageous noise the air,
> And all her entrails tore, disgorging foul
> Their devilish glut, chained thunderbolts and hail
> Of iron globes.   [6.585–90]

Like Earth, Air has "entrails," which cannonballs, like mining, tear, producing a gigantic fit of indigestion; she has a throat—gorge—that belches and vomits a glut

---

11   Sturtevant, *Metallica*, Preface, sigs. 2v–3v.
12   Evelyn, *Fumifugium*, 15, 18–19.

air pollution

of catastrophic artificial weather. This burlesque is suitable to Satan's enterprise, but thinking of air, like earth, as a living body is no less applicable to the pollutions and climate changes attributable to human activity.

The loyal angels combat this new kind of warfare by ripping up Heaven's mountains and hurling them at the rebels—an acknowledgment of the devastations of war—and the Son arrives on the third day in a living chariot, which has its own "smoke and bickering flame, and sparkles dire" (6.765)—Heaven's parodic response to demonic technology. The Son proves his creative power when the landforms that have been used as weapons obediently return to their places:

> At his command the uprooted hills retired
> Each to his place, they heard his voice and went
> Obsequious;[13] Heav'n his wonted face renewed,
> And with fresh flow'rets hill and valley smiled.   [6.781–4]

But air pollution continues apace in Hell, with its hill "whose grisly top / Belched fire and rolling smoke" (1.670–71) from whose metallic ore Mammon makes his first presumptuous construction, Pandemonium. Mammon personifies greed, the motive that Evelyn attributed to the producers of "infernal Smoake" caused by "sordid, and accursed Avarice."

Satan first fathers air pollution and then metaphorically becomes it. In Eden Ithuriel finds him "Squat like a toad" at Eve's ear trying to taint "th'animal spirits that from pure blood arise / Like gentle breaths from rivers pure" (4.800–806) as air pollution does in Evelyn's tract. In a parody of the ignition of the cannon from the rebel's "store" of "blackest grain" with "nicest touch" (6.515, 584), Ithuriel touches him lightly with his spear:

> up he starts
> Discovered and surprised. As when a spark
> Lights on a heap of nitrous powder, laid
> Fit for the tun some magazine to store
> Against a rumoured war, the smutty grain
> With sudden blaze diffused, inflames the air:
> So started up in his own shape the Fiend.   [4.813–19]

Milton acknowledges the bad air of his own city as Satan finds not-yet-fallen Eve among her roses sustaining "Each flower" and is as delighted with the change "As one who long in populous city pent, / Where houses thick, and sewers, annoy the air" (9.445–6). Approaching Paradise, Satan has enjoyed the fragrances borne by pure air that Evelyn says "have rendred some Men healthy and wise," but Satan's despair prevents his cure when "of pure now purer air / Meets his approach . . .able to drive / All sadness but despair . . . So entertained those odorous sweets the Fiend, / Who came their bane" (4.153–6, 166–7). After the bane succeeds, Death, with delight, upturns "His nostril wide into the murky air" at the gate of Hell and "snuffs the smell / Of mortal change on earth" (10.272–3).

---

13 A term, also applied to Eve's "obsequious majesty," meaning dutiful, not servile.

Coal fires reappear when the archangel Raphael enjoys earthly food and easily digests it:

> nor wonder; if by fire
> Of sooty coal th'empiric alchemist
> Can turn, or holds it possible to turn,
> Metals of drossiest ore to perfect gold
> As from the mine.   [5.439–43]

Since "empiric" experimenters have not succeeded with this project, gold is a divisive substance, and mining pollutes,[14] the simile casts doubt on the empirical enterprise. The point is, if empiricists believe in chemical transubstantiation, using the dirtiest fuel and drossiest substance to produce the purest metal, it should be easy for the wise to believe that angels, derived from "one first matter" like all created beings, can be nourished by food also made of that first matter; material food and spiritual substance are no farther apart, and more truly valuable, than dross and gold.

In Part III of *Fumifugium*, Evelyn turns to grass roots remedies for air pollution: the planting of a green belt and the cultivation of private gardens with fragrant and air-cleansing plants—Eve's exemplary task. The fields around the city should be enclosed by double palisades or hedges "elegantly planted, diligently kept and supply'd, with such Shrubes, as yield the most fragrant and odoriferous Flowers," such as "Periclymena's and Woodbinds; the Common white and yellow Jessamine, both the Syringa's of Pipe trees; the Guelder-Rose, the Musk, and all other Roses." The areas between the palisades should be "employ'd in Beds and Bordures of Pinks, Carnations, Cloves, Stock, gilly-flower, Primroses, Auriculas, Violets" and other plants "which upon the least pressure and cutting, breath out and betray their ravishing odors." The fields within these "Closures, or Invironing Gardens" should be planted with wild thyme, vegetable plots having peas and beans but not cabbages, and "blossom-bearing Grains," all "marketable at London," and the trees, shrubs, hedges, and flowers, and even the benign smoke of burning their prunings, would make everyone "sensible of the sweet and ravishing varieties of the perfumes" as well as providing places of recreation and noble prospects.

Fragrant gardening is what Eve is doing so self-forgetfully when Satan finds her alone

> Veiled in a cloud of fragrance, where she stood,
> Half spied, so thick the roses bushing round
> About her glowed, oft stooping to support
> Each flow'r of slender stalk, whose head though gay
> Carnation, purple, azure, or specked with gold,
> Hung drooping unsustained; them she upstays
> Gently with myrtle band.   [9.424–31][15]

---

14   Fallon comments that Milton "disarms objections to the truth of his own narrative by pointing to falsehoods once credulously and universally received" in *Milton among the Philosophers*, 164.

15   For illuminating discussions of this passage see Ann Gulden, "Is Art 'nice'?" and Karen Edwards, *Milton and the Natural World*, "Flourishing Colors," 166–81.

Her "graceful innocence, her every air / Of gesture or least action" (9.459–60) almost seduce Satan back to goodness. Her gentle upstaying of "Each flower" is her last innocent act of nurture, to be resumed with difficulty in the cursed ground (Gen. 3.17) of a torn world.

Water wars and riparian poetry

Earth, air, and water, the elements of life, were all altered by seventeenth-century technology, and watersheds massively rearranged. As Harander Singh Marjara notes, Paracelsus, Helmot, and Boyle all thought that, as in Genesis, water was the first element and gave it "the pre-eminent role . . . in the process of generation."[16] Milton writes of Genesis 1.9,

> The earth was formed, but in the womb as yet
> Of Waters, embryon immature involved,
> Appeared not: over all the face of Earth,
> Main Ocean flow'd, not idle, but with warm
> Prolific humor soft'ning all her Globe,
> Fermented the great Mother to conceive,
> Satiate with genial moisture.   [7.276–82]

Water then has both masculine and feminine properties. John Leonard glosses: "Earth is both the *Great Mother* about to *conceive*, and the foetus enveloped (*involved*) in protective waters. . . . *Prolific humour* [is] generative liquid. Earth's seas now act as penetrating seed as well as nursing fluid."[17]

Few English authors had as yet begun to describe what Ray called the "Terraqueous Globe"[18] (a concept represented in the early eighteenth century in Plate 3) in an integrated way, as Gilbert White would do, showing its geological history, the composition of its soils, the lay of the land, and the flow of the waters. But some personified the land as a living body and traced its veins. Among these are Michael Drayton (1622, to whom we shall return) and John Taylor, "The Water Poet" (1632).

Taylor was a practicing bargeman, and the title of his poem makes it clear that he thinks about watersheds as well as navigation:

> Taylor on Thame Isis:
> or the
> Description of the Two Famous Riuers of Thame and Isis, who being
> conioyned or combined together, are called Thamisis, or Thames.

> With all the Flats, Shoares, Shelues, Sands, Weares, Stops, Riuers, Brooks,
> Bournes, Streames, Rills, Rivolets, Streamelets, Creeks, and whatsoeuer helps
> the said Rivers have, from their springs or heads, to their falls into the Ocean.

---

16 Marjara, *Contemplation of Created Things*, 165.
17 Leonard's comments in Milton, *Complete Poems*, 807 nn. to 7.277 and 2.80.
18 Ray, *Wisdom of God*, 59.

As also a discovery of the hinderances which doe impeach the passage of
Boats and Barges, betwixt the famous University of Oxford , and the City of
London.[19]

Taylor begins with the process of weather led by the sun as Apollo, patron of
enlightened poets:

Our patron Phoebus, whose sweet influence,
Doth quicken all our reason, life, and sense,
Tis he makes grasse to grow, & Riuers spring,
He makes both my songs, subject, and me sing;

and represents the cycle of water from river to cloud to rain to river in an unstoppered
sentence:

His beames the waters doe extenuate
To vapours, and those vapours elevate
Into the middle Region, where they tumble,
And melt, and then descend and are made humble,
Moystening the face of many a spacious hill,
Where soaking deepe the hollow vaults they fill,
Where into Riuers they againe breake out,
So nature in a circle runnes about.

Like "face," but less decorously, the next lines analogize the land to the human body:
"Large Downes doe treasure vp great store of raine, / Whose bowels vent it in the
vales againe."

The poem follows the Isis from its springs in the Cotswolds, gathering streams
on the way, to Oxford, where it is joined by the Cherwell and later the Ock; finally
near Dorchester "her lovely Tame," personified as a disconsolate lover, "his Isis
doth embrace and kiss." Other waterways bring tribute to the conjoined lovers, and
we see the landscapes they nourish and clean, the fields they water, their breeding
beasts, fish, and fowl, the timber and coal they transport, and the towns and bridges
they pass. But all is not well, and Taylor proceeds to "tell the rivers wrongs" in hopes
that "good mindes" will amend the abuses of greedy persons who damage the river
by trying to control it. He asks two timeless questions that bear on enclosure and
draining as well as rivers:

Shall private persons for their gainfull use,
Ingross the waters and the land abuse [?]
Shall that which God and nature gives us free,
For use and profit in community,
Be barr'd from men, and damb'd up as in Thames [?]

He enumerates the "abuses" seen on a barge trip from Oxford to Staines and asks right-
minded persons to mend the numerous impediments to the independent bargeman's
way of life. These include turnpikes at Ifley and Stanford leaving "Weeds, shelves,

---

19 *Works of John Taylor The Water Poet*, 9.

and shoales all waterlesse and flat," dumping, ill-built locks, a quack spa, rearranged channels made too shallow or swift, a cistern that periodically floods and fouls Henley, and faulty weirs for private use that alter and pollute the river: "We found the river very foule below, / With weeds and hills of mud and gravell choak'd, / That with our Oares and staves we thrust and poake'd," while another "doth almost crosse the river all, / Making the passage straight and very small."

As Marc Reisner has shown in his account of the destructive politics of water exploitation in the American West,[20] Taylor's moral question still stands, writ large:

How can that man be counted a good liver
That for his private use can stop a river?

Troubling the Waters

Controversy produced by the draining of the fens or "levels," the wetlands of eastern England during the Stuart monarchies and the interregnum illustrates the politics of land issues and resonates in poems. Although the wildlife that the fens supported was mainly valued for food and income, Milton recognized that wetlands are breeding grounds of birds and attributes their production to the habitat itself: "the tepid caves, and fens and shores / Their brood as numerous hatch" (7.417–18); and he then describes not human uses or pleasures but the experience of the birds themselves. Marvell's metaphor of leveled fields as a model for Levellers in *Upon Appleton House* may ironically allude to the redistribution of the Levels, which Levellers protested.

Private or community draining has a long history, but these massive projects supported by "big government" made draining part of a widespread dispute between advocates of enclosure and defenders of common lands that was among the causes of the civil wars. Among supporters was the Duke of Newcastle, who, his wife Margaret Cavendish records, thought it "a part of prudence in a commonwealth or kingdom to encourage drainers; for drowned lands are only fit to maintain and increase some wild ducks, whereas being drained, they are able to afford nourishment and food to cattle, besides the producing of several sorts of fruit and corn."[21] But the seemingly sensible conversion to arable lands was devastating to fenlanders who wanted to preserve their hunting and fishing way of life. Protests were swept aside for the greater economic good of the country, but often for crown, court, and entrepreneurs in particular.

Drainage had undoubted benefits. Gilbert White speculates that "[l]ands that are subject to frequent inundations are always poor; and probably the reason may be because the worms are drowned." Of enclosure generally he remarks that some diseases, such as leprosy, nearly disappeared because of the better diet allowed by market gardening, private vegetable plots, and year-round fresh meat and dairy

---

20 Reisner, *Cadillac Desert: The American West and Its Disappearing Water.*

21 Cavendish, *The Life of the Thrice noble, high, and puissant Prince, William Cavendish* (1667), 224.

products made possible by winter fodder.[22] Eventually the fenlands became fertile croplands. But in the seventeenth century, when engineering of the fens put much communal land into private hands, and ditching isolated neighbors by cutting off long-used roads and paths, these changes felt to the commonalty like an invasion and a usurpation of the rights of traditional communities by implacable powers.

The pleasures of the fens appear in Michael Drayton's *Poly-Olbion* (1622)— Britain was anciently named for Albion, son of Neptune—which bears on its title page a queenly "Great Brittain" with scepter and cornucopia, robed in a pictorial map of rivers, trees, hills, and towns. As Wyman Herendeen points out, Drayton "formulates a historic nationalism based in geographical nature . . . ; instead of seeing the environment as a product of human presence, he sees people as a product of their environment." In the accompanying maps, "[m]issing are the signs of humanity's shaping influence usually included on Renaissance maps, the symbols depicting the religious, military, and civilizing presence of society and history"; "Hole's engravings . . . remove the social boundaries" from Christopher Saxton's maps of the counties so that "[t]he rivers are restored to nature."[23]

In the "Songs" of *Poly-Olbion*, the voices belong to the land itself. Holland, a section of Lincolnshire, describes "Fowling, and Fishing in the fen." The Washes (shallow parts of the estuary between Lincolnshire and Norfolk), where "Neptune every day doth powerfully invade / The vast and queachy soil with Hosts of wallowing waves," have the most abundant fowl; "Holland" tells of "The Duck and Mallard first, the Falconers onely sport," then turns to delights of the eye with a lesson in bird identification, describing their colors and habits: Gossander, Widgeon, Golden-Eye, Smeath, Coot, Water-Hen, Weasel, "The diving Dob-chick . . . Now up, now downe againe, that hard it is to proove, / Whether under water most it liveth, or above."[24] Drayton moves seamlessly to the delight of the palate, however:

> The Puffin we compare, which comming to the dish,
> Nice pallats hardly judge, if it be flesh or fish.

The osprey, a fellow hunter, apparently frightens his prey into a submission like that of Jonson's fish at Penshurst, though less glad, "Turning their bellies up, as though their death they saw, / They at his pleasure lye, to stuffe his glutt'nous maw."

But the chief "pleasure of the Fennes" is that they supply diverse human needs:

> The toyling Fisher here is tewing of his Net:
> The Fowler is imployd his lymed twigs to set.
> One underneath his Horse, to get a shoot doth stalke;
> Another over Dykes upon his stilts doth walke:
> There other with their Spades, the peats are squaring out,
> And others from their Carres, are busily about,
> To draw out Sedge and Reed, for Thatch and Stover fit,
> That whosoever would a Landskip rightly hit,

22 White, *The Natural History of Selborne*, 196 and 200–201.
23 Herendeen, *From Landscape to Literature*, 292–4 and 342–3, figs. 22 and 23.
24 Compare John Muir's water ouzel in *The Mountains of California*, 207–21.

Beholding but my Fennes, shall with more shapes be stor'd,
Then Germany, or France, or Thuscan can afford.[25]

These pleasures and commodities disappeared at an accelerated pace under Charles I and Cromwell. By 1654 John Evelyn could write that from the steeple at Peterborough "we viewed the fens of Lincolnshire, now much inclosed and drained with infinite expense, and by many sluices, cuts, mounds, and ingenious mills, and the like inventions; at which the city and country people about it consisting of a poor and very lazy sort of people, were much displeased."[26] Since this massive government-sponsored engineering project radically changed the land and was politically controversial in ways still with us, I think it worth recounting.

"Reclaiming" of marshland had gone on since Roman times,[27] and ordinances concerning wetlands and estuaries were established in the reigns of Henry III and his successors. The history of these laws is recounted in *The Charter of Romney Marsh*, an "Ancient Charter of King Henry the Third" concerning 24,000 acres in the County of Kent that became "the Pattern or Law for all other Sea-Borders, and great Marshes and Fens." It defined the powers of "the Governors, Bailiffs, and Conservators" and the surveillance of elected jurors "chosen by the Commonalty." Among the rights and duties of these officers are the prohibition of dams or fords impeding "the right course of the Waters"; levying taxes for repairs of sea walls and watergates; and determining who benefits from them and who is at fault when inundations occur in order to assign responsibility for repairs of walls, sluices, and ditches. The "Famous English Lawyer Sir Edward Cook in the Fourth Part of his Institutes of the Laws of England" commends this custom from which "all England receive[s] Light and Direction."[28]

Ideally, this charter made water management a community activity, so that one knew with what and whom one was dealing. When during the seventeenth century draining was accelerated, monarchs and professional drainers took it in hand, and commoners protested the loss of land and livelihood.

The parliamentary journal of Simonds D'Ewes during November through March of 1640–41 records a petition for Lincolnshire complaining of the draining of fens and taking of lands; petitions from Dr. Anthony Thompson, clergyman, who was deprived of his tithes, and of another resident for loss of an inheritance, by the draining of Sutton Marsh; and referral of other petitions to the Committee for Sutton Marsh formed by Dr. Thompson, including one protesting a project that would "entitle the King to all the lands in England betweene high-water and Low-water marke, which are worth 1,000,000£ per annum." Other petitions came from "the lords and gentry of the county of Cambridge against the Drayners of the great levell in that County" and "in the name of the six Counties wheere the levelling of the fenns lay" with an order that all the knights, citizens, and burgesses of those shires be

---

25 Drayton 512–14.

26 Evelyn, *Diary*, vol. 2, entry for 30 August 1654, 93–4.

27 Hoskins 78 and 95–100. Hoskins traces changes in the land from pre-Roman times to the twentieth century.

28 The Charter of Romney Marsh by "the Venerable Justice Henry de Bathe" (1686), sig. A3 and pp. 10, 40, 56–8, 72.

added to Dr. Thompson's "Committee touching Salt Marshes." Evidence was given that "one Henry Ruff" sent to London as a witness "about the draining of the fenns in Lincolneshire" had been arrested and imprisoned; and a grievance from Sir Hamond Strange and others of Norfolk complained "of ther salt marshes taken from them [which] was referred to Dr. Thompsons Committee but was not read."[29] The State Papers for 1660–1661, the first year of the restored monarchy, show how fenlands accrued to the crown and recount losses to landholders and commoners because of the unpaid war debts and previous extravagances of Charles I.[30] The use of land to pay for the royal jewels, for example, may remind us of the Lady's retort to Comus in Milton's *Mask* that Nature "means her provision only to the good / That live according to her sober laws, / And holy dictate of spare Temperance" (762, 764–7).

Engineers and entrepreneurs claimed that draining of the Levels would bring prosperity to all, but commoners and freeholders with grazing rights to common land felt their livelihood of small farming, grazing, hunting, and fishing threatened by those who wanted to make the land more profitable. According to Keith Lindley, the Dutch engineer Cornelius Vermuyden, contracted by Charles I (as lord of Hatfield, Epworth, and adjacent manors), was "a man of great resolution who ruthlessly, and, when necessary, unscrupulously pursued his objectives with scant regard for criticism and apparent indifference to the unpopularity which he deservedly earned in most of the enterprises with which he was associated," meanwhile protected by the patronage of James I, Charles I, and powerful courtiers.[31] In the following printed debate, J.L. speaks for the drainers and John Lilburne for the commoners in ways that demonstrate the politics of land use then and now. Milton writes of seabirds summing their pens; "J.L.", a Netherlander experienced in drainage and embankment, provides much penning of sums to prove the benefits of draining. In 1641 he addressed the English King and Parliament in a pamphlet offering to cure the "decay" of England's trade by draining and embanking to reduce the necessity of imported goods and increase local planting and manufacture. Vegetable oils from cole-seed and rapeseed, for example, should be used by woolen-cloth makers, tanners, and soap makers; in other countries soap made from animal fat is prohibited as a cause of disease. He calculates profits on flax for clothing, hemp for sailcloth, woad and madder for dyes, wheat, rye, barley, oats, peas, beans, onions, meadow and pasture for dairy cows and the breeding of cattle, horse and sheep, and acreage for houses, gardens, orchards, nurseries for trees, carrots, turnips, annis, coriander, and "Nardis seedes, and such like which cannot be valued." He argues that engineering a system of waterways throughout 12 counties would benefit the City of London and many towns. And he will answer the objections of those who promote the malice of "rude and ignorant peoples . . . out of a popular ambition."[32]

---

29 D'Ewes, *The Journal of Sir Simonds D'Ewes*, 19, 98, 178, 429, and 513.

30 *Calendar of State Papers*, Domestic Series, Charles II, vol. 1, 1660–1661: 120, 276, 296, 429, 253.

31 Lindley, *Fenland Riots and the English Revolution*, 23–4. For the earlier history of these issues see Joan Thirsk, "Enclosing and Engrossing."

32 J.L., *A Discourse Concerning the Great Benefit of Drayning and imbanking* (1641), sig. A2 and pp. 1, 3–4, 6.

To the objection that draining destroys fish and fowl, J.L. answers that fish would thrive if sluices are properly made, rape and cole fields would provide shelter for birds, and domestic fowl would increase along with hares and partridges. To the objection of insufficient skilled workers, he replies with an entrepreneurial tolerance like Bushell's that if liberty of religion "as in Queene Elizabeths time" were given to foreigners, low-country men would buy or rent these lands, and "natives" would soon become "better artists than their instructors." By these means "his Majesty for his share might have out of the great Levell" £100,000 a year and soon more.

To the objection that most of the profits would go to the developers, he answers that in the Earl of Lincoln's drained lands the commons now keep many more horses and cattle than before, but that those who refuse the work, when others take the risks and succeed, protest by "breaking downe banks, filling up draynes, destroying the works, and turning whole heards of cattle into the undertakers grounds to spoyle their cropps."

To the objection that the developers acquire and drain the best lands "but do rather drown then drayn the Commoners part," he answers that as many sluices were made, proportionably, for the commoners as for the undertakers; that banks were omitted on the commoners' side only for the purpose of winter inundation to improve fertility and to protect those who have only a cow or two from the overgrazing of the "great flocks of sheep" of the rich; and that most problems are caused by objectors to the progress provided by those who have made them roads and bridges and protected their houses and barns from floods; and that these objectors cut banks or make dams or let cattle tread down the drains and fail to maintain water courses, yet blame the undertakers for the results of their own unruliness and neglect.

To doubts about fertility and marketability, J.L. answers that Hatfield is very fruitful, and the Lord of Lindsey's draining had hopeful crops before the "uncivill actions" and even after them the "small pieces of dry ground remaining" produced enough cole-seed to make £12,000 worth of oil. To the question "yet why should these Fennes be drayned without the inhabitants willing consent, and part taken away, being their proper inheritance and freehold?" he answers that most of it is underwater and the rest unhealthy, so that cattle die of rot. If the quantity of land is lessened, the quality will be improved. If drained lands are "hassocky and moorish" industry will soon make them profitable, and if crops decrease the land will become excellent pasture. Summing up, J.L. reiterates that the project will employ thousands, aid trade, reduce imports, and increase the honor and wealth of the region and the commonwealth.[33]

In 1650, Keith Lindley notes, Sir John Maynard argued before the committee for the Lincolnshire fens that the fens already not only produced abundant meat, butter, cheese, hides, tallow, winter fodder, and dung for the upland fields, but also helped uplanders and adjacent counties save their cattle in dry summers. As to commodities such as "J.L." commends, these are "but trash and trumpery" compared with those of the fens as they are, which are "the Oar of the Commonwealth."

Enter John Lilburne.

---

33 J.L. 7–16.

Lilburne's case in 1651 was that the tenants of the manor of Epworth had been deprived of their 300-year-old rights to common pasturage and "waste grounds" when, in 1626, Charles I contracted with Vermuyden to drain these "wastes" once the King's Commissioners "had agreed with the Tenants and Commoners of the said Mannor for that right." Complications arose; the tenants were "unwilling to part with their ancient Inheritance, those Commonable grounds being extraordinary good for Milch Kine, and feeding fat Cattel, and breeding young Catel, though not for Corn," made better for grass by the winter inundations, and worth more left as pasture than plowed for grain.

Vermuyden had already drained the Manor of Hatfield; for example, he argued that his investment of £100,000 would be lost if the waste of the Manor of Epworth were not also "drayned through"; the Commissioners sided with Vermuyden and demanded over half the 13,400 hundred acres of common lands "under pretence that they had drayned their Commons for them"; though the undertakers had only drained the other manors through it, yet they took "by violence from the Commoners neer eight thousand acres . . . and set out for themselves the best ground [and] left to the Commoners only the worst ground."

The commoners, Lilburne continues, "used all lawful means" to retain their land, and when the drainers had enclosed some of their "Commonable grounds" by force and impounded their cattle, they lawsuits which in November of 1634 the Barons of the Exchequer stopped, leaving them without legal recourse. When they tried to meet force with force, they "were by the Tyranny and injustice of those Times condemned as Rioters." The Sheriff's forces killed some and wounded others, and took some to the Star Chamber where they were indicted as rioters, fined thousands of pounds, and made afraid to sleep in their own houses for fear of arrest. Many were terrorized into compromise and submission.

The drainers had use of these lands for 18, Lilburne points out, though the commoners took part of them back while in arms for Parliament in 1643. In 1646, when they tried to recover their lands legally, they were again denied. Some returned to their lands and destroyed the "poor houses" the drainers had built. Some quietly reoccupied the land and sought a legal trial, which after five years the Exchequer finally granted, but the drainers continued to prevent it on the grounds that losing their improvements would be bad for the Commonwealth. The commoners answered that although some land was now fitter for grain, they lost profit from summer pasture, navigation on the destroyed River Eidle, and fishing and fowling. Nevertheless, they were willing to help maintain the new drains and cut more. The drainers objected that the cost of their improvements entitled them to some of the grounds, though they had no right to "improve" them in the first place. The commoners replied that they had little benefit from what the drainers had done and that they were already "abundantly reimbursed," which Lilburne proves from calculations using the drainers' own figures.[34]

Lindley argues that the fenland protests called "riots" were "essentially defensive, conservative, and restrained," directed at specific local changes and resorted to only when law and custom were ignored. In the civil wars, many were fighting for

---

34 Lilburne, *The Case of the Tenants of the Mannor of Epworth* (1651), 1–6.

their lands against the undertakings of courtiers. Some works produced widespread flooding, and other places were "allegedly drained so dry that the commoners were forced to buy water for their cattle." Costs rose and wages declined. The commoners' petitions to the House of Commons and the undertakers' to the House of Lords were among the tensions that led to war; the protests helped convince "the ruling elite" of their need for monarchical rather than parliamentary rule; and fenmen were fighting against "enclosure, loss of common rights and enforced change, rather than with King or Parliament." Some fought on the Parliamentary side "to have power to destroy the Draining and Improvement" but were to be bitterly disillusioned when a victorious Parliament came to look with equal favor upon fenland drainage and enclosure" including Cromwell himself.

But Lindley sees a moral victory. After the Restoration, although Charles II praised the projects and needed land to pay his father's debts, Parliament approved only those of local landowners, while "courtiers who had ridden roughshod over property rights, local interests, and established conventions . . . remained permanently dispossessed of their fenland acres." By 1700, "Where the commoners' resistance had failed, nature was . . . more successful," and "all the surviving schemes" experienced "outfall difficulties and the progressive lowering of the fenland surface as the peat dried out and wasted away."[35]

The profits and losses of draining and embanking where seas and rivers encroach on inhabited land are often unfairly distributed. John Wesley Powell penned his sums to show how much land could be used for ranching in arid lands, and the United States Congress did not listen. The fenlands controversies forecast the politics of water wars to come.

Threats of over-management and pollution to people, places, plants, animals, justice, and the human spirit are contexts for numerous poems. Marvell describes degrees of management from moderate to minimal. In "Upon Appleton House" the Denton is a controlled river. When the watergates are opened to flood the meadows and increase fertility, "The river in itself is drowned" (1.471) but not for long: by evening "the waves are fall'n and dried, / And now the meadows fresher dyed," and the speaking "I" goes fishing on its bank, his feet among the osiers. In Milton's Paradise, free streams and rivers wander as the varied land carries them and his verse flows and pours and "runs diverse" like a watercourse:

> Southward through Eden went a river large,
> Nor changed his course, but through the shaggy hill
> Passed underneath ingulfed, for God had thrown
> That mountain as his garden mould, high raised
> Upon the rapid current, which through veins
> Of porous earth with kindly thirst up drawn,
> Rose a fresh fountain, and with many a rill
> Watered the garden; thence united fell
> Down the steep glade, and met the nether flood,
> Which from his darksome passage now appears;
> And now, divided into four main streams,

---

35 Lindley, 57, 20–21, 46 ff., 108, 141–2, 160–61, 221, 259.

Runs diverse, wandering many a famous realm
And country whereof here needs no account,
But rather to tell how, if art could tell,
How from that sapphire fount the crisped brooks,
Rolling on orient pearl and sands of gold,
With mazy error under pendant shades
Ran nectar, visiting each plant, and fed
Flowers worthy of Paradise . . . .   [4.223–41]

The sentence flows on for a total of 64 lines, many of them running into the next, a few rhymes and off-rhymes show "art" but not "nice" or punctilious art, and we see why Milton eschewed the rhymed and closed couplets of his contemporaries.

"Mazie error" is not an intimation that Nature is delusive. Waters-errant wander freely and mazily in order to visit "each plant," and these spring freely along the watercourses, not ordered in finicky plots and patterns. The "fresh fountain"—springing sapphire blue, like the sky—resembles Milton's metaphor for truth as "a streaming fountain" that must flow "in a perpetuall progression."[36] The wandering waters do their work as confined ones could not, and the verses run freely to express the paradisal freedom of streams and art and their implications for both truth and the means of life in a regenerate commonwealth.

In Sir John Denham's Coopers Hill (1642),[37] the Thames too strays at first among "wanton valleyes" but soon hastens "to pay his tribute to the Sea" (186, 189) banked by predominantly closed heroic couplets. In the rising storm of civil war, Denham makes the river a model of kingly liberality and the restraint of both sovereign and populace as he describes the temperate river's gifts to agriculture and trade. Other streams have "golden veynes" but the Thames gives "less guilty wealth" (191, 193):

Search not his bottome, but survey his shore;
O'er which he kindly spreads his spacious wing,
And hatches plenty for th' ensuing Spring.
Nor with a furious and unruly wave,
Like profuse Kings, resumes the wealth he gave:
No unexpected Inundations spoile
The Mowers' hopes, nor mock the Plough-man's toyle.   [194–200]

The analogy of kingship then turns to conquest and world commerce; "the wise King first settles fruitful peace / In his owne Realmes," and with this prosperity "Seekes warre abroad, and then in triumph brings / The spoyles of Kingdomes, and the Crownes of Kings"; the Thames brings to London not only "tributes" from nearby, but "from the East, / Spices he brings, and treasures from the West";

---

36 Milton, *Complete Prose Works* 12:543.

37 Denham, ed. Brendan O Hehir, in *Expans'd Hieroglyphicks*. Except where noted, I quote from the 1642 draft in this collection, which O Hehir designates the "A Text" and bases on the Oxford edition of 1643 collated with other versions.

Findes wealth where 'tis, and gives it where it wants,
Cities in Desarts, woods in Cities plants,
Rounds the whole Globe, and with his flying towers
Brings home to us, and makes both Indies ours:
So that to us no thing, no place is strange
Whilst thy faire bosome is the worlds Exchange:
O could my verse freely and smoothly flow,
As thy pure flood . . .   [205–20]

In the 1655 version Denham revised and extended this wish to what became a classic statement about neoclassical versification and landscape:

Oh could I flow like thee, and make thy stream
My great example, as it is my theme!
Though deep, yet, clear, though gentle, yet not dull,
Strong without rage, without o'erflowing full.   [1655, 1668: 185–92][38]

The first version demonstrates the lack of smoothness lamented, the second displays the smoothness desired. Rhymes and metrics flow easily, gently rocking the boat in balanced, symmetrical oppositions, and coming to a full cadence on "full."

Brendan O Hehir notes that Denham in his own copy of the 1668 version adds six handwritten lines after "Exchange"[39]:

Rome only conquerd halfe the world, but trade
One commonwealth of us and her hath made
And though the sunn his beame extends to all
Yet to his neighbour sheds most liberall
Lest God and Nature partiall should appeare
Commerse makes everything grow everywhere.

Denham hails widespread exchange of "exotic species" now known to be potentially disastrous to ecosystems, and profit-motivated manipulations such as John Taylor had complained of ten years earlier had made the Thames between Oxford and London far from free. Denham's concluding political metaphor opposes dams but reinforces channels: a commonwealth is happy "When Kings give liberty, and Subjects love" (318); when either runs to excess, "The Husbandmen" can reinforce the banks, but "if with Bays, and Dammes they strive to force / His channell to a new, or narrow course . . . he roares, and knows no bound."

Therefore their boundlesse power let Princes draw
Within the Channel, and the shores of Law,
And may that Law, which teaches Kings to sway
Their scepters, teach their Subjects to obey.   [351–4]

---

38 From O Hehir's "B Text."
39 O Hehir 150 n.

The ideal of a gentle and generous but controlled waterway—if you can ignore the blockages and pollutions it was already enduring—fits with Evelyn's tamed landscape, not Milton's heaving mountains and tumid hills, and with the ideal of order in neoclassical versification and political philosophy rather than the unbounded resonances of vitalist poets. Describing a landscape that, Ken Hiltner points out, was already giving evidence of pollution and overexploitation,[40] Denham joined Drayton in contributing to a genre in which "the environment" is itself a topos or "place" of invention. But commendation of the king who "Seekes warre abroad, and then in triumph brings / The spoyles of Kingdomes, and the Crownes of Kings" is contrary to Milton's unfettered streams in a Paradise where both nature and humanity work freely and where unfettered "connubial love" is the "Sole propriety" in a Paradise "of all things common else" (4.743, 751–2): the antithesis of monarchical appropriation of common lands.

Henry Vaughan, though loyal to the English king, identifies himself as the poet of a particular place; not London or Eden or an idealized *locus amoenus* but a Welsh valley through which a river runs. Vaughan too prefers God's management of waters to man's. In his translation of Psalm 104, God "curbs whole seas" with sand, yet

> . . . as thy care bounds these, so thy rich love
>   Doth broach the earth, and lesser brooks lets forth,
> Which run from hills to valleys, and improve
>   Their pleasure and their worth.
>
> These to the beasts of every field give drink;
>   There the wild asses swallow the cool spring:
> And birds amongst the branches on their brink
>   Their dwellings have and sing.
>
> Thou from thy upper springs above, from those
>   Chambers of rain, where Heaven's large bottles lie,
> Dost water the parched hills, whose breaches close
>   Healed by the showers from high.[41]

The title of *Olor Iscanus* means swan of the Usk, and the author identifies himself as "Silurist" from the ancient inhabitants of southeastern Wales, where the river Usk runs through Vaughan's native Brecknockshire.[42] The title page shows a large swan on a small, placid stream, with trees, flowers, and many bees, emblems of poets, as honey-gatherers and wax-makers, providers of sweetness and light. Below the title is a motto from *Georgics* II, *Flumina amo Silvasque, inglorius*, in which Vergil expresses his desire to live in the country and love inglorious rivers and woods, but with "amo" altered from Vergil's subjunctive "amem" since Vaughan actually lives beside the river he loves. Vergil's passage follows the expression of a higher desire, to be an inspired philosophical poet-prophet-priest of the muses, who understands

---

40   Hiltner, in progress.
41   Vaughan, in Rudrum, ed., *Complete Poems*, 258–9.
42   Alan Rudrum shows the importance of Vaughan's self-identification of "Silurist" in *Henry Vaughan* for the series *Writers of Wales*.

the depths of heaven and earth and the ways of stars, tides, eclipses, earthquakes, and seasons. But if "my heavy Blood restrain the Flight / of my free Soul, aspiring to the Height of Nature, and unclouded Fields of Light" (in Dryden's rather Horation translation),

> My next Desire is, void of Care and Strife,
> To lead a soft, secure, inglorious Life.
> A country Cottage neare a Crystal Flood,
> A winding Valley, and a lofty Wood.[43]

Vergil's simpler original diction fits his theme of the contentments of a simple life. Vaughan in his sacred poems aspires like Vergil to the fields of light, yet in the motto for the secular verses of *Olar Iscanus* he too seeks to live inconspicuously with river and woods.

To the River Isca is Vaughan's statement of his calling as a poet of place, and in it Vergil's alternative vocations become united. Poets divine and human from Apollo to Sidney, Vaughan begins, have brought forth flowers of poesie on the banks of rivers, where their protective *genii* still live. Poets "Hallow the place." Vaughan vows so to write that he will hallow the Usk valley where he was born and means to die.

> When I am laid to *rest* hard by thy *streams*,
> And my *sun sets*, where first it *sprang* in beams,
> I'll leave behind me such a large, kind light,
> As shall redeem thee from oblivious night.

Vaughan does not describe the river merely as a component of his own pleasure, but invokes blessings for the river so that "*vocal groves*" like Dodona's may grow there, "and all / The shades in them prophetical, / Where (laid) men shall more *fair truths* see / Than *fictions* were of *Thessaly*." His choice of place may be "ingloriosus" but he hopes his poetry will give it the right kind of fame. In the process of enumerating the blessings he invokes for the river—fair name, poetic praise, true lovers, mild weather, "The *turtle's voice, joy* without fear," freedom from real or emblematic evets,[44] toads, and snakes (not all Vaughan's animals are equal)—he also wishes the Usk freedom from pollution, specifically from mining.

> No *nitrous clay*, nor *brimstone-vein*
> Mix with thy *streams*, but may they pass
> Fresh as the *air*, and clear as *glass*[.][45]

The nearest thing to a mercantile image Vaughan produces, in contrast to Denham, is "the factor-wind," a factor being, Alan Rudrum points out, "a mercantile agent . . . bringing the odours from far";[46] but this merchant, who may remind us of Herbert's "sweet commerce" between Christ and the soul, brings only "spicy whispers."

---

43 Dryden, *Georgics* 2:685–91, in *Works* 5:203.

44 Rudrum explains *evet* as "the Greater Water-Newt," in Vaughan, *Complete Poems*, 470 n. 51.

45 Vaughan, *Complete Poems*, 70–72.

46 Rudrum, in Vaughan, *Complete Poems*, 471 n. 61.

Vaughan's final fervent wish for the river alludes to the civil war that had so disturbed his own peace, also a link with Vergil. He hopes for freedom from lifeless temporal things and for an order that is different from Hobbes's and other fellow royalists' ideas of order, in that even the state may be a "toy" and the liberation and peace of the land itself, including a willingness to live a materially inconspicuous life, is a primary responsibility of the body politic:

> . . . what ever *Fate*
> Impose elsewhere, whether the graver state,
> Or some toy else, may these *loud, anxious cares*
> For *dead* and *dying things* (the common wares
> And shows of time) ne'er break thy *peace*, nor make
> Thy *reposed arms* to a new war *awake*!
> > But *freedom, safety, joy and bliss*
> > *United* in one loving *kiss*
> > *Surround* thee quite, and style thy borders
> *The land redeemed from all disorders*!

Vegetable gold: I sing of the forest political

If mines tear Earth's womb, and dams clot her arteries, deforestation damages her lungs and defaces her landscapes. John Beale wrote to Samuel Hartlib, "All our hills have sometimes borne Oaks, or few failed, and I conceive most are very apt for it. But of late the Iron-Mills have devoured our Glory, and deflower'd our Groves."[47] Just as poets wrote in the contexts of mining, coal-burning, damming, and draining, they also wrote among real trees and the politics of their use. Deforestation was a crisis for which each side in the civil wars—quite rightly—blamed the other. Arboreal writings by Gerrard Winstanley, Samuel Hartlib, Gerrard Boate, John Evelyn, and Nehemiah Grew describe the kinds, social importance, historical misuses, necessity to human well-being, anatomy, restoration, and care of trees and woodlands, and poets' descriptions however pastoral or metaphorical are laden with a sense of real and wounded trees.[48]

In Marvell's "The Garden," "all flow'rs and all trees do close" (both unite and agree) "To weave the garlands of repose," and the lover of trees resolves, "Fair trees! whers'e'er your barks I wound, / No name shall but your own be found." In Milton's Eden, God "caused to grow / All trees of noblest kind for sight, smell, taste; / And all amid them stood the Tree of Life, / High eminent, blooming ambrosial fruit / Of vegetable gold" (4.215–20). Adam and Eve were given this and all other fruit- and nut-bearing trees to eat from except one, reserved as an exercise in temperance and faith, a reminder that trees are not mere timber. "Vegetable" indicates a real tree, not an emblem, marking the literality so important to Milton's interpretation of the Bible's natural imagery, and "gold" thus modified indicates a preciousness exceeding all the ornaments of Oriana. The repeated "all" by each poet, and the assignment of

---

47   Beale (b. 1603), *Herefordshire-Orchards* (1730), 520.

48   A history of attitudes towards woodlands may be found in Robert Pogue Harrison, *Forests: The Shadow of Civilization.*

highest value to trees, spoke to their contemporaries' awareness of increasingly rapid deforestation as trees fell victim to Moloch and Mammon.

In Drayton's *Poly-Olbion*, where the Muse makes a Progress over the topography of England and places speak, Waltham Forest, "still in prosperous estate, / As standing to this day (so strangely fortunate)," speaks to her sister Hatfield about changing landscapes:

> The Ridge and Furrow shewes, that once the crooked Plow,
> Turn'd up the grassy turfe, where Oakes are rooted now:
> And at this hour we see, the Share and Coulter teare
> The full corne-bearing gleabe, where sometimes forrests were;
> And those but Caitifes are, which most doe seeke our spoyle,
> Who having sold our woods, doe lastly sell our soyle.[49]

In *The Muses Elizium*, Jean Brink points out, Drayton's "ideals have become tarnished" just as Felicia, or Albion, has been "'defac'd,'" "'Braveries gone wherein she did abound, / With dainty Groves, when she was highly grac'd / With goodly Oake, Ashe, Elme, and Beeches croun'd (85–88)'". Her people "ignorant of their own history," Brink continues, "have become contemptuous of the poetry that gave voice to their heroic ideals. They have even turned upon the land and begun to deface and ravage its beauty": "This cruell kinde thus Viper-like devoure / That fruitfull soyle which them too fully fed."[50] That people "contemptuous of poetry" should "deface and ravage" the beauty of the land holds, in an acorn shell, the argument of the book you are reading.

Attitudes towards forests were intervolved with politics, but again, poetry cannot be politicized along party lines. On the Royalist and Royal Society side, in Aemelia Lanyer's "The Description of Cooke-ham" the mistress of the estate literally kisses a tree goodbye; Henry Vaughan thought trees were always in God's eye; Margaret Cavendish gives an oak threatened with the ax a voice to plead for its life; John Evelyn thought that the chief recreation of estate owners, rather than hunting, should be tree-planting competitions; and Nehemiah Grew argued that trees' vitality and sexuality were more like ours than we imagine. Jurisdiction over forests was by long tradition royal or aristocratic,[51] and it is not surprising that the most ardent writers on behalf of saving and replanting trees come from that tradition, or that botanists are members of the Royal Society. The republican Samuel Hartlib and the radical Gerrard Winstanley express (so far as I know) no spiritual kinship with trees; the issue was who possessed them.

Timber means specifically "Wood for the building of houses, ships, use of carpenters, joiners, and other artisans" and "Trees growing upon land, and forming part of the freehold inheritance," especially oak, ash, and elm of 20 years or more, or others as locally defined (*Oxford English Dictionary*). *Forest* is the legal term

---

49 Drayton, *Poly-Olbion*, Song XIX, ll. 27–8 and 41–2, p. 398. For a literary history of rivers, see Herendeen, *From Landscape to Literature*.

50 Brink, *Michael Drayton Revisited*, 126.

51 On the politics and poetics of forests see Jeffrey S. Theis, "'The pulieus of heaven': Milton's Eden as Pastoral Forest."

for a royal preserve, whether wooded or not, for the recreation of princes—in view, John Manwood says, of the "continual study and care that Kings and Princes have in great and mighty affairs of matters of Commonweal, for the good of their Subjects, whereby they are oftentimes wearied with the toyl of the same." Manwood defines a forest as "a certain Territory of woody grounds, and fruitful pastures, privileged for wild beasts and fowls of Forest, Chase, and Warren, to rest and abide in, in the safe protection of the King, for his princely delight and pleasure," demarcated by "unremovable marks, meers, and boundaries" though not enclosed; "And also replenished with wild beasts of Venery or Chase, and with great coverts of Vert, for the succour of the said wild beasts, to have their abode in." A forest consists chiefly of "vert, venison, particular laws and privileges" and officers appointed to preserve it "for a place of recreation and pastime meet for the royal dignity of a Prince."[52] The commonalty received severe penalties for poaching.

During the seventeenth century, Britain's forests were not disafforested (deregulated) but deforested. Trees were cut by both sides in the civil wars and by both monarchs and Protector to pay the King's and the Commonwealth's war bills, to feed and warm the poor in hard times, and to replenish the naval fleet and increase trade. Motives for preserving and restoring forests were mixed all along the political spectrum. Both royalists and republicans took a managerial approach to nature, and no party can claim all the credit or blame either for the new respect for trees that began to spring up as they were cut down or for the centuries of deforestation which, though charcoal was being replaced by toxic mineral coal, was accelerated by shipbuilding, war, overplowing, overbuilding, and the land wars of the interregnum. Trees were financial and political pawns, and habitats were destroyed without consideration of their non-human inhabitants except those classed as game.

Proponents of putting all possible land under the plow argued that barren lands and idle hands could profitably mend each other. Agricultural projectors published numerous proposals for cultivating all land that could be plowed, draining wetlands, improving soil, rotating crops, and increasing the fertility of both land and plants. Many of these were published by Samuel Hartlib, the correspondent who evoked Milton's *Of Education*, in which the Latin "Authors [of] Agriculture, *Cato, Varro, and Columella*" are part of the curriculum.[53]

Like Bushell in his project to save drowned mines, agricultural projectors had beneficent motives, but no room for the wild. A pre-war writer of this kind is Gabriel Plattes, author of *Subterraneall Treasure*, who also wrote a book called *A Discovery of Infinite Treasure* (1635) urging that "corne, and fruits" are "the chiefest of all riches," while "Gold that Great Commander" is "a good Art," but "lucrous in these times." His suggestions include ways to grow trees as timber without using land suitable for agriculture: "There is a Law in Spaine, that he that cutteth downe a tree, shall plant three young ones for it; and by this meanes there are builded in two provinces, both not so great as Yorkeshire, twentie ships yearely, and yet the wood increaseth: If this Law were observed here, how happie would it be for the

---

52   John Manwood, *A Treatise of the Laws of the Forest* (1665) a4 verso, 40–41.

53   Milton, *Of Education*, in *Complete Prose Works* 2:387–8; see DuRocher "Careful Plowing" and *Milton Among the Romans*.

posteritie?" But "I would have all Timber trees planted in hedgerows, and by this means no ground will be lost: but all woods and thornie grounds may be turned into fruitfull fields and pastures, and are apt to be made fertile by my new inventions."[54]

For Plattes among others, trees are not living things, but money in the bank. A tract of 1643 tells its story in its title: *An Abstract . . . of a Grant and Conveyance proposed to be made by His Majesty for securing of the payment and discharge of divers debts and sums of money lent, and which hereafter shall be lent to His Majesty, or secured . . . for His Majesty's use and service: assigning New Forest, Sherwood Forest and Park, Beskwood Park, Clarendon Park, and Bowood park to commissioners for payment of the King's debts.*[55] A parliamentary ordinance of the same year (in response to the siege of Newcastle that reduced air pollution and benefitted trees as reported in Evelyn's *Fumifugium*) provides government supervision of tree-cutting; indicates protests against both unauthorized destruction of timber and appropriation of trees by the state (which disafforested the woods belonging to recusants and ousted church officials while protecting other private owners); authorizes bringing out the troops to aid officials in enforcing the rules of felling; and provides punishments for infringers.[56]

Apparently, opportunistic clear-cutters were not lacking during the Commonwealth. The *Calendar of State Papers* records that on 22 April 1655, the Earl of Clare, Lord Warden of Sherwood Forest, reported to Mr. Montague, of the Council,

> I beg you to acquaint [his Highness] with . . . a report that Mr. Clark has leave to sell for his own use 28,000 trees . . . ; that he sets on all the workmen that can be got at very high wages, and before the bark will peel, contrary to statute, and sells at very low rates, like Solomon's harlot that would have the living child divided. He sweeps clean, leaving no standards according to law, which will bare of timber a forest that stands near 2 navigable rivers, the Trent and Idle, and render it in the same condition as the Forest of Dean was endeavoured in the late King's time, by malevolent persons, to weaken our wooden walls of shipping.

The Earl attaches a report of 16 April 1655 that "the forest is ruined, especially Clipston Woods, where the inhabitants have right of estovers, by Mr. Clark, on pretence of a grant from the Committee for sale of Traitor's Estates. He has felled 1,000 trees, and daily fells more, and sold 300 to Phillips of Bawley, for ship timber. He fells in the heart of the forest, where the deer have their greatest relief. There is much good ship timber in the forest. Rob. Baskerville, late Woodward General, has died; another should be appointed or the woods will suffer much."[57]

Other excerpts from the *State Papers*:

1654–55: A petition to the Protector and Council from those living near Needwood Forest, designated as recompense for military service, that the forest may not be sold, or else that they may establish legal rights and be compensated, especially since the county had

---

54 Plattes, *A Discovery of Infinite Treasure* (1635), 10.

55 *Calendar of the Clarendon State Papers Preserved in the Bodleian Library*, 247.

56 *An Ordinance. . . For the cutting and felling of Wood within threescore miles of London* (3 October 1643), 1–6.

57 *Commonwealth* 8 (1655): 137.

already paid £8,000 to the disbanded soldiers. "Former Kings took 10 parks from the chase," the rest has little value, and its sale or enclosure would rob them of their ancient right to use a landlord's woods for necessary repairs to houses and fences.

1655: Sale of forest lands for payment of bills for fitting the treasury at Worcester House; and a petition from hundreds who had lent money to the Protector asking to be paid "from debtors' estates, as promised by Parliament, or from forest lands, excise, or customs, or any speedy way."[58]

1656: "We are running deeply into debt to send our fleet to sea. There is great expectation of action this year; our forests, and the remainder of our Deans and Chapters' lands and impropriate tithes will soon be sold."[59]

Margaret Cavendish says of her husband, the Duke of Newcastle, who fought against Fairfax, that after the restoration, "Of eight parks, which my Lord had before the wars," he found only one "not quite destroyed, Welbeck Park"; the rest "were totally defaced and destroyed, both woods, pales, and deer; amongst which was also Clipston Park, of seven mile's compass, wherein my Lord had taken much delight formerly, it being rich of wood, and containing the greatest and tallest timber-trees of all the woods he had . . . . It was watered by a pleasant river that runs through it, full of fish and otters" and "well-stocked" with deer, hares, partridges, poots, pheasants, and "all sorts of water-fowl," affording "all manner of sports, for hunting, hawking, coursing, fishing, &c., for which my Lord esteemed it very much." Although the Duke did not complain, "yet when he beheld the ruins of that park, I observed him troubled . . . there being not one timber-tree in it left for shelter."[60]

The Duke managed to repale the woods and restock its wild animals, or game; the Duchess expresses quite different feelings about hunting and felling in "The Hunting of the Hare" and "A Dialogue *between an* Oake, *and a* Man *cutting him downe*."[61] Given the symbolism of oaks as royalty, the dialogue might possibly be thought to speak for Charles I, but it certainly speaks for trees. Why, the oak asks, does the man cut the tree that protects him from heat, rain, and snow, invites the birds to sing for his pleasure, and lets him lean his "weary head" amid the gentle sounds of leaves and cooling air? "And will you thus requite my Love, Good Will, / To take away my Life, and Body kill?" The oak describes this violence as Ovid describes violence to the ox: "For all my Care, and Service," must I be laid on the fire?

Cavendish likens the tree to a human body, as does Marvell and (as we shall see) Nehemiah Grew, and even alludes to the wounding of Christ:

First you do peele my Barke, and flay my Skinne,
Hew downe my Boughes, so chops off every Limb.
With Wedges you do peirce my Sides to wound,
And with your Hatchet knock me to the ground.
I minc'd shall be in Chips, and peeces small,
       And thus doth Man reward good Deeds withall.

---

58 *Commonwealth* 8:31 and 242.
59 *Commonwealth* 9 (1655–1656): 363.
60 Cavendish, *Life*, 135–6.
61 Cavendish, in *Poems and Fancies*, 66–70.

The man replies that the old King of the Wood should make way for young acorns who "Long for your Crowne, and wish to see you fall," but the oak wants to "live the Life that Nature gave" regardless of its subjects' opinions. The man says the oak is ignorant from lack of travel and offers to make a trafficking ship of it, so that "thy sharpe Keele the watry Wombe doth teare." But the oak replies "I am contented well, / Without that Knowledge, in my Wood to dwell / and simple be," rather than risk being sunk by the over-freighting of greedy merchants: "I care not for that Wealth, wherein the paines, / And trouble, is farre greater then the Gaines./ I am contented with what Nature gave."

The man offers to make the oak into "a Stately House" where he could enjoy entertainments more lavish than nightingales', but the oak, again waxing biblical, is "sore afraid" of burdensome preferment and "Nailes, and Hammer strong" that "pierce my Sides, to hang their Pictures on." This bathetic crucifixion does not work as an allegory of Charles, with his love of pictures and preferment. The oak adds,

> More Honour tis, to be in Natures dress,
> Then any Shape, that Men by Art expresse.
> I am not like to Man, would Praises have,
> And for Opinion make my selfe a Slave . . . .

Finally the man offers the oak a victory: "If you, as Man, desire like Gods to bee, / I'le spare you Life, and not cut downe your Tree." So Cavendish grants the Man and the King of the Wood a kind of equality—with a wry glance perhaps at the Tree that cut down Man in Eden for too much "desire like Gods to bee," and with a critique of over-consumption that aligns her with the builders in Marvell's estate poem rather than those whose opulent houses "forests did to pastures hew."

From the point of view of the Leveller and Universalist Gerrard Winstanley, all private property including forests was a usurpation of "the righteous Law of Creation." Shortly after the King's execution in 1649 he defended the right of the landless poor to cultivate common land. "A Declaration to the Powers of England, and to All the Powers of the World, shewing the cause why the common people of England have begun . . . to digge up, manure, and sowe corn upon George-Hill in Surrey" begins with a statement somewhat like Adam's response to the story of Nimrod in *Paradise Lost*:

> In the beginning of Time, the great Creator Reason, made the Earth to be a Common Treasury, to preserve Beasts, Birds, Fishes, and Man, the lord that was to govern this Creation; for Man had Domination given to him, over the Beasts, Birds, and Fishes; but not one word was spoken in the beginning, That one branch of mankind should rule over another.

Since "Every single man, Male and Female, is a perfect Creature of himself; and the same Spirit that made the Globe, dwels in man to govern the Globe" when the flesh is subdued to "Reason his Maker," he needs no other teacher or ruler.

Winstanley's plan is modest, "To dig up Georges-Hill and the waste Ground thereabouts, and to Sow Corn, and to eat our bread together by the sweat of our brow." But he also has larger views: he wishes to abolish money and berates those who "follow the subtle art of buying and selling the Earth, meerly to get the Treasury thereof into their hands" while letting those with equal creation-rights starve.[62] Although Winstanley would disagree with Karl Marx about the abolition of religion, his proposals are consonant with, though more modest than, those of the *Communist Manifesto* for "the bringing into cultivation of waste-lands" and the "gradual abolition of the distinction between town and country."[63] Winstanley and his fellow Diggers aim "to cut and fell . . . the Woods and Trees, that grow upon the Commons" in order to plant crops to sustain themselves and the poor until the harvest. They will not "meddle" with private property "till the Spirit in you, make you cast up your Lands and Goods," got and kept "by murder, and theft." They will take these possessions peaceably "from the Spirit, that hath conquered you, and not from our Swords, which is an abominable, and unrighteous power, and a destroyer of Creation."

The Declaration accuses some Lords of Manors of having trees cut for their own use on common lands already overgrazed by the sheep and cattle of rich landowners, leaving little for the poor yet preventing them from cutting "Wood, Heath, Turf, or Furseys." But "if the Common Lands belongs to . . . the poor oppressed, surely the woods that grow upon the Commons belong to us likewise: therefor we are resolved to try the uttermost in light of reason, to know whether we shall be free men, or slaves." They have paid their taxes and given their lives for "the Nation's freedom as much as you . . . . And if we strive for freedom, and your murdering, governing Laws destroy us, we can but perish." They propose to take common lands and woods for livelihood, and "look upon you as equal with us." Lords of Manors who fell common trees for private use should desist, and no one including wood mongers should buy trees from those Lords of Manors who by "the murdering and cheating law of the sword" have stolen the common land, but should buy them from and for the poor.

On 9 June of the same year, Winstanley sent a letter to the Lord General Thomas Fairfax and his Council of War on behalf of the diggers of George-Hill, seeing the controversy about it as "plainly a pitched battaile between the Lamb and Dragon." He protests that some of Fairfax's soldiers had beaten and robbed a boy and a man who were alone on George-Hill, and had "fired our house." But his larger plea is ardently political: the efforts of the Diggers are the continuation of the war against slavery that Fairfax himself had led. Charles I was successor to William the Conqueror, who "turned the English out of their birthrights"; monarchical laws still keep the common people "under slavery"; the Lords of Manors are the successors of the Conqueror's colonels and officers; and the Norman yoke has been thrown off under the Lord General Fairfax's leadership—yet not for all. His mission is to make the newly liberated commonwealth more inclusive.

This letter to the Lord of Nunappleton should be considered as we read Marvell's poems of estates where trees are conserved and the owner chooses to withdraw from government. Winstanley's view of creation-rights and the "Fall" into possession of property resembles the morality of Traherne's "Adam," but with political intent: "Before the fall, Adam, or the Man did dresse the garden, or the earth, in love,

---

62   Winstanley, *Works*, 270, 251, 257, 272–4.
63   Marx, *The Communist Manifesto*, 75.

freedom, and righteousnesse, which was his rest and peace"; but covetousness made man "set himself one man above another." The story of Cain manifests "the two powers that strive in the man Adams heart" since "he consented to that serpent covetousnesse" bringing in "particular propriety" upheld by the sword. Winstanley believed that "mankind in all his branches is the lord over the Beasts, Birds, Fishes, and the Earth," which is "free for every son and daughter of mankind to live free upon."[64] But he fights with apocalyptic zeal against the covetousness that destroys the creation.

Samuel Hartlib considered the instrumental understanding of nature as made for man's use as an element of liberty. Gerard Boate's *Ireland's Naturall History* (1657) was published by Hartlib and dedicated to Oliver Cromwell and Charles Fleetwood, Cromwell's commander of the English forces in Ireland who brutally suppressed the Irish rebellion. Hartlib's preface argues that no kind of learning is "more profitable in Nature, than that of Husbandry," and nothing is more useful to commerce than "the knowledge of the Natural History of each Nation." He says of the relation of science and liberty, with allusion to Bacon:

> These great and mighty Changes, which God is making in the Earth, do tend to break the yokes of Vanity, and to weaken the Power, which hath wreathed the same upon the necks of the Nations . . . and [to] the advancement of the ways of Learning, whereby the Intellectual Cabinets of Nature are opened . . . .

This new understanding will make clear "the right use" of nature and fulfill the promise *that the Earth shall be filled with the knowledge of the Lord, as the waters cover the sea, & that we shall be taught of God, from the least to the Greatest.* Like Winstanley, he associates the right use of nature with a "breaking of yoakes." By "more perfect knowledge, both in Natural and Spiritual things, wee may see the drawing neer of the promises, which will in their own times Constitute *the day of Salvation unto all the Earth, wherein all flesh shall see the glory of the Lord together* [Isaiah 40.5.]."

Unlike Milton and other vitalists, Hartlib was a dualist: "There is a twofold body, and a twofold life in man, which God hath created, the one is Naturall, the other Spirituall, & the Apostle tells us, *that the Spirituall is not first, but the Naturall, and afterward that which is Spirituall* [I Cor. 15.46]." But he defends the importance of the natural world and, like Milton and Vaughan, believed in the restoration of the earth expected in Romans 8.19, "in the time of *the Restauration of all things*": when "the works of the Devill, whereby he hath brought us, & the whole Creation, under the bondage of Corruption, shall be destroied, & when Nature & right use of the Creature by his meanes obscured, shall be revealed, then also the properties and application of the Creature *in the glorious liberty of the sonnes of God,* shall be subjected unto Grace." God is weakening the political power that lays yokes "upon the necks of the Nations" in order to advance liberty and learning "whereby the Intellectual Cabinets of Nature are opened" and the right use of the creation made plain to all.

---

64 Winstanley, Letter to Fairfax, *Works*, 281–9, 290.

Hartlib hopes to see Ireland replanted by both investors and Protestant exiles, and to further the settlement that the "Natural History of that Countrie" will serve.[65] Liberty and the breaking of yokes seem not to apply to the Irish. The replantation of their deforested land was an opportunity to increase commerce and the Protestant population.

Boate's history of deforestation begins with Giraldus Cambrensis's report that during the first conquest under Henry II in 1171, Ireland was wooded everywhere; but the English settlers nearly destroyed the Woods "partly to deprive the Theeves and Rogues . . . of their refuge and starting-holes, and partly to gain the greater scope of profitable lands." The English expelled the "Wild Irish . . . into the desart wood and mountains," but between warring among themselves and taking up indigenous "wild fashions" they were reduced to the "English Pale" of four counties and the great cities. Since subduing of the rebellion at the end of Queen Elizabeth's reign and the 40-year Peace that followed,

> the remaining Woods have very much been diminished, . . . not for the ordinary uses of building and fitting . . . but to make merchandise of, and for the making of Charcoal for the Ironworks. [A] mighty Trade was driven in Pipe-staves . . . and whole ship-loads sent into forrein countries yearly; which as it brought great profit to the proprietarie, so the felling of many thousands of trees every year as were employed that way, did make a great destruction of the Woods in tract of time. As for the Charcoal, it is incredible what quantity thereof is consumed by one Iron-work in a year: [and] there hath been a very great number of them erected since the last Peace in sundry parts of every Province; the which to furnish constantly with Charcoal, it was necessity from time to time to fell an infinite number of trees.

As a result, the inhabitants of Ireland lack wood for burning and even for building; many counties are nearly bare of trees.[66]

Boates' history sounds wry against Hartlib's ideal of liberty and education. In it, the English see the Irish as American expansionists would see the First Nations, as barbarous and in need of reformation, and the forests as so much fodder for industry. Under James I, "the whole Island was reduced under the obedience and government of the English Lawes, and replenished with English and Scotch Colonies," but the name "the English Pale" remains even since "this last bloody rebellion" in which inhabitants of English descent "have conspired with the Native Irish, for to stake off the Government of the Crown of England, and utterly to extinguish the Reformed Religion."[67] He considers the draining of bogs as one of England's gifts to Ireland for which that "brutish nation" returned ingratitude and "a horrible and bloody conspiracie." Regarding the remaining "Bogs, Barren-Mountains, and Woods," Acts of Parliament have been made on behalf of the investors "for the reconquering of the revolted part of that Kingdom." As elsewhere, the conquest of nature and the conquest of native inhabitants are joined even among the proponents of liberty.

---

65 Hartlib in Boate, A3–A4–A5v.
66 Boate 114–22.
67 Boate 7–8.

John Evelyn exposed deforestation as well as air pollution. *Sylva* (1664) is *A Discourse of Forest-Trees, and The Propagation of Timber in His Majesties Dominions* describing their species and culture, a subject perhaps "too sordid and vulgar for Noble Persons and Gentlemen to busie themselves withal, and who oftner find ways to fell down and destroy their Trees and Plantations, than either to repair or improve them." But the brunt of Evelyn'e attack is aimed at "our late prodigious Spoilers, whose furious devastation of so many goodly Woods and Forests have left an Infamy on their Names and Memories" so that some of the "Gallant and Loyal Gentry" were "compell'd to add yet to this Waste, by an inhumane and unparallel'd Tyranny over them, to preserve the poor remaines of their Fortunes, and to find them Bread." The revolutionaries not only destroyed "that beautiful Grove under Green-wich Castle," but proposed to their Council of State "that the Royal Walk of Elms in St. James's Park, 'That living Gallery of aged Trees' (as our excellent poet calls it)" [Gloss: "Mr. Waller's Poem of St. James's Park"] should be "cut down and sold, that with the rest of His Majesties Houses already demolish'd and mark'd for destruction, His Trees might likewise undergo the same destin[y], and no footsteps of Monarchy remain unviolated."

Evelyn's tract is a model for sustainable forestry. He mocks the shortsighted revolutionary parliament's waste of "that Material, which being left intire, or husbanded with discretion, had prov'd the best support of it"; this despoliation was not caused by the chaos of war as they claim, but "cold deliberation" and a "barbarous resolution" after their victory, in contrast the generals and statesmen of antiquity who in their wars spared trees, and in their retirements cultivated them. And he pleads to his countrymen, "May such Woods as do yet remain intire be carefully Preserv'd, and such as are destroy'd, sedulously Repair'd."[68]

Evelyn asks the Royal Society to preserve timber for repairing the naval fleet and opposes the agricultural principles of the Hartlib Circle and the Levellers: timber has been reduced by "the disproportionate spreading of Tillage, caused through that prodigious havock made by such as lately proffessing themselves against Root and Branch" (a woodsy literalization of Cromwell's metaphor urging the destruction of the episcopacy) who "were tempted, not only to fell and cut down, but utterly grub up, demolish, and raze, as it were, all those many goodly Woods, and Forests, which our more prudent Ancestors left standing, for the Ornament, and service of their Country." That is, like agricultural deforesters today, they destroyed the woods' ability to regenerate themselves. Regrowth "would cost (besides Inclosure) some entire Ages repose of the Plow"; but such is the epidemical "waste, and destruction of our woods that I conceive nothing less then a universal Plantation of all the sorts of Trees" from seed in nurseries, and especially of the oak, under whose shade cattle and deer may graze, and "for the great, and masculine beauty which a wild Quincunx, as it were, of such Trees would present to your eyes."[69]

As in *Fumifugium*, Evelyn argued in *Sylva* for conservation through political action. While persuading Parliament and the Royal Society of the utility of his

---

68 Evelyn, "To the Reader," sigs. A–B1v. See further Parry, "John Evelyn as Hortulan Saint," in Leslie and Raylor 130–50.

69 Evelyn 1–3 and 114.

proposals, he also wished to enhance the beauty of the ravaged land. Limes, firs, and elms should crown and encircle estates. Lieutenants and rangers should take delight "as much in the goodliness of their Trees, as other men generally do in their Dogs, and Horses, for Races and Hunting; neither of which Recreations is comparable to the Planting, either for Virtue or pleasure."[70] Evelyn's prescient tract gives detailed instructions for that universal replanting that he hopes will, and that to some extent did, restore England to something nearer the "green, yet-growing Ark" that the Parliamentary revolutionary Lord General Fairfax had, for a while, preserved.

---

70 Evelyn 115.

Chapter 4

Hylozoic Poetry
The Lives of Plants

The trees of the Lord are full of sap; the cedars of
Lebanon which he hath planted;
Where the birds make their nests: as for the stork,
the fir trees are her house.

Psalm 104

The bodies of plants and the bodies of words

Most early modern poets would be familiar with Pliny's praise of trees in his *Natural History*, and their less learned readers with Philemon Holland's translation. In his preface Pliny reflects that trees were Nature's supreme gift, furnishing all needs, before, through pride, "wee must needs cut through great mountaines for to meet with marble," travel to China for silk, "dive down into the bottom of the red sea for pearls," and "sinke deepe pits even to the bottom of the earth, for the precious [Emerald]." From "pride and vanity . . . we have devised means to pierce and wound our ears: because, forsooth, it would not serve our turns to weare costly pearles and rich stones . . . unless they were engraven also, and cut into the very flesh of our bodies." Pliny's wry comments on luxury goods (costing trees for shafts, ships, and fuel) resonate in seventeenth-century satire on what Andrew Marvell in "The Mower against Gardens," calls "Luxurious man."[1]

Pliny begins his encomium, "In old time, Trees were the very temples of the gods" and "we ourselves" adore the forests and their silences. Trees provide houses, the finest food, and ships for commerce, and were made into images of the gods before men used "the costly Anatomy of the elephant; yet now we make our tables even of the same yvory that we see the faces of gods are portraied of, as if we had our warrant from them to begin & maintain our riot and superfluity." He recounts the story that the Gauls invaded Italy because of the fruits, oil, and wine brought back by a Swiss traveler, a good excuse, Pliny opines, even for war. His extensive catalogue, peppered with anecdote, concerns the cultivation, importation, sexual reproduction, and products of trees and other plants for spices, perfumes, medicines, fruits, oils, wines, and triumphal wreaths. These themes recur in early modern tracts and poems with attention to plants' inner processes and their relationships with ourselves, as well as to woods and their sacred silences.[2]

---

1   Pliny, *The Historie of the World,* trans. Holland (1601, rpt. 1634), Book 12, preface.
2   Pliny 1.356–7.

Perhaps because trees are so vital to sustenance, shelter, and a sense of sacred, they are etymologically associated with matter itself and with the "matter," as in Hamlet's "What is the matter?" (*Hamlet* 2.2), of reading. The Greek word for both wood and matter is υλη, *hyle* or *hyla*: forest, woodland undergrowth, timber, firewood, and, in Aristotle, twigs for nests. It also means material, "the stuff of which a thing is made" and "matter for a poem or treatise."[3] The Latin *materia*, timber or building material, has a similar development. Hylozoism is a theological concept with a name rooted in trees. In late Greek and early Christian writing *hyle* came dualistically to mean non-divine matter, with the connotation of "sinful, hostile to God,"[4] perhaps with reference to wooden idols and pagan groves. The history of the word reflects the philosophical contentions of seventeenth-century theology.[5]

The *Oxford English Dictionary* defines *hylozoism* as "The theory that matter is endowed with life, or that life is merely a property of matter." Of these alternatives, Christian vitalist poets may be suspected of the former but not the latter. Other words from this root include *hylopathism*, "the doctrine that matter is sentient"; *hylomorphism*, (υλη+ μθρφη, form), "the doctrine that primordial matter is the First Cause of the universe," a teaching obviously incompatible with Hebraic and Christian accounts of God as First Cause; and *hylotheism*, "the doctrine that God and matter or the material universe are identical," a kind of pantheism also capable of idolatrous interpretation. These words carry trees in their etymologies as Greek columns carry them in their forms. Christian vitalist poets retain a hylozoic sense of the origins of matter and the materials of language in their words and forms while omitting the atheistic denial of God and the pantheistic denial that God transcends, as well as giving his own substance to and being immanent in, the natural world.[6]

The Latin *silva* also means materials or supplies and woods, forest, or foliage—and books have folios, leaves, pages (from *pagina*, vine-trellis). Seventeenth-century titles such as Milton's *Sylvarum Liber* and Cowley's *Sylva* follow classical precedents for miscellanies, and Ben Jonson in *Underwood* explains that "the ancients called that kind of body Sylva, or Hule, in which there were works of diverse nature" as we call "timber-trees, promiscuously growing, a wood or forest." Book 6 of Cowley's *Plantarum*, also called *Sylva*, concerns a parliament of trees, and Bacon's *Sylva Sylvarum* collects observations about natural history. John Evelyn in *Sylva* literally teaches the best ways of planting and caring for various species of trees and the importance of preservation of woods, and also allies them to language, stating in Book IV that "standing Woods and Forests were not only the Original Habitations

---

3   Liddell and Scott, *A Greek-English Lexicon.*

4   Arndt and Gingrich, *Greek-English Lexicon of the New Testament.*

5   Homer, *Iliad* 11.155 and *Odyssey* 5.257; copse, brushwood, undergrowth as opposed to timber (Xenophon, *Oec.* 16.13, 17), timber, firewood, twigs for nests (Aristotle *H. A.* 559a); in Aristotelian philosophy, matter, later "mostly opposed to the intelligent and formative principle (νους)"; also "matter for a poem or treatise" (Liddell and Scott, *A Greek-English Lexicon*). In New Testament Greek, forest, timber, non-divine matter (Arndt and Gingrich, *Greek-English Lexicon*). One sees an element of dualism in late Greek and early Christian connotations, perhaps in response to idol worship.

6   See discussion of Milton's monism, Chapter 3.

of Men, and fore Defence and Fortresse, but the first occasion of that Speech, Polity, and Society which made them differ from the Beasts."[7]

Stephen Fallon defines vitalism as "the belief that life is a property traceable to matter itself rather than to either the motion of complex organizations of matter or an immaterial soul"; "Animist materialism—the belief, shared by Milton, that matter can possess the traits of mind—is an extension of vitalism."[8] What I am calling hylozoic poems by vitalist or animist materialist poets are literally about plants, are concerned with the matter of life and the matter of language, and are, in various degrees, organically constructed—not wooden icons but alive with new shoots at each reading. Given the ways that poetic texts make us conscious of the fibers from which they are made, I want to look at poems about plants in the contexts of the philosophy of matter, empirical discoveries about their inner processes, and the practical and political responses we have seen to the early modern deforestation of Britain and Ireland, beginning by observing ways poets increasingly went beyond emblematic uses of plants to heed the processes of their lives.

Robert Herrick's "Divination by a Daffadill" is perfectly emblematic, the flower providing a spiritual lesson in visible form:

> WHEN a Daffadill I see,
>   Hanging down his head t'wards me;
> Guesse I may, what I must be:
> First, I shall decline my head;
> Secondly, I shall be dead;
> Lastly, safely buryed.[9]

What is remarkable is the way the last three lines not only visibly decline but do so without diminishment, all having the same number of syllables. "Safely," and a flower that grows from a buried bulb, also suggest rebirth.

In "Providence," George Herbert treats nature as God's providence to man, who should learn from the bees to be more careful of it.

> Bees work for man; and yet they never bruise
> Their masters flower, but leave it, having done,
> As fair as ever, and as fit to use;
> So both the flower doth stay, and hony run.

The thought, not the form (except the buzzing rhyme-words), makes bees emblematic. In "Man" Herbert notes carelessness of medicinal herbs: "More servants wait on Man / Then he'll take notice of: in every path / He treads down that which doth befriend him, / When sicknesse makes him pale and wan."[10] Despite the personification, this statement is not emblematic but hortatory, with a principle urgent today as deforestation destroys herbal species not taken notice of.

---

7   Evelyn, *Dendrologia: An Historical Account of the Sacredness and Use of Standing Groves*, 324.

8   Fallon, *Milton among the Philosophers*, 111.

9   Herrick, in *The Complete Poems*, ed. Grosart, 1:64.

10   Herbert, "Providence" and "Man," in *English Poems*, 131 and 107.

Sometimes Herbert wants to *be* a tree, when, Christopher Hodgkins writes, he "feels the pain of his uselessness and exclusion": "I reade, and sigh, and wish I were a tree; / For sure then I would grow / To fruit or shade: at least some bird would trust / Her household to me, and I should be just" ("Affliction" (I) ll. 57–60); and "Oh that I were an Orenge-tree, / That busie plant! / Then should I ever laden be, / And never want / Some fruit for him that dressed me" ("Employment" (II) ll. 21–5).[11] And in "Confession" (ll. 7–9) he seems to have felt their pain: "No scrue, no piercer can, / Into a piece of timber work and winde, / As Gods afflictions into man."

Herbert and Vaughan both call attention to our kinship with trees, grass, and flowers, and incorporate creature-frailty into the hope of rebirth, in ways that go beyond the emblematic into the hylozoic. Herbert represents himself as a tree in God's Garden in "Paradise" and as a flower in "The Flower."

Paradise

I blesse thee, Lord, because I GROW
Among thy trees, which in a   ROW
To thee both fruit and order   OW.

What open force, or hidden   CHARM
Can blast my fruit, or bring me HARM,
While the inclosure is thy   ARM?

Inclose me still for fear I START
Be to me rather sharp and TART
Then let me want thy hand & ART.

When thou dost greater judgements SPARE,
And with thy knife but prune and   PARE,
Ev'n fruitful trees more fruitfull   ARE.

Such sharpness shows the sweetest FREND:
Such cuttings rather heal than   REND:
And such beginnings touch their   END.[12]

Herbert represents God's forestry of souls, which he protects and prunes in a "garden inclosed" (Song of Solomon 4.12), the fence being God's non-exclusive arm. The five stanzas may recall the ancient practice of planting trees in a quincunx or formation of five. Sir Thomas Browne was to recommend this practice in *The Garden of Cyrus* and also remarks on the quincuntial structures of plants, with leaves "set after a Quintuple ordination" (1.195) and oak branches whose "foundation is five-cornered in the tender annual sprouts and manifest[s] upon incision the signature of a Starre" (1.201). Herbert's form, in which the last word of each line is pruned to disclose another word enclosed within it, represents both the "cuttings," or discipline, and the enclosing, or protecting, of the souls that the trees represent. The

---

11 Hodgkins, *Authority, Church, and Society in George Herbert*, 201–2.
12 Herbert, *English Poems*, 143–4.

"end" or purpose of the poem is thus mimed in the line-endings, which like branch-endings are the site of prunings that encourage fruitfulness.

Similarly, while "The Flower" speaks to anyone's states of depression and revival, flowers, as traditional emblems of poetry, are particularly suitable to the coming and going of the poet's ability to "relish versing." In contrast to poems in which flowers represent the frailty of beauty, Herbert's does not stop with the life and death of flowers on the surface of the earth. His imagination goes underground with them.

> Who would have thought my shrivel'd heart
> Could have recover'd greenesse? It was gone
>   Quite underground; as flowers depart
> To see their mother-root, when they have blown;
>   Where they together
>   All the hard weather
> Dead to the world, keep house unknown.

Herbert's sense of unity with the unobservable winter lives of perennial flowers turns the emblem of poetry into a kind of herbal healing.

Henry Vaughan writes most truly hylozoically about the literal stuff of which a book of his time was made: flax, wood, and leather. Part of ecological thinking is knowing where our artifacts come from, with what cost to the earth, to habitats, to species, to individuals of those species, and in human labor.[13] Vaughan's book required materials from an oak, a cow, and a field of flax, all of them a kind of sacrifice. His poem too is a sacrifice—a making-sacred.

> The Book
>
> Eternal God! maker of all
> That have lived here, since the man's fall;
> The Rock of ages! in whose shade
> They live unseen, when here they fade.
>
> Thou knew'st this *paper*, when it was
> Mere seed, and after that but *grass*;
> Before 'twas *dressed* or *spun*, and when
> Made *linen*, who did *wear* it then:
> What were their lives, their thoughts & deeds
> Whether good *corn*, or fruitless *weeds*.
>
> Thou knew'st this *tree*, when a green *shade*
> Covered it, since a *cover* made,
> And where it flourished, grew and spread,
> As if it never should be dead.
>
> Thou knew'st this harmless *beast*, when he

---

13 The latter lesson is given to Voltaire's *Candide* by the slave who has lost his right hand in the sugar mill and his left leg for trying to run away, and who says "It is at this price that you eat sugar in Europe" (*Candide*, 60).

Did live and feed by thy decree
On each green thing; then slept (well fed)
Clothed in this *skin*, which now lies spread
A *covering* o'er this aged book,
Which makes me wisely weep and look
On my own dust; mere dust it is,
but not so dry and clean as this.
Thou knew'st and saw'st them all and though
Now scattered thus, dost know them so.

O knowing, glorious spirit! when
Thou shalt restore trees, beasts and men,
When thou shalt make all new again,
Destroying only death and pain,
Give him among thy works a place,
Who in them loved and sought thy face!

Alan Rudrum points out that "To see the world of nature *as* a book was a Medieval and Renaissance commonplace; Vaughan's originality is to see the world of nature *in* a book."[14] Rudrum compares Vaughan to the Hermetic philosophers, of whom the poet's brother Thomas was one, quoting Paracelsus: "It is opposed to all true philosophy to say that flowers lack their own eternity. They may perish and die here, but they will reappear in the restitution of all things. Nothing has been created out of the Great Mystery which will not have a *form* beyond the aether."[15] In "The Book" Vaughan does not speak in abstractions, but of this grass, this tree, this skin, this book. At the same time, he invests his contemplation of them with sacramental vitalism, including his belief that "Thou shalt restore trees, beasts and men, / When thou shalt make all new again," as promised in Revelation 21.1 and expected by "the creature" in Romans 8.19. The living cow, grass, and tree are still in God's mind and will be restored; and the man—who also, like all mortal life, is grass (1 Peter 1.24)— asks for a place among them, in whom the speaker has sought not God's power or magnificence but God's face: not transcendental dualism but love of creatures *in* whom he finds the face of the holy.

In form, the poem itself is constructed like a book. The couplets suggest a folio, made of sheets folded in two; the stanzas are gathered in three parallel signatures, one for each name, and enclosed in the front and back matter of biblical human time, from creation to apocalypse, within the covers of the prayer to the Rock of Ages.[16] Although the book in the speaker's hand need not be identified as a Bible or a prayer

---

14 Vaughan, *Complete Poems*, 641 n.

15 Paracelsus, *The Hermetic and Alchemical Writings*, ed. A.E. Waite, I:269; quoted in Rudrum, "Henry Vaughan's 'The Book,'" 166 n. 13.

16 Barbara Kiefer Lewalski points out, "The book of the Creatures is here treated as the physical embodiment of the Book of the Scriptures": *Protestant Poetics and the Seventeenth-Century Religious Lyric*, 347.

book—it could be any book[17]—the poem's construction binds together the scope and the liturgical form of those two chief books of the poet's time.

What is the matter?

I have raised the matter of hylozoism because it seems to me that some vitalist poets may be considered as Christian hylozoists, for whom the substance of all living things contains spiritual vitality. It should not be confused with hylomorphism; hylozoism only claims that matter is alive, while atheist hylomorphism makes matter the cause of the universe and holds that matter and form, the hyle- and the -morph, are all there is. But a religious form of hylomorphism exists as well, at least as applied to humanity and sometimes to all earthly lives. Caroline Walker Bynum, arguing for the importance of the body in medieval spirituality, states, "One of the most important philosophical formulations of the thirteen century, Thomas Aquinas's statement of the hylomorphic composition of the human person, was a new attempt to come to terms with matter. The doctrine says that what the person *is*, the existing substance *man*, is form and matter, soul and body." (Milton would carry further the point that both are necessary to constitute a person by denying the divisibility that "soul and body" implies.) Visionary women, Bynum adds, "reflected in their visions a general sense of body as necessary for salvation" and some thought the possibility of salvation extended to all bodily lives: "The author of the nuns' book of Unterlinden . . . commented that *homo* (our humanity) really includes all creatures." Mechtild of Hackeborn "saw a vision of the celebrating priest in which his vestments were covered with every blade and twig, every hair and scale, of the flora and fauna of the universe. As she looked in surprise, she saw that 'the smallest details of creation are reflected in the holy Trinity by means of the humanity of Christ, because it is from the same earth that produced them that Christ drew his humanity.'"[18]

Conceptions of matter contribute, like cosmology, to both philosophy and poetic form. Opponents of hylozoism in the seventeenth century were dualists worried about its potential for either denial of the spiritual or transference of it to the material. In the nineteenth century, Samuel Coleridge, at the romantic crux of faith impelled by further scientific and political revolutions, felt that "the hypothesis of Hylozoism is the death of all rational physiology and indeed of physical science."[19] This post-Enlightenment reversal of emphasis shares alarm with seventeenth-century Platonism about mixing the spiritual and the physical.

For the Cambridge Platonist Ralph Cudworth in 1678, hylozoism was one kind of philosophical atheism, atomism being the other: "Hylozoism. . . makes all Body, as such, and therefore every smallest Atom of it, to have Life Essentially belonging to it (natural perception and appetite)."[20] The red flags here are "as such"

---

17 Lewalski suggests however that this book is "the Bible, subject of the poem immediately following" (*Protestant Poetics*, 347).

18 Bynum, *Holy Feast and Holy Fast*, 254, citing Mechtild's *Liber specialis gratiae*, Book 4, Chapter 3, p. 260.

19 Coleridge, *Biographia Literaria* 63 (1817), quoted in *Oxford English Dictionary*.

20 Cudworth, *True Intellectual System* (1678); from 1845 edition, 1.iii.144.

and "Essentially." Christian hylozoists, if they may be so called, would not go so far, since for them material bodies originate in God, whether as divine substance or as separate material informed by his breath and indwelling spirit, and corporeal forms are continuous with, not opposed to, spiritual origins. Man and woman, created in the image of God (Genesis 1.27), bear the divine imprint and attributes most fully (and so are responsible for the rest), but all created things are made of the same matter and participate in its divine origin. They are not divinities to be worshipped, however, and they share the suffering brought by human vanity under which, since the Fall, creation groans. Seventeenth-century writers who wanted to save representations of the life of nature from both atheism, impugned to hylozoism, and the death of nature, contrived by mechanists, had an ally in Pierre Gassendi, a Catholic priest whose *Animadversiones* on Epicurus was published in 1649, and who wanted to reconcile Epicurean atomism with Christian belief in free will, responsibility, and an incorporeal soul. Stephen Fallon relates,

> [The] value of Gassendi's hypothetical atomist model was the simple explanatory power that applied to all corporeal phenomena, an explanatory power that Hobbes easily transferred to the will. . . . Gassendi worked himself out of this impasse of mechanism with two apparently conflicting strategies: hylozoism and incorporealism. The hylozoist Gassendi argued for a nonmechanical principle of causation in matter, ultimately traceable to the motion given to atoms at their creation but not limited to rectilinear motion.[21]

Cudworth's objection to hylozoism is that it leaves "no necessity . . . either of any incorporeal soul in men to make them rational, or of any Deity in the whole universe to solve [or explain] the regularity thereof." But he cautions that "as every Atomist is not therefore necessarily an Atheist, so neither must every Hylozoist needs be accounted such. For whoever so holds the life of matter, as notwithstanding to assert another kind of substance also, that is immaterial and incorporeal, is no ways obnoxious to that foul imputation." He finds atomism preferable to hylozoism, however, because atomism is naturally conjoined to incorporealism and only "violently cut off" by the atheism of Democritus; whereas hylozoism corresponds with corporealism, and so is more capable of leading to denial of spirit. His anxiety resembles that to be produced by Darwin: "if all matter . . . have not only such a life, perception, and self-active power in it, as whereby it can form itself" into stars, planets, and various animals, "but can also improve itself into sense and self-enjoyment; it may as well be thought able to advance itself higher, into all the acts of reason and understanding in men; so that there will be no need either of an incorporeal immortal soul in men, or a deity in the universe."

In order to refute both "Cosmo-plastic and Hylozoic Atheisms," Cudworth offers his hypothesis of "the plastic life of nature," that serves as intermediary between God and matter as the efficient cause of nature directed by the First Cause, or God. "Plastic" has the active sense "capable of shaping or moulding formless matter" (*Oxford English Dictionary*), and the concept "plastic nature" was partly an attempt to solve the problem agitating many incorporealists of how spirit can act on matter. Without this intermediary, Cudworth argues, either everything happens fortuitously,

---

21   Fallon, *Milton among the Philosophers*, 43.

Plate 1 The Rail or Daker Hen and other birds, TAB. XXVIIII, from John Ray's *Ornithology*, 1678.

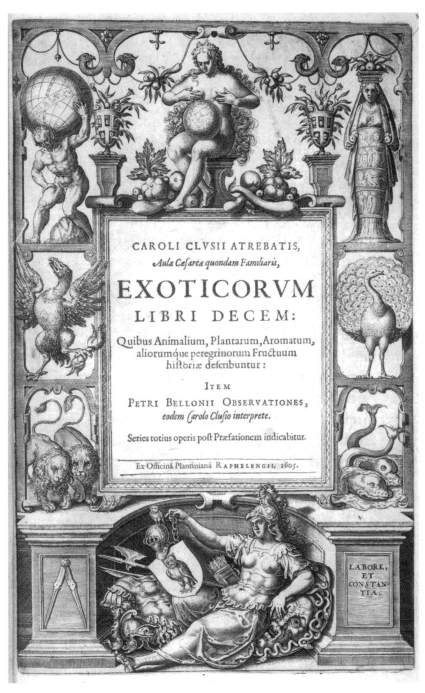

Plate 2 Natura nurturing Earth. Title page from Carolus Clusius, *Exoticorum LibriDecem*. Plantin Press, 1605.

Plate 3 *Terra Dei.* Illustration to Job 38.4–6 by I. G. Pintz, designed by J.M.Füssli, from Johanne Jakob Scheuchzer's *Physica Sacra.* Augsburg and Ulm, 1731–1735.

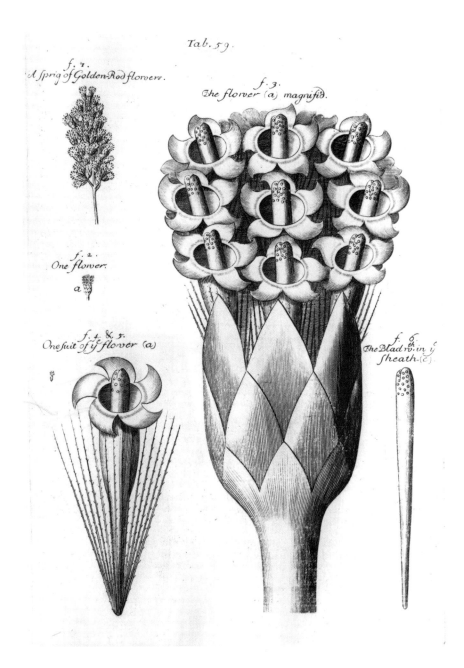

Tab. 59.

f. 1.
A sprig of Golden-Rod flowers.

f. 3.
The flower (a) magnifid.

f. 2.
One flower.
a

f. 4. & 5.
One suit of ye flower (a)

f. 6.
The Blad rv: in ye
sheath. (c)

Plate 4   Reproductive parts of Goldenrod, Tab. 59, from Nehemiah Grew,
The Anatomy of Vegetables Begun, London, 1672.

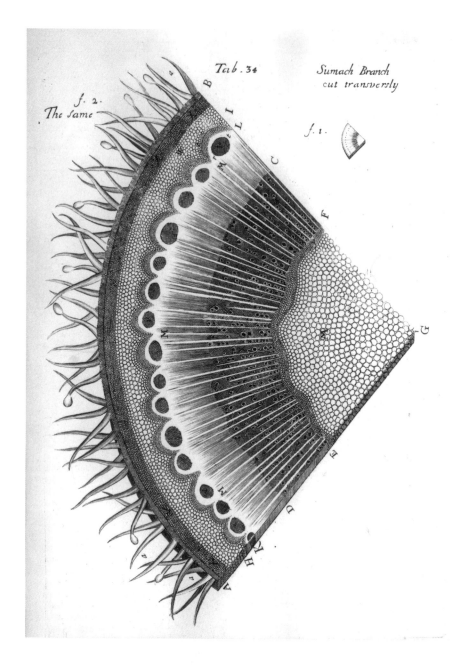

Plate 5   *Sumach Branch*, from Grew, Tab. 34, *The Anatomy of Vegetables Begun.*

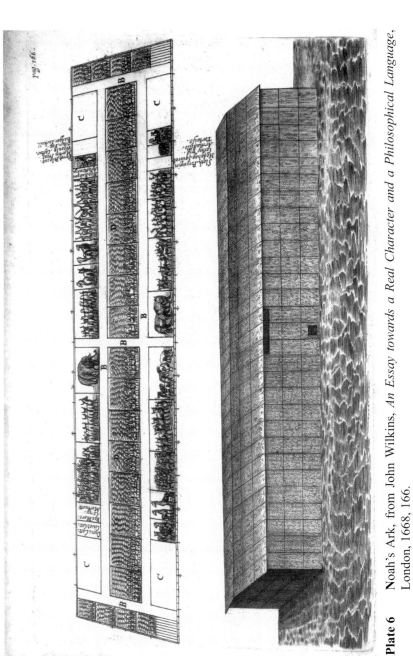

Plate 6 Noah's Ark, from John Wilkins, *An Essay towards a Real Character and a Philosophical Language*, London, 1668, 166.

Plate 7   Nets and traps, from John Ray's *Ornithology*.

Plate 8 Nicholaes de Bruyn. *Orpheus Playing to the Animals*. c. 1600.

Plate 9   Interroga Aves.   Illustration to Job 12.7 by G. Lichtenteger, designed by J.M. Füssli, from Johanne Jakob Scheuchzer, *Physica Sacra*, 1731–1735.

Ornamenta novo, iam constant omnia Mundo   Ergò capit Requiem septena luce potenti, 7
Ille Opifex, nil, quod efficiatur, habet.   Constituens, dextra, Sabbatha dia, sacrat.

Plate 10   The Blessing of the Seventh Day, from Guillaume Du Bartas, *Oevvres* (Paris, 1614): headpiece to "Le Septiesme Jour." The Bridgewater copy has "Brackley" handwritten on the title page.

an idea that does not correspond with the observable regularity of the universe; or else "God himself doth all immediately, and, as it were with his own hands, form the body of every gnat and fly, insect and mites, as of other animals," an employment he finds inconsistent with God's dignity. Since such things could not be "administered, with such exact regularity and constancy every where . . . by those inferior spirits, d[a]emons or angels," then "besides the divine will and pleasure, there must needs be some other immediate agent": "Wherefore the divine law and command, by which the things of nature are administered, must be conceived to be the real appointment of some energetic, effectual and operative cause for the production of every effect."

This idea of an incorporeal agent also disputes the mechanists, who make God merely "an idle spectator of the various results of the fortuitous and necessary motions of bodies; and render his wisdom altogether useless and insignificant, as being a thing wholly inclosed and shut up within his own breast, and not at all acting abroad upon any thing without him." Mechanists make "a kind of dead and wooden world," while "those who are considerative" see "that there is a mixture of life or plastic nature, together with mechanism, which runs through the whole corporeal universe." In addition, "Besides this plastic nature which is in animals, forming their several bodies artificially [artfully], as so many microcosms or little worlds, there must be also a general plastic nature in the macrocosm, the whole corporeal universe, that which makes all things thus to conspire every where, and agree together into one harmony." This power is "a spirit, and a living and generative nature . . . distinct from the Deity, but subordinate to it and dependent on it."[22]

Cudworth, then, supplied God with an unconscious but obedient agent to save him from the indignity of constant attention to detail and from the mechanist atomist heresy that God stands apart from a clockwork creation. Milton had already proposed a more elegant explanation of the relation of God to matter, the creation *De Deo* rather than *ex nihilo*. Other vitalist poets had supposed that God needed no help in managing a living universe and wrote poems that assume the vital life of plants as well as animals, bringing the two "kingdoms" nearer together. Cudworth's rejection of mechanism and preference for hylozoism is useful, however, in helping us see the issues.

Poets who write with a hylozoic sense of living materials without being atheists could be supposed merely to be using a traditional language of personification and metaphor reserved for poetry. Instead, I find them to be drawing on natural philosophy to represent energy, purpose, and responsiveness in plants, animals, and the elements themselves, with vitality directed toward a *telos* of their own, not necessarily subservient to man. Even when an image of a plant or animal is emblematic, it can have a careful regard for the natural life of the being itself. That regard makes a better metaphor, gives it organic form, honors each kind of life, and allies us more closely with them.

Henry More, Cudworth's colleague among the Cambridge Platonists, expresses a vitalist opinion of the activity of the earth in the origination of plants:

---

22 Cudworth, *True Intellectual System* (1678); 1845 edition, 1.iii.145, 217–21, 260–61. The quotation near the end is from "De Mundo," a supposed follower of Aristotle.

> God prepared the matter of earth so, as that there was a vital congruity of the parts thereof, with sundry sorts of seminall forms of trees, herbes, and choicest kinds of flowers; and so the Body of the Earth drew in sundry principles of Plantall Life, from the World of Life, that is at hand every where.[23]

More's student Lady Anne Conway opposes the dualistic separation of body and spirit in *The Principles of the Most Ancient and Modern Philosophy*, a vitalist theodicy insisting that a living God would not create dead matter or withhold life from the infinity of creatures he is able to make:

> God does not make death. It is equally true that he did not make any dead thing, for how can a dead thing come from him who is infinite life and love? Or, how can any creature receive so vile and diminished an essence from him (who is so infinitely generous and good) that it does not share any life or perception and is not able to aspire to the least degree of these for all eternity?

In a statement that looks back to Lucretian atomism and forward to modern particle physics, she states that "an infinite number of creatures can be contained and exist inside the smallest creatures," both "mutually impenetrable bodies" and subtler "spirits" that can "penetrate grosser and more corporeal ones." She rejects the idea of a finite creation in which all creatures can be numbered and the mechanistic model of a measurable universe. What her editors call her "spiritual monism"[24] opposes both Hobbes's materialism and Descartes' dualism. "Cartesian philosophy," she states, "claims that body is merely dead mass, which not only lacks life and perception of any kind but is also utterly incapable of either for all eternity. This great error must be imputed to all those who say that body and spirit are contrary things and unable to change into one another, thereby denying bodies all life and perception."

Finding perhaps in her own chronic pain a reason to wonder why the spirit suffers with the body if it has no corporeality, she states, "But if one admits that the soul is of one nature and substance with the body, although it surpasses the body by many degrees of life and spirituality . . . one may easily understand how the soul and body are united together and how the soul moves the body and suffers with it and through it."[25] Like Milton and Vaughan, she also believed that all creatures would share eternal life, for "how can anything be annihilated since the goodness of God towards his creatures always remains the same and since the preservation or continuation of his creatures is a constant act of creation?"[26]

Vital lives: Milton's monist animism

In *Paradise Lost*, God says "Let th'Earth / Put forth the verdant grass, herb yielding seed, / And fruit tree yielding fruit after her kind; / Whose seed is in herself upon the earth" (7.309–12). In this paraphrase of Genesis 1.11, Milton changes the Authorized

---

23   *Conjectura Cabbalistica* (1653), 27–8.
24   Introduction to *Principles*, xxx.
25   Conway, *Principles*, 17, 45, 63, 58.
26   Conway, 33.

Version's "bring forth" to the more potent "put forth" and replaces the pronouns of "the fruit tree yielding fruit after his kind whose seed is in itself" to feminine ones. Milton's active verbs give plants an energetic part in their birth from Earth's Body as well as in their own reproduction:

> Forth flourished thick the clust'ring vine, forth crept
> The swelling gourd, up stood the corny reed
> Embattled in her field: and the humble shrub,
> And bush with frizzled hair implicit: last
> Rose as in a dance the stately trees, and spread
> Their branches hung with copious fruit; or gemmed
> Their blossoms: with high woods the hills were crowned,
> With tufts the valleys and each fountain side,
> With borders long the rivers. That earth now
> Seemed like to Heav'n, a seat where gods might dwell,
> Or wander with delight, and love to haunt
> Her sacred shades.   [7.320–31]

"Forth flourished. . . forth crept . . .up stood . . . rose . . . spred . . . gemmed" are all actions of plants. The contranym "[e]mbattled" faintly echoes the careful ploughman's doubts about his "hopeful sheaves" and perhaps the poignant simile of Ceres seeking her lost child (4.268–72); it means either fortified or under attack, and again reminds us that the welfare of the Garden is a matter choice. Shrubs are crisply curled, and "stately," "gemmed" and "crowned" suggest that Earth's natural adornment surpasses the state of queens. "Gemmed" is a strong verb, coming from "gen- to produce" (*Oxford English Dictionary*) as in generate, and also invoking the beauty and value of precious things, as does "vegetable gold" (4.220), vegetation being more precious than minerals of dubious uses. Put "embattled" with "stately" and "sacred" and we may remember how England's fields and forests had been embattled in the recent revolutionary and religious "civil" wars—trampled, felled, sold for war debts—and that the fall of Adam and Eve would wound Earth's body, so that "Earth trembled from her entrails, as again / In pangs" (9.1000–1001).

"Swelling gourd" was emended by Richard Bentley from the "smelling gourd" of both the editions printed during Milton's lifetime.[27] Other images appeal to sight, and the sounds of the lines to hearing and kinesis: in "Forth flourished thick the clust'ring vine" we hear the motion of the leaves, and in "forth crept / The swelling [or smelling] gourd, up stood the corny reed" the enjambment at "crept" gives impetus to the vine's motion and the spondee of "up stood" gives stability. If one is reading aloud, the sounds are tactile as well.

Bentley was a brilliant and uncompromising dualist who in the first series of Boyle lectures made an absolute division between matter and spirit.[28] His edition of *Paradise Lost* suggests emendations of what he called the original printer's

---

27 Gourds served as drinking vessels and water bottles for pilgrims. James Patrick McHenry points out in *A Milton Herbal* that northern gourds are tasteless and "generally unpalatable" (70). "Smelling" suggests a more aromatic variety.

28 Bentley, *A Defense of Natural and Revealed Religion* (1692).

"slips"; these emendations show us what Milton was doing that a more orthodox and unecosophical person could not grasp. For example, Adam and Eve "haste" to their work

> Among sweet dews and flow'rs; where any row
> Of Fruit-trees over-woody reach'd too far
> Their pamper'd boughs, and needed hands to check
> Fruitless embraces; or they led the Vine
> To wed her Elm; she spous'd about him twines
> Her marriageable arms.   [5.212–17]

Bentley expostulates, "This is a Monster of a Printer's Production: I can see whence he mistook his *Embraces*; but the Words adjoining quite puzle [sic] me. I suspect the Author gave it thus;

> With pruning hands they check
> The fruitless Branches; or they lead the Vine.

Unless we put it, they check; the Sentence has no Exit, and no work is done in the overwoody Rows. Branches for Embraces: as Spenser, V. 11.

Apparently Bentley was unable to read and punctuate "they haste . . . where any row . . . needed hands" as a clause because of the semicolon after "flow'rs," which he could merely have changed to a comma, and also dislikes the vitalism of "embraces" and believes that Milton should not alter any phrase reminiscent of Spenser. He continues,

> V. 217. Her marriageable arms.] Marriageable? capable of future Marriage? Why she was wed, spous'd already in the Verse before. And why her arms more marriageable, than the rest of her Substance? One may suppose, He gave it Manageable; that can twine and twist in any Situation. But that will not please. Among several ways of Alteration, this may be one:
>
> She spous'd about him twines her Arms Lascivious.
> Spenser, speaking of the Ivy Tree, II.12,61.[29]

Bentley misses the point that Adam and Eve are enacting the marriage as natural priests; a declaration of marriageability is part of the nuptial ceremony. He apparently finds the idea of arboreal embraces repellently irrational, and he accuses vines of being lascivious by nature, and thereby reinforces traditional stereotypes, which Milton's poem repeatedly shatters, of both Eve and the natural world as primordially unreliable and seductive. And Bentley suggests manageability when Milton, throughout, represents Adam and Eve as assistants, not manipulative managers, of nature.

Bentley's revisions de-animize nature and add a moralization unsuitable before the fall. His management of the poem displaces fresh perspectives with customary attitudes. Unscrutinized custom was a monster of Errour that Milton—who drew

---

29   Bentley, *Milton's Paradise Lost. A New Edition* (1732) 151, 154–5.

more from Spenser than revisable phrases—often honed his verbal sword to slay, and the image of nature as manipulable mistress is one of his targets.

Milton's language and its appeal to the senses suggest our kinship with the plants. This relation is startlingly literalized in Sir Thomas Browne's meditation on the verse "All flesh is grass, and all the glory of man is as the flower of grass. The grass withereth, and the flower thereof falleth, But the word of the Lord endureth forever" (1 Peter 1.24–5). Browne writes,

> Now for the wals of flesh, wherein the soule doth seeme to be immured before the Resurrection, it is nothing but an elementall composition, and a fabricke that must fall to ashes; "All flesh is grasse," is not onely metaphorically, but literally true, for all those creatures [which] we behold, are but the hearbs of the field, digested into flesh in them, or more remotely carnified in our selves. Nay further, we are what we all abhorre, Anthropophagi and Cannibals, devourers not only of men, but of our selves; and that not in an allegory, but a positive truth; for all this masse of flesh which wee behold, came in at our mouths: this frame we looke upon, hath beene upon our trenchers; In briefe, we have devoured ourselves [and yet do live and remaine our selves].[30]

While for Browne we are what we eat, for Milton we are all, whether animals, plants, or angels, made of the same matter, originating in God's own substance. The archangel Raphael reveals his angelic knowledge of this kinship in his description to Adam and Eve of the tree of being in *Paradise Lost*. The passage is quintessentially hylozoic, being about matter, and using the anatomically correct figure of a tree to show how matter turns to spirit without separating from its root. The beginning of this speech concerns the monistical kinship of all being through its derivation from God:

> one Almighty is, from whom
> All things proceed, and up to him return,
> If not depraved from good, created all
> Such to perfection, one first matter all,
> Endued with various forms, various degrees
> Of substance, and in things that live of life;
> But more refined, more spiritous, and pure,
> As nearer to him placed or nearer tending
> Each in their several active spheres assigned,
> Til body up to spirit work, in bounds
> Proportioned to each kind. [5.469–79]

The emphatically repeated "all" of this statement, though biblical, is heretical to dualists who believe that bodies and non-human life forms are not eternal (in spite of the orthodox belief in the resurrection of the body), and that only human beings can expect union with God. In Milton's passage, body is not contrary to but "works" up to spirit, within the sphere of activity of each species or "kind."

"Each in their several active spheres assigned" retains some of the Aristotelian idea of a scale of nature ranked by degrees of perfection or capability; the more a

---

30 Browne, *Works* 1:47–8; bracketed final words added to manuscript.

creature can do the higher it ranks. But Milton's "active spheres" also indicate two things important to his theology of nature. First, all beings retain the integrity of their species in the process of working up to spirit; no entity will be lost.[31] Milton's God delights in diversity. For maximum diversity all degrees of life are given being, and whether one is an angel, a lark, or a sponge differently circumscribes one's "active sphere." But, second, all are "active": not the mechanically determined things of Hobbes or Descartes, but beings whose activity springs from themselves. All bodies, then, work "up to spirit" while retaining their special nature, "in bounds / Proportioned to each kind." John Leonard discerns a contranym in "bounds": "both 'limits' and 'leaps' . . . Milton's universe is both hierarchical and dynamic."[32]

All species, then, are kindred, made of the same "first matter," are various in activity as well as form, and proceed from God and eventually return to him as "spirit": not a denigration of body but a process of refinement and increasing freedom from corporeal limits, without losing, but rather having actively participated in developing, the identities they have achieved.

As the passage continues, Raphael teaches Adam and Eve how the "one first matter" from which diverse beings come is refined to spirit, and applies the process to human beings using the natural homology of a fruit-bearing plant, especially fitting because the participants in this after-dinner discourse are actually digesting "fruit of all kinds" (5.341) gathered by Eve, and the conversation, initiated by Adam's courteous comment on the angel's savoring of earthly food, began with Raphael's description of the whole universe as a system of nurture.

This Tree of Life is a metaphor assimilating the working of bodies up to spirit with the way the matter of fruit is transubstantiated into the soul of man; but it also behaves like a living tree, which is one of the "all things" spoken of and so an actual part of the process Raphael is describing; and his sounds and syntax imitate the manner of growth of a real plant:

> So from the root
> Springs lighter the green stalk, from thence the leaves
> More aery, last the bright consummate flow'r
> Spirits odorous breathes: flow'rs and thir fruit
> Man's nourishment, by gradual scale sublim'd
> To vital spirits aspire, to animal,
> To intellectual, give both life and sense,
> Fancy and Understanding, whence the Soul
> Reason receives, and reason is her being,
> Discursive, or Intuitive; discourse
> Is oftest yours, the latter most is ours,
> Differing but in degree, of kind the same. [5.479–90]

Raphael begins at the root, grounded at the end of a line by the spondaic entangling consonants of "root / Springs," so that "Springs lighter" does what it says: the

---

31 *Complete Prose Works* 6:307–10.

32 Leonard, ed., in *Milton: The Complete Poems*, 781 n. Leonard is also my source for the word "contranym."

quicker syllables of "lighter" spring from the groundedness of "root" and the energy wound into the double consonants and framing sibilants of "springs." "Green stalk," another spondee, is lightened by its longer vowels but retains the solidity of clustered consonants. "From thence the leaves / More aery" has airier consonants, while "last the bright consummate flow'r / Spirits odorous breathes" rises like fragrance in rounded vowels and aspirates that themselves "breathe." The whole sentence does something syntactically tree-like as well; it begins with long phrases and branches into shorter ones, each growing out of the one before, then further divides into compounds to show the difference and yet relatedness of human discourse and angelic intuition, to which the matter of the plant has been refined. Raphael notices how plants grow and how that growth corresponds with the growth of mind and soul he is describing, and his sentence grows to match.

The perfection of a metaphor is its fidelity to the thing that provides the comparison and the integrity with which the poet develops its capacity for enriching thought. Allegorical readings of this metaphor have a long and noble history. But if we look at this passage through the lens of the botanist Nehemiah Grew, who also takes up the theme of the kinship of species, we find that Milton's passage is remarkably congruent with Grew's account of the growth of an actual tree.

Grew wanted to know about inner processes: how sap can ascend, how flowers can make the same mix of minerals produce adjacent contrasting tinctures as different as white and red, what part their "attire" or stamens had in sexual reproduction (Plate 4). His language demonstrates a sense similar to Milton's of the energetic motions, relations, continuity, and, oft-repeated, "Elegance and Variety" of plants. He takes such pleasure in them that, although he became a Fellow of the Royal Society, admired Wilkins, dedicated his magnum opus "To His Most Sacred Majesty Charles II," and practiced dissection (but the most ardent vegetarian does that on every dinner plate), he stands apart from the unmetaphorical and static language the Royal Society's language-manufacturers sought. His sense of *telos*, a purposeful and energetic unfolding toward completion, makes each plant a microcosm analogous to a human body. He deliberately diminishes the difference between plant and animal. His descriptions and drawings of plants seen through a microscope show their fabric to be as beautiful as the most lavish needlework (Plate 5).

Grew's interest is not in the systematic cataloguing of discrete kinds, but in relation. His tracts, published by the Royal Society between 1672 and 1682, are gathered in folio as *The Anatomy of Plants* (1682) not in order of publication but "more according to their Nature or Relation to one another." The splendid engraved plates represent magnification of "not the Barque, Wood, or Pith of a Root or Tree, by it self; but at least some portion of all three together: Whereby, both their Texture, and also their Relation one to another, and the Fabrick of the whole, may be observed at one View."[33]

In 1670 Grew gave the first study, *The Anatomy of Vegetables*, to Henry Oldenburgh, secretary of the Royal Society, who sent it to "that excellent Person Dr. John Wilkins then Bishop of Chester" who read it to a meeting of the Royal Society

---

33 Preface to *The Anatomy of Plants*.

and encouraged Grew to continue his work.[34] When Grew states his intention to "enquire into the visible Constitutions and Uses of their several parts," we may suppose him about to describe their usefullness to man, but (although in later tracts he also mentions their alimentary, medicinal, and commercial uses) he turns out to mean, unlike other herbalists, the uses of each of their parts to the plants themselves. He also, like Vaughan, helps us think about the once-living materials we hold in our hands. The stuff of a walking stick "is so exquisitely fine, that no Silk-worm is able to draw any thing so small a Thre[a]d. So that one who walks about with the meanest Stick, holds a Piece of Natures Handicraft, which far surpasses the most elaborate Woof of Needle-Work in the World."[35]

Former botanists, Grew says, had looked only at the outsides of plants. He looks at—and feels, smells, tastes, and chews—all their materials, structures, and processes, beginning with a neglected, because invisible, part: the root. The themes of his work are the continuity of substance, all parts of a plant being forms of the same matter; the variety and relations of parts; and the process of refinement by which a plant transforms minerals in the soil (Satan's "crude materials") into "the bright consummate flow'r" and "fruit / Man's nourishment, by gradual scale sublim'd." He organizes his book according to "the Method of Nature her self . . . from the Seed sown, to the formation of the Root, Trunk, Branch, Leaf, Flower, Fruit, and last of all, of the Seed also to be sown again."[36]

The choice both Milton and Grew make to proceed from the root up may seem merely obvious, but the analogy goes further. Grew emphasizes the energetic life of the plant as a system of nurture formed by a process of purification through fermentation and filtration; as a bean plant (his representative example) draws nutriment from moist soil, the sap first passes through the planted bean's two coats "by due degrees; but also in a purer body," whereas "were the Bean naked, the sap would be overcopious and crude, as not being filtered through so fine a Cotton as the Coates be." The sap "next enters the Body of the Bean" and is "by mediation of the Cuticle, again more finely filter'd, and so entereth the Parenchyma it self . . . passing towards the Seminal Root . . . which is of a more spatious content; besides the benefit it hath of a farther percolation, it will also find room enough for a more free and active fermenting and maturation herein." Having passed through five different "governments" by the time it reaches the "Seminal Root," the sap has become very "delicate" and "with its highest Tincture and Impregnation thus enriched."[37]

In addition to the process of purification, Grew, like Milton, emphasizes continuity of substance: "As to their Continuity . . . as the Skin is continuous with the Parenchyma of the Barque; and this Parenchyma likewise, with the Insertions in

---

34 Grew, *The Anatomy of Vegetables Begun* (1672). Although Milton and Grew could have heard of each other through Henry Oldenberg, I am not suggesting influence, only congruity.

35 Grew's comparisons are borne out by 83 elegant engravings (see Plates 4 and 5), some from his own drawings, in which he is concerned with their dynamic life; he says in the Preface, "Some of the Plates, especially those which I did not draw to the Engravers hand, are a little hard and stiff: but they are all well enough done, to represent what they intend."

36 Grew, *Anatomy of Vegetables*, 2.

37 Grew, *Anatomy of Vegetables*, 20–24.

the Wood; so these Insertions again, running through the Wood, are also continuous with the Pith. So that the Skin, Parenchyma, Insertions, and Pith, are all One entire piece of Work; being only filled up, in divers manners, with the Vessels."[38]

In Grew's language, all parts of plants are full of energy. Particles of sap "by the vigour of their own motion from the Center . . . impress an equal tendency on some of the inner parts of the Lignous Body next adjacent to the Pith, to move with them." Forms of leaves give them "Elegancy and Security, . . . in taking up, so far as their Forms will bear, the least room; and in being so conveniently couch'd, as to be capable of receiving protection from other parts, or of giving it to one another."[39]

"[F]low'rs and their fruit / Man's nourishment, by gradual scale sublimed / To vital spirits aspire": Using the example of an apple, Grew explains that though it is only a continuation of the bark, "yet the plenty and purity of its Sap being likewise effectual to the fulness and fineness of its growth, it thus becomes a soft and tender meat." And "If it be asked, how the Fruit becomes, generally above all the other Part, so pleasant a Meat? It is partly from the Sap, the grosser portion thereof being deposited in the Leaves, and so the purer hereunto reserved; partly from the Globular Figure of the Fruit; for the Sap being thus in a greater quantity herein, and all parts equally diffused, the Concoction hereof is with greatest advantage favoured and promoted." In Milton's words, "The grosser feeds the purer" (5.416). In such ways, and in his reiterations concerning the variety of kinds produced from these principles, Grew confirms the organicity of the metaphoric Tree of Life that grows in the midst of Milton's epic.

Milton takes these processes further; the purification or "sublimation" continues as fruit is concocted to "vital spirits . . . to animal, / To intellectual," which give "life and sense, / Fancy and Understanding, whence the Soul / Reason receives . . . Discursive, or Intuitive," to all of which these nutrients "aspire" (the word sharing its root with "spirit" and "respiration"). Since the difference between human and angelic reason, like other differences between species, is a matter of degree of refinement, and in the Garden of Eden vegetation feeds them all, Raphael's metaphor of the tree is the perfect similitude for that which refines matter to spirit—which are states of the same substance—and true to the nature of the thing made metaphor. Those who aspire to reason, moral wisdom, spiritual refinement, and love grow rootedly towards God, like a tree.

Sensitive plants: Marvell and Grew

Andrew Marvell looked upon the old-growth forests of Nunappleton as a "green, yet-growing ark," in which Noah might have found "Fit timber" (*hyle, materia*). Conferring among the birds and plants he nearly becomes them; "Or turn me but, and you shall see / I was but an inverted Tree." The inversion of syntax is an instance of organic form; and "was" may suggest that an inverted tree is what he has always been. Rosalie Colie in "*My Ecchoing Song*" reproduces emblems of the idea that a

---

38 Grew, *Anatomy of Plants*, 119.
39 Grew, *Anatomy of Vegetables,* 26, 106, 115.

man is an upside-down tree, a source of much symbolism. Marvell literalizes the metaphor; he is not only nearly metamorphosed into a tree, but is thus returning to his true nature.

Nehemiah Grew later argued that plants are more like us than we acknowledge. In the dedicatory letter to Charles II of *The Anatomy of Plants*, he states,

> Your Majesty will here see, That there are those things within a Plant, little less admirable, than within an Animal. That a Plant, as well as an Animal, is composed of several Organical Parts; some whereof may be called its Bowels. That every Plant hath Bowels of divers kinds, conteining divers kinds of Liquors. That even a Plant lives partly upon Aer; for the reception whereof, it hath those Parts which are answerable to Lungs.

And he concludes with a metaphor of the book: "So that a Plant is, as it were, an Animal in Quires; as an Animal is a Plant, or rather several Plants bound up into one Volume."

Grew makes us feel empathy with the lives of plants by analogizing them to our own bodies: "For considering, that both of them came at first out of the same Hand; and were therefore the Contrivances of the same Wisdom: I thence fully assured my self, that it could not be a vain Design; to seek it in both." In Book III, "Of Trunks," he shows how plants breathe. Air enters and expires through pores in all parts; in some trunks, these are large enough to see with the naked eye, as in good walking sticks. But the chief entrance is through the root: "What the mouth is to an Animal; that the root is to a Plant."[40]

The analogy between plant and human is striking in his discussion of plant sexuality and reproduction. Chapter V, "Of Fruits," concerns "the Seed-Case or Membraneous Uterus" (186) and Chapter VI, "Of the Generation of the Seed." Grew chooses "an Aprecock" (interestingly, given the association of that fruit with pregnancy as in *The Duchess of Malfi*) "as very apt and convenient, to observe and represent the Method which Nature taketh in its Generation." The first step "is to make a fit Uterus. Both to keep the Membranes of the Foetus warm, and succulent, till it be formed: and to preserve and secure the Foetus it self afterwards, till it come to be born into the Ground . . . . The Stone being made hard and dry; it could never be so sufficiently softened by lying underground, but that, it would keep the Seed a perpetual prisoner, unless it were also made pretty easily to cleave in two." If you cut a young Aprecock you can see the skin "to be doubled inward from the two Lips of the Fruit, and so to be continued "through the pulp and the stone . . . . Nature having thus provided a convenient Uterus, She next taketh care about the Membranes of the Foetus."[41]

Breaking down of the Aristotelian boundaries between vegetative, sensitive, and rational beings was furthered by Martin Lister's report to the Royal Society concerning plant circulation, sensitivity, and animation. Lister found that plants have both motion and sense. Discussing two kinds of sap, the Limpid or Alimental and the Milkie or Venal, he writes:

---

40   Grew, *Anatomy of Plants*, 127.
41   Grew, *Anatomy of Plants*, 186, 209–10.

As to the motion of these Juices, these things are certain;

1. That the Milkie Juice alwais moves and springs briskly upon the opening of a vein; the Limpid sap but at certain seasons, and as it were by accident, and not (as I judge) from any vital principle of fermentation of its own.

2. The venal juice hath a manifest intestine motion or fermentation within it self; witness (besides what hath been just now said of it) it contributing (and the long continuance of) that motion to the most insensible of liquors; and likewise its thick and troubled bleeding, like the rising of yeast, which yet in a few hours after drawing falls, and the juice becomes transparent, as the Gum of the Virginian Rhus, etc.

At the present state of knowledge we must suppose that plant juices move by a far different contrivance of parts from that of Animals; not yet here discovering any uniting of the veins into one common Trunk, no Pulsation, no sensible stop by ligature, no difference in veins, &c. All of which difficulties notwithstanding may, I hope, in time be happily overcome; and the Analogie betwixt Plants and Animals be in all thing else, as well as the motion of their juice, fully clear'd.

This hope of a totalizing "Analogie" is consonant with other Royal Society investigations into the unifying principles of things. Lister continues immediately,

There seem to be in Plants manifest Acts of Sense. We see instance in the suddain shrinking of some Plants; the frequent closing and opening of flowers; the critical erecting of the heads of Poppies from a pendulous posture, and particularly the Vermicular motion of the Veins when exposed to the air. Again, the Veins of Plants may indeed be different, though at present we cannot tell wherein they are so. The Arteries within our heads are hardly to be known by the eye from the Veins. Further there are natural and spontaneous excretions or venting of superfluous moisture in plants, visible and constant, in the Crown Imperial, Rorella, Pinguicula, &c. distendable.

Finally, we must either deny "the other reasons given of the necessity of the Circulation of the blood in Animals, viz. the hindring of its breaking and clodding; or we must grant the same motion to the Venal juice in Plants"; and "undeniable Experiments" show that when drawn from their veins "the Venal juice of Plants and the Blood of Animals" both "break and coagulate" and the serum in both "becomes a still gelly by a little standing."[42]

The homology of human bodies and the bodies of trees was not new, but in an age when plants and animals were increasingly objectified and classified, Grew's and Lister's reinforcement of it approaches the sense of creature kinship found among poets. The observations of plants responding to their environments and even to human touch make the poetry of sympathetic trees, if not less fanciful, at least something more than projections of human fancy.

---

42 Lister, *Philosophical Transactions* 7–8.90:5131–7: "A further Account concerning the Existence of Veins in all kind of Plants; together with a Discovery of the Membranous substance of those Veins, and of some Acts in Plants resembling those of Sense; as also of the Agreement of the Venal Juice in Vegetables with the Blood of Animals, &c. Communicated by Mr. Lister in a Letter of Januar 8. 1672/73. and exhibited to the R. Society," 5136–7.

In "Upon the Hill and Grove at Bilborough" Marvell writes of the sentience of the Lord General Fairfax's "plump of agèd trees" and his protection of them: "No hostile hand durst ere envade / With impious steel the sacred shade." Although he did make the "wounds" of writing his beloved Vera's name in their bark, no other wounds were allowed, and "ere he well the barks could part / 'Twas writ already in their heart." This claim is the pretext for a vitalist assertion about trees:

> For they ('tis credible) have sense,
> As we, of love and reverence,
> And underneath the coarser rind
> The genius of the house do bind.
> Hence they successes seem to know,
> And in their Lord's advancement grow;
> But in no memory were seen,
> As under this, so straight and green.

That is, under this Lord, the trees throve as under none other. Here, as in *Upon Appleton House*, Marvell literalizes the family tree. The metaphorical grove is also an actual grove on that symmetrical hill that because of real care survived the civil wars and the war debts and rebuilding that devastated other British woods. Another use of hill and timber adds complexity and grief to this preservation: in Fairfax's war against absolute monarchy, "Through groves of pikes he thundered then, / And mountains raised of dying men." And the saved trees say

> 'For all the civic garlands due
> To him, our branches are but few.
> Nor are our trunks enow to bear
> The trophies of one fertile year.'[43]

The trees cannot hold all the prizes of weapons and armor won from the enemy, nor, perhaps, would suffice for the coffins of so many "dying men."

In "The Garden," Marvell literalizes the allegorical passage from the Song of Solomon, "My love is a garden enclosed," and makes an enclosed garden his love. Putting us through mazes of wordplay, Marvell mocks the vanity of those who put themselves though mazes of toils to win the narrow garlands that both braid up and mock their labor; he prefers the living garland of a whole garden over the wreathes of palm, oak, and bay, the symbolic rewards of heroic or spiritual, royal or civic, and poetic champions.[44] He claims that the sacred plants of quiet and innocence, if to be found on earth, "Only among the plants will grow"; that, unlike lovers who "Cut in these trees their mistress' name," he would cut only their own names—and that

---

43   Marvell, *Complete Poems*, 71–3.

44   Rosalie L. Colie characterizes Marvell's "unmetaphorizing" as "one of the marks of a poet critical of traditions, attempting to see into their meaning some basis in actuality," in *"My Ecchoing Song"* 79 n.2. She also reproduces an emblem from Joachim Camerarius's *Symbolorum et Emblematum* of three intertwined garlands, with the olive of peace instead of the palm of victory (Colie, fig. 14). See also Anna K. Nardo, *The Ludic Self*, chapter 6: "Andrew Marvell Recreating the Self."

mythical nymphs changed to plants and trees are improved by their metamorphoses: "No white nor red was ever seen / So am'rous as this lovely green." Like his figure of the "inverted tree," Marvell's playful sympathy with trees draws us closer to our woody cousins; but "No name shall but your own be found" brings us back to the problem of naming—what names? Their common names, their nymph names, their new-made botanical names—none their own?

Nigel Smith, citing Jacob Boehme's *Signatura Rerum*, explains that Marvell "alludes to the notion, commonly found in occult writings and nature mysticism (especially Paracelsus), of . . . the doctrine [that] God put into each piece of creation a distinct sign, which was the true name of that object, and which most perfectly expressed what it was." Correspondingly, "God put into Adam's mind a mental impression of each signature so that he would be able to name and hence know every object in creation. This was the basis of the Adamic knowledge so celebrated in the Hermetic tradition."[45] Marvell lived into the age of scientific naming represented by John Ray and leading to Linnaeus. An exquisite attender to words, he must have been aware of the questions his Adamic persona was raising about naming. His friend and colleague John Milton also raised them; he catalogues common names of flowers in *Lycidas*, Adam names the animals "and understood their nature," and Eve names the flowers in "tribes"—floral relatives.[46]

The common names of flowers and trees (which have usurped the *Signatura Rerum* in the fallen world) are linked to characters in Greek and Latin myth and come notably from Ovid's *Metamorphoses*, reminding us of loss and mutability. When "The gods, that mortal beauty chase, / Still in a tree did end their race," mortal beauty became immortal art. "Apollo hunted Daphne so, / Only that she might laurel grow," and Pan pursued Syrinx "Not as a nymph, but for a reed." The laurel provides the laureate wreath, those perplexed bays renounced (ironically, in a poem) in stanza one; and with the name Laura, Petrarch began a tradition of praising white and red of brow and lip in the kind of poetry that Marvell's speaker now metamorphoses back into the praise of vegetable green—though the name, *l'aura*, also suggests what Milton called "vegetable gold" (4.220). Syrinx provides the stuff of panpipes or reed flutes. Trees and reeds are the *hyle*, the materials from which viols and pipes are made; these originary myths tell of art emerging from pain. The poet-speaker recognizes that without nature there is no art, and will write only the trees' own "signatura" on their bark, but with the admission, "I wound."[47]

The poem continues with a delicious catalogue of sensuous pleasures. "The luscious clusters of the vine / Upon my mouth do crush their wine"—what rhyme words could more fittingly wind together than vine and wine? What sounds could come nearer to the taste of wine than that rich yet edgy assonance and consonance, or make one more aware of one's palate than those luscious clusters of words?

---

45 Nigel Smith, ed., in *The poems of Andrew Marvell*, 156.

46 See especially Leonard, *Naming in Paradise*.

47 Robert N. Watson in *Back to Nature* interestingly and wittily discusses this and other poems by Marvell as part of an epistemological questioning in the late Renaissance raised by post-Copernican doubts of sense perception and the possibility of right naming.

As to contemplation, in this garden, "The mind, that ocean where each kind / Does straight its own resemblance find"; every "kind," or species has its replication in us. But Marvell does not say "that ocean where we find / resemblances of every kind." Instead of having us look into the mirror of the natural world, he has each species look into the mirror of the human mind and find "its own resemblance." The difference may be small, but the quick trick of reversed perspective is a pattern of Marvell's poems that makes us see ourselves through other eyes, even the eyes of other species.

The mind, however, is the organ of imagination and transcendence:

> Yet it creates, transcending these,
> Far other worlds, and other seas,
> Annihilating all that's made
> To a green thought in a green shade.

Again a curious doubleness: "Annihilating all that's made" is a shocking reminder of Lear and Macbeth desiring to destroy the very germens, yet depicts beautifully, though not without vanity, the state of the meditative soul that casts "the body's vest aside" and glides into the boughs where

> like a bird it sits, and sings,
> Then whets, and combs its silver wings;
> And, till prepared for longer flight,
> Waves in its plumes the various light.

The deliberate echo of Genesis in the next stanza contradicts the opinion of God that "it is not good for the man to be alone." Then the transcendent speaker comes abruptly back to local earth and the hylozoic sundial—a "fragrant zodiac" of "herbs and flow'rs"—and we emerge refreshed by both the garden of plants and the garden of words.

At a time when gardens were almost universally praised in poetry, Marvell takes a different stance in "The Mower against Gardens." The hybridizing and grafting to which the mower objects has since burgeoned into large-scale importation of exotic species, interbreeding, and genetic engineering with sometimes dire consequences. Marvell's mower worries about such things. In this age of elaborate gardens, he prefers his flowers wild, "Where willing nature does to all dispense / A wild and fragrant innocence." The small "all" should not be missed. Nature is egalitarian in her dispensations, while luxurious man is busy producing an unnatural elite.

The mower of those "sweet fields" and "meadows" he loves inevitably reminds us of the Great Leveller; Marvell never shuns irony. Nature spirits in contrast take care of meadows "More by their presence than their skill," a genius they share with Mary Fairfax in *Upon Appleton House* and with Eve in Milton's Eden, where plants respond to both her presence and her skill. Nehemiah Grew loved gardens and believed in the improvement of fertility, but was remarkably uninterested in commodification of plants as luxuries. Both poet and botanist find joy in nature and seek temperance in her use. "Luxurious man," the mower says, "first enclosed within the garden's square / A dead and standing pool of air." "Enclosed" is politically charged, and the poem's closed couplets fit it, along with the squared garden and its stagnant air—the opposite of what Evelyn promoted gardens for. The pink grows "double," like the rhymes. And the alternation of ten-syllable and eight-syllable lines might remind us that ten is the number of law, the decalogue, regulation, rules, and the eight of the octave, the symbol of heaven and earth and their joining by grace.

"The Garden" has rhymed couplets too, but more are enjambed. It has squarish stanzas, each having eight lines mostly of eight syllables, also suggesting an octagon, the form of fountains in paradisal gardens. And it has nine stanzas, the number of celestial harmony, in which the eight lines form octaves. "The Garden" and "The Mower against Gardens" draw a fine line between cultivation and preservation—dressing and keeping. Luxurious man over-manages; contemplative man, up to a point, lets be, as at the beginning of *Upon Appleton House* where the luxurious man overbuilds and the wise man, like the tortoise, does not.

Marvell's Garden and Mower poems are hylozoic in being about plants and poetry, but are not georgic. Although "The Garden" alludes to the lost Paradise, including snares but excluding Eve, it tells us nothing about how to garden. The visitor's relation to trees and his sensuous enjoyment of fruit are intimate, but nothing is known of the gardener except that he contrived the herbal sundial. The mower, oddly, is even less interested in controlling nature. Apart from the annual shearing of meadow grass (which is not so radical as felling trees, since grasses regenerate annually), he prefers to let nature be—though with Marvell's usual ironic multiple vision. Though the two poems work as two sides of a debate, they are unified in their suspicion of the kind of dominion over all the earth that the agricultural projectors and Dryden's version of the *Georgics* vigorously promoted.

Planting our name: Royalist poetry of place

Milton and Marvell were both commonwealth men and both entered with full sympathy into the living processes of plants and animals. Loyalists too could be good stewards and empathetic poets of nature. John Evelyn was an eloquent and learned natural historian of plants, advocate of vegetarianism, and proponent and teacher of conservation and reparation. To some extent Abraham Cowley shared Evelyn's ethic. George Herbert was a courtier, Henry Vaughan adhered to the established church and state even after both were dismantled, and Margaret Cavendish was surrounded by noblemen and philosophers of dominion such as Descartes and Hobbes and thought that "Democracy is more Wild and Barbarous than Monarchy."[48] However, other royalist poets treated nature, people, and language as subjects to be ruled, and these attitudes may be seen in their diction and forms.

Edmund Waller's poem *On St. James's Park, As Lately Improved by His Majesty*, to which Evelyn alludes in *Sylva*, was published in a slim folio with *Of our late War with Spain* in 1661 and celebrates (or satirizes) the Restoration in a language of control over nature that suits (or mocks) an absolute monarch or a Baconian projector or a voluntarist God. Here beside the tidal Thames, in a possible allusion

---

48 Cavendish, *CCXI Sociable Letters*, 137.

to Dedham's *Cooper's Hill*, "The Sea which always served his Empire, now / Pays tribute to our Prince's pleasure, too." Providently, "For future shade young Trees upon the banks / Of the new stream appear in even ranks," while in his "living Gallery of aged Trees" Charles II

> . . . contrives the ordering of his States,
> Here he resolves his Neighboring Princes' Fates:
> What Nation shall have Peace, where War be made,
> Determined is in this oraculous shade:
> The world, from *India* to the frozen North,
> Concerned in what this solitude brings forth.

The trees of this sacred grove or brigade wear the language of violence as "Bold sons of earth that thrust their arms so high, / As if once more they would invade the sky." Looking out towards Whitehall, the "seat of Empire," the courts of justice, and the "house" of Parliament "where all our ill were shaped," the king sees "His flock subjected to his view below." In his walks he ponders "How peaceful Olive may his Temples shade, / For mending Laws, and for restoring trade; / Or how his Brows may be with Laurel charged / For Nations conquered, and our bounds enlarged." Like an agricultural projector, he will "Reform these Nations, and improve them more, / Than this fair Park, from what it was before."[49] Evelyn reports to the Royal Society in 1662 that the puritans had proposed "to the late Council of State (as they called it) that "the Royal Walk of Elms in St James's Park should be cut down and sold to remove the "Footsteps of Monarchy."[50] How does the king's attitude toward nature in this poem, or the puritans' in Evelyn's report, compare with those of Mary Fairfax or Milton's Adam and Eve? What are the implications for planting colonies, in "Nations conquered"?

The reformation of nature is also the subject of Abraham Cowley's ode "To the Royal Society" printed in the second edition of Thomas Sprat's *History*, in which Cowley calls natural philosophy the only kind of human knowledge "unforfeited" by "Man"s rebellious Sin." Unconventionally designating Philosophy "he" because "It a Male Virtue seems to me," the ode explains that until now Philosophy's guardians have kept him "in Nonage" lest his powers outweigh theirs, tutoring him with "wanton Wit" and "Desserts of Poetry" instead of "solid meats," with "pleasant Labyrinths of ever-fresh Discourse" instead of "vigorous exercise," and with "painted Scenes, and Pageants of the Brain" instead of "Natures endless Treasure." Bacon has rescued Philosophy from these idols by banishing the phantom "Authority" from his sacred grove, which now all may enter. Yet, Cowley continues, we still seek the forbidden fruit of trying to find knowledge in our own minds without grounding in the senses, as only God can do. The Baconian revolution has transferred authority from words to "Things, the Minds right Object," alluding perhaps to the Society"s motto, "Nullus in Verbis." The wine of knowledge can only be vinted from real grapes:

---

49 Waller, *A Poem of St. James Park* (1661), sigs. B and C.
50 Evelyn, *Silva* (1706), 346.

Like foolish Birds to painted Grapes we flew;
He sought and gather'd for our use the Tru;
And when on heaps the chosen Bunches lay,
He prest them wisely the Mechanic way,
Till all their juyce did in one Vessel joyn,
Ferment into a Nourishment Divine,
The thirsty Souls refreshing Wine.

While Cowley's promotion of empirical observation is salutary, his image of mechanism brings to mind another image of "Nourishment Divine," the one (sometimes used on the title pages of Bibles) of Christ in the Winepress, his blood pressed out by a literal machine.

Cowley's totalizing "one vessel" is to be filled not by the ideas and images copied from others or one's own fancy but "The real Object." Bacon, the Moses of wandering philosophers, brought us to the promised land; the Champions he addresses must now lead us to those undiscovered Guianas where "instead of Nature, we / Her Images and Idols worship'd see: / These large and wealthy Regions to subdu." God's armies of learning by their "glorious Fight" and "victorious Lights" lead where "New scenes of Heven already we espy, / And Crowds of golden Worlds on high; / Which from the spacious Plains of Earth and Sea, / Could never yet discover'd be." Now, neither distance nor smallness can obscure Nature's works:

Y' have taught the curious Sight to press
    Into the privatest recess
Of her imperceptible Littleness.
She with much stranger Art than his who put
    All th'Iliads in a Nut,
The numerous work of Life does into Atomes shut.

Cowley's excitement about new perceptions possible through astronomy and micrography matches Marvell's, but (unlike Marvell or Anne Conway) he uses a militant and voyeuristic language reminiscent of Ralegh and of the chemic in Herbert's "Vanitie (I)" to represent the dominion of atomic mechanism. The ode concludes with an imprecation against scoffers and praise for Sprat as fit Historian, for, as the empiricists purge philosophy from error, he purges language: "His candid Stile like a clean Stream does slide."[51] From an ecological point of view, Cowley wins points for praising firsthand views of nature intelligibly expressed, rather than inherited speculations. But he uses the old authoritarian language of nature as treasury and introduces a new one of the conquest of mechanist philosophy and plain speech over "fresh Discourse."

Cowley assigns blame for deforestation to the rebels in Book 6, *Sylva*, of his six-book Latin poem *Plantarum* (1668). Although he says in his preface that he means to write of trees themselves, his *Sylva* is frequently allegorical and political. In Aphra Behn's translation we read that when "Royal Charles that Prince of Peace

---

51 Sprat, *The History of the Royal-Society of London*, sigs. B–B3.

. . . / Sway'd England's Scepter with a God-Like Hand, / Scattering soft Ease and Plenty o'er the Land," the people in their pride

> To a base Plebeian Senate gave
> The arbitrary Priv'lege to enslave;
> Who through a Sea of noblest Blood did wade,
> To tear the Diadem from the sacred Head.   [60–72]

Until then, Peace had made her nest "In *British* Groves," where she hatched a Golden Age; but Luxury destroys virtue, England became "sick with Ease," and in spite of portents the English oaks, symbol of royalty, were torn from their soil. While for Milton King Charles was the aggressor, and for Marvell the woods in the care of Fairfax, who fought on the side of Parliament, were green and growing, for Cowley, with the Interregnum, "The dismal Shade with Birds obscene were fill'd" (198).

It is fitting that Cowley dedicated his poem "The Garden" to John Evelyn, the ecologically minded royalist whose *Fumifugium* taught air-cleansing planting and whose *Sylva* taught the reforestation of the nation. Cowley writes charmingly of the garden as Horatian or Dioclesian retreat from the fractious world of ambition and avarice. He commends nature's harmony, both ideal and audible in wind, water, and the songs of birds, who, like poets, live "Without Reward, or Thanks for their obliging Pains," and adds hylozoically,

> But to our Plants, Art's Musick too,
>   The Pipe, Theorbo, and Guitar we owe;
> The Lute it self, which once was green and mute;
>   When Orpheus strook th'inspir'd Lute,
> The Trees danc'd round, and understood
>   By Sympathy the Voice of Wood.

As in *Fumifugium*, sweet air vies with city smoke:

> Who would not among Roses and Jasmin dwell,
>   Rather than all his Spirits choak
> With Exhalations of Dirt and Smoak?
>   And all th'Uncleanness which does drown
> In Pestilential Clouds a populous Town?

Unlike the many country house poems whose tables, like Vetellius's, hold "As many Creatures as the Ark of old," to whose "Fiscal Table . . . ev'ry Day / All Countries did a constant Tribute pay," the virtuous Epicure's holds his own produce;

> The wanton Taste no Fish, or Fowl can chuse,
>   For which the Grape or Melon he would lose,
> Tho' all th'Inhabitants of Sea and Air
>   Be listed in the Glutton's Bill of Fare [.]

But empire over nature comes back in a stanza on grafting trees, where art most "over-rules" nature and "is her Master":

Who would not joy to see his conqu'ring Hand
   O'er all the Vegetable World command?
And the wild Giants of the Wood receive
   What Law he pleas'd to give?[52]

Waller and Cowley make the order and servitude imposed on the land the metaphor of good government. But Cowley's preference of local produce to animal food and the "Fiscal Table" of imported luxuries is salvific. Royalist poets sometimes censure excess, but I don't find them speaking anti-oppressively, as Milton, Marvell, Vaughan, and Cavendish do, of non-human living things as our kindred in sentience and consciousness, or using language that acknowledges their inward forms and potencies, their patterns of growth, or their connections to their habitats.

I have said that hylozoic poets are concerned with the matter of life. Milton, Marvell, and Vaughan are literally so, and their descriptions of trees and woods are also descriptions of the matter of poetry, the structures and textures of words that represent the structures and textures of the things for which they are signs. I do not find this quality in the poems of Lucy Cavendish and Anne Finch, though written on behalf of trees, but they show two women with royalist alliances whose animist arboreal verse protests more felling than that of Charles, the Royal Oak.

In *Philosophical and Physical Opinions*, Margaret Cavendish questions the Aristotelean and mechanist limits to sentience.

> There may be in Nature More Sensitive Passages or Organs, than the Sensitive Organs in Animals, and not only More Sensitive Passages or Organs, but more Various; for though Animals cannot see Outward Objects without an Eye, yet certainly Nature can, and hath made Different Organs in Different Creatures . . . . for it is not probable, that the several Works in Nature can be in Obscurity to most, and only be Divulged to some particular Sorts or Kinds.[53]

Cavendish may be working out the hylozoism of Pierre Gassendi, whose Christianizing of Epicurus was promoted by Walter Charleton, a member of the Newcastle circle. Gassendi, as Stephen Fallon explains, argued from both hylozoism and incorporealism, proposing Epicurean atomism and mechanism but believing in divine creation, free will, responsibility, and an incorporeal soul on the grounds that if we can do nothing unavoidably, there is no reason for human life.[54] He taught that the Epicureans "did not consider atoms, which they said are the matter of all things, as inert or motionless, but rather as most active and mobile, so much so that they held them to be the first principle from which things take their motion."[55] And he proposed a teleology for each created thing: "Each natural agent tends to a certain end . . . . You say, therefore, must a certain cognition be attributed to the seeds, not only of animals, but also of plants, stones, and other things? But if you wish me to

---

52 Cowley, "The Garden," stanzas 4–6 and 10, in *Complete Works* 2:326–9.

53 Cavendish, *Philosophical and Physical Opinions*, "To the Reader," sig. Nnn2.

54 Gassendi, *Ethics*, in *Opera*, 2:831; Fallon, *Milton among the Philosophers*, 43.

55 Gassendi, *Syntagma philosophicum*, *The Physics*, Book 4, in *Selected Works*, 411–12; Fallon, 44.

deny this, explain therefore how they finish their own operations so exquisitely."[56] Lucretius, a disciple of Epicurus, taught that "All created things have come / From their own definite kinds of seed, they move / From their beginnings toward the shores of light / Out of their primal motes. . . . each kind / Of substance has its own inherent power, / Its own capacity."[57]

Given Cavendish's *Philosophical and Physical Opinions*, we can read "*A Dialogue between an Oake, and a Man cutting him downe*,"[58] as neither merely sentimental nor strictly allegorical. Though her form and syntax are not particularly witty, her choice of oak as oracle is. Vergil calls it "oracula quercus" (2.26), which Dryden renders "vocal Oke / Where Jove of old Oraculously spoke." The man's language is managerial, the oak's simple and wise.

Anne Finch, Countess of Winchelsea (not to be confused with an earlier Anne Finch, the brilliant student of Henry More who became Viscountess Conway) also considers reciprocity with nature in "The Tree." She writes her poem to reciprocate the tree's "delightful Shade" and tells how others make grateful returns: the birds repay shelter with music, travellers waiting out storms in its protection give praise, the shepherd escaping the scorching sun "Tunes to thy dancing Leaves his Reed; / Whilst his lov'd Nymph, in Thanks, bestows / Her flow'ry Chaplets on thy Boughs." Her own garland is a blessing-poem, wishing the tree a natural death.

> Shall I then only Silent be,
> And no Return be made by me?
> No; let this Wish upon thee wait,
> And still to flourish be thy Fate,
> To future Ages may'st thou stand
> Untouch'd by the rash Workman's hand;
> 'Till the fierce Winds, that vainly strive
> To shock thy Greatness whilst alive,
> Shall on thy lifely Hour attend,
> Prevent the Axe, and grace thy End;
> Their scatter'd Strength together call,
> And to the Clouds proclaim thy Fall;
> Who then their Ev'ning-Dews may spare,
> When thou no longer art their Care;
> But shalt, like ancient Heroes, burn,
> And some bright Hearth be made thy Urn.[59]

Cavendish and Finch contest an attitude toward nature that appears to some extent in Dryden's translation of Vergil's *Georgics* 2, on the cultivation of trees, which I will compare with the more vitalistic modern translation by L.P. Wilkinson. Vergil begins by saying that some plants grow of their own accord, without human control, while others profit both from kinds of care that Nature ordains and others

56 Gassendi, *Physics*, from Sarasohn, "Motion and Morality," 372, in Fallon, 43–5.

57 Lucretius, *The Way Things Are* [*De Rerum Natura*] trans. Rolfe Humphries, 1.168–74.

58 Cavendish, "*A Dialogue between an Oake, and a Man cutting him downe*," in *Poems and Fancies*, 66–70. This poem is discussed at length in Chapter 3.

59 *The Poems of Anne Countess of Winchilsea*, ed. Reynolds, 266–7.

discovered by experiments. On propagation by planting suckers, Vergil writes "hic plantas tenero abscindens de corpore matrum / deposuit sulcis" (2.23); Wilkinson translates "one tearing suckers from / The mother's tender body buried them in furrows" (ll. 23–4); Dryden writes "Some cut the shoots, and plant in furrow'd ground" (l.30). What Vergil calls "Silvestrem animum" (l. 51) Wilkinson translates "Their wildwood spirit" (l. 51) and Dryden "their salvage [wild] Mind" (l.71). Both render clearly the management of nature, and the need to match stocks to the proper ground and tend them, as a moral imperative, but with different emphases; in the spirit of seventeenth-century agricultural tracts Dryden admonishes "Much labour is required in Trees, to tame / Their wild disorder, and in ranks reclaim."[60]

John Rogers thinks that the "Vitalist Moment" Margaret Cavendish represents was a brief though lively phenomenon of the mid-seventeenth century, soon to be replaced in ways Dryden's language reflects.[61] Yet John Muir as a young naturalist wrote in his diary of 1867, "Plants are credited with but dim and uncertain sensation, and minerals with positively none at all. But why may not even a mineral arrangement of matter be endowed with sensation of a kind that we in our blind exclusive perfection can have no manner of communication with?"[62] The vitalist sensibility continues in current poetry and art and in the work of philosophical scientists such as Rupert Shelldrake; and many people who doubt the sensate life of Earth can still see nature responding to human alterations in ways that recommend the ethic vitalist poets expressed.

---

60 Dryden, *Works*, 5.182–3; Wilkinson, *Georgics*, 77–8. Draymen's translation is from Tonson's edition, 1697, as is the illustration of tree-planting with evenly spaced trees in square beds appropriate to Draymen's kind of neoclassicism.

61 Rogers, *Matter of Revolution*, 1–2, 8–17, et passim.

62 Muir, "A Thousand-Mile Walk to the Gulf," *The Eight Wilderness Discovery Books*, 161.

Chapter 5

Zoic Poetry
Animals, Ornithology, and the
Ethics of Empathy

By love our souls are married and soldered to the creatures,
and it is our duty like God to be united to them all.

Thomas Traherne, *Meditations* 2.66

Cabinets, fragments, and the lives of animals

René Descartes reasoned that non-human animals did not have reason or significant feelings, a view that promoted scientific experiments but that Charles Darwin two centuries later was to deny.[1] The dualism that considers the soul or anima separate from the body it animates, and that only human beings have rational and immortal souls, suggested that animals are automata, moved by the action of animal spirits—physical emanations of the blood—on their material bodies, and enabled by instinct to carry out their tasks of survival and reproduction, but having negligible capacities for suffering and joy. That opinion broke away from deep roots of poetry and moral philosophy, and was to be contested by some natural philosophers as an impulse of empathy began to grow. Michel de Montaigne, whose *Essays* appeared in English in 1607, opposed a strictly instrumental attitude to any living thing on moral grounds: "There [is] a kinde of respect, and a general duty of humanity, which tieth us not only unto brute beasts that have life and sense, but even unto trees and plants."[2] While some proto-scientists were developing an abstract language free of imagination and feeling, poets developed a language of empathy and particularity; and natural historians themselves, even in the process of collecting and dissecting, often exclaimed at the beauty or divine wisdom or possible inner lives of the objects of their study, and eventually began to think that animals had a right to enjoy their lives.

At first the empirical study of animals was literally fragmentary. If you walked into John Tradescant's personal museum in South Lambeth during the Interregnum, you could see numerous bodies and fragments of birds and beasts, including "Sixteen several strange beaks of Birds from the East India's"; "A legge and claw of the Cassawary or Emeu that dyed at S. James's, Westminster"; "Beavers skin, teeth,

---

1 See Descartes, *Philosophical Writings I: Description of the Human Body*, 317, and *Discourse on Method*, 134, 139–40.

2 Montaigne, "Of Crueltie," in *Essays*, trans. Florio, 2:126.

testicles"; a "Foot of a Ginny Dogge," a "Lions head and teeth," an "Elephants head and tayle," "The Rhinocerous—horn, jaw-bone, back-bone," "A Dolphins head," "Sea Horses—head, teeth, pissle"; and some whole animals, including a "Hippopotamus," an "alegator or Crocodile, from Aegypt" and a "Dodar, from the Island of Mauritius; it is not able to flie being so big."[3] This dodo wound up as fragments too, its head and one foot having been rescued when the trustees of the Ashmolean Museum ordered it burnt in 1755 because it was in poor condition. By that time, the exhibit could not be replaced.[4]

The Tradescants' house was known as "The Ark." Popular interest in this collection illustrates the seventeenth-century enthusiasm for global natural history out of which grew, on the one hand, a commodification of nature that has reduced thousands of species to the fate of the dodo, and on the other hand, the biological sciences with their contributions to medicine and other kinds of human and animal welfare and eventually to an understanding of ecosystems and of the hazards of fragmentary thinking about the natural world.

Pieces of exotic animals were also treasured at the Museum of the Royal Society in Gresham College. In its catalogue, published in 1685, Nehemiah Grew includes a fine engraving of the skeletal "HEAD OF THE ALBITROS" and describes birds with meticulous measurements, but is unable to complete those of "The Lesser HUMING BIRD" because "His Head is lost."[5]

In a "Proposition for the Advancement of Experimental Philosophy" (1661), Abraham Cowley rejoices that "the industry of Men has ventured to go abroad, out of Books and out of themselves, and to work among God's own Creatures." To advance this work he proposes a college that would have among its facilities "An Anatomical Chamber adorned with Skeletons and Anatomical Pictures, and prepared with all conveniences for Dissection," and "A Gallery to walk in" containing "the stuft skins of as many strange Animals as can be gotten."[6] What are we to make of this mixture of piety, empiricism, and indifference to the experience of "God's own Creatures" themselves?

Sir Thomas Browne writes in *Religio Medici*, "I hold that there is a general beauty in all the works of God, and therefore no deformity in any kind or species of creature whatsoever."[7] While many natural historians would agree, deformity was their necessary mode of description and display. Descriptive biology verbally, and museum exhibits literally, dealt with fragments, and often birds illustrated in Ray's *Ornithology*, some provided by Dr. Browne, are clearly dead.

Collecting parts of animals was not new. Medieval churches contained them, along with parts of saints. According to David Murray, two claws of a griffin reside in the

---

3   Tradescant, *Museum Tradescantium, or A Collection of Rarities Preserved at South-Lambeth near London* (1655) in Allan, Mea, *The Tradescants: Their Plants, Gardens and Museum*, Appendix II, 247–312.

4   Allan, *The Tradescants*, 24.

5   Grew, *Musaeum Regalis Societatis: Or A Catalogue and Description of the Natural and Artificial Rarities Belonging to the Royal Society* (1685), p. 62 and Table 6.

6   Cowley, *A Proposition for the Advancement of Experimental Philosophy*, (1661) in *Complete Works*, ed. Grosart, 288.

7   Browne, Sir Thomas, *Religio Medici*, in Works 2:25–6.

Treasury of Durham Cathedral, which skeptics allege to be antelope horns, and other collections claimed whale bones that once held Jonah and elephants' bones thought to have come from the giants in Genesis 6.[8] Nor was detached description newly invented; pre-Baconian natural historians regularly wrote such entries as Topsell's after Aldrovandus describing the blackbird (Gesner's Birckamsel) and ending, "They are gratefull meate at table. And so much for this kind."[9] But collecting and cataloging was stimulated by global exploration and by Francis Bacon's program in the *Novum Organon* and his vivid fable in the *New Atlantis*, where the Father of Salomon's House explains, "The End of our Foundation is the knowledge of Causes, and secret motions of things; and the enlarging of the bounds of Human Empire, to the effecting of all things possible."[10] Among these,

> We have also parks and enclosures of all sorts of beasts and birds, which we use not only for view or rareness, but likewise for dissections and trials; that we may take light what may be wrought upon the body of man. Wherein we find many strange effects; as continuing life in them, though divers parts, which you account vital, be perished and taken forth; resuscitating some that seem dead in appearance; and the like. We try also all poisons and other medicines upon them, as well of chirurgery as physic. By art likewise, we make them greater or taller than their kind is; and contrariwise dwarf them, and stay their growth: we make them more fruitful and bearing than their kind is; and contrariwise barren and not generative. Also we make them differ in colour, shape, activity, many ways. We find means to make commixtures and copulations of different kinds; which have produced many new kinds, and them not barren, as the general opinion is. We make a number of kinds of serpents, worms, flies, fishes, of putrefaction; whereof some are advanced (in effect) to be perfect creatures, like beasts or birds; and have sexes, and do propagate. Neither do we do this by chance, but we know beforehand of what matter and commixture what kind of those creatures will arise . . . Besides we have heats of dungs, and of bellies and maws of living creatures, and of their bloods and bodies.[11]

Anyone aware of the suffering from ignorance and superstition in Bacon's time, the deaths of children from infections now controllable, the pain endured from common ailments such as gout and kidney stone, will understand the sense of urgency that spurred medical investigations. In any case, animal suffering was already caused by the superstitious and useless abuses of the bodies of animals that Bacon's experimental program proposed to test and rectify. But nothing is said about mitigating the suffering of experimental animals, and many of the experiments go beyond human necessity or the remedy of disease.[12]

Ethical and proto-ecological attitudes toward other sentient beings were at hand in moral philosophy of which so learned a man as Bacon can hardly have been ignorant.

---

8   David Murray, *Museums:Their History and their Use*, 9–10.

9   Topsell, *The Fowles of Heaven*, 96.

10   Bacon, ed. Vickers, 480.

11   Bacon, ed. Vickers, 482–4.

12   Bacon's notes in the *Sylva Sylvarum*, with which the *New Atlantis* was published in 1627, suggest that these are Bacon's own views; and James Spedding declares that "The description of Solomon's House is the description of the vision in which he lived . . . of our own world as it might be made if we did our duty by it." Bacon, *Works* 3:22.

He would surely have known Lucretius' *De Rerum Natura*; Ovid's *Metamorphoses*, in which Pythagoras finds animal sacrifice and consumption morally abhorrent; and Plutarch's *Moralia*, which contains essays on the reasoning and suffering of animals and on the motives and effects of eating them. He may have known Porphyry's *Abstinentia animalium* from the paraphrase of Marsilio Ficino;[13] and he would have known about the debate on the intelligence of animals that, Bruce Boehrer points out, James I attended in Cambridge in 1615[14] when Bacon was James's Attorney-General and about to be his Privy Counselor.

When in 1668 John Wilkins, Anglican cleric and founding Fellow of the Royal Society, published his categorical *Essay towards a Real Character and a Philosophical Language*, he needed to assure readers that nature is finite and capable of being catalogued, and included with his classification of animals a "Digression" to prove mathematically that all air-breathing species and their provisions could fit into the Biblically prescribed dimensions of Noah's Ark (Plate 6). He states that although it is "most probable" that no animal was carnivorous before the Flood (citing Gen. 1.29, 30 and 9.3), yet since "a captious Adversary" might "question, whether the Rapacious kinds of Beasts and Birds, who in the natural frame of their parts are peculiarly fitted for the catching and devouring of their prey, did ever feed upon herbs and fruits . . . I shall be content to suppose that those Animals which are now Praedatory were so from the beginning." Given that "the carnivorous beasts were twenty pairs" he calculated that "five Sheep must be allotted to be devoured for food each day of the year, amounting to 1,825." Predators would occupy the first level of the ark, raptors the third, and the sheep to be eaten the second.

Wilkins comments neither on the theological problem of original rapacity nor its implications for the typology of the Ark as the church. He does pause for an ethical consideration: although "there might seem no just exception, if these beasts should be stor'd close together," as is usual in shipping them, "yet I shall not take any such advantage, but offer them such fair Stalls or Cabins as may be abundantly sufficient for them in any kind of posture, either standing, or lying, or turning themselves, as likewise to receive all the dung that should proceed from them for a whole year." Birds, being "of small bulk," could be pigeon-holed or stacked in cages. After fitting these animals mathematically into the dimensions of ark architecture, Wilkins finds nearly 200 feet left over, but this excess is no defect of God's arithmetic; divine providence has allotted the extra space for any animals that might be found in the "undiscovered parts of the world."[15]

Wilkins' ark is an excellent metaphor for his invented language. By parceling "all things and notions" into compartments, he hoped to make language hold still, or barely move, so that accurate global communication based on Western logic and management could go on forever. His categorical tables provide a hierarchical arrangement dependent on dualistic oppositions, dividing Being into God and the World; the World into Spirit and Body; animals and plants by method of reproduction

---

13   Ficino, in *Iamblichus de mysteriis* (Lyon, 1570). Harold Skulsky translates selections in *Milton and the Death of Man*, 166 and 248 n. 87.

14   Boehrer, "Milton and the Reasoning of Animals," *Milton Studies* 39 (2000): 52.

15   Wilkins, b verso, b3, 162–8.

and animals by number and shapes of feet, which aid recognition but also the construction of nets and traps. The scheme necessarily lacks the sense of process and mutability that enlivens seventeenth-century poetry and cosmology, and limits empathetic expression.

The Bible and the liturgy generated various attitudes;[16] in the creation poem of Genesis 1 God blesses his work, pronounces it (in the English translation of 1611) "very good," and grants "dominion" to man and woman. In view of the injunction to "dress and keep" the garden, dominion (lordship) is primarily interpretable as stewardship: God's human gardeners taking care of their domain of earth as the habitat of all the creatures God has just blessed.[17] But many in the age of global and scientific exploration took the subduing of the earth as warrant not just to encourage the fertility of plants and domesticate appropriate animals for mutual benefit, but to gain absolute control over them. The monistic vitalism or animist materialism of Milton, Marvell, Margaret Cavendish, and Henry and Thomas Vaughan embodies ethical principals Baconians refused.

Although Margaret Cavendish was a royalist and entertained Hobbes and Descartes at her table, in "A Discourse of Beasts" she mocks the philosophers with the notion that animals, and even fish, may be better astronomers, meteorologists, and chemists than they are. The poem may been a response to a letter to her husband from Descartes, dated 23 November 1646, disagreeing with the opinion of Montaigne that animals may be able to think:

> I cannot share the opinion of Montaigne and others who attribute understanding or thought to animals. I am not worried that people say that men have an absolute empire over all the animals . . . . I know that animals do many things better than we do, but this does not surprise me. It can even be used to prove that they act naturally and mechanically, like a clock which tells the time better than our judgement does. Doubtless when the swallows come in spring, they operate like clocks."[18]

Margaret Cavendish questions this opinion:

> Who knowes; but Beasts, as they do lye,
> In Meadowes low, or else on Mountaines high?
> But that they do contemplate on the Sun,
> And how his daily, yearely Circles run.
> Whether the Sun about the Earth doth rove,
> Or else the Earth upon its owne Poles move.
> And in the Night, when twinkling Stars we see,
> Like Man, imagines them all Suns to bee.
> And may like Man, Stars, Planets number well,
> And could they speak, they might their Motions tell.
> And how the Planets in each Orbe do move:

---

16   See for example Jeremy Cohen, '*Be fertile and increase, fill the earth and master it*'; Andrew Linzey, *Animal Theology*; Chris Fitter, *Poetry, Space, Landscape*.

17   On the Hebrew terms for dressing and keeping see Jeffrey Theis, "The Environmental Ethics of *Paradise Lost*."

18   Descartes, *Philosophical Letters*, trans. and ed. Anthony Kenny.

'Gainst their Astrology no Man can prove.
For they may know the Stars, and their Aspects,
What Influence they cast, and their Effects.[19]

Birds may know where storm winds come from and what thunder and falling stars are, and fish may understand their element better than we:

Who knows, but Fishes which swim in the Sea,
Can give a Reason, why so Salt it be?
And how it Ebbs and Flowes, perchance they can
Give Reasons, for which never yet could Man.

Henry Vaughan, interested in both piety and empiricism, goes abroad among "God's own Creatures" and speaks to a bird in a storm:

Hither thou com'st: the busy wind all night
Blew through thy lodging, where thy own warm wing
Thy pillow was. Many a sullen storm
(For which course man seems much the fitter born,)
    Rained on thy bed
    And harmless head.

And now as fresh and cheerful as the light
Thy little heart in early hymns doth sing
Unto that Providence, whose unseen arm
Curbed them, and clothed thee well and warm.[20]

June Sturrock explains Vaughan's omission of names and details of species: "He cares chiefly for their dynamism and for their characteristic activity . . . . To him, 'that's best / Which is not fixed but flies, and flows.' "[21]

I am comparing natural history and poetry not to claim that animals should not be employed but because the language produced by poetry and natural philosophy did in the seventeenth century and can now, in an age when talk is so often about manmade things and apt to be mechanical or "fixed" itself, encourage awareness of the sentient active lives of other beings. What follows looks at the effects of exploitative and fragmentary thinking about animals in seventeenth-century ornithologies, zoological works, and micrography, at poets' accounts of animals within these contexts, and in the next chapter at the ethics that began to develop in natural philosophy as well as poetry. I'll begin with a brief history of thought about an animal especially unable to speak for itself.

---

19   Cavendish, "A Discourse of Beasts," "Of Fish," and "Of Birds," in *Poems and Fancies*, 105.

20   Vaughan, "The Bird," in Rudrum, ed., *Complete Poems*, 260–61.

21   Sturrock, "'Cock-crowing,'" 152.

Speaking of animals: The case of the tortoise

During the Renaissance, when representations of animals were often allegorical lessons, the tortoise was a model of domesticity because she is always at home. When Zeus gave a banquet, the story goes, the tortoise came late because she preferred her own house (*Oikos*, the root of *ecology*), and Zeus sentenced her to carry it on her back. Among the popular sixteenth-century *Emblemata* of Andreas Alciati is an emblem titled "Matrimonium" showing a woman indoors, fully clothed, and identified as Venus, with her foot on a tortoise. Its motto is "A woman's reputation, not her beauty, should be known to the world," and the accompanying poem explains that the Greek artist Phidias fashioned Venus this way to teach that women should stay at home and keep silence."[22] But if you are a man, according to an English emblem from Thomas Combes's *Theater of Fine Devices* (1614),[23] the tortoise represents your shield of virtue, which will protect you from the stings of fortune wherever you go.

The tortoise appears in sixteenth- and seventeenth-century paintings and engravings of Adam and Eve before the Fall to assure us that they were happily married, though some interpreters might add "as long as Eve kept silent." An illustration by Adrien van de Venne to a work by Milton's Dutch acquaintance Jacob Cats (1643) clearly makes domesticity the central virtue.[24] The tortoise is also prominent in Jan Theodore de Bry's illustration to Du Bartas (Plate 10) and Nicolaes de Bruyn's *Orpheus Playing to the Animals* (Plate 8) and present in the conjugal life of Adam and Eve after the Fall in Jan Sadeler's *The Family of Adam*.[25]

The turning point from primary interest in allegory to primary interest in the animal itself may be seen in the *Historia Animalium* of the Swiss natural historian Konrad Gesner,[26] translated and amplified by Edward Topsell in 1607.[27] Gesner combines ancient lore, especially Pliny's, with new observations, and comments that "the tortoise fights vipers and serpents,"[28] perhaps another reason why it appears so prominently with Adam and Eve. Topsell's English version of 1607 poses the riddle: "although I am mute or dumb, yet do I make many voices"; Jubal's "corded shell," as Dryden writes in "A Song for St. Cecilia's Day" (1687), was thought to be the first musical instrument. Topsell shows how tortoises have been coveted since ancient times, "especially of their cover or shell, and likewise of their flesh . . . . the ancient ornament of Beds, Chambers, Tables, and Banquetting houses . . . called Carvilius . . . was framed in gold and silver, brasse and wood, Ivory and Tortoise-shels; . . . Ryot [that is, excess] . . . caused Tortoise-shells to be deerly bought, and thereof also complained the Poet Juvenal."[29]

---

22 Alciati, *Emblemata*, Lyons, 1550.

23 Thomas Combes, *The Theater of Fine Devices*, emblem XXVIII.

24 I have reproduced this image in both *Milton's Eve* and *A Gust for Paradise*.

25 Reproduced in McColley, *A Gust for Paradise*, fig. 20.

26 Gesner, *Historiae Animalium Liber* 2.

27 Topsell, *The Historie of Foure-Footed Beastes* and *The History of Serpents*; the tortoise in Gesner is in Book 2, Oviparous Quadrupeds, but in Topsell is in *Serpents*.

28 Gesner, Book 2: "Testudo contra viperas & serpentes pugnat," 168.

29 Topsell, *History of Serpents* (1658) 796 and 795; Dryden, "A Song for St. Cecilia's Day," 1687, l.17.

In Juvenal's Eleventh Satire the speaker invites a guest to feast on wild asparagus and eggs fresh from the nest with straws still stuck to the shells, and praises simpler times when "No one . . . thought it of any importance / What kind of tortoise shell swam in the waves of the ocean, / Destined to prop up the pates of our noblemen," for "couches used to be small, their sides unadorned," and everything was "perfectly simple, / Furniture, household, and food."[30] Vergil, commending the simple life in the *Georgics*, mentions the arrogance of doors "inlaid with varied tortoiseshell."[31] Topsell also reports a newly discovered culture for which tortoises provide food, roofs, and row boats, and adds that the sea-tortoises "eyes are most clear and splendent, casting their beams far and near, and also they are of white color, so that for their brightness and rare whiteness, the Apples are taken out and included in Rings, Chains, and Bracelets."[32]

Most writers of global exploration—unsurprisingly in an era of long voyages and no refrigeration—thought of most non-human flesh as food. Thomas Harriot, the historian of Sir Walter Raleigh's Roanoke expedition, notes "there are many Tortoyses both of lande and sea kinde . . . their head, feete, and taile . . . seeme ougly as though thy were . . . venemous: but notwithstanding they are very good meate."[33]

Du Bartas in his *Devine Weekes*, in Joshua Sylvestre's translation of 1611, revels in the variety of sea life but values the tortoise for its usefulness:

> The *Tyrian* Marchant, or the *Portuguez*
> Can hardly build one Ship of many Trees:
> But of one Tortoise, when he list to float,
> Th'Arabian Fisher-man can make a Boat.
> And one such shell, him in the stead doth stand
> Of Hulk at Sea, and of a House on land.[34]

As global exploration sought commodities and natural historians sought knowledge, they also sought an objective and utilitarian language. Among the binomial categories of John Wilkins' *Essay* of 1668 tortoises are in the first category of oviparous animals and their "progressive motion" is "Gradient; having four feet; the figure of their bodies being . . . Broad; whose outward covering is . . . Crustaceous; belonging either to the Land: or to the Water."[35] But writers increasingly observed this animal with respect and affection.

When Andrew Marvell unfavorably compares owners of showy houses to tortoises, "who dwell / In cases fit of tortoise shell",[36] he declares that the fit uses of tortoise shells are to house tortoises and teach human beings to live with proportional fitness. *Paradise Lost* (both 1667 and 1674) dignifies the tortoise's genus when God

---

30 Juvenal, *The Satires of Juvenal*, 138–9.
31 Vergil, *Georgics* 2.462–3, trans. L.P. Wilkinson.
32 *History of Serpents* (1658 edition), 795–6.
33 Harriot, *A briefe and true report of the new found land of Virginia*, 21.
34 Sylvester, *Du Bartas His Deuine Weekes and Workes Translated*, 116.
35 Wilkins, *Essay* (1668), 161.
36 Marvell, *Upon Appleton House*, stanza 2.

begins the creation of animal life with words "let the Waters generate / Reptil with Spawn abundant, living Soule."

John Evelyn writes to the Royal Society in 1684 with perhaps a touch of sorrow,

> My *Tortoise*, which by his constant burying himself in the Earth at approach of Winter I look upon as a kind of *Plant-Animal*, happening to be obstructed by Vine-root, from mining to the depth, he was usually wont to interr, is found stark dead, after having many years escaped the severest Winter.[37]

Nehemiah Grew's entry on tortoises, in his catalogue of the Museum of the Royal Society of London in 1685, consists mostly of measurements and uses, some quite brutal, though with a flicker of pity and perhaps envy: "In Generation, the embraces of the Male and Female continue for a whole Lunary month. [Men] take them, by turning them on their Backs with staves, in which posture they lie, till they are fetch'd away. As they lie on their Backs, they will sometimes fetch deep sighs, and shed abundance of Tears. They kill them, by laying them on their backs, and so ripping them up round about where the Back and Belly-pieces meet. The flesh hereof maketh a most pleasant jelly. . . . the Belly-part . . . , baked, is an excellent Dish. . . . The Legs. . . are a most experienced Remedy in Gout."[38] The catalogue's illustration of empty tortoise shells shows what became of most *chelonia* who encountered homo sapiens.

Thomas Heyrick's poem of 1691 remarks on sea tortoises' instinctive navigation as they

> Do with unwearied Feet repair
> Unto the Place, where they were bred,
> Or where before their Eggs they laid;
>
> And without Guide, but Nature being their Friend,
> Thro devious ways are without Pole-star led:
>   And upon barren Desolate Isles,
>   They stupidly unto the Care
> Of Hatching Sands their shelly Brood commend,
> Or to the Sun's auspicious Smiles.[39]

Turtle migration is still a mystery to evolutionary scientists like Stephan Jay Gould. Having rejected various theories, Gould concludes, "While the world's best scientists struggled to invent the tools of navigation, *Chelonia* looked at the skies and proceeded on course."[40]

---

37 Evelyn, "An Abstract of a Letter," in *Philosophical Transactions of the Royal Society of London* 14 (1684): 559–63.

38 Grew, *Musaeum Regalis Societatis*, 39.

39 Thomas Heyrick. *Miscellany Poems* (1691): "The Submarine Voyage," 37. "Stupidly" may mean indifferently.

40 Gould, *The Panda's Thumb* (New York and London: W.W. Norton, 1980), 30–34.

Empirical observation was beginning to produce varied opinions of turtle perception and even intelligence. For John Ray, in 1691, the behavior of the Sea-Tortoise seems "to argue something of Reason, in him, and more than a bare Instinct" because rather than sinking to escape being caught, "by a wonderful Sagacity and Caution [he] dares not let the Air out of his Lungs . . . because he fears that his Shell being wet, it should become so heavy, that he . . . might never have power to reascend. If this may be the reason why he exposes himself to the danger of being taken . . . it is clear, that he is endued with an admirable Providence and Foresight, and a Power of Argumentation."[41]

The trend continues: in the early eighteenth century, Marc Catesby depicted a truly speaking likeness of a sea turtle covering her eggs; Christopher Smart in *Jubilate Agno* bids "Let Elihu bless with the Tortoise, which is food for praise and thanksgiving," though in the Hebrew Bible the tortoise is an unclean beast[42]; Gilbert White in *The Natural History of Selborne* reports watching a neighbor's tortoise dig its "hybernaculum" with a slowness "suitable to the composure of an animal said to be a whole month in performing one feat of copulation," and becomes "much taken with its sagacity," for it "distinguishes the hand that feeds it, and is touched with feelings of gratitude" (140).[43]

Living soul: The animal creation

Probably the most frequently represented topics of human beings and other beings together in the visual arts, partly because of their frequency in illustrated bibles, are from the story of Adam and Eve (Plate 10 being an example); and the major English poem that draws them most fully and closely together is *Paradise Lost*.

Unlike Bacon's intention of empire over nature, Wilkins' ark of static taxonomy, and the Tradescants' Ark of dried parts, Milton, in part through mimetic prosody, draws us into sensuous and muscular sympathy with other creatures. As Adam and Eve rest after gardening, the description of the animals that "frisking played" before them reports their perceptions and engages ours by rhythmically recreating the rearing and gamboling animals in energetic trochaic and dactylic accents;

> Sporting the lion ramped, and in his paw
> Dandled the kid; bears, tigers, ounces, pards
> Gambolled before them.

Pronouncing "th'unwieldy elephant, / To make them mirth used all his might, and wreathed / His lithe proboscis" causes us to wreath our lips lithely and invites us to join the merriment and feel a kinetic kinship with the elephant.

John Wilkins's description appeals to mercantile interests and has no empathy for elephants:

---

41   Ray, *The Wisdom of God*, corrected 5th edition, 1709, 108–10.
42   Smart, *Jubilated Agno*, l.52.
43   White, *The Natural History of Selbourne*.

ELEPHANT, Ivory. Multifidous kind; having little prominencies at the end of the feet, representing toes, being of the greatest magnitude amongst all other beasts, used for the carriage and draught of great weights, and more particularly esteemed for tusks.[44]

Edward Topsell, after describing the elephant's intelligence, sociability, virtue, wisdom, piety, and benevolence as known from ancient times, describes an entertainment, familiar to Milton's audience from Roman history, that gives added poignancy to Milton's lines. "[H]is trunck called Proboscis and Promucis, is a large hollow thing hanging from his nose like skin to the groundward"; and "Their trunck or hand is most easie to be cut off," as was done "in the aedility or temple-office of Claudius, Antonius, and Posthumus being Consuls, and afterward in the Circus"; "when Pompey was Consul the second time . . . Gentulians fought with them with Spears and Darts" and a wounded soldier crept between the legs of an elephant to "cast up the Darts over his head into the beasts belly, which fell down round him, to the great pleasure of the beholders."[45] "Proboscis" might prompt readers to remember, in contrast to the harmless pleasures of Adam and Eve, the pain of Roman cruelty and compare the natural government of Adam and Eve to Roman tyranny over man and beast.

The language of Milton's creation poetry contrasts radically with both the allegorical tradition and descriptions by natural historians living under conditions that Genesis attributes to the Fall. Adam and Eve enjoy the companionship of animals "since of chace," hunted after the loss of innocence. But Milton does not consider innocence—not-nocence, non-toxicity—as something gone forever. He presents Eden not only as a paradise lost by the original sin but as an arena of original righteousness to be renewed: "the inner man is regenerated by God through the word and the spirit so that his whole mind is restored to the image of God, as if he were a new creature."[46] More than Bacon's Utopian academy,[47] Milton's Garden is what Spedding calls "our own world as it might be made if we did our duty by it."

The theology that makes all creatures different but kindred, seen in the Archangel Raphael's account of creation from "one first matter" (5.472), is supported by the same angel's empathetic narrative of the creation of the animals (7.387–498), which contrasts strikingly with collectors' catalogues, parts of John Ray's *The Ornithology of Francis Willughby* (1678; originally so called in tribute to Ray's friend who was working on it when he died), and Hakluyt's compendium of global exploration,[48] whose writers are largely concerned with the use of animals for food and fur.

---

44 Wilkins, *Essay towards a Real Character and a Philosophical Language* (1668), 156.

45 Topsell (1658), 153 and 161. For descriptions of elephants by English travelers such as Thomas Coryat, see M. G. Aune, "Elephants, Englishmen, and India."

46 Milton, *Christian Doctrine*, chapter 18, in *Complete Prose Works* 6:461.

47 In *Areopagitica* Milton objects to "Atlantic and Eutopian polities" (*Prose Works* 2:526). Barbara Lewalski interprets:" The fanciful utopias of Plato, Bacon, and More are, like sequestered virtue, useless" (*Life*, 194).

48 Richard Hakluyt, *Principal Navigations* (1589). I have discussed attitudes toward animals that Milton opposes in "Ecology and Empire," in Rajan and Sauer, eds, *Milton and the Imperial Vision,* 112–29.

Although John Ruskin's phrase "pathetic fallacy" concerns poetic integrity, it is popularly used to censure the projection of human sentiments onto beings unlikely to have them. Milton's language avoids such projection. The narrator angel describes fish and crustaceans, birds, and land animals from their own literal points or places of view and reenacts their actions through mimetic sound. Raphael's lack of anthropocentrism (or angelocentrism) and his sense of habitat are striking in both what he says and what he does not say. The animals of Eden are not selected for serviceability: lion, bear, tiger, ounce, pard, elephant, whale, crane, nightingale, swan, leopard, stag, hippopotamus, crocodile, ant, bee, and, more generically, reptile, cock, cattle, worm, and serpent. The latter is "Not noxious, but obedient at thy call" (7.498)—though we never hear such a command until Eve says "Lead, then" to a usurped serpent (9.631). Of this list, only bees might perform a direct service to Adam and Eve—though worms and animal manure improve the soil—and of animals that would later become domesticated or made beasts of burden, few are mentioned by name and none is subjected to their interference. Animals provide beauty, wisdom, innocent mirth, and delight in otherness to their human and angelic observers by being themselves. But neither are they chosen for obvious megafaunal attractiveness. Creatures great and small from reptile and oyster to ant and worm are generated by water or earth, and Milton's prosody helps us feel the experience of their bodies in their natural elements.

On the fifth day of creation,

> And God said, Let the waters generate
> Reptile with spawn abundant, living soul:
> And let fowl fly about the earth, with wings
> Displayed on the op'n firmament of heav'n.   [7.387–90]

"Displayed" (L. *displicare*, unfold, extend, open to view) calls attention to the act of perception itself, and also means to place with limbs extended (*Oxford English Dictionary*), as in a museum exhibit; Milton's fowl display their wings in the open sky, and such figures of freedom pervade Milton's description of the animal world as well as his hopes for the body politic. "Reptile"—creeping animals—as the first kind of "living soul" God's voice calls forth sheds its denigratory meanings. As we have seen, the sea tortoise is of particular interest as part of the debate about the intelligence of animals, in which Milton's God takes a strong position: "They also know, and reason not contemptibly" (8.373–4).[49]
Raphael's narrative continues:

> And God created the great whales, and each
> Soul living, each that crept, which plenteously
> The waters generated in their kinds,
> And every bird of wing after his kind;
> And saw that it was good, and blessed them, saying,
> Be fruitful, multiply, and in the seas

---

49   For an interesting account of this topic see Bruce Boehrer, "Milton and the Reasoning of Animals: Variations on a Theme by Plutarch."

And lakes and running streams the waters fill;
And let the fowl be multiplied upon the earth.

"And God created the great Whales" evokes the spacious and weighty consonance of the 1611 Genesis, and the close paraphrase reminds us that every creature was made, blessed, and found good by God, a refrain that did not permeate the early modern idea of "dominion." In Hakluyt's *Principal Navigations*, Edward Haies describes "Abundance of whales, for which also is a very great trade . . . where is made Trane oils of the whale."[50] Grew lists whales and manatees among "Viviparous Fishes" and notes that whales produce whale-bone "which Taylors in Denmark use in making of Cloaths" and "In I[ce]land they are so commonly taken, That the hard Bones are there used for the impaling of Houses and Gardens."[51] In the eighteenth century, the Royal Society took an interest in building a better harpoon.

Milton's version of the generation of the waters onomatopoetically incorporates kinetic, sensuous, and conceptual mimicry:

Forthwith the sounds and seas, each creek and bay
With fry innumerable swarm, and shoals
Of Fish that with their fins and shining scales
Glide under the green wave, in schools that oft
Bank in the mid sea: part single or with mate
Graze the sea-weed their pasture, and through groves
Of coral stray, or sporting with quick glance
Show to the sun their waved coats dropped with Gold,
Or in their pearly shells at ease, attend
Moist nutriment, or under rocks their food
In jointed armour watch: on smooth the seal,
And bended dolphins play: part huge of bulk
Wallowing unwieldy, enormous in thir gait
Tempest the ocean: there Leviathan
Hugest of living creatures, on the deep
Stretched like a promontory sleeps or swims,
And seems a moving land, and at his gills
Draws in, and at his trunk spouts out a Sea.   [7.387–416]

Even though "sounds" turns out to be a feature of marine geography, it alerts us to Raphael's virtuosic display of sounds, and by similar wordplay "glance" alerts us to sight, "Graze" to touch, and "part" to motion, for the caesura mimes "part" meaning separate, while the sense is "a portion." While alerting both the senses and the wits by these syntactic puns, Milton uses sound to connect our senses and wits with the design of the creatures and their elements. Alliterations mime the sounds of seas and swishing fish. At "schools that oft / Bank the mid Sea" Milton imitates those amazingly simultaneous turns in the flick of his enjambment, and "on the Deep / Stretched" stretches across the lines. The pause, or rest, of "at ease, attend" suspends

---

50 Haies, in Hakluyt, *Principal Navigations*, 689. Trane or train-oil was pressed from animal fat and used for soap and lamp-oil.

51 Grew cites the Museum Romanum.

the verse to attend the conclusion in the next line. "Fry innumerable swarm" stirs with fricatives and labials while "Glide under the green Wave" employs a gliding tongue. One can scarcely read "sporting with quick glance" without speeding up, nor "wallowing unwieldy" without slowing down, feeling enormity on our lips. When "part of huge bulk / Wallowing unwieldly, enormous in thir Gait, / Tempest the Ocean," Leviathan springs dangerously alive, while the passage rhythmically allies him to our own breath when he "at his Gills / Draws in, and at his Trunk spouts out a Sea."

Raphael sees "the Seal, / And bended Dolphins play." Thomas Candish in Hakluyt's *Voyages* reports that "Seales are. . . monstrous of shape" and give "their yong milke," with no sympathy for fellow mammals: "their yong are marveillous good meat."[52] John Hawkins describes "Dolphins which are of very goodly colour and proportion to beholde, and no lesse delicate in taste." Among other sea and riparian animals, Thomas Harriot's "Marchantable Commodities" of furs and hides include "Otters, which being taken by weires and other engines made for the purpose, wil yeeld good profit." One kind of language promotes delight; the other, when taken beyond the needs of human survival, promotes extinction.

An ordinary lark net: Ornithological poetics

At the creation of the birds, Milton's understanding of wetlands as breeding grounds takes ecological and social resonance from the project of draining the fens. He imagines the experience of parent birds as their naked young emerge from their shells, and recreates their perspective and sensations in flight.

> Meanwhile the tepid caves, and fens and shores
> Their brood as numerous hatch, from the egg that soon
> Bursting with kindly rupture forth disclosed
> Their callow young, but feathered soon and fledge
> They summed their pens, and soaring th' air sublime
> With clang despised the ground, under a cloud
> In prospect; there the eagle and the stork
> On cliffs and cedar tops their eyries build:
> Part loosely wing the region, part more wise
> In common, ranged in figure wedge their way,
> Intelligent of seasons, and set forth
> Their airy caravan high over seas
> Flying, and over lands with mutual wing
> Easing their flight; so steers the prudent crane
> Her annual voyage, borne on winds; the air
> Floats, as they pass, fanned with unnumbered plumes.   [7.417–32]

When the shorebirds hatch their numerous brood, the energy produced by the trochaic reversal on "Bursting," the double meaning of "kindly rupture"—according

---

52 Candish (Cavendish), in Hakluyt, *Voyages, Navigations, Traffiques, and Discoveries of the English Nation* 3 (1600): 805.

to kind, as well as merciful—and the pun on "disclos'd" let us share the moment of liberation for the young and recognition by the parents, and "callow," literally meaning unfledged, shows their vulnerability and the humorous sympathy of the fully fledged angel-narrator. When the fledglings "summ'd thir Pens, and soaring th'air sublime / With clang despis'd [literally, looked down on] the ground, under a cloud / In prospect," Raphael gives Adam and Eve the birds' point of view, even to the clang, or resonant sound, by which flocks keep together, and the "prospect" or seeing ahead (with a verbal glance ahead to the prudence of the crane). When they set forth in wise commonality "the Air / Floats, as they pass, fanned with unnumber'd plumes"[53] and the airy assonance and the alliteration of fricatives make us feel the sensation of flight while giving us a tiny lesson in aerodynamics. At the same time "Unnumbered plumes" may raise the image of an army with plumes on their helmets as signs of victory or conquest, a use of birds' bodies that sums the "pens" of human vanity and violence.

Milton's "prudent crane" may have been suggested by Pliny, who claims for cranes prudence both practical and political: they begin their long migrations with "a counsell called before, and a generall consent. They fly aloft, because they would have a better prospect to see before them, and for this purpose a captain they chuse to guide them, whom the rest follow. In the rereward behind there be certaine of them set and disposed to give signall by their manner of crie, for to raunge orderly in rankes, and keep close together in array [Milton's "clang"]: and this they do by turnes each one in this course."[54]

The *Ornithology* of Willughby and Ray describes the crane with a different emphasis: "But that which is most rare, and especially remarkable, yea, wonderful in this bird, is the conformation of the Wind-pipe. . . . The flesh is very savoury and well-tasted, not to say delicate."[55]

Milton's language is especially playful at "sum their pens," gather their pinions for flight, lightly reminding us of one of the things our species—and Milton's amanuensis at that very moment of composing—used birds' feathers for. When they fan these plumes, the fricatives let us hear what the birds hear and feel. We may think of the arithmeticians of nature and commerce who pen their sums—the draining of the fens caused much penning intended to prove its benefits—and anatomists writing diagrams on the wings of birds and numbering their dissected parts [Plate 9] and the swishy scratch of quill on paper as the blind bard dictates his words. "Unnumbered" is also a pun about writing, meaning unmetrical; Adam and Eve pray in "prose or numerousl verse" (5.150), and Milton calls his verses "harmonious Numbers" (3.38).

John Wilkins' classification defined birds as animals "which have two leggs and two wings, whose bodies are covered with feathers, being oviparous, whose proper motion is flying."[56] The engraved illustration to Job 12.7 (Plate 9), in which

---

53 Angels, too, are "unnumbered."

54 Pliny, *The Historie of the World*, trans. Holland (1634), 281.

55 Ray, *Ornithology*, 274.

56 Wilkins, *Essay*, 121. In spite of his claim to objectivity, Wilkins divides them into "more elegant and beautiful" (the peacock) and "less beautiful" (the turkey), 148.

Job advises his friends to "ask . . . the fowls of the air, and they shall tell thee," incorporates the new natural history. Job sits by an estuary contemplating the birds, the four winds and the water acknowledging habitat, while the divine light startles a shorebird who is not the Holy Spirit yet reminds the viewer of that person of the Trinity who broods upon the waters in Genesis and hatches life. Measuring devices, diagrams showing motion of wings and head, and a row of quills and bones suggest that the wisdom of God is manifested in accurate empirical observation—these plumes are numbered. Catalogues like Nehemiah Grew's consisted very largely of numbers, measurement being the safest mode of description. Milton's "Unnumbered plumes" suggests the differences between classification and birds in flight.

Milton's description of the swan may be compared with a statement in the chapter on words in John Locke's *Essay Concerning the Understanding* (1671). In *Paradise Lost* water fowl

> on silver lakes and rivers bathed
> Their downy breast; the swan with archèd neck
> Between her white wings mantling proudly, rows
> Her state with oary feet: yet oft they quit
> The dank, and rising on stiff pennons, tower
> The mid-aerial sky: others on ground walked firm . . . . [7.437–43]

According to Locke's 1671 draft,

> the idea which an Englishman signifies by the name swan is white colour, long neck, red beak, black legs, whole feet, with a power of swimming in the water, and making a certain kind of noise, and perhaps, to a man who has long observed those kind of birds, some other properties, which all terminate in sensible simple ideas.[57]

In Milton's description, instead of a blazon of body parts we see the actions of arching, mantling, rowing, quitting, rising, and towering, many gaining propulsion by being placed at the end of enjambed lines, all self-activating, done at the swan's own choice. "State" confers dignity: she rows as on a royal progress, without ornament or expense,[58] and we are made aware of what she is aware of and we may not perceive, the movement of "her oary feet."

Milton's birds that "on ground / walked firm" (with an imitative spondaic foot) are cock and peacock. In the wild, such birds are especially vulnerable to human captors. In Hakluyt, Haies describes "Partridges most plentiful . . . which our men . . . did kill with cudgels, they were so fat and unable to flie," and David Ingram says that penguins "are of the shape and bignesse of a Goose . . . and cannot flie: You may drive them before you like sheepe: They are exceeding fatte and very delicate meate." Similarly the dodo, according to the *Ornithology*, is "a slow-paced and stupid bird, . . . which easily becomes a prey to the Fowlers"; Bontius reports that "The flesh, especially of the Breast, is fat, esculent, and so copious, that three or four

---

57 Locke, *An Essay Concerning the Understanding*, ed. Rand, 128.

58 In England swans belong to the monarch, and so were protected. (American trumpeter swans were hunted nearly to extinction for powder puffs.)

Dodos will sometimes suffice to fill an hundred Seamens bellies." The authors report "a Leg thereof cut off at the knee" residing in Leyden and saw the dodo "dried, or its skin stuffed, in Tradescants Cabinet."[59]

Next in Milton's catalogue come the birds most beloved of poets, their fellow singers, their emblems, and often their figures for freedom.

> From branch to branch the smaller birds with song
> Solaced the woods, and spread their painted wings
> Till ev'n, nor then the solemn nightingale
> Ceased warbling, but all night tuned her soft lays.   [433–6]

Three "smaller birds," two of song and one of "painted wings" more newly discovered, have special associations with the arts, so that ornithologists' and poets' ways of speaking about them offer striking comparisons: the lark, the nightingale, and—since all species dwelt in Eden—the hummingbird.

The plight of the "smaller birds" in Milton's time may be seen in the *Ornithology*. Ray as an observer of the way things fit together is ultimately a hero of this story. Keith Thomas calls Ray and Willughby "the first English naturalists to emancipate themselves explicitly from the emblematic tradition," a service to poetry as well as the development of ecological thought, and points out that Ray's work on fossils undermined the assumption that all creatures were made for human use.[60] Clarence Glacken calls Ray's *The Wisdom of God Manifested in the Works of Creation* (1692) "probably the best natural theology ever written." He quotes Ernst Cassirer's observation that the "Cambridge Platonists wish to look upon nature as plastic rather than mechanical, proceeding from the whole to the parts, and show how the one original vital force governing nature is infinitely exemplified, yet not lost," and finds that Ray "in turning to Cudworth divorced himself from the doctrine, stressed by Bacon, that final causes have no place in science"—that is, science can not suppose a God-given teleology. This turning "represented . . . an insistence on the unique qualities of life, a rejection of the idea that life processes were like those of a machine, an impatience with the crudities in Descartes's ideas of universal physiology. For to him they were nothing more than machines."[61]

With this conversion in mind, we can observe without malice that in the *Ornithology* Ray sets a tone not entirely attributable to Willughby by appending—at the beginning —*An Epitome of the Art of Fowling*, culled "partly out of Olina's *Uccelleraia* but mostly out of Gervase Markham, *Hungers prevention*," with illustrations. Hunger must be taken into account; but Ray (or Olina) depicts fowling as a sport or an exercise in commercial songbird-herding. In "How they take Birds in Italy by night" he writes "This sport is most used in the Champain of Rome. The Net is of the Mash of an ordinary Lark-net" (Plate 7). Instructions follow for making the net and a lantern with which "they also search bushes, hedges, and low trees, where they think Thrushes and other Birds pearch, and having discovered them, strike them down with an Instrument called Ramata, made like a Racket with a long handle, or

---

59 Ray, *Ornithology*, 154.
60 Thomas, *Man and the Natural World*, 67 and 168.
61 Glacken, *Traces on the Rhodian Shore*, 379, 393–4; Cassirer, *The Platonic Renaissance*, 51.

if they be out of reach of that, shoot them with a Cross-bow." (The engraving shows two men: one with a long-handled scoop-shaped net and the lantern, open on one side, and the other with a gun, approaching a huddle of small birds.) In "How to take Larks with Nets, called by the Italians Pantiere," we are told how to set up a net on stakes "two hours before Sun-set, for the Evening-driving; and for the Morning driving, before break of day; in stubble-fields":

> About a Musket-shot from the nets two men on foot holding a rope of twenty or twenty five yards long, one at one end, the other at the other, must begin and walk towards the Nets, drawing the Rope over the stubble, and so raising the Larks that lie scatterd up and down the field: the which will not take wing, but run forward before the rope, till at last they come within the Nets, which being not stretched out streight, but easily running up, the more they struggle and fly about, the more they are entangled. [62]

Ben Jonson in "Inviting a Friend to Supper" entices his guest with them: "And though fowl now be scarce, yet there are clerks, / The sky not falling, think we may have larks."[63] But Abraham Cowley laments human violence to song birds, who like other poets get no reward for their music; indeed "Tis well if they become not prey";[64] and in Margaret Cavendish's "Dialogue of Birds" the larks complain that men "luxuriously us eate, till they be fill'd: / And of our Flesh they make such cruell wast, / That but some of our Limbes will please their tast," though "The smaller Lark they eate all at one bite."[65]

In Milton's *L'Allegro*, the sprightly speaker rises

> To hear the lark begin his flight,
> And singing startle the dull night,
> From his watch-tower in the skies,
> Till the dappled dawn doth rise;
> Then to come in spite of sorrow,
> And at my window bid good morrow,
> Through the sweet-briar, or the vine,
> Or the twisted eglantine.   [410–48]

One might recall Jules Breton's painting "The Song of the Lark"[66] in which a girl with a scyth stands struck to the soul with its song; or Shelley's blithe spirit pouring "thy full heart / In profuse strains of unpremeditated art"; or Daffyd ap Gwilym's description of "The world's early riser, a boiling of gold song / Towards the sky,"

---

62 Ray, *Ornithology,* 35–6, 39; engraving, unnumbered, at end of volume.

63 Jonson, "Inviting a Friend to Supper," in *Complete Poems.*

64 Cowley, "The Garden" ("Essay" to John Evelyn), in *Works,* 117.

65 Cavendish, *Poems and Fancies,* 70–75. Knightley and Madge in *Pocket Guide to the Birds of Britain* estimate a decrease in skylarks from 25 million birds in 1990 to 2,500,000 pairs in 1998.

66 Breton, oil on canvas, 1884, The Art Institute of Chicago, cat. no. 1894.1033.

or Hopkins's "Caged Skylark" who needs for song "his own nest, wild nest, no prison."[67]

Poets have long taken nightingales as sharers of both their art and their need for freedom: an emblematic yet sympathetic and observant affinity. Milton invokes one in his first sonnet, and in the epic sings in his blindness and exile "Nightly," as "the wakeful bird / Sings darkling, and in shadiest covert hid / Tunes her nocturnal note"(3.38–40). When Adam leads Eve to their nuptial bower, Adam says, "the amorous bird of night / Sung spousal" (8.518–19). Ann Finch tells the nightingale:

Poets, wild as thee, were born,
Pleasing best when unconfine'd,
When to Please is least design'd,
Soothing but their cares to rest;
Cares do still their Thoughts molest,
And still th' unhappy Poet's Breast,
Like thine, when best he sings, is plac'd against a Thorn.[68]

In Richard Crashaw's "Music's Duel" musician and nightingale meet "art with art" until the nightingale falls dead on the musician's lute, a poignant outcome consonant with the fate of other avian musicians.

The nightingale, says the *Ornithology*, is "the chief of all singing birds . . . The Guts are about ten inches long." Ray has a fine passage on the beauty of the nightingales' song, taken from Pliny, and a great deal of advice on how to capture them, largely out of Olina, and on cages, diseases, and "How to provoke a Nightingale to sing." He instructs those trying to find and capture a nest of nightingales to "put meal-worms on a thorn and see where the cock carries them." Further, "To take old nightingales, make a Trap-age or Net-trap baited with worms or maggots. Tie the tips of his wings with some brown thread, not straining it too hard, that he may not have strength to beat himself against the top and wires of the Cage."[69]

Marvell's description of the Nunappleton nightingale emphatically puts the bird in her chosen habitat: birds and poets need freedom, and kings, represented by oaks, and councils, represented by elders, should listen to them.

The nightingale does *here* make choice
To sing the trials of her voice.
Low shrubs she sits in, and adorns
With music high the squatted thorns.
But highest oaks stoop down to hear,
And listening elders prick the ear.
The thorn, lest it should hurt her, draws
Within the skin its shrunken claws. [stanza 65, italics mine]

67 Daffyd ap Gwilym, "The Skylark," in *Poems*, trans. Richard Morgan Loomis; Hopkins, *Poems*, 70–71.

68 Finch, "To the Nightingale," in *The Poems of Anne Countess of Winchilsea*.

69 Ray, *Ornithology*, 220–27.

The *Ornithology* takes a description of the "Humming Bird or Tomineio" from Josephus à Costa's *Natural and Moral History of the West Indies*. The Tomineo is so called "perchance because it is so light, that it weighs only one Spanish Tomino, that is, twelve grains." It is also called "Ourissia, (that is, a Sun-beam)," and is in size "the least of all birds." This description apparently inspired Thomas Heyrick's "On an Indian Tomineios, the Least of Birds," in which the hummingbird speaks for itself: "The Indians me a sunbeam name, / And I may be the child of one: / . . . And, like a sunbeam from the sky, I can't be followed by the quickest eye. . . ."

> I'm the true bird of paradise,
>   And heavenly dew's my only meat:
> My mouth so small, 'twill nothing else admit.
>   No scales know how my weight to poise,
>   So light, I seem condensèd air;
> And did at the end of the creation rise,
>   When nature wanted more supplies,
>   When she could little matter spare,
> But in return did make the work more rare.

The poem's moral is that the same hand made all things, expressed with an appropriately light touch. The *Ornithology* adds that this "least of all birds" is "nourished with honey, dew, and the juice of flowers, which it sucks out with its bill . . . so that, being taken alive, they cannot be kept for want of food, but die in a short time." The most elegant of the nine kinds has a head and neck that shine "as if a Rubine were illustrated by the Sun-beams: But the Throat and underside of the Neck do resemble pure, polished, Hungarian gold, shone upon by the Sun-beams." And "Of the feathers of these and other birds of beautiful colours the Indians make the likenesses (for Pictures we must not call them) of Saints, and other things so dextrously and artificially, and to the life that one would think they were drawn with a Pencil in colours, of which we have seen many in the Cabinets of the Virtuosi."[70]

John Evelyn saw a collection of rarities in Oxford at the "Anatomy School" that had "a prodigious large parrot" and "two humming birds, not much bigger than our humble-bee, which indeed I had not seen before, that I remember."[71] Grew's entry on the "huming Bird" in the catalogue of the Royal Society's Museum draws from Clusius and de Laet out of Lerius, "as he from Oviedus" (61), Marggravius, Thevetus, Linschot, and Piso, many of whom are also cited in the *Ornithology*. "The Huming-Bird is every where ill pictur'd," Grew complains, "even in Mr. Willughby, for want of the bird it self"; and certainly among the *Ornithology*'s illustrations the lively "Tomineio" (TAB XLII) looks especially enervated. Grew confirms that "His Feathers are set in Gold by Embroydorors, and sold at a great rate. The Indians make of them very artificial Images. They take them by mazing them with Sand shot at them out of a Gun." By his count "one of them with its Neast weighs but two Tomino's," that is, 24 grains altogether, a grain being the weight of a dried grain

---

70 Ray, *Ornithology*, 230. "Pictures" would suggest icons.
71 Evelyn, *Diary* 2:78

of wheat (*Oxford English Dictionary*).[72] Even the arithmetical Mr. Grew does not calculate the weight of the feathers if you remove the nest and the bird, or tell how many hummingbirds must be stunned and plucked for an embroidered cloak or a splendidly artificial image.

As noted before, Marvell's speaker in his old-growth forest, who knows each leaf individually, makes one of his lightly mordant comparisons:

Out of these scatter'd sibyl's leaves
Strange prophecies my fancy weaves:
And in one history consumes,
Like Mexique paintings, all the plumes.

"Mexique paintings" are among things that Bacon in *Sylva Sylvarum* commends that "work upon the Spirits of Man by secret Sympathy and Antipathy "including "The Pictures of Indian Feathers" as "comfortable and pleasant to behold."[73] Bacon has no compassion for individual hummingbirds and no conception that the ornamental and commercial use of feathers could extinguish species. Marvell knew that such uses can consume "all the plumes."

Clods now calved

At the creation of land animals in *Paradise Lost*,

The grassy clods now calved, now half appeared
The tawny lion, pawing to get free
His hinder parts, then springs as broke from bonds,
And rampant shakes his brinded main; the ounce,
The libbard and the tiger, as the mole
Rising, the crumbled earth above them threw
In hillocks; the swift stag from under ground
Bore up his branching head: scarce from his mould
Behemoth biggest born of earth upheaved
His vastness; fleeced the flocks and bleating rose,
As plants: ambiguous between sea and land
The river-horse and scaly crocodile.   [7.468–74]

When "clods . . . calve" the alliteration concurs with the relatedness of earth and offspring. The lion's rupture from earth, like the bird's from its shell, is a struggle and liberation we feel in the syntax as it delays and then leaps into swifter syllables, and the enjambments at "free / His hinder parts," "mole / Rising,"[74] "from under ground / Bore up" and the weightily alliterated "Behemoth biggest born. . . upheaved / His

---

72 Grew, *Musaeum Regalis Societatis*, 62.

73 Bacon, *Sylva Sylvarum*, in *Works* 2:661. Ray commends paintings made of the feathers of hummingbirds and other birds (*Ornithology*, 232).

74 The mole is a significant example in both Henry More's *Antidote against Atheism* and Ray's *Wisdom of God*, which asks "What more palpable Argument of Providence than she?" (1692, 131).

vastness" also reproduce this sense of struggle and liberation: Milton mimes the birth of the animals as consonant with his politics and theology. The land mammals emerge from Earth's "fertile Womb" as "perfet forms . . . As from his Lair the wild Beast where he wons / In Forest wild . . . Among the trees in Pairs they rose, they walk'd"; when the "Tawny Lion, pawing to get free / His hinder parts, then springs as broke from Bonds, / And Rampant shakes his Brinded main," the syntax lets us share his accomplishment. Harriot, however, tells us that "The inhabitants sometimes kill the [new world] Lyon and eat him" and some of his company have tasted wolves.[75] The flocks that rise "As plants" may give us pause. Is Milton thinking of the "vegetable lamb" that some believed Adam and Eve must have used for meat?[76] Grew's account of the similarities between plants and animals had not been published, but the fancy of fleecy flocks rising from their fields like the grass they feed on again calls attention to the generative earth and the natural habitats of her offspring.

Richard Bentley supposes that repetitions underlining the vitality of the wild are editorial errors or unauthorized interpolations.

> V. 458. *The Wildbeast where he wons In Forest wild.*] The *wild* Beast
> in the *wild* Forest? miserable Jejunity! The Author gave it,
> *The Wildbeast where he wons In Forest* WIDE.

Because he thinks a good poet would not use the same word twice in one sentence, Bentley misses the point about the connection between the Wildbeast and the wild forest; and the wildness of both, though harmless in Eden, perhaps disturbs his managerial mind.

> V. 463. *The grassie Clods now calv'd, &c.*] Here we are come to a whole Dozen of Verses, which are demonstrably an Insertion of the Editor's, without the Poet's knowledge. I shal first join together the Lines that are genuine; and their Connexion will appear so inseparable, that the Lines intermediate must be voted spurious; though they were as elegant, as they'll be found silly. He had spoke of the Generations of Beast, both Wild and Tame:

> > *Those rare and solitary, These in flocks*
> > *Pasturing, at once and in broad herds, up sprang:*
> > *At once came forth whatever creeps the ground,*
> > *Insect or worm.*

> Let anyone, either gifted with Poetry, or conversant in good Poets, determine; if this Repetition, At once, At once, did not follow thus close . . . nothing intervening. And now let's examine what the Editor would palm upon us. . . .

> > *The grassy Clods now calv'd.*

> *Calv'd* is a Metaphor very heroical, especially for wild Beasts. But had not the Author express'd it, and much better, before?

---

75 Hakluyt, *The Principal Navigations*, 542 (Hawkins), 751 (Harriot), 689 (Haies), 560 (Ingram), 757 (Harriot).

76 See Karen Edwards, *Milton and the Natural World*, 122–4.

> *The Earth obey'd, and straight*
> *Op'ning her fertil Womb teem'd at a birth.*

Would a Man, that had once said *Teem'd*, have doubled and polluted it with *Calv'd?* He goes on, *the Lion pawing to get forth his hinder parts.* The poor Lion stuck fast in the Passage: he was form'd, it seems, in the Earth, without any Cavity for him. And his Hinder parts being much thinner than his Foreparts: if these were once out, he needed not to paw and struggle to free *the Hinder* ones, which could not possibly stick at all.[77]

Bentley cannot accept the idea that Earth is in some sense all womb, and brings forth living things from her own substance; nor that her "calves" could participate in their own emergence.[78] Henry More, more akin to Milton's vitalism, thinks that plants and animals were the generations or productions of the Earth, "the Seminal Forms and Souls of Animals insinuating themselves into the prepared matter thereof, and Suns, Planets, or Earths were the generations or productions of the Heavens, vigour and motion being imparted from the world of Life to the immense body of the Universe."[79] For Milton, Earth, like woman, is not merely a vessel. Earth's womb is the soil in and from which lives are formed, and animals' energies are self-activated in the process of emergence.

Milton's version of the creation of the large animals begins with the whale and ends with the elephant (behemoth), the hippopotamus, and the crocodile. These were the four candidates for "Behemoth" and "Leviathan" in the Book of Job, that resounding retort to those who interpreted the warrant of dominion in Genesis to mean that all of nature could be subdued. By Milton's time it had become clear that these two creatures were not the tamable elephant and non-aggressive whale but the hippopotamus and the crocodile: in Job's time neither tamable nor endangered, in Milton's noted for ferocity but already exploited. According to Grew's catalogue the royal museum contained the skull of a hippopotamus, "which in the Book of Job is called BEHEMOTH; as is solidly proved by Brochart, in his Hierozoican. He is almost every where described very falsely." As to his uses, "Rings made of his Teeth, are believed to be very effectual against the Cramp. Those that sell Artificial Teeth, usually make them of the long Teeth of this Animal, as being supposed the best for this purpose."[80]

The Voice from the Whirlwind in Job brings down the pride of man by the strength and virility of Behemoth: "Behold now behemoth, which I made with thee; he eateth grass as an ox. Lo now, his strength is in his loins, and his force is in the navel of his belly. He moveth his tail like a cedar: the sinews of his stones are wrapped together" (Job 40.15–17). Grew describes "A PISLE said to be that of the HIPPOPOTAMUS. . . . 'Tis in length, above a foot. The Glans even now it is dry, above seven Inches

---

77 Bentley, ed., *Milton's Paradise Lost. A New Edition* (1732), 234–5.

78 Perhaps Bentley was thinking of Lucretius: "In that time past earth was indeed prolific, / With field profuse in teeming warmth, and wet, / And so, wherever a suitable place was given, / Wombs multiplied, held to the earth by roots," *De Rerum Natura*, trans. Humfries, 5.805–25. See also Richard DuRocher *Milton among the Romans*, 21.

79 More, *Cabbalistica*, 35.

80 Grew, *Musaeum Regalis Societatis*, 14–15.

about. The other end very slender." However impressive these measurements may be, one feels that the Royal Society has tamed the pride of Behemoth.[81]

Grew's crocodile

> differs not much from a Lizard; chiefly in his Bulk. In the Museum Romanum, there is a Tragical Relation of a very great one that devoured a Virgin, Cap. 6. The same Animal which in the Book of Job is called the Leviathan, and hath been commonly taken to be the Whale; but falsly, as Brochart hath demonstrated. . . . He is esteemed good meat, not only by the Natives in Brasile, but also by the Hollanders there. He is taken thus; They fasten a thick long Rope to some Tree by the Waterside, and to the other end, a strong iron Hook, which they bait with a Weather.

His body parts are used for medicines and his testicles "smell like Oyntment" and "sell very dear." In Brazil the "lesser sort . . . come into the Houses, and let the Children play with them harmlessly."[82] So much for the lessons of Job—nothing escapes the dominion of imperial man. But the idea that wild beasts can be harmless was also beginning to emerge as reverse lessons of colonization; George Sandys had already observed that "there is a nation at this day in the East-Indies, (with whom our Merchants frequently trade) who are so farre from eating of what ever had life, that they will not kill so much as a flea; so that the birds of the air, and beasts of the Forrest, without feare frequent their habitations, as their fellow Cittisens."[83]

Bacon's animals

Milton's empathetic and libertarian language about animals entered a century in which dissections crowded the reports of experimental anatomists. Karen Edwards, making the point that for natural historians the empirical scrutiny of the Book of Nature is comparable to close-reading of the Book of Scripture, cites Robert Boyle's account of overcoming his aversion to dissections by their instructiveness, so that "I have often spent hours much less delightfully, not only in courts, but even in libraries, than in tracing in those forsaken mansions the inimitable workmanship of the omniscient Architect."[84] Milton's correspondent Samuel Hartlib dissents: "To mangle tyrannise etc over the Creatures for to trie exp[e]riments . . . as Verul[amus]

---

81   Grew, 14–15.

82   Grew, 41–2. Herodotus wrote in the fifth century B.C.E. that crocodiles were caught in some parts of Egypt, stating that hunters caught them for food by baiting a hook with chines of pork and beating a live pig whose squeals attracted the crocodile to take the hook, drew it ashore, and plastered its eyes with mud to subdue it. In and around Thebes, where the crocodile was sacred, they tamed it, "putting rings made of glass or gold into its ears and bracelets round its front feet, and giving it special food and ceremonial offerings," treating it with kindness, and when it died they embalmed and entombed it (*Histories*, 129). "Weather" probably refers to "wether," a male sheep.

83   Sandys, *Ovids Metamorphosis* [sic] *Englished, Mythologiz'd, and Represented in Figures*, 513.

84   Boyle expresses a radically non-anthropocentric attitude toward animals, however, in a letter quoted by Alan Rudrum in "Ethical Vegetarianism" to be further discussed in Chapter 6.

p[re]scribes is a meere drudgery curiosity and Impiety and no necessity for it."[85] Due to experiments on animals, we no longer fear diseases that used to be fatal and can obtain rehabilitating repairs to our bodies. Some modern research uses guidelines meant to minimize animal suffering, but Bacon expresses no compunction; he promotes and Descartes supports the attitude that animals are ingredients of a pharmacopoeia and a stock of research materials that can also provide luxurious merchandise.

In *Sylva Sylvarum*, as part of the program described in *The New Atlantis*, Bacon collects what "is said" and needs to be tested about the medicinal uses of animals and plants. In the chapter on "sympathies and antipathies recommended by the writers of Natural Magic" (early experimental chemistry that did not separate the physical from the mystical), Bacon reports:

> It is said that the Guts of Skin of a Wolf being applied to the Belly do cure the Colick. It is true, that the Wolf is a Beast of great Edacity and Digestion; and so it may be the Parts of him comfort the Bowels. . . . It is reported by some, that the Head of a Wolf, whole, dried and hanged up in a Dove-house, will scare away the Vermin, such as Weasils, Polcats, and the like. It may be that the Head of a Dog will doe as much; for those Vermin with us know Dogs better then Wolves.

> The brains of some Cretures (when their Heads are rosted) taken in Wine are said to strengthen the Memory: as the Brains of Hares, Brains of Hens, Brains of Deer, &c. And it seemeth to be incident to the Brains of those Creatures that are fearful.

> The Ointment that Witches use is reported to be made of the Fat of Children digged out of their Graves. . . .

Bacon does not suggest an experiment for the latter report, recommending soporific herbs instead. But human bodies are not exempt from medicinal uses; "Mummy" and herbs growing upon a human skull stanch blood. He reports that "Writers of Natural Magick" see much efficacy to "the parts of living Creatures, so as they be taken from them, the Creatures remaining still alive, as if the Creature still living did infuse some Immateriate Virtue and Vigour into the part severed," but endorses only the idea "that any part taken from a living Creature newly slain, may be of greater force than if it were taken from the like Creature dying of it self; because it is fuller of Spirit."

The chapter contains some useful and long forgotten observations, such as that wine and tobacco consumed by a pregnant woman can endanger the wits of her child. Some cures from "natural magic" that Bacon mentions are still practiced, such as the medical use of snake venom; and herbal and animal cures studied by ethnobiologists give reason to preserve vanishing cultures and species.

That Bacon's experimental program lacks an ethic for the mitigation of suffering is not unusual. Topsell jumbles the elephant's noble virtues together with human cruelty and exploitation without comment, except by juxtaposition, on the experience

85 Edwards, *Milton and the Natural World*, 60–61. Edwards cites Boyle, *Works* 2:7, and Hartlib, *Ephemerides, Three Hartlib Papers* (CD-ROM [Ann Arbor, MI: UMI, 1995], 30/4/54A).

of the animals themselves. Pliny's censure is directed toward human moral failures and greedy excesses, rather than toward the sufferings of the creatures misused, though the animals' observed qualities contrast tellingly with human abuse of them. Wilkins and Grew content themselves with physical description and uses. Bacon justifies experiments on the grounds that "the general Root of Superstition" is "that men observe when things Hit, and not when they Miss." But accurate testing takes place, for example, if to find out whether the destruction of part of a creature would destroy the rest by "sympathy," or an invisible connection, "you should cut off part of the Tail or Leg of a Dog or a Cat, and lay it to putrefie, to see whether it will fester, or keep from healing, the part which remaineth." One experiment he tried on himself: when an outbreak of warts on his hands was treated by rubbing them with a piece of lard, then nailing it up (with the skin still on it) in the sun, not only did the warts disappear in five weeks, which they might have done anyway, but another which he had had for many years disappeared as well. Bacon suggests the trial of rubbing corns and wens "with some parts of living Creatures that are nearest the nature of Excrescencies; as the Combs of Cocks, the Spurs of Cocks, the Horns of Beasts, &c," by "cutting off some piece of those parts, and laying it to consume, to see whether it will work any effect towards the Consumption of that part which was once joyned to it."[86]

Such "trials," by not working, dispel superstition and so reduce animal suffering, though that result is not among Bacon's motives. His "sympathy" does not include the fellow-feeling with other sentient beings expressed by Cavendish, Vaughan, and especially Milton, whose monistic theology and language of empathetic particularity achieve the recognition of creature kinship while promoting self-understanding and respect for otherness. What Adam and Eve do *not* do to animals in *Paradise Lost* is part of the definition of felicity.

Minims of nature and the uses of micrography

The work of the Sixth Day in Genesis does not end with megafauna and man; between them come "every creeping thing that creepeth upon the earth" (Gen. 1.25), including insects and amphibians, with the refrain "and God saw that it was good." Disturbance to a hierarchical view of nature was also noted by the micrographers, who discovered in the tiny lineaments of insects the most absolute perfection. John Ray finds another "Argument of the admirable Art and Skill of the Creator and Composer of them from the incredible Smalness of some of those natural and enlivened Machines." Minute craft in works of art is much admired, "But what are these for their fineness and parivity" compared with those "*Animalcula*, not long since discovered in Pepper-water by Mr. Lewenhoek," as confirmed by Robert Hook, who found up to 45,000 "little living Creatures in a quantity of Water no bigger than a grain of Millet." And how much smaller are their individual organs! If Pliny could have seen them, "How would he have admired the immense subtilty

---

86   Bacon, *Sylva Sylvarum* (1664), 216; *Works* 2:660.

. . . of their Parts"; he would have been "rapt into and Extasie of Astonishment and Admiration."

> Where hath Nature disposed so many Senses in a Gnat? . . . . Certain it is, that the Mechanism by which Nature performs the Muscular Motion, is exceeding small and curious; and to the performance of every Muscular Motion, in greater Animals at least, there are not fewer distinct parts concerned than many Millions of Millions, and these visible through a Microscope."[87]

Milton writes of creeping things (7.475–92):

> At once came forth whatever creeps the ground,
> Insect or worm; those waved their limber fans
> For wings, and smallest lineaments exact
> In all the liveries decked of summer's pride
> With spots of gold and purple, azure and green:
> These as a line their long dimension drew,
> Streaking the ground with sinuous trace; not all
> Minims of nature; some of serpent kind
> Wondrous in length and corpulence involved
> Their snaky folds, and added wings.

Readers will not have missed the living jewels, the waving of the syntax at the airy "fans / For," or the visual appropriateness of the shape of the alliterated letter *w* for a pair of wings—there is even a waving gesture in the Latinate "those" (insect) and "these" (worm, the closer word)—or the fact that the worms draw out their long dimensions in one unbroken line, and their long bodies extend liquidly in the repeated l's and contract tactilely with the harder dentals of "dimension drew."

> First crept
> The parsimonious emmet, provident
> Of future, in small room large heart enclosed,
> Pattern of just equality perhaps
> Hereafter, join'd in her popular tribes
> Of commonalty: swarming next appeared
> The female bee that feeds her husband drone
> Deliciously, and builds her waxen cells
> With honey store:

Putting ants and bees into the same category as "serpent kind" is conventional; in Topsell's *History of Serpents* a serpent is anything that can sting. Here the vowels swell spaciously at "in small room large heart enclos'd"; while the p's and t's patter through the passage like a quick heartbeat or minute provident feet.

Although emblematic uses of animals declined as empiricism increased, ants and bees were particularly susceptible to political allegory. Thomas Muffet or Mouffat writes "Of the Politick, Ethick, and Oeconomick virtues of Bees":

---

87 Ray, *Wisdom of God*, 159–62.

Bees are swayed by soveraignty not tyranny, neither do they admit of a King properly so called, by succession or by lot, but by due advice, and circumspect choice; and though they willingly submit to regall authority; yet so, as they retain their liberty; because they still keep their Prerogative of Election; and when their King is once made sure to them by oath, they do in a principal manner love him. And if he chance to find amongst his young ones any one that is a fool, unhandsome, hairy, of an angry disposition, ill shapen, or naturally ill conditions, by the unanimous consent of the rest, he gives order to put him to death, lest his souldiery should be disordered, and his subjects being drawn into faction should be destroyed.[88]

If Muffet (father of the famous tuffet-sitter) wished allegorically to commend the absolute power of a sitting King, he is distant from Milton, whose "just equality" glances at the Restoration's lack of it, while Raphael's "perhaps/ Hereafter" acknowledges that unfallen Adam and Eve, justice already written in their hearts, do not yet, if ever, need such a pattern. The "perhaps" is weighty with choice.

According to Topsell's Gesner, bees are the only venomous Insect "made for the nourishment of mankinde," all others serving only for medicine, "delight of the eyes, delectation of the ears, and the ornament, trimming, and setting forth of the body." He agrees with Muffet about the election of monarchs (like Muffet and Vergil in *Georgics* 4, he supposes the head bee to be male, though both wrote or translated first in the reign of Elizabeth, to whom Muffet dedicates his work); "and although they willingly submit their necks under a Kingly government, yet notwithstanding they still keep their ancient liberties and privileges," mainly the prerogative of giving their opinions. They are also "studious of peace."[89]

In "The commendation of Pismires" Topsell extolls ants or emmets for intelligence and virtue; "the beauty of their body follows the goodnesse of their minde." In comparison with "the profuseness of Caius Julius Caesar, the luxury of Caligula, the prodigality of Nero, the excessive gluttony of Apicius, and the great waste of Heliogabalus . . . I exceedingly commend the wit and ingenuity of the Pismire, and prefer her prudence before that of Man. [The wasters] lived sweetly, and with fat patrimonies from their fathers," yet by "new use of baths, dangerous kindes of meats, curiosity in banquets, ships made of cedars adorned with Jewels, the drinking of pearls they wasted as much in one year, as they could extort tributes and customes, or by plunder, both at home and abroad all their life time." The ant, provident and temperate, "is never tortured with poverty or the effects of an unhealthy superfluous diet."[90] These writers do not know about the findings of E.O. Wilson regarding our planet's dependence on ants, but the planet is still dependent on those who imitate the ant and damaged by those who imitate Caligula and Heliogabalus.

The micrographers who alerted the world to the beauty of insects of course dissected them, but with difficulty: Robert Hooke finds the "Ant or Pismire" most "troublesome to draw" because it wouldn't hold still:

---

88   Mouffet, *The Theater of Insects* (1658), bound and consecutively paginated with Topsell, 1658.

89   Topsell, *History of Serpents*, 637 and 639.

90   Topsell, *History of Serpents*, 1074.

Whilst it was alive, if its feet were fetter'd in Wax of Glew, it would so twist and wind its body, that I could not any wayes get a good view of it; and if I killed it, its body was so little, that I did often spoile the shape of it, before I could throughly view it: for this is the nature of these minute Bodies, that as soon, almost, as ever their life is destroy'd, their parts immediately shrivel, and lose their beauty.

Hooke made his uncooperative specimen drunk with brandy several times, after which it remained immobile for hours, then revived, a kind of experiment that might be useful "for the discovery of the Latent Scheme, (as the Noble Verulam calls it) or the hidden, unknown Texture of Bodies." Its "two protuberant eyes" were "pearl'd like those of a Fly."

Like Ray's tortoise, Hookes ants perform "seemingly rational actions." He puts out his finger, and they run towards it,

stand round about it, at a certain distance, and smell, as it were, and consider whether they should any of them venture any further, till one more bold then the rest venturing to climb it, all the rest, if I would have suffered them, would have immediately followed: many such other seemingly rational actions I have observ'd in this little Vermine with much pleasure.[91]

The delight and amiable irony of Hooke's language draws sympathy to "vermin" who usually met with disgust. The book-worm "appears to the naked eye, a small glistering Pearl-colour'd Moth," seen while moving books "very nimbly to scud, and pack away to some lurking cranney." The microscope reveals a carrot-shaped body to be divided into fourteen "shells . . . tiled over with a multitude of thin transparent scales, which, from the multiplicity of their reflecting surfaces, make the whole Animal appear of a perfect Pearl-colour" consisting of "laminated orbiculations" that give "a very pleasant reflection of light." It eats the "husks of Hemp and Flax" in old paper; considering the "heap of Saw-dust or chips this little creature (which is one of the teeth of Time) conveys into its intrails" Hooke admires "the excellent contrivance of Nature"

in placing in Animals such a fire, as is continually nourished and supply'd by the materials convey'd into the stomach, and fomented by the bellows of the lungs; and in so contriving the most admirable fabrick of Animals, as to make the very spending and wasting of that fire, to be instrumental to the procuring and collecting more materials to augment and cherish it self, which indeed seems to be the principal end of all the contrivances observable in bruit Animals.[92]

For Henry Power the microscope confirmed the conjectures and experiments that "the Atomical and Corpuscularian Philosophers durst but imagine," since naturalists had before described only the larger animals and "regardlesly pass'd by the Insectile Automata, (those Living-exiguities) with only a bare mention of their names, whereas in these pretty Engines (by an Incomparable Stenography of Providence) are lodged all the perfections of the largest Animals." Moreover,

---

91 Hooke, *Micrographia*, 203–204.
92 Hooke, 210.

that which augments the miracle, is, that all these in so narrow a room neither interfere nor impede one another in their operations. . . . Ruder heads stand amazed at those prodigious and Colossean pieces of Nature, as Whales, Elephants, and Dromedaries; but in these narrow Engines there is more curious Mathematicks, and the Architecture of these little Fabricks more neatly set forth the wisdom of their Maker.[93]

Power's adherence to "the ever-to-be-admired Des-Cartes"[94] appears in "Automata" and in his simultaneous admiration and brutality. The common fly

is a very pleasant Insect to behold; her body is as it were from head to tayl studded with silver and black Armour, stuck all over with great black Bristles, like Porcupine quills, set all in parallel order, with their ends pointing all towards the tayl; her wings look like a Seafan with black thick ribs or fibers, dispers'd and branch'd through them, which are webb'd between with a thin membrane or film, like a slice of Muscovy-glasse: She hath a small head which she can move or turn any way: She hath six legs, but goes onely but upon four; the two foremost she makes use of instead of hands, with which you may often see her wipe her mouth and nose, and take up any thing to eat. . . . But of all things her eyes are most remarkable, being exceeding large, ovally protuberant and most neatly dimpled with innumerable little cavities like a small grater or thimble, through which seeming perforations you may see a faint reddish colour (which is the blood in the eyes, for if you prick a pin through the eye, you shall finde more blood there, then in all the rest of her body.)

Similarly, the eye of "The Gray, or Horse-Fly" is "an incomparable pleasant spectacle: 'tis of a semisphaeroidal figure; black and waved, or rather indented all over with a pure Emerauld-green, so that it looks like green silk Irish-stitch, drawn upon a black ground, and all latticed or chequered with dimples like Common flyes, which makes the Indentures look more pleasantly: Her body looks like silver in frost-work, onely fring'd all over with white silk: . . . . After her head is cut off, you shall most fairly see (just at the setting on of her neck) a pulsing particle (which certainly is the heart) to beat for half an hour most orderly and neatly through the skin." And of the firefly:

Take hold of her horns, and you may draw out her eyes and cut them out, and so lay them on your object-plate and see them distinctly. This is that Night-Animal with its Lanthorn in its tail; that creeping-Star which seems to outshine those of the Firmament, and to outvye them too in this property especially; that whereas the Coelestial Lights are quite obscured by the interposition of a small cloud, this Terrestrial-Star is more enliven'd and enkindled thereby, whose pleasant fulgour no darkness is able to eclipse.[95]

Milton, though blind, acknowledges the "lineaments exact" of insects (7.477) and the beauty that micrographers praised, but prefers to describe them alive. Raphael's description of "serpent kind" concludes, addressing Adam,

---

93 Power, *Experimental Philosophy* (1664), Preface, sig. B2v–b3.

94 Power, Preface, sig. C.

95 Power, 4–5, 6–7, 24.

the rest are numberless,
And thou their natures know'st, and gav'st them names,
Needless to be repeated; nor unknowne
The serpent subtlest beast of all the field,
Of huge extent sometimes, with brazen eyes
And hairy mane terrific, though to thee
Not noxious, but obedient at thy call.   [7.492–8]

The serpent raises a problem of theology. Did—or why did—God create venomous animals? Was venom part of their equipment before the fall? The question connects to the problem of predation, which I defer to the next chapter. All serpents are among the things God pronounced good, though one was to become "nocent" later, and whatever good things in the Edenic garden could be used to do harm need not be: the garden is an arena of choice for the exercise of observation and reason. Sir Thomas Browne believed that ingredients of plants and animals now poisonous could do no harm before the Fall because perfect temperance was joined to perfect immunity.[96] According to Topsell, some heathen and heretics think that a good God cannot have created the "hurtful Beasts," but these must have good purposes though "in the barrenness of our understanding, we cannot conceive or learn them." But Man was given authority over all the creatures, and even snakes when tamed [James 3.7] are "no ways enemies to mankinde, but friendly, and endued with sociable respect."[97] The more upright we are, the less the other creatures are our enemies.

Medicines made of serpents often participate in "sympathetic magic" such as applying body parts similar to the ones affected, and Topsell includes recipes for preservation against venom and against leprosy. Their skin, fat, blood, heads and tails—the latter two minced into chicken feed and ingested by eating the chickens—cure almost everything. Moreover—and here their suggested uses slide from curative to chic—"The bloud of a Serpent is more precious then Balsumum, and if you anoint your lips with a little of it, they will look passing red: and if the face be anointed therewith, it will receive no spot or fleck, but causeth to have an orient or beautifull hew."[98]

These micrographers experienced empathy enough to personify the objects of their study and analogize them humorously or satirically to their own species, but they still considered animals "automata" and "mechanisms" and "fabricks." By 1692, John Ray had come to the opinion, expressed earlier by Henry More, that God did not make all creatures only "to be serviceable to Man, but also to partake themselves of his overflowing Goodness, and to enjoy their own Beings." If they were "mere Machins or automata, to have no life, no Sense of Perception of any thing, then . . . being uncapable of pleasure or pain, they can have no enjoyment"; and the unholy concept that God would create sentient beings incapable of joy is one of his reasons for not inclining to that theory.[99]

---

96 Browne, *Pseudodoxia Epidemica*, in *Works* 2:344.
97 Topsell, *History of Serpents*, 591.
98 Topsell, 605.
99 Ray, *The Wisdom of God*, part 2, 142–3.

Earlier, in *Paradise Lost*, animals are responsive "living souls" and their relation to Adam and Eve is one, though not of equality, of a commonwealth of differentiated "first matter" with rights as what Sandys calls "fellow Cittisens." If we take the unfallen state as Milton's ideal model for a regenerate one, the epic promotes a polity that does not subject animals to unnecessary suffering or pesticides of mass destruction. As the loss of free and biologically diverse lives threatens to produce cultural aphasia, Milton's and other poets' anti-oppressive language is worth reviving. As each image enters our imaginations, and our voices respond to the forms and motions of other beings, the sound that embodies that image forms a bond with our flesh. As we shall see in the following chapter, a thoughtful literature of the possible "rights" of animals had begun to develop earlier in the century, and along with the poetry supplies an ethic for human relations to other sentient beings.

Chapter 6

Animal Ethics and Radical Justice

> There is a kinde of respect, and a general duty of humanity,
> which tieth us not only unto brute beasts that have life and sense,
> but even unto trees and plants.

Michel de Montaigne, *Of Crueltie*

Why is homo "sapiens" such a violent species? Is violence between human beings related to violence from and toward the rest of the natural world? Are we inured to human suffering by disregard for the suffering of other sentient beings?

Classical, Biblical, post-Darwinian, and non-Western philosophies hold diverse answers to the problem of human violence, with violence towards and by animals among the correlatives. Lucretius, Plutarch, and Porphyry questioned the sacrifice of animals either to the divinities or to our own appetites. For the atomist materialist Titus Lucretius Carus (born c. 95 B.C.E.), human vanity results from fear of death and animal sacrifice from fear of the wrath of the gods. His purpose is to release human beings from superstition and the violence to which it leads. Propitiation by substitute victims leads to not only "sprinkling the altars with the blood of beasts" but the sacrifice of "a girl's blood"—Iphigenia's. The gods, however, are too aloof and serene to care for such things. If human beings would accept their mortality, they would not be driven to atrocities by fear.[1]

The writers of the Book of Job and portions of the Psalms and Gospels questioned human tyranny over God's other creatures, and the propitiation of Jesus abolished ceremonial animal sacrifice for most of his followers. Seventeenth-century poets and natural historians would have been familiar with both the biblical passages and the philosophical arguments, which were widely available in early modern editions and translations. Ovid's representation of the views of Pythagoras in *Metamorphoses*, for example, was vividly translated by Arthur Golding, George Sandys, and John Dryden. Readers may be surprised by the passionate promotion of vegetarianism, the theological responses to the problem of predation, and the advocacy for animal rights to be found among early modern poets and natural philosophers, and by both the ethics and the obliviousness in aristocratic tracts and poems of feasting, hawking, and hunting.

---

1   Lucretius, *The Way Things Are*, trans. Humphries, 5.1202 and 1.87.

Orpheus and the animals: Classical traditions

Nicholas de Bruyn's *Orpheus Playing to the Animals* (Plate 8) illustrates a classical topos of the ability of the artist to create harmony, whether among warring human passions or among the denizens of the natural world. Orpheus, distraught after the death of his beloved Eurydice, so charms Pluto and Persephone with his music that they agree to release her from death, on condition that as she follows him up to the light he must never look back. Of course, he does. This breaking of the taboo has many interpretations, one being that Orpheus could not control his intense need to know that she was still there. In Ovid's version, he retreats into the woods with his viol, and the animals, and even the trees, gather peaceably around him, so drawn are they by his song, and this act shows them not only sentient but to some degree rational—music appeals to the mind, not just the senses. To a degree, the animals represent the beasts within us, brought by art into what Donne called "an Arke where all agree."[2] But in de Bruyn's illustration they are also carefully observed real animals, and the illustration suggests that human culture matters to other inhabitants of the natural world. During the early centuries of modern science, according to Emmet Robbins, Orpheus "presides over the transformations and interaction of poetry and science."[3] It is no wonder that Milton took Orpheus for his emblem of poetry or that, as Peter Thomas has eloquently shown of Henry Vaughan, physician and poet, "Orpheus (archetypal singer) emerges as one of the most powerful of his evoked ghosts."[4]

Aristotle argues from observation that most animals have senses like ours: "Now man and the footed Vivipara, and in addition the blooded Ovipara, all plainly possess all these five [senses]," except when they are stunted, as sight in the mole, in whom impaired eyes are found under the skin. Fish, as is clear from their behavior, have the senses of taste, hearing and smell, though the organs are not visible; and "the Cephalopods, the Crustacea, and the Insects possess all the senses." All animals have touch. Testacea have smell and taste; some appear to have sight and hearing by burrowing or closing at the approach of a finger. When huntsmen encircle a pod of dolphins with their canoes and make a noise on the sea, the dolphins to take flight and beach themselves, and are captured while bewildered by the noise; "And yet the dolphin has no visible organ of hearing."[5]

Nevertheless, Aristotle approves of human dominion over all of nature and links it with dominion over women, slaves, and nations. In the words of the first English translation of the *Politics* (1598), "[It] is most expedient for all [beasts], both tame and wild to be in subjection to man: sith therein consisteth their safety. Moreover, . . . by natures law the male as better commaundeth, and the female as inferiour obeyeth, and is subject." Those who, like beasts, "understand not reason, but serve their owne affection" are "servantes by nature"; and "the use of servants and bruit beasts hath but small diversitie; for we are holpen of each of them by their bodies

---

2   Donne, "To Sr. Edward Herbert. At Julyers," in Shawcross, ed., *Complete Poetry*, 233.
3   Robbins, "Famous Orpheus," in *Orpheus: The Metamorphosis of a Myth*, 4.
4   Peter Thomas, "Henry Vaughan, Orpheus, and The Empowerment of Poetry," 235.
5   Aristotle, *Historia Animalium,* 2.69, 71–3, and 63–5.

. . . in our necessary businesse. . . . Therefore may wee conclude, that some men are borne to libertie, and other to bondage, to whome it is profitable and just to serve."[6] The commentary to this translation, published at a time when advertisement for colonization ran high, adds,

> There be not onely particular men disposed to servitude, by reason of the rudenesse of their wit and small understanding, unable to doe any service but by the strength of their bodies: but also there be whole Nations naturally more servile then others as Aristotle in his 3. booke of Government, Chapt. 10 and Hippocrates in his booke of the Aire, of Waters, and Difference of place, doe report of the people of Asia to be.

Aristotle's chapter "Of Possession" treats hunting and war as "Art[s] of Acquiring." If nature makes nothing in vain, "it necessarily followeth, that she hath made all things for mens behoofe," and therefore hunting "must be practised, not only against beasts, but also against such men as by their nativity ought to live in subjection, and yet seek to shake off the youke of their obedience: for that kind of warre is g[r]ounded upon just and lawfull cause." The 1598 commentary adds,

> It is certaine, that by the skill of Chivalrie or Militarie discipline, are gotten the chiefest things of this world; as great kingdomes, Empires, and other states . . . and the warre is permitted as just and lawfull, when it is justly and lawfully undertaken; as, to the intent to subdue such persons as are borne to obey and be ruled.[7]

The assumptions of Aristotle's analogy of animals and slaves served the colonial enterprise, turning up in descriptions of inhabitants of the New World who were "clothed in beasts skins, did eate rawe flesh, and spake such speach, that no man could understand them, and in their demeanor like to brute beasts."[8]

John Streater's commentary on the *Politics* (1654) connects Aristotle's position to the Biblical story of Nimrod, also both a hunter of animals and a hunter of men. Like Calvin, Streater traces the beginning of empire to Nimrod, who "got together many people, under a pretence of hunting of wild beasts to make room for the increase of mankind" and "with those bands made himself Lord of many large countries"; small cities under "paternal government" were forced by "the growing great of their neighbors, whose greatnesse received its foundation by the hand of *Nimrod* that mighty Hunter," to band together and "subject themselves to an absolute monarchical government" to defend themselves from tyrants. Moreover, "*Nimrod* . . . began his Tyranny with drawing of a curtain of Religion, as well as a curtain of pretences of publick good, and publick necessity upon his intention, two Vizards

---

6   *Aristotles Politiques*, trans. Loys Le Roy.

7   *Aristotles Politiques* (1598), 25, 30, 31, 37, 42. Huntington Library copy from the Bridgewater Library, with which Milton and other poets would have been familiar. J.M. Evans discusses the application of "Aristotle's theory of natural slavery" in the works of Oviedo and Sepúlveda (100) and other apologists for conquest in *Milton's Imperial Epic*.

8   Richard Hakluyt, *The Principal Navigations* (1589), 515. Huntington Library copy from the Bridgewater Library, with the signature "Tho. Egerton."

used since *Nimrod* as well as by *Nimrod*."[9] Milton recounts a similar history in *Paradise Lost* (12.7–62), and Satan makes the tyrant's plea that "public reason just, / Honor and Empire with revenge enlarg'd / By conquering this new World, compels me now / To do what else though damn'd I should abhor" (4.389–92).

Against this aspect of Aristotle stood successors of Pythagoras such as Ovid, Plutarch, and Porphyry, in whose works animal slavery and slaughter are also linked to human slavery and slaughter, but as unjust practices. Ovid in his story of Pythagoras, and Plutarch and Porphyry in tracts on the eating of flesh, teach that the just man does not cause suffering to other sentient beings for his own pleasure, and eating flesh, except from dire necessity, is unjust, uneconomical, unhealthy, and of course carnal, incapacitating the philosophical capabilities of the mind.

Vergil and Ovid trace humanity's decline from the Golden Age, ruled by Saturn, to the beginnings of violence, war, crime, and lust for gold in the Bronze and Iron ages. Vergil speaks in the *Georgics* of the impious Age of Bronze when people began to sacrifice and feast on bullocks. Saturn had not accepted such sacrifices: in Dryden's translation "The good old God his Hunger did assuage / With Roots and Herbs, and gave the Golden Age."[10] The philosopher Pythagoras in Ovid's *Metamorphoses* 15 (finished in 8 C.E.) declares that the first meat-eater, perhaps after killing an animal in self-defense or witnessing a lion eating his prey, "led the way toward death and infamy."[11] One of Pythagoras' arguments for respect for animals is the possible transmigration of souls, but Ovid and other followers did not make reincarnation an important part of his ethic. Plutarch and Porphyry taught the Pythagorean tradition of nonviolence to animals for ethical and philosophical reasons that opposed Aristotle's view of dominion. These philosophers along with some natural historians and theologians gave moral support to seventeenth-century poets in their empathetic descriptions of the lives of animals.

Ovid's *Metamorphoses* in Renaissance translations by Arthur Golding and George Sandys provided widespread knowledge of Ovid's version of Pythagoras's views. Ovid introduces the exhortation of Pythagoras against eating flesh (Book 15) with the story of his exile from Samos because he hated tyrants and servility, and vividly presents his teaching that shedding the blood of animals issues in human brutality. The transmigration of souls is a small part of this argument, but the principal points are the suffering of the animals and its cost to human civility. At the end, the wise prince Numa brings this philosophy to Rome and teaches a savage race the arts of peace.

Golding's Elizabethan version makes no bones about the eating of flesh. Our "moother / The earth" yields "gentle foode, and riches too content bothe mynde and eye . . . . Oh what a wickednesse / It is to cram the mawe with mawe, and frank up flesh with flesh," as if nothing "myght delyght / Thy cruell teethe too chawe uppon, than grisly swoundes." Before human beings began to stain their mouths with blood, birds could safely fly and fish could safely swim, the hare "unscaard of hound / Went

---

9   Streater, *Observation Historical, Political, and Philosophical, upon Aristotles first Book of Political Government* (1654), 42–3.

10   Vergil, trans. Dryden, *Georgics*, 2, ll. 791–2, in *The Works of John Dryden*, 5.207.

11   Ovid, *The Metamorphoses*, trans. Gregory, 417.

pricking over all the fields" (like a Spenserian Knight errant) and all things were free of guile and treason and full of "freendshippe, love, and peace." The first who "[to] cram that cruell croppe of his with fleshmeate did not spare, / He made a way for wickednesse." How could anyone find it in his heart to slaughter guileless oxen, releasing his fellow "tilman" from the plow only to cut the throat whose skin is worn with laboring for him? Yet people blame this wickedness upon the gods, imagining that they delight in death, placing between his horns "The eares of corne that he himself hath wrought for in the clay" and staining with his blood the knife that the ox may have seen reflected in the basin; then

> Immediatly they haling out his hartstrings still alive,
> And poring on them, seeke therein Goddes secrets too retryve.
> All this comes of men's own greedy appetite for meat;
> but whensoever you doo your Oxen eate,
> you devowre your husbandmen.[12]

George Sandys's translation of 1632 (one wonders how this work might have been received at the lavish Caroline court and country estates) links flesh-eating with other cruelties:

> How horrible a Sin,
> That entrailes bleeding entrailes should intomb!
> The greedie flesh, by flesh should fat become!
> While by one creatures death another lives!
> Of all, which Earth, our wealthie mother, gives;
> Can nothing please, unlesse thy teeth thou imbrue
> In wounds, and dire *Cyclopean* fare renue?
> Nor satiate the greedy luxury
> Of thy rude panch, except an other die.

The first man "that cramb'd his guts with flesh, set ope the gates / To cruell Crimes." The first slaughter may have been not have been impious, but defense from "salvage beasts, which made our lives their food." They were not to be eaten, however. Even the more audacious sin of sacrificing the boar who uprooted grain, and goats who browsed on vines, is understandable. But—he turns to address the animals—

> You Sheepe, what ill did you? a gentle beast,
> Whose udders swell with Nectar, borne t'invest
> Exposèd man with your soft wooll, and are
> Alive, th[a]n dead, more profitable farre.
> Or what the Oxe, a creature without guile,
> So innocent, so simple; borne for toyle.
> Hee most ungratefull is, deserving ill
> The gift of corne; that can un-yoke, then kill
> His painefull Hinde: that neck with axe to wound
> In service gall'd, that had the stubborne ground
> So often tild; so many crops brought in.

---

12 *The. xv.Bookes of P. Ouidius Naso, entytuled Metamorphosis*, trans. Arthyr Golding (1567), 15:296–7.

As if that were not crime enough (with a nod to Lucretius), men

> ascribe the sinne
> To guiltless Gods: as if the Powres on high
> In death of labour-bearing oxen joy.

An especially beautiful animal is chosen ("'Tis death to please") and standing by the altar decked in ribbons and gold sees "the meale upon his fore-head throwne, / Got by his toyle"; we share the tricked-out animal's last glimpse of the bloody knife he had seen reflected in water of the laver, and then watch the throbbing body disemboweled for the diviners. "Whence springs so dire an appetite in man / To interdicted food? O Mortals . . . dare you feed on flesh? henceforth forbeare . . . :

> When limmes of slaughtred Beeves become your meat;
> Then think, and know, that you your Servants eat.[13]

Sandys's commentary produces witnesses. For the Roman agricultural writer Varro,

> the various beings in various parts of the world al derived from God, or the greater Soule; and participat[ed] in his divine nature. He was so pittifull even to irrationall creatures, that he exclaimed against the killing, much more detested the eating of any; as proceeding from injustice, cruelty, and corruption of manners; not knowne in that innocent age which was called the golden.

In the Bible, "before the deluge men fed not on flesh; but onely of such hearbes and fruits as the earth produced;" [flesh-eating] was "a privilege granted after Noah; because they had lost much of their nourishing vertue";

> Yet there is a nation at this day in the East-Indies, (with whom our Merchants frequently trade) who are so farre from eating of what ever had life, that they will not kill so much as a flea; so that the birds of the air, and beasts of the Forrest, without feare frequent their habitations, as their fellow Cittisens.[14]

Dryden also translates Pythagoras's exhortation against flesh-eating in *Metamorphoses* 15, sometimes strikingly:

> O impious use! to nature's laws opposed,
> Where bowels are in other bowels closed;
> Where fattened by their fellows' fat they thrive;
> Maintained by murder, and by death they live.
> 'Tis then for naught that mother earth provides
> The stores of all she shows, and all she hides,
> If men with fleshly morsels much be fed,
> And chew with bloody teeth the breathing bread. [125–32]

---

13 Ovid, *Ovid's Metamorphosis Englished*, trans. G[eorge] S[andys] (1632), 492–4. Dedicated to Charles I. The Latin *Metamorphosen* was edited with extensive commentary by the Jesuit Jacobus Pontanus (Antwerp, 1610); Garland reprints the 1618 edition.

14 Sandys 513.

How can men be other than vicious when they begin with bloodshed,

> Deaf to the calf that lies beneath the knife,
> Looks up, and from her butcher begs her life;
> Deaf to the harmless kid, there ere he dies
> All methods to procure thy mercy cries,
> And imitates in vain thy children's cries.   [686–90] [15]

Plutarch (46–120 C.E.) asked *Whether it be lawfull to Eat Flesh or No* in a tract translated unsympathetically 1603 by Philemon Holland, who shows his affinity with Aristotle by praising James I for increasing the dominions of Elizabeth "in greater measure, proportionable to the dignity of Sex." Holland allows Plutarch the rational motive of "abridging of the great excesse and superfluitie in purveying, buying, and spending of viands" in his time. But he debunks the topic of the tract as a dialogue such as children practice at school for argument's sake, maintaining "paradoxes and strange opinions." He attributes Plutarch's zeal to an ignorant belief in reincarnation and says that this mistake should instruct all men "not to glory and vaunt themselves, but in the mercy of him, who calleth them to a better life, wherein the brute beasts, (created onely for our use, and for the present life, with which they perish for ever) have no part nor portion at all."[16]

But in fact, Plutarch's argument is straightforwardly ethical:

> I againe do marvell, what affection, what manner of courage, or what motive and reason had that man, who first approached with his mouth unto a slaine creature, who durst with his lips once touch the flesh of a beast either killed or dead; or how he could finde in his heart to be served at his table with dead bodies . . . to make his food and nourishment of those parts and members which a little before did blea[t], low, bellow, walk, and see. How could his eies endure to beholde such murder and slaughter, whiles the poore beasts were either sticked or had the throats cut, were flaied and dismembred? how could his nose abide the smell and sent that came from them? how came it that his taste was not cleane marred and overthrowen with horrour, when he came to handle those uncouth sores and ulcers, or receive the bloud and humours, issuing out of the deadly wounds.

The first "monstrosities" of flesh-eating were "contrary to nature" and done from necessity by those would envy the plenty of Ceres and Bacchus that makes them needless: "You call lions and libards savage beasts; meane while your selves are stained with bloudshed, giving no place to them in crueltie, for where as they doe worie and kill other beasts, it is for verie necessitie and need of food; but you do it for dainty fare. Though we slay wild animals in self-defense, we eat them not," instead we kill "the innocent, the harmelesse, the gentle and tame . . . although nature seemeth to have created them, onely for beautie and delight." Human hearts are hard, unmoved by "the faire and beautifull colour, or the sweet and tunable voice, or the quicknesse and subtiltie of spirit, or the neat and cleane life, or the vivacitie of wit and understanding, of these poore seelly creatures; and for a little

---

15 Dryden, *Of the Pythagorian Philosophy* (a translation of *Metamorphoses* 15) from *Fables* (1700); from *John Dryden*, ed. Walker, 5.220–21, 234.

16 Holland, in Plutarch, *The Philosophie, commonlie called, The Morals*, 571, 561–2.

peece of flesh we take away their life, we bereave them of the sunne and of light" and "those lamentable and trembling voices which they utter for feare, we suppose to be inarticulate or unsignificant sounds, [but are] nothing lesse than pitifull praiers, supplications, pleas & justifications of these poore innocent creatures, who in their language everie one of them crie in this manner: If thou be forced upon necessitie, I beseech thee not to save my life: but if it be for that thou wouldest feed more delicately, hold thy hand and let me live."

Those who think men meat-eaters by nature, Plutarch continues—though lacking carnivore's teeth and claws—should slay their prey with their own hands and teeth and eat it alive, rather than disguising it with cooking and sauces. Besides, eating meat makes our bodies torpid and diseased, our souls "fat and grosse" and our moral sense debased: the way we treat animals predicts the way we will treat our own kind: "[W]ho would ever finde in his heart to abuse & wrong a man, who is affectionate, gentle, and milde, to the very beasts which are of a strange kind from us, and have no communication of reason with us?"[17] This latter clause, an opinion of Aristotle that descended to Christianity through Thomas Aquinas, is turned against its more frequent use as an excuse for unstinted exploitation.

The third-century Greek philosopher Porphyry lays out all sides of the debate in *Abstinence from Animal Food*. Opponents of animal rights such as the Aristotelians and Stoics, he explains, say "that justice will be confounded, and things immoveable be moved, if we extend what is just, not only to the rational, but to the irrational nature; conceiving . . . an alliance between us." Porphyry thinks rather that our relation to animals should benefit both us and them, and gives the example of beekeeping as "mutually profitable to bees."[18] He concedes that slaying dangerous animals is not unjust, but neither self-defense nor sacrifice—probably initiated by famine—makes it necessary for us to eat them.

To the point that plants are equally violated by being eaten, Porphyry replies that plants are not unwilling, that they "would spontaneously drop their fruits" if we did not pick them and that gathering does not destroy the plant, while animals lose "their animating principle." If we reject slaying animals for food, we shall increase our mutual security, for those averse to destroying members of other species would surely "abstain from injuring those of their own kind." It would best to repent, like Empedocles, of feeding "on the dire nutriment of flesh." Instead of sacrificing animals, fruits should be offered to the gods "and to the Earth, by whom they are produced. . . . all of us, reclining on her surface, as on the bosom of our mother and nurse, should celebrate her divinity" and thus be worthy of residing "with all the celestial Gods." God needs nothing "external to himself," nor does "the soul of the world"; they should be thanked with inanimate sacrifices, like the Pythagorians' offerings of the study of numbers.[19]

Perhaps the most violent image of animal slaughter appears in the epyllion of Aristaeus in Vergil's *Georgics* 4, on beekeeping, in which Aristaeus loses his bees as punishment for attempting to rape Eurydice and so causing her death by a serpent's

---

17 Plutarch, *The Philosophie, commonlie called, The Morals*, 572–5.

18 Porphyry, *Select Works*, 53.

19 Porphyry, *Select Works*, 3, 53, 67–9, 74.

sting as she flees. In the ancient "useful Science" of restoring a hive, Vergil recounts, a young bullock is beaten to death, flowers and herbs are strewn about and under his body, and the corpse ferments and produces bees. In Dryden's translation, after building "A narrow Flooring, gutter'd, wall'd, and til'd,"

> A Steer of two Years old they take, whose Head
> Now first with burnish'd Horns begins to spread:
> They stop his Nostrils, while he strives in vain
> To breath free Air, and struggles with his Pain.
> Knock'd down, he dyes: his Bowels bruis'd within,
> Betray no Wound on his unbroken Skin.   [4.418, 421–6][20]

Dryden's couplets, though painful, lighten the tone of this event, and "Knock'd down" is less violent than Vergil's "tundere," meaning both to beat and to thresh. The story of Aristaeus's loss of his bees, givers of sweetness and light, through moral blindness, and of redemption by this brutal method, is perhaps an analogue of other forms of animal sacrifice.

Eyelids of the morning: The biblical traditions

In the Hebrew Book of Beginnings, God makes and blesses all species, and gives man and woman the mandate to take care of their domain, the earth and its other occupants: "Be fruitful, and multiply, and replenish the earth, and subdue it: and have dominion over the the fish of the sea, and over the fowl of the air, and over every living thing that moveth upon the earth." The commandment sets the worshippers of one Creator-God apart from the worshippers of nature spirits, releases them from superstitious fear of nature's power, and gives warrant to cultivation and civilization. The words "subdue" and "dominion" are nevertheless troubling because they can be used to excuse excesses of dominion that make the natural world merely an instrument or a collection of raw materials, without consideration of the lives of other beings.

Rabbinical and Christian interpretations do not warrant greed or cruelty,[21] and other biblical texts acknowledge God's providence to all his creatures. In Genesis, God creates all kinds of beings and declares them good, and then makes man "in his own image, in the image of God created he him; male and female created he them" (Gen. 1.27); that is, among other things, the human race is made in the image of the creator who has made and blessed all things and seen that they were good. God then gives to man and woman "every herb bearing seed which is upon the face of all the earth, and every tree, in which is the fruit of of a tree yielding seed; to you it shall be for meat" and also to "to every beast of the field, and to every fowl of the air, and to everything that creepeth upon the earth, wherein there is life, I have given every green herb for meat" (Gen. 1.29–30), (*meat* being a general word for food not yet

---

20 Dryden, *The Fourth Book of the Georgics*, in *Works* 5:252.
21 See Cohen, *'Be fertile and increase, fill the earth and master it'* and Linzey, *Animal Theology.*

including the flesh of animals). In some interpretations, all creatures are blessed both by God and by human presences made in the image of the creative "Dominus," and "dominion" is the stewardship of what God has made; the decline to violence results from defiance of the creator; and a striving toward the regenerate "peaceable kingdom" foretold by Isaiah (Isaiah 65.25).

God's odd preference of the animal sacrifice of Abel the shepherd over the vegetable sacrifice of Cain the farmer prefigures Christ's sacrifice and perhaps the incompatibility of fields and herds. Cain (perhaps meaning "smith"[22]) is more territorial. Joan Blythe writes, "Cain's plowing of the earth and raising of crops suggested to commentators that he was of the earth and violated the earth to get material wealth. Abel as shepherd was seen to deal with living things that did not have to be killed to provide sustenance. Pastoral work is preparatory to true leadership of peoples."[23]

Milton's fallen Adam imagines, before Michael sets him right, that God will not be found outside the lost garden, where he could have reared "grateful altars" of "grassy turf" and lustrous stones and offered "sweet smelling gums and fruits and flow'rs" (11.326–7). But after the Flood, "Noah builded an altar unto the Lord; and took of every clean beast, and of every clean fowl"—brought or born in the ark?— and "offered burnt offerings on the altar. And the Lord smelled a sweet savour; and the Lord said in his heart, I will not again curse the ground any more for man's sake; for the imagination of man's heart is evil from his youth; neither will I again smite any more every thing living, as I have done' " (Gen. 8.20–22).[24] God then delivers every bird, fish, and animal into the hands of Noah and his sons and into "dread"; he gives permission to eat them, excepting the blood—and also requires the blood of man "at the hand of every beast . . . and at the hand of man" and of "whoso sheddeth mans blood . . . for in the image of God made he man" (Gen. 9.1–6). God tests Abraham's willingness to sacrifice even his son Isaac, but then supplies a ram instead, both testing Abraham's faith and separating the chosen people from those who practiced human sacrifice, such as the worshippers of Moloch. Leviticus 1–7 codifies the practice of animal sacrifice, with burnt offerings from the herds and the fowl—no part of which is to be eaten—with elaborate rituals of slaying, butchering, burning, and sprinkling of blood.

Yet in Psalm 50, a Psalm of Asaph, God speaks to his people Israel:

> I will take no bullock out of thy house, nor he goats out of thy folds.
> For every beast of the forest is mine, and the cattle upon a
>   thousand hills.
> I know all the fowls of the mountains: and the wild beasts of the
>   field are mine,
> If I were hungry, I would not tell thee: for the world is mine, and
>   the fulness thereof.

---

22 *Oxford Companion to the Bible*, ed. Metzger and Coogan, 97.

23 Blythe, "Cain and Abel in *Paradise Regained*: Fratricide, Regicide, and Cultural Equity," 72.

24 Lindzey in *Animal Theology* cites interpretations that show respect for the animals sacrificed, 103–6.

Will I eat the flesh of bulls,
> or drink the blood of goats?

Offer unto God thanksgiving; and pay thy vows unto the most
> high.

And in Psalm 51, A Psalm of David,

> For thou desirest not sacrifice; else would I give it: thou
>> delightest not in burnt offering.
> The sacrifices of God are a broken spirit: a broken and a
>> contrite heart, O God, thou wilt not despise.

The Prophet Isaiah teaches that the Lord rejects propitiatory oblations as vain: "I delight not in the blood of bullocks, or of lambs, or of he-goats . . . your hands are full of blood. Wash you, make you clean . . . cease to do evil. Learn to do well; seek judgment, relieve the oppressed, judge the fatherless, plead for the widow. . . . though your sins be as scarlet, they shall be as white as snow" (Isaiah 1.11–18). Sacrifice by substituting animals is to be replaced by the mending of one's ways. Christians completed the process of abolishing ritual bloodshed by instituting the sacrifice of Christ as sufficient propitiation for the sins of man.

Seventeenth-century commentary attributes the eating of flesh to violence issuing from the Fall, and illustrations to Genesis present the animals as God's works, not man's pantry. "When the earth was filled with *crueltie*," cries Samuel Purchas, "as men escaped not beastly butchery, so beasts escaped not butcherly inhumanity."[25] Andrew Willet writes that "this slaughter and killing of beasts, upon what occasion soever, whether for food, for knowledge, or pleasure, belongeth unto the bondage of corruption, which by sinne was brought into the world."[26] Edward Topsell reprehends the arrogance of those who "made no account of those beasts, which broght not profit to their purse."[27]

To return to the Book of Job, the Voice from the Whirlwind (chapters 38–41) delivers a stunning rebuke to the presumption that animals are "created only for our use" when the Voice from the Whirlwind displays the dynamic power of nature and the wild energies of animals, culminating with Behemoth and Leviathan, as antidotes to human pride. Who can lay out the measurements of the earth, or bound the sea, or search its depths, or cause rain in the wilderness, or make ice and snow or lightening, or stop floods, or understand the wild beasts, or tame them? Many of these lessons in humility and admiration proto-scientific projectors took rather as challenges and set out to perform the things declared impossible.

Job's advice to his friends is generally explained as a lesson in God's sovereignty and providence: "Ask the beasts, and they shall teach thee; and the fowls of the air, and they shall tell thee: or speak to the earth, and it shall teach thee: and the fishes

---

25 *Pvrchas his Pilgrimage* (1613), 13.

26 Willet, *Hexapla in Genesin* (1608), 18, 31.

27 Topsell, *The Historie of foure-footed Beastes* (1607), sig. A4. ("Beasts," from *bestia*, wild animal, is not necessarily a degrading term.)

of the sea shall declare unto thee. Who knoweth not in all these that the hand of the Lord hath wrought this?" (Job 12.7–9; Plate 9) George Sandys paraphrases:

> Ask thou the Citizens of pathlesse woods;
> What cut the ayre with wings, what swim in floods;
> Brute beasts, and fostering Earth: in generall
> They will confesse the power of God in all.[28]

By calling wild animals "Citizens," as in his commentary on Ovid, Sandys—a benefactor of the Tradescants' Ark and a treasurer of the Virginia Company—implies that wild animals have rights as well as teachings.

John Calvin held animals to be instrumental to human use, but his commentary on Job views animals as instrumental to man's moral understanding as well as his temporal life. We lost dominion over the beasts

> from Adams sinne and our own naughtinesse, in that wee be stubborne against him that had made us Princes of the worlde, and put all creatures into our hande. Let us consider this and be sorie for our sinnes: and as oft as the wilde beasts do us any harme, let us bethinke us thus: Behold, God sheweth us our owne wants: and thereupon lette us pray him to graunt us the grace to obey him in such wise, as we may beare his mark, that the beasts may know the power which he hath given us as his children.

But animals have an even higher reason for being:

> [N]ow a man might aske a question, why God keepeth still such kind of beastes [as Behemoth and Leviathan], seeing they do men no service. For it shoulde seeme that the cause ceasseth why God shoulde nurrish them any longer: but let us marke, that they ceasse not to be as beautifyings of this world, to the end that men might behold the majesty of God in them. And that is one reason sufficient ynough of it selfe . . . . God sheweth us diverse sightes in them, to teach us by that varietie to understand his power, goodnesse, and justice the better. On the other side, they are a good instruction to us, bicause that sith we cannot have the use of them, we must not presume to exalt our selves too high.[29]

The Anglican cleric Joseph Caryl, while agreeing that "all cretures . . . reade us divinity lectures of Divine Providence," adds "the least as well as the greatest, the Mouse as well as the Elephant or the Lyon; the shrimp as well as Leviathan . . . *the hand of the Lord hath wrought this, and . . . all these are in the hand of the Lord.*"[30]

John Wilkins did not need to fit into his measurements for the Ark the creature that the Voice from the Whirlwind holds out as utterly untamable:

> Canst thou draw out leviathan with an hook?
> or his tongue with a cord which thou lettest down?

---

28 George Sandys, *A Paraphrase vpon Iob,* in *A Paraphrase vpon the Divine Poems* (1638), chapter 12, p. 7.

29 *Sermons of Master Iohn Calvin, vpon the Booke of Job*, trans. Arthur Golding (1574), 782.

30 Caryl, *An Exposition with Practicall Observation . . . of the Book of Job.* London, 1649): 211 and 215.

Canst thou put an hook into his nose?
Or bore his jaw with a thorn?

Will he make many supplications unto thee?
will he speak soft words unto thee?

Will he make a covenant with thee?
wilt thou take him for a servant forever?

Will thou play with him as with a bird?
or wilt thou bind him for thy maidens?

Shall the companions make a banquet of him?
shall they part him among the merchants?

Canst thou fill his skin with barbed irons?
or his head with fish spears?

Lay thy hand upon him,
remember the battle, do no more.

This rebuke to human pride sounds ironic now that several crocodilians have been hunted nearly to extinction. One could in fact lay one's hand upon the dead body of a crocodile at the Tradescants' Ark, which also had a hippopotamus, and the Museum of the Royal Society had a crocodile, a "head of hippopotamus or Behemoth" and "skin" from the buttock of a rhinoceros. Evelyn saw an "extraordinary greate Crocodile" in Naples, hanging from the ceiling in the collection of Ferrante Imperato, of which Karen Edwards provides an illustration from Imperato's *Dell' historia naturale* (1599).[31] As the Voice continues, the crocodile—whom we recognize when the Voice says "his teeth are terrible round about. His scales are his pride, shut up together as with a close seal"—takes on numinosity:

By his neesings a light doth shine,
and his eyes are like the eyelids of the morning.
....
He maketh a path to shine after him;
one would think the deep to be hoary.
When he raiseth up himself, the mighty are afraid;
by reason of breakings , they purify themselves.
Upon earth there is not his like,
who is made without fear.
He beholdeth all high things;
he is a king over all the children of pride.

Calvin (and Beza after him) identified Behemoth and Leviathan, two highly untamable beasts, as the elephant and the whale. The elephant he thinks "a terrible

---

31 Edwards, *Milton and the Natural World*, 118; Evelyn, *Diary*, February 1645, ed. Dobson, 1:225.

houge beast, and ynought too feare us out of our wittes."[32] Natural historians decided that Leviathan is neither a myth nor a whale but a crocodile, and understood Behemoth, which means large animal, as the hippopotamus rather than the elephant. These identifications fit both the descriptions and the moral of the passage, since Asian elephants can be made obedient to human government, and the whale has long been parted among the merchants.

Leviathan, often pictured, as in the mosaics of San Marco, as neither whale nor crocodile but a snouted sea-creature, is often associated with the monster of the deep, a remnant of chaos, found in creation myths competing with, but seeping into, the Hebrew one.[33] Calvin's biblical literalism gives credit to the real beast. He denies that either Behemoth or Leviathan is an allegory of the devil. Rather, they "shewe vs Gods mightie power in the things that are too bee seene . . . we must take this text simplie as it standeth, and not shiftingly." God's intention was "to teache men after a grosse and homely maner, according to their owne small capacitie, . . . to the end that his mightie power should be the better proved unto them. . . thereby too skorne their pryde, in sending them to the brute beasts: but this could take no place, if it were spoken of the diuell . . . . When a man hath vaunted himselfe to the uttermost, let him but come to encounter with a whale, and the whale shall have more cause to vaunt himselfe than he."[34]

The Reformers' biblical literality contributed to the de-allegorization of actual animals, helping to bring them into the ark of poetry as "living souls." Milton's Leviathan, in whose hide sailors, mistaking him "haply slumb'ring on the Norway foam" for an island, are said "oft" to anchor their ships, a simile applied to Satan, yet the simile does not demonize the natural animal. The pilot "Moors by his side, under his lee" and waits for daylight. The real animal is unsubduable, but in this case does no harm. It is Satan who has "dark designs" (1.204–8, 213).

Another correction to the theme of subduing the earth occurs in the Song of Solomon (who was himself reputed to be a natural historian): that erotic poem interpreted as a marriage song of God and his people, in which the bride is likened to an enclosed garden and to the land of Israel. "[T]he Song is concerned as much with the relationship between man and nature," writes Francis Landy, "—his alienation from it through language and consciousness, and his participation in it—as it is with that between human beings. . . . [T]he Song is a reflection on the story of the garden of Eden, using the same images of garden and tree, substituting for the traumatic dissociation of man and animals their metaphoric integration. Through it we glimpse, belatedly, by the grace of poetry, the possibility of paradise."[35]

32　Calvin, 800. See Grew's disagreement in Chapter 5 above.

33　See Neil Forsyth, *The Old Enemy: Satan and the Combat Myth*, and Regina Schwartz, *Remembering and Repeating*, 28–31. Forsyth associates the end-time monstrous enemy with the "political figure of the cosmic rebel" in times of "apocalyptic thinking" (146).

34　Calvin, 800–801.

35　Landy, "The Song of Songs," in *The Literary Guide to the Bible*, ed. Alter and Kermode (1990), 306 and 319.

The creatures' communion and the rights of animals

The Bible, a work of heuristic openness, can be interpreted self-servingly, and the moral teachings of the classics ignored as pagan productions where the moral did not fit the mores. But the view that violence to animals is wrong was also held by hermeticists, writers of natural magic whose version of chemistry took the vital life of nature into account, and by orthodox Christian advocates of human community with the creatures and even the rights of animals.

Alan Rudrum applies the "Cosmic Sympathy" of hermeticists such as Paracelsus, Jacob Boehme, and Thomas Vaughan to seventeenth-century poetry, particularly that of Thomas Vaughan's twin brother Henry. Rudrum finds that "the hermetic philosophy is so organic that we cannot feel any poem as fully 'hermetic' unless it embraces the Trinity of God, Man, and Nature."[36] He points out that although analogies between human "spiritual aspirations" and those of plants and animals are apt to be taken as allegorical, Thomas Vaughan, following Paracelsus's teachings that "as souls are pre-existent, so flowers emerge from the 'Great Mystery' and have their own eternity," and that "everything has an appetency for its source . . . sees those aspirations as part of a whole cosmic seeking for eternity."[37]

A strong statement of human communion with all the creatures comes from Godfrey Goodman's *The Creatures Praysing God* (1622), which attributes natural religion to all created things, so that their spontaneous worship makes them part of the community of believers. What better humility than "to stoope to the basest wormes, and together with them, to associate thy selfe in God's service?" Following the Benedicite and Psalm 148, Goodman includes among the worshippers "Fire and hail, snow and vapours, storms, winds, fulfilling his word: Mountains and all hilles, fruitfull trees and all Cedars, Beasts and all cattell, wormes, and feathered fowles." He is not opposed to their dying for us, but wants us to understand this death as a sacrifice and part of the communion of all creatures through which they or their elements will accompany us to eternity as part of the body of Christ. "Though they are ordained for [Man's] naturall use, for his food clothing, labour: so it should seeme, they were appointed for his spirituall use, to serve him in the nature of Chaplaines"—anthropocentricity, but different from Calvin's, Willet's, or Bacon's. "Then let us conceive that all the workes of God make one corporation, and are as members of one body, under one common government." Since theirs is "a testifying faith," and moreover "they use our tongues to set forth God's praise . . . stirring vs up to praise him," there is not only "a communion of Saints, but a communion of Creatures, who joyne together in one naturall service of God." The birds are the choir, singing chorally and antiphonally at the set times of morning and evening

---

36 Rudrum, "An Aspect of Vaughan's Hermeticism," 131. See also "Henry Vaughan and the Theme of Transformation."

37 Rudrum, "The Influence of Alchemy," 473. Rudrum's "Henry Vaughan, the Liberation of the Creatures, and Seventeenth-Century English Calvinism" traces the confrontation of Calvinism with this belief, which Calvinists, like Thomas Aquinas, deemed heretical.

prayer, and unlike us, but like the Angels, they are "sealed and confirmed in their state and Condition."

Goodman's definition of "Sacrifice" is being "ordained for [God's] Service . . . . More particularly: Nothing in it selfe, contains in it selfe the use and end of it selfe, but hath some reference beyond it selfe"; what are "incense and odoriferous perfumes" of plants but "natures Sacrifices?" Further, since "man's body . . . is the Temple of God's Spirit" those creatures whose "use" is slaughter "are indeed consecrated and become a sacrifice." Like Milton and Vaughan, Goodman believes in the conservation of all species in the renovation of nature. The "dumbe Creatures" offered up by the Jews "were only types and shadowes of a true Sacrifice, the sacrifice of Christ." Since we as men partake of Christ as man, all creatures participate in the "one common matter, or substance, in the body of Christ," so that "the whole world, the great world in the little world, becomes a true and reall sacrifice"; and "They are not without hope of reward for their service, . . . For certain it is of all the dumbe Creatures, that at the generall day or our Resurrection, they likewise, though not in themselves, yet in their owne elements and Principles, shalbe renewed."

Goodman continues:

> Creatures were first created in Paradise. Then surely they were not so much ordained for slaughter, and mens use, as for the setting forth of Gods glory. Now since our fall, they groane and travell in paine together with vs, under the burthen of our sinnes, and our miseries, the punishments of sinne, Rom. 8 22. Yet they still continue innocent in themselves, they are often imployed in Gods service, alwaies praysing God in their owne kinde, never incurre the breach of his law, but are patient, notwithstanding our immoderate and inordinat abuse. Then surely, by a course of justice . . . though not. . . in the fiercenesse, malignity, and corruption of their nature, yet in their owne first elements and principles, or as they have now entered into mans body, and are become parts of mans flesh, all the Creatures in general shal partake with us, in our future intended renovation.

This view, with its curious possibility that we may transport animals to heaven by eating them, opposes Calvin's and Willet's claim that "the bruit creatures which now onely serve for our necessarie use, shall not be partakers of the glorie of the Sonnes of God; [since] there shall then be no use of them, . . . it is probable, that they shall be abolished." Goodman agrees with later monists in concluding that

> when we consider how the dumbe Creatures are sanctified, and proove to be *Sacramentalia*, fit to enter into the Holiest of Holies, to be unto vs as meanes and conduit-pipes of grace, which seems to imply, that nature and grace being now incorporated, there was surely some Deity incarnate, by vertue whereof, the whole materiall nature is combined to the Spirituall nature; not by consanguinity, but by alliance, by the nuptials of those two natures in his one person, who was both perfect God nd perfect Man, this is a most deepe and profound mysterie in Theology.

The contemplation of created things leads, as Milton's Adam exclaims, not to making the creatures objects and secular commodities, but to God.[38]

---

38 Goodman, *The Creatures Praysing God*, 3–4, 20–21, 26–32.

It may be from such preachers as Goodman that the young Robert Boyle, despite his later commitment to vivisection, drew ideas he expressed in a letter to a friend. Alan Rudrum quotes from a Royal Society "manuscript draft of a letter to an unnamed friend" in which Boyle argues from various sources that "the Soul of every Beast, does as immediately descend from God as our's"; "that Beasts do participate of Reason"; "that in the Greate Renovation at the Last Day /of all things/ [the] Beasts also shall receave & be preferred to a more exhalted Nature; & in their respective Degrees be sharers with us in our future. . . Happynesse" (with reference to Romans 8.19–22); that theologians teach "that all God's Creatures. . . glorify their Creator. . . either by our employing them to his Glory that made them, or by some secret expressions of their Thankfulnesse in a way & Language unknowne to us tho naturall to them."

Rudrum comments, "The conclusion Boyle draws, is that in mistreating animals, 'we pervert and prostitute the Creature to the service of our exorbitant and unruly Passions' and in that we disturb 'their Gratitude & Devotion' to God. . . . Boyle explicitly addresses the question of man's dominion over the creatures . . . which had been stronger before the Fall and which Bacon's program was to recover as far as possible, in the despotic mode suggested by his image of leading Nature with all her children to bind her to our service and make her our slave: "we deceive our selves, to fancy a Right in man to any other Dominion over the Creature, than what will make us through them more instrumentall to the Glory of. . . God. . . our Common Maker."

Boyle continues, "give me a Charity that extends to the whole Creation of God," who both declared them good and commanded Noah to save them in the Ark, and not just those useful to man: God "commands Noah to . . . nourrish them in the Arke; tho the Species, were, and still be, never so venemous or noxious to man." Clearly, as Ray and other empiricists came to understand, the creatures were made "for other Ends, besides Man's Service & Advantages."[39]

Henry More in *Antidote against Atheism* (1655) responds to objections that "Animals preying one upon another, and Man upon them all . . . is inconsistent with that Eternal Goodness that we profess to have created and ordered all things." More writes that God is bountiful and benign and takes pleasure that all his Creatures enjoy themselves that have life and sense. He says rather lamely at first: the "Sovereign goodness" was content to let some animals suffer so that the "several kindes of terrestrial Creatures, more exactly might be happy in their animal nature" while leaving "The *Species* of things in the mean time being still copiously enough preserved." This account of the mind of God differs from the Gospel of Luke, who says "Are not five sparrows sold for two farthings, and not one of them forgotten before God?" (Luke 12.6)

More himself was fond of hunting and may say with a certain empathy,

---

39 Boyle, Royal Society manuscript draft described and quoted by Alan Rudrum in an Appendix to "Ethical Vegetarianism Seventeenth-Century Britain," 87–9, with the permission of Professor J.J. Macintosh of the University of Calgary, "who read a paper on "Robert Boyle on Animal Rights" at a Simon Fraser Philosophy Seminar, and kindly sent me a transcript from the Royal Society manuscript on which his paper was based."

Now it is evident that the main powers of the *Animal life*, are natural craft, strength and activity of body, and that any purchase by these is far more pleasant to a living Creature, then what easily comes without them. Wherefore what can be more grateful to a terrestrial Animal, then to hunt his prey and to obtain it? But all kindes of Creatures are not capable of this special happiness. Some therefore are made to feed on the fruits of the Earth, that they may thus not only enjoy themselves, but occasionally afford game and food to other Creatures. In which notwithstanding the wisdom of God as well as his goodness is manifest, in that, while they are thus a sport and prey to others, yet they are abundantly preserved in their several generations.

Like Milton and Vaughan, More provides arguments for animal immortality.

[I]f the Souls of Brutes prove immortal (which the best of Philosophers have not been averse from) the Tragedy is still lesse horrid; but yet that ought not to animate us causlessly and petulantly to dislodge them, because we know not how long it will be till they have an opportunity to frame to themselves other bodies: and the interval of time betwixt is as to them a perfect death, wherein they have not the sense nor enjoyment of any thing. And for my own part I think, that he that slights the life or welfare of a brute Creature, is naturally so unjust, that if outward Laws did not restrain him, he would be as cruel to man.

To his argument that preying removes animals offensive to us, objectors say that it would be more providential not to have made them at all. More replies that this argument rests on the "false Principle *That the world was made for man alone*, when as assuredly the Blessed and Benign Maker of all things, intended that *other* living Creatures should enjoy themselves as well as *Men*, which they could not it they had no existence:

Therefore Providence is more exact, in that she can thus spread out her goodness further, even to the enjoyments of the more inferior ranks of the Creatures, without any considerable inconvenience to the more noble and superior. Besides, all these Creatures that are thus a prey to others are their sport and sustenance, and so pleasure others by their death, as well as enjoy themselves while they are yet in life and free from their enemy.

As to "the swarms of little Vermine, and of Flyes" More writes, with remarkable magnanimity, "we should rather congratulate their coming into Being, then murmure sullenly and scornfully against their Existence." "Those little Souls" are as capable of receiving God's benignity "as the Ox, the Elephant or Whale. For it is sense, not bulk, that makes things capable of enjoyment." He concedes however that "if they grow noysome and troublesome to us, we have both power and right to curb them."[40]

By 1692, John Ray had also come to the opinion that God did not make all creatures only "to be serviceable to Man, but also to partake themselves of his overflowing Goodness, and to enjoy their own Beings." If they are "mere Machins or automata, . . . they can have no enjoyment"; the unholy concept that God would create sentient beings incapable of joy is one of Ray's reasons for not inclining to Cartesian mechanism.[41]

---

40 More, *Antidote against Antheism*, 124–5.
41 Ray, *The Wisdom of God*, part 2, 142–3.

In 1688, Thomas Tryon could indict the human species in the court of natural law: "From whence did thou derive thy authority for killing thy inferiours, merely because they are such, or for destroying their natural rights and privileges?"[42] In *Wisdom's Dictates* (1691) he provides a vegan menu and lists among his aphorisms:

39. Refrain at all times such Foods as cannot be procured without violence and oppression.

40. For know, that all inferior Creatures when hurt do cry and send forth their complaints to their Maker or grand Fountain from whence they proceeded.

41. Be not insensible that every Creature doth bear the Image of the great Creator according to the Nature of each, and that he is the Vital Power in all things.

42. Therefore let none take pleasure to offer violence to that Life, lest he awaken the fierce wrath, and bring danger to his own Soul.

. . . .

48. Refrain Hunting, Hawking, Shooting, and all violent oppressive Exercises, and instead spend your spare time in Gardening, Planting, and Cultivating the Earth, which will afford both an innocent Pleasure and Profit to Body and Mind."[43]

Anyone minded to take this advice would find abundant guidance in John Evelyn's *Aceteria: Or, a Discourse of Sallets*, a compendious history and passionate recommendation of vegetarianism, in which Evelyn quotes the passage from Milton "As our Paridisian Bard introduces Eve, dressing of a Sallet for her Angelic Guest" and argues from Biblical and classical history, health, longevity (proven by numerous long lives including his own), morality, and pleasure—alluding to John Ray's *History of Plants*—that "Certainly Man by Nature was never made to be a *Carnivorous* Creature; nor is he arm'd for Prey and Rapine, with gag's and pointed Teeth, and crooked Claw, sharpened to rend and tear: But with gentle Hands to gather Fruit and Vegetables, and with Teeth to chew and eat them." [44]

Bird cage walk: Royal animals

Tables heaped with birds and animals are a *topos* of royalist poetry of praise that does not appear in Marvell's accounts of Bilbrough and Appleton House and that Milton mocks in *Paradise Regained* by making the Devil the founder of the feast.

Thomas Carew, Gentleman of the Privy Chamber and Sewer in Ordinary to Charles I, wrote a graceful and witty compliment to the generosity of the family and estate of Sir John Crofts in "To Saxham," extending Jonson's conceit in "To

---

42 Tryon, "Complaint of the birds and fowls of heaven to their Creator" in *The Countryman's Companion*, 141–73. Quoted from Linzey, 20.

43 Tryon, *Wisdom's Dictates, or, Aphorisms*, 6–7.

44 *Aceteria: Or, a Discourse of Sallets*. In *Silva, or a Discourse of Forest Trees*, 1706, 173, 197 (citing Ray, *History of Plants*, Book 1, Chapter 24).

Penshurst" of fish and birds vying for preferment at the master's dinner table. The grateful prayers of the poor "have made thy table blest / With plenty far above the rest," so that the sky becomes an aviary and earth an ark of willing burnt offerings to that one lord:

> The season hardly did afford
> Course cates unto thy neighbor's board,
> Yet thou hadst dainties, as the sky
> Had only been thy Volary;
> Or else the birds, fearing the snow
> Might to another deluge grow:
> The pheasant, partridge, and the lark
> Flew to thy house, as to the Ark.
> The willing ox, of himself came
> Home to the slaughter, with the lamb,
> And every beast did thither bring
> Himself to be an offering.
> The scaly herd, more pleasure took,
> Bathed in thy dish, than in the brook:
> Water, earth, air, did all conspire,
> To pay their tributes to thy fire.

Fires like suns burn in every room, adding forests to the liberality of consumption. One thinks of the displays of animals in Dutch *vanitas* paintings, which typically feature dead deer, hares, fish, and wild birds of great beauty fully feathered or plucked, trussed, and hung, not looking happy at all.

Ben Jonson in "Inviting a Friend to Supper" promises a modest meal, to be accompanied by Roman poetry, of mutton, "a short-legged hen, / If we can get her, full of eggs," a rabbit, and larks, and adds a list of other scarce birds he wishes they could dine on as well:

> And though fowl be scarce, yet there are clerks,
>   The sky not falling, think we may have larks;
> I'll tell you of more, and lie, so you will come:
>   Of partridge, pheasant, woodcock, of which some
> May yet be there; and godwit, if we can;
>   Knat, rail, and ruff, too.[45]

We have seen ways the regimentation of plants corresponds with the regimentation of peoples in Waller's "On St. James's Park." The park also contained the King's menagerie, including the cassowary before it migrated into the Tradescant collection and the Indian Crane reported "among his Majesties rare Birds kept in St. James Park near Westminster" in Ray's *Ornithology*.[46] Alastair Fowler recounts the Park's history as part of a royal hunting grounds, having "a menagerie with crocodiles" and "aviaries near Birdcage Walk (1667)." He comments, "As many seventeenth-century

---

45 Jonson, "Inviting a Friend to Supper." Compare Marvell's rail.
46 *Ornithology*, 275

Dutch paintings of country houses illustrate, domesticated exotic birds were a status symbol, displaying wealth and imperial reach. In the case of the Park, the birds were gifts of the John (later East India) Company or of foreign ambassadors."[47]

Waller promises,

> *All* that can living feed the greedy eye,
> Or dead the Pallat, here you may descry;
> The choicest things that furnisht *Noahs* Ark,
> Or *Peters* sheet, inhabiting this Park.

Noah becomes the savior of heaped boards. In Peter's vision of unforbidden food (Acts 10), a great bundle is let down from heaven "Wherein were all manner of fourfooted beasts of the earth, and wild beasts, and creeping things, and fowls of the air. And there came a voice to him, Rise, Peter, kill, and eat." Peter, though "very hungry," refuses three times on the grounds that some of the animals are unclean in Jewish law, but the voice assures them that "What God hath cleansed, that call not thou common." Peter's response to the vision is striking renunciation of the divisive effects of religious practices: "God hath showed me that I should not call any man common or unclean . . . . Of a truth I perceive that God is no respecter of persons: But in every nation he that feareth him, and worketh righteousness, is accepted with him." He renounces the use of dietary laws to separate people on grounds of ceremonial rather than moral law. In Waller's witty poem, this world-changing lesson becomes an invitation to gluttony and the winding sheet of edible animals.

Fowler describes the convention of boards groaning with animal fare:

> In the entertainment poems, the quantity of dead game is often dwelt on surprisingly. We might distinguish between the abundance of a Hondecoeter game-piece and the gross slaughter of Edwardian shooting-parties; but in the Renaissance few seem to have felt such a distinction. Cornucopias could not be poured too profusely. At the Duke of Newburgh's entertainment, "various bodies . . . thick are strowed / Cov'ring his tables like another wood"; at Wrest, the liberal board is piled with meats "till his oaken back / Under the load of piled-up dishes crack." Who is to say how far this was generosity, how far ostentation, how far 'gluttony' (Jonson), how far 'harmony' (Leigh)."[48]

Royalist poets do not all commend rapacious carnivorousness. Margaret Cavendish and Henry Vaughan suggest something close to animal rights, and John Evelyn, though no lover of the wild, is a "wise use" conservationist. Yet the Kings' and nobles' caged birds and animal-laden tables provide a setting that must have made consuming them seem normal. Perhaps it is not surprising to see Bacon, a courtier, and Hobbes, a supporter of sovereign power invested in a royal person, and later the members of the Royal Society, supported by the King's patronage—many of them powerful figures of church and state—taking a cavalier attitude toward the lives of animals. If the court, the owners of great estates, and global adventurers had followed the teachings of Pythagoras and Plutarch, would their society and ours

---

47 Fowler, *The Country House Poem*, 192–3.
48 Fowler, *The Country House Poem*, 10.

have been both better preservers of the health of nature and less prone to human bloodshed, as these philosophers claimed?

Hawking, hunting, and fishing

The fish, flesh, and fowl that arrived so willingly at the tables of the rich did not arrive on their own, and the wild ones were trapped or shot. Hunting was and is a debated topic. Margaret Cavendish took the side of the hunted, and Andrew Linzey, in *Animal Theology*, presents the argument for ethical hunting but rejects it on the grounds that hunting and meat-eating are now unnecessary and therefore wanton.[49]

As we have seen, in the seventeenth century the great forests that belonged to the monarch and the landed aristocracy were in a sense protected habitats,[50] the draining of the fens put much wildlife habitat into the hands of the already landed, and Levellers and Diggers argued for equal rights for commoners cut off from common lands. The controversies were not over the rights of animals but over who had a right to eat them. Milton's description of animals in Eden, "since wild, and of all chase" (IV. 341) takes a shot at hunting as a fallen activity, while acknowledging, with classical writers, that violence towards animals may have begun in self-defense. After the Flood, the beasts turn wild—God "requires" man's blood from them (Gen. 9.5)—and later hunting escalates for human luxury.

Jonson's *To Penshurst* begins and ends with hunting scenes, and in his "Praises of a Country Life" (translating Horace's Epode ii) the happy man

> drives with many a hound
>   Wild boars into his toils pitched round;
> Or strains on his small fork his subtle nets
>   For the eating thrush, or pitfalls sets;
> And snares the fearful hare and new-come crane,
>   And 'counts them sweet rewards so ta'en.[51]

Margaret Cavendish's biography of her husband, when assessing the damage to Clipston Park during his exile, states, "It was watered by a pleasant river that runs through it, full of fish and otters; was well-stocked with deer, full of hares, and had great store of partridges, poots, pheasants, &c., besides all sorts of water-fowl; so that this park afforded all manner of sports, for hunting, hawking, coursing, fishing, &c., for which my Lord esteemed it very much."[52] But her empathetic poem, "The Hunting of the Hare," follows the hare's experience through fear and exhaustion as he is pursued by baying hounds and trumpeting horns and galloping hunters who

---

49   Linzey, chapters 7, "Hunting as the Anti-Gospel of Predation," and 8, "Vegetarianism as a Biblical Ideal."

50   The definitions and laws of forests are stated by John Manwood in *A Treatise of the Laws of the Forest* (1665), revised and enlarged from his *Treatise and Discourse of the Laws of the Forest*, 1598.

51   Jonson, "Praises of a Country Life," in Rudrum et al., *Broadview Anthology*, 159.

52   Cavendish, *The Life of the Thrice noble, high, and puissant Prince, William Cavendish*, 135–6. Quoted from *The Life of William Cavendish* (1886).

"shout for Joy , /And valiant seeme, *poore Wat* for to destroy," until "the *Dogs* so neere his *Heeles* did get, / That they their sharp *Teeth* in his *Breech* did set" and the men whoop triumphantly. Cavendish joins Ovid and Pythagoras with an added barb for hunting: Men think that God gave all creatures their lives for men's luxury and recreation,

> Making their *Stomacks*, *Graves* which full they fill
> With *Murthe'd Bodies*, that in sport they kill.
> Yet Man doth think himselfe so gentle, mild,
> When *he* of *Creatures* is most cruell wild.
> And is so *Proud*, thinks onely he shall live,
> That *God* a *God-like Nature* did him give.
> And that all *Creatures* for his sake alone,
> Was made for him, to *Tyrannize* upon.[53]

The first printed English works on hunting, hawking, and fishing are attributed to Dame Juliana Berners, Prioress of Sopwell Nunnery,[54] by the printer, Wynken de Word, in *The Boke of St. Albans* (1486), famous as the first book in England printed in color. Many reprints and editions followed. A paraphrase appeared in 1614 as *A Iewell for Gentrie*. Its title page shows three men with hawks and hounds and the preface calls it "The childe of the most excellentest Father that ever begot, in memory, any worke of this nature."

Like Xenophon, this redaction of Dame Juliana's work teaches these arts from the ground up, telling anglers for example how to make and dye their lines and what shape to make hooks for various kinds of fish. She describes the habits and habitats of the hunted and commends consideration for the animals who work with the human hunter: "When your Hawke hath slaine a Fowle, and that you have rewarded her as before, let her flye no more till she hath rejoiced her." She makes careful observations of the hunted, as in "Of the Hare, and her rights" (that is, her nature and the right way to hunt her); "The Hare is the King of all beasts of venerie, and in Hunting maketh the best sport, breedeth the most delight of any other, and is a beast most strange by nature, for he often changeth his kinde, and is both male and female." She assigns classes of hawks to classes of hunters, prescribing "What kind of hawk is for a king, a prince, a duke, an earl, a baron, a knight, a squire, a lady, a young man."[55]

Dame Juliana's book on angling, which is bound into the 1614 edition without acknowledgment, invented a genre for future writers. According to the introduction to the 1880 facsimile, Walton took his "jury of flies" from its "xij flyes wyth whyche ye shall angle to the trought & grayllyng." Burton, "that universal plunderer, has extracted her eloquent eulogy on the secondary pleasures of angling" in the *Anatomy of Melancholy*. To this "earliest account of the art of fishing . . . belongs the credit of having assigned in popular estimation to the angler his meditative and gentle nature." Donne, Wotton, and Herbert "have . . . found that not their bodily health

---

53 *Poems and Fancies* (1653), 110–13; quoted from Germaine Greer et al., *Kissing the Rod*, 170.

54 Opinions as to authorship are cited in the *Dictionary of National Biography*, which finds no evidence against hers (4:13–14), nor does the preface to the 1966 facsimile.

55 *Iewell for Gentrie* (1614) c3v and F2.

only, but also their morals, were improved by angling. It became a school of virtues, a quiet pastime in which, while looking into their own hearts, they learnt lessons of the highest wisdom, reverence, resignation, and love."

The treatise ends by commanding conservation: "Also ye shall not be to ravenous in takying of your sayd game as to moche at one tyme" which would be easy if you followed this treatise "in every poynt. Whyche sholde lyghtly be occasyon to dystroye your owne dysportes & other mennys also. As whan ye have a suffycynt mese ye sholde coveyte nomore at that tyme." And it adds piously but unecologically that you should "nourish the game by all that ye may: & to dystroye all such thynges as ben devourers of it. And all those that done after this rule shall have the blessynge of god & saynt Petyr whyche he theym graunte whatwyth his precyous blood vs boughte."[56]

The year of the 1614 paraphrase also saw the publication of a book of hawking and hunting songs by Thomas Ravenscroft, who published several of John Milton Senior's Psalm-settings. The songs urge "Our murdering kites" to strike down partridges and so "Yield pleasure fit for kings." The names of the chorus of hunting dogs include Duty, Beauty, Jew, Damsel, Dido, Civil, Carver, Courtier, Ruler, and German. Benjamin Britten set this song for his song cycle *Our Hunting Fathers* in 1936, one of the singers whispering two of the names at the end: "German. Jew."[57]

Dame Juliana urges conservation, and Edmund Waller probes the ethics of hunting since the invention of gunpowder in a prefatory poem to Christopher Wase's translation of Gratius Falisci's *Cynegeton*, a Latin poem on hunting. The preface compares it to Vergil's *Georgics* and Waller makes the hunt a metaphor for the poem:

> The Muses all the Chase adorne,
> My Friend on Pegasus is borne,
> And young Apollo winds the horne.

Waller commends the lessons "How to chuse Dogs for sent or speed, / And how to change and mend the breed"; "What armes to use, or nets to frame, / Wild beasts to combat or to tame, / With all the Mystery's of that game," but draws the line at the use of guns.

> But (worthy friend) the face of warr
> In ancient times does differ farr
> From what our fiery battels are.
>
> Nor is it like (since powder knowne)
> That man so cruell to his owne
> Should spare the race of Beasts alone.

---

56 Berners, *A Treatyse of Fysshynge wyth an Angle* (1496, facs. 1880), Preface pp. vii–viii and conclusion.

57 Ravenscroft, "Hawking for the Partridge," in *A Briefe Discovrse* (1614); The Huntington Library copy, shelfmark 69078, is from the Bridgewater Library and has a long handwritten inscription to "To the honorable knight Sir John Egerton," whose "noble inclination to Musicke" is among the virtues commended. Probably Milton and certainly his collaborator Henry Lawes, music tutor to the Egerton family, would have seen this volume.

No quarter now, but with the Gun
Men wait in trees from Sun to Sun
And all is in a moment done.

And therefore we expect your next
Should be no Comment but a Text
To tell how moderne Beasts are vext.[58]

Wase's commentary finds hunting poems more wholesome than those that inflame youth to lasciviousness, ambition, "love of War, and seeds of anger." (The legendary alliance of hunting and chastity accords with the virgin goddess Diana, praised here for teaching mortals to defend themselves from wild beasts). Hunting dissuades from "sloth and softness" without, when "us'd with moderation," causing hard-heartedness, "but rather enclines men to acquaintance and sociablenesse." It inures one from childhood to hardships and discomforts and provides "innocent and natural delights" like seeing daybreak, hearing "the chirping of small birds pearched upon their dewie boughs," and breathing in the fragrance of pastures and cool morning air. The hunter's delight in tracking the "amazed beast . . . by the intelligence he holds with Dogs" is "most pleasant and as it were a master-piece of Naturall Magique"; then the triumph of returning "with Victory and Spoiles, having a good title both to his meat and repose." But one must not "become altogether addicted to Slaughter and Carnage . . . For as it is the privilege of man, who is endued with reason, and authorized in the Law of his Creation to subdue the Beast of the field, so to tyrannize over them is plainly brutish."

Like Juliana, Falesci advises hunters to make their own weapons, where to find best flax for nets and snares, how to plant hemp and use lines of feathers to balk deer and of other animal parts for "Gins and Fetters." Making weapons of wood begins with the right ordering of trees in nurseries. The work also teaches breeds and breeding, diseases of hunting dogs, the care of pregnant bitches and their young, how to cure hounds' wounds and diseases by natural and divine means, how to choose a good hunting nag. A good huntsman, courageous and skilled, arms himself "with weapons to cast at distance" and "to charge with at hand, either to cut up hedges, or to open his Beast."[59]

The aristocratic entertainment of the chase saved forests and practiced a tradition of ethics, allied to the habit of command, which requires some temperance. One begins with a field of hemp and a nursery of trees and gives "game" a fighting chance. But royal and aristocratic entertainments do not suggest communion with animals as fellow worshippers or fellow sufferers. The awakening of human consciences to the effects of violence on other species and its possible relation to violence toward our own belonged to those poets, preachers, and philosophers who interpreted the observations of Aristotle or Bacon or Ray or classical and biblical teachings or their own eyes as cause for compassion and responsibility towards the works of the biblical fifth and sixth days of creation.

---

58   Waller, *Cynegeticon*, sigs a5–a6 recto.
59   Wase, sigs A1v and a8r–9r and p. 13.

Chapter 7

Milton's Prophetic Epics

Nature first gave signs, impressed
On bird, beast, air, air suddenly eclipsed
After short blush of morn.

Paradise Lost 11.182–4

Many injustices to Milton's epics arise from applying interpretations of Genesis with which Milton did not concur. Biblical literature—the Hebrew and Greek testaments—leave space for interpretation; by learnedly liberating the literal texts from assumptions and allegories of intervening centuries and re-presenting them newly imagined, Milton sets perceptions of mother Earth, mother Nature, and mother Eve on new trajectories.[1] As a defender of the liberty of the educated conscience, he divorces monotheism from the authoritarianism that sometimes claims it.

Paradise Lost represents the wounding of the earth in epic form and provides a pattern for the regeneration of humankind on which other species depend. Milton's theology of matter is material to his epic. He holds that all species issue from divine substance and renders the vocation of the species gifted with discursive reason, articulate speech, and a capacity for magnanimity as caring for the habitation they share. The first human beings were put into a pristine place "to dress it and to keep it" (Gen. 2.15) and expected by increasing and multiplying to extend this care through "more hands" (9.207) to the whole earth. The desertion and renewal of earth-care are part of what the story of the "mortal fruit" is about.[2]

Early poems

Milton's early interest in natural knowledge appears in *Poems . . . Both English and Latin* (1645). His boyhood metrical paraphrase of Psalm 114 amplifies the Hebraic sense of nature's rejoicing with those liberated from slavery in the Exodus: "The high, huge-bellied mountains skip like rams / Among their ewes, the little hills like lambs"; with youthful prosodic mimesis he exhorts the earth to shake in the presence

---

1   This process is more fully discussed by Ken Hiltner in *Milton and Ecology*. My argument may be found in *Milton's Eve*.

2   Anthony Low in *The Georgic Revolution* points out that pastoral poetry is essentially arisocratic, and that georgic poetry had to overcome a snobbish disdain towards manual labor.

of him who "glassy floods from rugged rocks can crush, / And make soft rills from fiery-flint-stones gush."[3]

While the poems Milton wrote during and shortly after his college days often retain suggestive allegory, they tilt toward natural knowledge and a sense of responsibility for the natural world. In the Nativity Ode, the Lord of Nature enters nature and banishes proprietary deities that had to be propitiated by animal and human sacrifice. *L'Allegro* and *Il Penseroso* draw opposites together, as Milton does other polarized archetypes, and resolves the old debate about whether the active or the contemplative life is better by making these persona two sides of one complete person. "L'Allegro" favors sensuous perception and "Il Penseroso" draws abstract wisdom closer to the particular virtues of actual things. The happy man wakes to the song of the lark, enjoys a country ramble, and ends the day with comic theater and lyric song. The pensive man immerses himself in the philosophical and cosmic worlds, beginning with the song of the nightingale and ending with sacred anthems and tragic drama. He studies at midnight

> in some high lonely tow'r
> Where I may oft outwatch the Bear,
> With thrice-great Hermes, or unsphere
> The Spirit of Plato to unfold
> What worlds, or what vast regions hold
> The immortal mind that hath forsook
> Her mansion in this fleshly nook.

The body is subordinated in this early poem—Milton has been immersed in Neoplatonic Cambridge—as the mind's small stopping-place ("mansion") where the wise man studies astronomy and both Platonic and hermetic philosophy, with the sympathetic correspondences of "those daemons that are found / In fire, air, flood, or under ground, / Whose power hath a true consent / With planet, or with element." But in old age it is visible nature that the contemplative man contemplates, seeking a hermitage

> Where I may sit and rightly spell,
> Of every star that heav'n doth show,
> And every herb that sips the dew;
> Till old experience do attain
> To something like prophetic strain.

"Rightly spell" may suggest a wary attachment to hermetic natural magic and an interest in the new search for an accurate scientific language based on experience. Prophetic poetry evolves from right knowledge of nature, from "every star" to "every herb"—not only genus and constellation but each individual orb and plant.

In 1632, at the age of 23, Milton was asked to contribute to an aristocratic entertainment for the dowager Countess of Derby, with the pastoral title of *Arcades*. He furnished three songs and a remarkable speech by "the Genius of the Wood," a

---

3   This is the passage about which Ruskin says "all feverish and wild fancy becomes just and true."

local nature spirit whose task is to protect and nurture a particular place.[4] The Genius of the Wood is clear about his vocation.

> For know by lot from Jove I am the pow'r
> Of this fair wood, and live in oaken bow'r,
> To nurse the saplings tall and curl the grove
> With ringlets quaint, and wanton windings wove.

"Quaint" and "wanton" retain their early definitions of "elaborate" (*Oxford English Dictionary* 3) and "unrestrained" (*Oxford English Dictionary* 3). As enjoined in Genesis 2.15, in addition to dressing plants, he keeps or protects them.

> And all my plants I save from nightly ill,
> Of noisome winds winds, and blasting vapours chill.
> And from the boughs brush off the evil dew,
> And heal the harms of thwarting thunder blue,
> Or what the cross dire-looking planet smites,
> Or hurtful worm with cankered venom bites.

The Genius combines astrology with agricultural advice resembling Gabriel Plattes's for preventing mildew on field crops: "let two men with a cord between them shake off the dew before sunrise."[5] He does what instructors from Xenophon onward say a good farmer does and more, making his rounds morning and evening to "Number my ranks, and visit every sprout," and does so "With puissant words, and murmurs made to bless." The Genius talks to his plants, while visiting each one like the waters of Eden in the epic, and like Eve.

A Mask Presented at Ludlow Castle 1634 (printed in 1637; also known as *A Masque* and *Comus*) was performed on the Feast of St. Michael and all Angels, the harvest festival and the day when public officials took office, to celebrate the inauguration of the Earl of Bridgewater as Lord President of Wales. In it Comus, lord of misrule, tries to entice the Lord President's young daughter, Lady Alice Egerton, playing herself, to a life of avaricious sensuality by promoting reckless consumption. The *Mask* educates the Egerton children about good government, starting with government of the self and including the responsibilities of governors for economic and environmental justice as well as the social justice to which Leah Marcus has drawn attention.[6] The habit of temperance that Comus mocks is both a personal virtue and the moral foundation of justice in the body politic.

The *Mask* locates the action in the geographical environs of its performance, Ludlow Castle, rather than a generalized Arcadia or Albion. Its title is place-based, a significance obscured by the generations of critics who called it "Comus." John Demaray notes the "real places in the text" and describes Ludlow Castle, "the residence of the lord president of Wales and the seat of government for six English

---

4   Ken Hiltner illuminates this figure in "The Portrayal of Eve in *Paradise Lost*: Genius at Work."

5   Plattes, *A Discovery of Infinite Treasure* (1635).

6   Marcus, "Justice for Margery Evans: A 'Local' reading of *Comus*," in Walker, *Milton and the Idea of Woman*, 66–85.

and four Welsh counties": "The walls facing away from the town surmounted a rocky height which dropped sharply to the united waters of the Teme and Corve." From its towers, the view "to the west was the meandering stream flowing southward toward the Severn River."[7] Ruins of the castle and sparse remainders of the woods, as well as the rivers, may still be seen. Stella Revard identifies the guardian and the rescuer of the children in the Mask, the Attendant Spirit and Sabrina, as "divinities of sky and water, who play their roles as the local gods of the English borders and protectors of the children of an earl of 'mickle trust and power,'" and Sabrina's associates as also deities of place. Sabrina is "a divinity who heals," whose task is "not only to purify, but also to detoxify."[8]

In his "stately Palace, set out with all manner of deliciousness," Comus offers the Lady "orient liquor" that turns human beings into "Monsters headed like sundry sorts of wilde Beasts, but otherwise like Men and Women, their apparel glistering,"[9] and when she refuses it he tries to convert her to a life of predatory consumption:

> Wherefore did Nature powre her bounties forth,
> With such a full and unwithdrawing hand,
> Covering the earth with odours, fruits, and flocks,
> Thronging the Seas with spawn innumerable,
> But all to please, and sate the curious taste?
> And set to work millions of spinning worms,
> That in their green shops weave the smooth-haired silk
> To deck her Sons, and that no corner might
> Be vacant of her plenty, in her own loins
> She hutch't th'all-worshipt ore, and precious gems
> To store her children with.   [710–20]

George Sandys uses similar imagery to describe "the wicked" in his paraphrase of Job 27–8, published a year later than *A Mask*:

> Although he gather Gold like heaps of Dust,
> The fuell of his Luxury and Lust:
> His Cabinets with change of Garments fraught
> By silke-wormes spun, and Phrygian Needles wrought:
> Yet for the Just reserv'd; who shall divide
> His treasure, and divest him of his pride.
> . . . Torne Rocks the sparkling Diamonds unfold;
> The blushing Ruby, and pure graines of Gold.
> Those gloomy vaults no wandring soule descries:
> . . . But where above the Earth, or underground,
> Can Wisedom by the search of Man be found?[10]

---

7   Demaray, *Milton and the Masque Tradition*, 54 and 97.
8   Revard, *Milton and the Tangles of Neara's Hair*, 130–31, 138–40.
9   Stage directions after lines 658 and 92.
10 Sandys, *A Paraphrase vpon the Divine Poems* (1638), 34–5.

Both Milton and Sandys allude to favorite interests of colonial projectors, silkworms and the Golden Calf of "all-worship't ore." Silkworms were much advertised by promoters of investment in Virginia,[11] and Samuel Hartlib was to publish elaborate instructions for raising them in England.[12] Comus's attitude toward them is the metonymy of his attitude toward the natural world and the explorers' attitudes toward the animals of the New World: they are slaves in nature's shop.

In *Paradise Lost*, Raphael takes an interest in the life of a worm and gives us the kinetic sense of being one. "These as a line their long dimension drew," he says in one unbroken line, "Streaking the ground with sinuous trace" (7.480–81); we feel on our tongues their long bodies extend liquidly in the repeated l's, contract tactilely with the harder dentals, draw themselves sibilantly over the earth and leave their trail. Comus's slippery lines imitate not the experience of a worm or snake or caterpillar but that of a wearer of silk: Dalila, for example, who in *Samson Agonistes* comes forth like a queen decked in all the riches of Guiana. He is not interested in the life of the caterpillar, or anyone else, but in corruption by luxurious commodities. His claim that without greedy consumption Nature "would be quite surcharg'd with her own own weight, . . . Th'earth cumber'd, and the wing'd air dark't with plumes" is the argument Porphyry attributes to "plebeians and the vulgar," who believe that without hunting "the earth will not be able to bear the multitude of animals."[13] Comus represents exploitative attitudes towards women, animals, and others Aristotle thought "disposed to servitude," represented in the "rabble" he turns his victims into.

In spite of her youth, the Lady is aware (and if Lady Alice Egerton is not, her lines teach her) that temperance is the field in which justice is sown. When Comus chides her "well-governed and wise appetite" as an ungrateful abstinence by which nature would be "strangled with her waste fertility," she makes an ethical reply:

> Impostor do not charge most innocent Nature,
> As if she would her children should be riotous
> With her abundance; she good cateress
> Means her provision only to the good
> That live according to her sober laws,
> And holy dictate of spare Temperance:
> If every just man that now pines with want
> Had but a moderate and beseeming share
> Of that which lewdly-pampered Luxury
> Now heaps upon some few with vast excess,
> Nature's full blessings would be well dispensed
> In unsuperfluous even proportion,
> And she no whit encumbered with her store,
> And then the giver would be better thanked,
> His praise due paid, for swinish gluttony
> Ne're looks to Heav'n amidst his gorgeous feast,

---

11   J. Martin Evans provides discussion and bibliography in *Milton's Imperial Epic*.

12   Hartlib [Publisher], *The Reformed Virginian Silk-Worm* (1655).

13   *Select Works of Porphyry* (1823), 11, 13.

But with besotted base ingratitude
Cramms, and blasphemes his feeder. [762–79]

Although temperance has a long literary history as a matter of personal morality and social conscience, Milton's "Lady" advocates justice to human beings founded on justice toward "innocent Nature." Temperance is the virtue that on the ethical level preserves the earth; of the spiritual sphere, where "the sun-clad power of Chastity" (782) knits the soul to God, the Lady deems Comus too corrupt to hear.

The Lady earns her rescue from Comus by her eloquent resistance, but it is effected by the genius Sabrina, who "with moist curb sways the smooth Severn stream." As we have seen, other hydraulic engineers, Thomas Bushell in mining and Cornelius Vermuyden in draining, curbed more imperially. Sabrina is the virgin granddaughter of the Brutus thought to have founded Britain, now transformed to the Goddess of the crystalline river Severn in the Lord President's domain of Wales. A figure of grace operating through local nature, Sabrina links moral probity with the health of the earth; she especially helps "Ensnared chastity" but also "Visits the herds along the twilight meadows / Helping all urchin blasts" and healing with "pretious viald liquors" that are the opposite of Comus's cup.

The Lady's chastity is not merely a self-regarding virtue; it concerns the temperate use of nature and the government of the self, in her case as a member of a ruling family and potentially of a fruitful marriage. In several regards, *A Mask* resembles Shakespeare's *The Tempest*. Both concern good government, both are tinctured by Vergil's *Georgics* and *Aeneid*, and, like the Forbidden Tree, both link temperance with justice. Prospero's masque (4.i.60–139) transforms an aristocratic and pastoral genre into a georgic one: Iris, the rainbow after the tempest, addresses Ceres as the patroness of a landscape with many signs of labor, and they exclude from their company the fallen and divisive Venus, "Mars's hot minion," who had plotted the rape of Proserpine "which cost Ceres all that pain" (*Paradise Lost* 4.271); but they welcome Juno, patroness of marriage, who promises that Ferdinand and Miranda will prosper. Ceres offers

Earth's increase, foison plenty,
Barns and garners never empty,
Vines with clust'ring bunches growing,
Plants with goodly burden bowing.

Shakespeare's Ferdinand applauds this combination of wedded and tedded fertility: "So rare a wond'red father and a wise / Makes this place a Paradise." Milton's Lady defeats her enemy with Sabrina's help, and Prospero gives his enemies opportunity to deliver themselves by "heart's sorrow / And a clear life ensuing" (3.iii.81–2).[14] At the end, nymphs join "sunburned sicklemen" in a "graceful dance," nature and labor combining in a harvest celebration, though the festivities must be broken off to await Prospero's harvest of souls.[15] Milton's rural courtly *Mask* also explores the relations

---

14 *The Tempest*, ed. Robert Langbaum (1963).
15 Whether Caliban benefits from Prospero's temporary colony or his gift of language is a matter of dispute.

among temperance, chastity, fecundity, and justice and incorporates country dancers near its end. It also regenerates Venus, placing her (in the printed version) in the Garden of Adonis from which, in Spenser, all creatures flow, where the Adonis of wounded sexuality is "waxing well."

Creaturehood and creature kinship: Satan and the son

The action that initiates the drama of *Paradise Lost* is the Son's appointment as Vicegerent, which precipitates the War in Heaven. This announcement, I shall argue, is preparatory to the Creation of the World. The Son is the "the Omnific Word" (7.217) who calls all creatures into being—"by whom," Abdiel retorts to Satan's objections, "As by his Word the mighty Father made / All things, ev'n thee, and all the Spirits of Heav'n / By him created in their bright degrees" (5.835–8) and who, in the scene of this anointing, becomes the mediator between divine and created beings. Envious Lucifer, the archangel who becomes Satan the adversary, objects, and persuades his legions that the new Vicegerent is a tyrant who will impose new laws, while the faithful angels respond with dance and song. The angels' attitudes toward the new creation include Satan's view of nature as engine against the Almighty and Mammon's as commodity, Raphael's empathetic respect for all "living souls" and their habitats as he relates the creation story, and Michael's assurance of God's presence in them all when Adam laments his dismissal from the Garden. These positions are incipient in the choices the angels make during that originary moment.

Michael's view of divine immanence may seem to be at odds with the divine transcendence insisted on in attributes of Milton's God that often trouble readers: his unapproachable throne, his absolute justice, and, particularly, the implacable proclamation concerning the Son that motivates Satan's rebellion:

> your Head I him appoint;
> And by myself have sworn to him shall bow
> All knees in Heav'n, and shall confess him Lord;
> Under his great Vicegerent Reign abide
> United as one individual Soul
> Forever happy: him who disobeys
> Mee disobeys, breaks union, and that day
> Cast out from God and blessed vision, falls
> Into utter darkness, deep ingulfed, his place
> Ordained without redemption, without end.[16]   [5.606–15]

This God would seem to be defending his transcendent authority. Yet Michael's understanding of God's Omnipresence "in every kind that lives" (11.337) reinterprets human dominion over other creatures as a sacred responsibility for their well-being, and the appointment of the Son as intermediary between the divine Other and a human race responsible for other others draws the whole creation closer to

---

16 Allusions are to Psalm 2 and Hebrews 1.6.

the creator.[17] God's creativity issues from his transcendence, the principle of free otherness out of which others come. But it is enacted by the Son, "the Omnific Word" who speaks forth lives.

Although the epic action begins with the anointing of the Son, an earlier event predicts its course. Newly fallen Satan, declaring that "Space may produce new worlds," remembers "a fame in Heaven" that God intended to create one, "and therein plant / A generation, whom his choice regard / Should favour equal to the sons of Heav'n." Indeed, this prophecy may be the first rankling of the yet unfallen Lucifer's potentiality for pride and envy and a motive for his rebellion. In the Infernal consultation on revenge that follows their fall, Beelzebub recalls:

> There is a place
> (If ancient and prophetic fame in Heav'n
> Err not) another world, the happy seat
> Of some new race called *Man*, about this time
> To be created like us, though less
> In power and excellence, but favoured more
> Of him who rules above; so was his will
> Pronounced among the gods, and by an oath,
> That shook Heavn's whole circumference, confirmed.   [2.345–53]

Methods of defrauding the new planet and its less rapacious inhabitants issue from Mammon, that least erected spirit at whose suggestion "impious hands / Rifled the bowels of their mother Earth / For Treasures better hid" (1.686–8).[18] As the chief demons debate in the counsel chamber of Pandemonium, built by his directions, Mammon counsels neither resuming war nor "our splendid vassalage" but finding a way to live splendidly in Hell by means of an agenda that demonically parodies Milton's own idea of liberty:

> Let us . . . seek
> Our own good from ourselves, and from our own
> Live to ourselves, though in this vast recess,
> Free, and to none accountable, preferring
> Hard liberty before the easy yoke
> Of servile pomp.   [249...257]

---

17   Mary Ann Radzinowicz states, "Milton . . . enthrones the Son in a meritocracy of which the natural political result is a loosening of God's empire and a strengthening of ties among creatures. And, finally, although he attributes this arrangement to God's calculated relinquishment of power, not to His tightening of it, the arrangement is held to be valuable for its reasonableness (it promotes unity and happiness), not for its divine binding." "The Politics of *Paradise Lost*," in Patterson, ed., *John Milton*, 127.

18   Alan Rudrum and Christopher Fitter show that the biblical mandate of "dominion" over all the earth, earlier interpreted as stewardship, was swayed to instrumentalism by followers of Calvin, the growth of global commerce, and a managerial attitude towards property as profit: Rudrum, "Henry Vaughan, The Liberation of the Creatures, and Seventeenth-Century English Calvinism," 33–54; Fitter, *Poetry, Space, Landscape*, chapters 4 and 5. On the earlier history of interpretation see Jeremy Cohen, *'Be fertile and increase, fill the earth and master it.'*

But the speech on labor and endurance that follows ends in mere acquisitiveness:

> This desert soil
> Wants not her hidden lustre, gems and gold;
> Nor want we skill or art, from whence to raise
> Magnificence; and what can Heav'n show more?   [2.270–73]

Satan's mouthpiece Beelzebub doubts their success in either Heaven or Hell but combines Mammon's plan with the earlier prophecy of a new world they might usurp, either

> To waste his whole Creation, or possess
> All as our own, and drive as we were driven,
> The puny habitants, or if not drive,
> Seduce them to our party, that their God
> May prove their foe, and with repenting hand
> Abolish his own works.   [2.365–8]

Raphael, in contrast, is free of envy; the unfallen angels, he tells Adam, "inquire / Gladly into the way of God with Man: / For God we see hath honor'd thee, and set / On Man his Equal Love" (8.225–8). Refusal to love the goodness and felicity of others, even in a state of just equality, begets evil.

The Son's elevation to anointed leader of the angels created by his agency would seem, then, to be connected to his previously predicted forthcoming agency as maker of this new creation, which the angels will serve: "Man he made," Satan complains later, and

> O indignity!
> Subjected to his service angel wings,
> And flaming ministers to watch and tend
> Their earthy charge.   9.154–7]

His refusal to serve the Son includes a refusal to serve his fellow creatures in an order where the higher serves the lower: God gives life, and angelic beings serve God by serving human ones, who serve by tending and keeping the creation. At the anointing, Lucifer sees his identity threatened. That identity does indeed dwindle, but only when he becomes Satan, a vengeful abuser of other creatures, initiating the individual and collective pain under which, the Apostle writes to the Romans, not only the human race but every kind that lives, "made subject to vanity, by reason of mans vanity," must groan.

Feeling injured by the Son's promotion, Satan pretends or jumps to the conclusion that the Son is going to exercise a legalistic and repressive dominion by imposing new laws. His subordinate Abdiel disagrees: this headship is provident of their good, and the Son merits it, because by him the Father created "All things, ev'n thee." Their glory is not obscured by the Son's vicegerency "But more illustrious made, since he the head / One of our number thus reduced becomes" (5.836–43).

Satan denies that he is a creature at all. "We know no time when we were not as now; / Know none before us, self-begot, self-rais'd / By our own quick'ning power" (5.859–61). And from this moment of denying that he is a creature—though sometimes he nearly repents—Satan assumes the right to exploit and destroy the creation from which he exempts himself.[19] The prototype of those who feel themselves superior to other races and believe that other species exist only for their use, he plots with his colleagues, especially Mammon, to appropriate the human race and other forms of flesh.

Raphael's more brotherly response to the creatures arises from his acceptance of eternal monistic materialism in which all living creatures from seraphim to seedling, though differing in degree, are made from "one first matter all" (5.472). For those who agree that the Son reigns by right of merit as the artist of their making, diversity of species expands the arena of love.

Satan despises fleshly creatures. Like a perverse parody of a natural historian, he has "with inspection deep / Considered every creature," but only to find "which of all / Most opportune might serve his wiles" (9.83–5). He uses animal bodies—cormorant, lion, leopard, toad, a magnificent snake—for disguise, to spy on and corrupt his human prey: a haughtily spiritual being in animal dress who hates being incarnated and mixed with "Bestial slime" (9.165). Eventually he and his followers will exploit all nature, including human flesh.

John Tanner writes of Satan's "ontological individualism," summed up in his vaunt that "The mind is its own place, and in it self / Can make a Heav'n of Hell, a Hell of Heav'n" (1.254–5), that "Satan's claim to possess such freedom presupposes two dubious premises that were to become common after Descartes: (1) the sharp rift between subject and object and (2) the priority of subject to object."[20] Satan's claim is a demonic form of the subjectivism that Ruskin argues against in his discourse on the pathetic fallacy, and the reverse of the empathetic identification with "the object" of perception that Milton's Edenic imagery and prosody invite.

The Father is the source, the density of originary light too strong to be looked upon even by Seraphim: "God is light," says the invocation to Book 3, "And never but in unapproachéd light / Dwelt from eternity." He is, and invents, otherness. Like the Voice from the Whirlwind, he gives his intellectual creatures the mind-stretching experience of an unimaginable Other who produces other others: the behemoth to whom the mountains bring forth food and who drinks up a river, the untamable crocodile whose "eyes are like the eyelids of the dawn" (Job 41.18). His transcendence gives to his creatures that vivifying panic awe of the holy that stretches the imagination of Job beyond the assumptions of human reason. Because of his transcendence, God is a free creator, able to call the matter of chaos into ordered substances enabled to produce beings endowed with selfhood and freedom. His invention of difference is the invention of free selves and of responsiveness to what is not oneself, the fundamentals of love and art.

The Son, on the other hand, participates in both divinity and creaturehood from the time of his appointment as head of the angels. Phenomenal light—the "Bright influence of bright essence increate" that is the emanating substance of the physics

---

19   See John Tanner on Satan's "fantasy of self-creation," in *Anxiety in Eden*, 152–4.

20   Tanner, *Anxiety in Eden*, 161. See also Wendell Berry, *Poetry and Place*, in *Standing by Words*.

of creation—proceeds, the Bard says tentatively, from the "Eternal Coeternal beam." This radiance has many meanings,[21] among them the relation of the Son to the Father as "Light of Light . . . By whom all things were made."[22] Because the Son is "anointed" Raphael calls him "Messiah," and his Messiahship is a kind of angelification. Like the Incarnation, the Messiah's vicegerency is a descent, at least in Abdiel's view, bringing "the Omnific Word" "more near." The appointment of the Son as vicegerent preserves the transcendent power that makes unhampered making possible while bringing divinity closer to, and eventually into, creaturehood. (Satan despises flesh; the Son becomes it.) By his mediation, God's Omnipresence can be "in every kind that lives" without being polytheistically confined within the natural world and subjected to vagary and necessity.

Some political and ecological critics blame monotheistic conceptions of divine transcendence for an exploitative attitude towards nature. Milton takes the opposite view. After the appointment of the Son as vicegerent, Satan both refuses to acknowledge God's transcendence and objects to God's modification of it through the mediation of the Son; he resents the proliferation of species, and his refusal to serve the Son is of a piece with his refusal to serve as a flaming minister to the "puny" beings whose creation has already been predicted. In contrast to the colonization and exploitation represented by Satan, Beelzebub, and Mammon, those puny beings, Adam and Eve, actually take care of the Garden. When they too aspire to transcendence at Satan's prompting, they fail to accept their creaturehood and its responsibilities.

For those characters who discern what Michael calls "the track divine" in nature, God's transcendence does not oppose his immanence in all beings, but is the condition of otherness out of which all variety comes. It also makes possible a kind of general providence that nature deities cannot provide. But Milton's natural world, unlike that of Emersonian Transcendentalism, is not a phenomenal simulacrum of the spirit, but a first substance God makes of himself, departs from, and calls into individuated being, and into which he chooses to re-enter, and in which he offers to dwell. In this way, nature can be holy without being worshipped and can be served without being idolized.

Natural calling: Preserving habitats

A Mask and *Paradise Regained* demonstrate renewals of justice to the household of nature after the violation of the "one restraint" in Paradise. *Paradise Lost* represents the Garden of Eden before that lapse as "A happy rural seat of various view" (4.247) shared with all kinds of interactive lives which, until the Fall, feed on the renewable parts of edible plants. For Adam and Eve, caring for this garden, contributing their mild arts to its prosperity and beauty, enjoying their companionship with each other and all the creatures (including angels and their music), is bliss. But that is not to say that the epic is not problematic. Adam seems to be echoing Bacon when he speaks

---

21 Hughes mentions several in his Introduction to *Paradise Lost*, section 56, in *Complete Poems and Major Prose*.

22 As expressed in the Nicene creed.

to Eve of "power and rule / Conferred upon us, and dominion giv'n / Over all other creatures that possess / Earth, air, and sea." (4.429–32). I don't mean to whitewash this statement, but to show that Milton perplexes and redefines it as part of his dialectic procedure, his reopening of many questions within the representation of a paradisal state where they could have been worked out without doing evil. Milton represents a full spectrum of attitudes towards the natural world in the voices of his narrator and characters, but with a pervasive consciousness of the value of keeping nature whole that we call "ecology." He satirizes the concept of nature as an insensate storehouse of "resources," the idea that the "dominion" conferred in Genesis gives permission to usurp species and habitats, and the commercial exploitation of the New World by attributing these ambitions to Satan, Beelzebub, and Mammon.

Adam's speech to Eve on human dominion continues:

> Then let us not think hard
> One easy prohibition, who enjoy
> Free leave so large to all things else, and choice
> Unlimited of manifold delights:
> But let us ever praise him, and extol
> His bounty, following our delightful task
> To prune these growing plants, and tend these flow'rs,
> Which were it toilsome, yet with thee were sweet.   [4.432–9]

Adam earns his moral leadership partly by understanding that other creatures "possess" their habitats. We read also that "the sov'reign Planter . . . framed / All things to man's delightful use" (4.691–2). Adam's and Eve's and our own care of the earth depends on what uses of the natural world we consider delightful; in their case, "delightful task" and "delightful use" are very nearly the same.

In Genesis 1.28, God enjoins the first man and woman to "Be fruitful, and multiply, and replenish the earth, and subdue it," and to "have dominion" over every living thing; in Genesis 2.15 he puts the first man into an earthly paradise "to dress it and to keep it" and creates woman to be his meet (fit) help in this employment.[23] Of the various verbs in these verses, "keep" has received least attention.[24]

The "dressing" or improvement of nature for human use was the object of scientific societies, including the Hartlib circle and the beginnings of the Royal Society. Writers like Samuel Hartlib, Robert Hooke, and John Ray connected scientific observation to the spiritual as well as the economic life of humankind and exclaimed at the beauty of divine craftsmanship, but did not imagine the possibility of extinction by exploitation. Milton recommended moderation: the Archangel Raphael warns against a surfeit of scientific and speculative knowledge unintegrated with land and community—"this Paradise / And thy fair *Eve*" (8.171–2)—, yet provides a great

---

23 Quotations are from the "Authorized" or "King James" Bible of 1611.

24 On the ecological implications of dressing and keeping see Jeffrey S. Theis, "The Environmental Epic in *Paradise Lost*" and Theis's discussion in "Milton's Principles of Architecture" of ways the paradisal bower relates to the the natural environment "and how this relationship represents and influences one's actions in the world" (103).

deal of it well integrated with moral wisdom; and Adam and Eve have an elementary technology, "guiltless of fire" (9.392).

In spite of the biblical calling to tend the Garden, no previous literary or iconographic tradition described or depicted Adam and Eve actually doing so before the Fall.[25] Their presence "subdued the earth" in the sense that, in medieval and Renaissance Genesis poems and plays, animals pay fawning obeisance to Adam and plants bloom to adorn Eve, but the idea that dressing and keeping the Garden before the Fall was an active employment was oddly overlooked. Commentators considered labor either allegorically as the cultivation of inner virtues, or disciplinarily as prevention of idleness in which temptations breed, or punitively as retribution for the original sin, or occasionally as a need to keep the beasts from damaging the plants, but not literally as a responsibility toward the creation and a joyous activity that gave interest and purpose to paradisal life.[26] Milton's Adam and Eve actually take care of the Garden. Both take earth-keeping seriously, especially Eve, who lets nothing—including the threatening presence of the Foe—deter her.

When Eve proposes to Adam, in a passage already discussed,[27] that they work apart for three hours, she says, "Let us divide our labours, thou where choice / Leads thee, or where most needs . . . while I . . . find what to redress till noon" (9.214–19). Her strong sense that nature needs them, that their work is essential to the Garden's well-being and their own, and that although their work is usually mutual, she has personal responsibility and creativity, is revolutionary among treatments of this story. Her suggestion of winding of woodbine or ivy around props is not mere domestic tidiness; growing in shade, vines need to climb for light and are constructed to clasp. Nehemiah Grew writes of

> the Claspers of Vines; the branches whereof being very long, fragile and slender, unless by their Claspers they were mutually contain'd together, they must needs by their own weight, and that of their Fruit, undecently fall, and be also liable to frequent breaking. So that the whole care is divided betwixt the Gardener and Nature; the Gardener With his ligaments of leather secures the main branches; and Nature, with these of her own finding, secures the less.[28]

Adam and Eve do not of course use leather, but train vines on trees and support flowers "gently with myrtle band" (9.431). But, if allowed, vines can choke trees. The image is horticultural, but also an emblem of marriage that illustrates both their need for mutual support and Eve's concern that erotic and conversational pleasure should not obscure their responsibilities to other beings.

Like Raphael's, but with the purpose of actual care, Eve's language shows her consciousness of the forms and needs of created things. Syntactically, the thought winds from enjambed verse to verse around the pole formed by the beginnings of

---

25 The few images I have been able to find that hint at useful activity before the Fall are mentioned and illustrated in *A Gust for Paradise*.

26 On the history of attitudes toward agricultural work, see Anthony Low, *The Georgic Revolution*.

27 See the beginning of Chapter 4.

28 Grew, *The Anatomy of Plants*, 100–101.

the lines, as Eve suggests winding the woodbine and the ivy around the trunks of the living trees that form their arbor.[29] The form recognizes the habits of these plants and their need for tending. It also puts "choice," "wind," and "direct" at the ends of enjambed lines, giving impulsion to these energetic ideas. "Where choice / Leads thee, or where most needs" leads the thought from line to line: specifically to a line that contains a choice and imitates choosing by its alternatives. Eve's syntax mimes not only the action of guiding the plant to the form it was formed for but also the thought at the heart of her suggestion to Adam of dividing their morning's work: the pattern of "choice" that she wants to preserve.

The debate that follows (9.226–375) is partly political, working out a form of government that will preserve their freedom even in the face of the Satan's predatory invasion, of which Raphael has warned them. They are looking for a balance "betwixt the Gardener and Nature," in Grew's words, between management and liberty. Adam stresses support; Eve wants neither fear nor love to make them neglect the other lives in their care. We may feel sympathy with Adam at this point—what can be more delightfully compelling than love?—and a sinking heart, knowing that Eve will in fact fall. But if either love's sweet compulsion or the fear of evil were, in the long run, to become an idol, it could impede their liberty, their calling, and their love. Like the horticulturists who linked gardens with restorative virtues, but in language more responsive to the plants themselves, Eve combines horticulture with ethical choice.

Satan has no interest in vines or trees except for the harm he can do with them. Having purloined the body of a snake, he lies to Eve about an experience he has not had, claiming that eating the forbidden fruit gave him speech and reason.

> About the mossy trunk I wound me soon,
> For high from ground the branches would require
> Thy utmost reach or Adam's; Round the tree
> All other beasts that saw, with like desire
> Longing and envying stood, but could not reach.   [9.589–93]

Milton avoids winding the line to say "About the mossy trunk / I wound me soon"; the Serpent, who makes "intricate seem straight" (9.32), speaks in one straight line, and adds flatly, "Round the tree / All other beasts . . . stood, but could not reach." His lines do not imitate his action: "Stood" is not end-stopped, and "reach" is not enjambed. His language is disconnected from experience. One can also lie convolutedly and tell the truth in plain speech, but the organic connectedness of truth-speaking to natural experience, both one's own and others', is the weft on which Milton's paradisal language weaves. This wovenness produces not silken tongues but the fabric of ecological consciousness.

---

29   Arbour, 3: "A bower or shady retreat, with sides and roof formed mainly by trees and climbing plants" (*Oxford English Dictionary*).

Horticultural poetics

Milton's garden has fragrant plants that John Evelyn recommends in *Fumifugium*, but not the orderly design that Evelyn loved. More even than Marvell, Milton commends Nature's freedom. He tells—or says he would tell "if art could tell"—

> How from that sapphire fount the crispéd brooks,
> Rolling on orient pearl and sands of gold,
> With mazy error under pendant shades
> Ran nectar, visiting each plant, and fed
> Flow'rs worthy of Paradise which not nice art
> In beds and curious knots, but Nature boon
> Poured forth profuse on hill and dale and plain . . . .   [4.236–43]

The jewel imagery is iconic of spiritual treasures, but playfully so, I think, since it is exactly what art had done to nature imagery in the past—we are back to the paradise of *Pearl*—until at "visiting each plant" Milton uses plainer speech. By wandering, these unchartered waters do their work of nourishing each plant.[30] The unfallen couple "wander" in Eden and visit each plant as well, both to tend and to taste (7.48–50), one plant excepted.

Francis Bacon's pattern in "Of Gardens" is contrived, with clipped lawns and geometrical walks. However, he too dislikes "knots" and topiary pruning and suggests a "heath" to be "framed, as much as may be, to a natural wildness" with "thickets made only of sweet-briar and honeysuckle, and some wild vine amongst; and the ground set with violets, strawberries, and primroses, . . . not in any order," with artificial mole-hills set with separate kinds of flowers, and "standards" of roses and other bushes "to be kept with cutting, that they grow not out of course."[31]

God's garden is not mown or geometrical. Adam's and Eve's angelic instructor Raphael approaches

> through groves of myrrh,
> And flow'ring odours, cassia, nard, and balm;
> A wilderness of sweets; for Nature here
> Wantoned as in her prime, and played at will
> Her virgin fancies, pouring forth more sweet,
> Wild above rule or art; enormous bliss.   [5.292–7]

Until they fall, Adam and Eve take care of a Garden that is both "a wilderness of sweets" and "A happy rural seat of various view" (4.247), "rural seat" lightly inviting comparison with country house poems. Satan approaches like an escapee from the polluted city "Where houses thick and sewers annoy the air, . . . to breathe / Among the pleasant villages and farms / Adjoined, from each thing met conceives delight, / The smell of grain, or tedded grass, or kine, / Or dairy" (9.445–51); Stevie

---

30 Gardner Campbell notes, "John Cary says of *Paradise Lost* that '[w]ander' is one of its key verbs, and it belongs to the lost, the fallen'"; Campbell refutes this notion on grounds from *Areopagitica*: in "Paradisal Appetite and Cusan Food in *Paradise Lost*," 246.

31 Bacon, "Of Gardens," in Vickers, ed., *Francis Bacon*, 430–45.

Davies uses this rural scene to commend the superiority of fallen civilization over prelapsarian life, but nothing in *Paradise Lost* suggests that culture could not have been developed without the Fall and its devastation.[32]

Sweet wilderness may be too tame for present lovers of the wild but would have seemed an oxymoron to many of Milton's contemporaries. Lucy Hutchinson includes sinister notes in the first creation, "Where every greater fish devours the less, / As mighty lords poor commoners oppress," ravens and owls have "ill-boding throats," and "jays and crows against each other rail."[33] J. Martin Evans remarks that "the theme of nature's abundance has a sinister overtone" in the *Mask* and that in *Paradise Lost* the "wild luxuriance of the garden has equally ominous implications." Gardner Campbell finds to the contrary, with comparisons to *Areopagitica*, that "This Paradise produces itself as a perfect good endlessly produced, endlessly eaten, and endlessly desired . . . . The ontological provocation of life in the garden of Eden is much too much—and thus just enough."[34] Perhaps for this very reason, temperance is given exercise by the forbidden tree.

Although some Puritan writers thought that wilderness "embodied the Satanic forces which the children of God were required to resist,"[35] I see no evidence that Milton thinks any quality of created nature "ominous." The "dolorous region" of Hell has "many a frozen, many a fiery alp, / Rocks, caves, lakes, fens, bogs, dens, and shades of death" (2.620–21), and God's new-made Earth has all of these but frost, volcanoes, and death, including "umbrageous grots and caves" and the "shaggy hill" (4.224) through which flows the river that provides the spring and streams that water the Garden. Even Heaven has hills with "shaggy tops" (6.645), which must surprise readers who suppose Heaven immaterial and untextured. The protective mount of Paradise is a "steep and savage hill" that impedes Satan's passage with "shrubs and tangling bushes" (4.172–76), which he lightly leaps over. But the admission of wilderness into the Garden itself expresses a pleasure in nature's freedom and uncontrived variety that presages John Clare's love of mice and rough commons.

Evan Eisenberg remarks, "Humans, the Bible says, were put in the Garden 'to work it and protect it.' But from what do we protect Eden if not from our own work?"[36] Milton makes sure that Adam and Eve do not tyrannize over nature. They lightly humanize parts of it with walks, arbors, borders, and plantings, but otherwise only aid natural processes. Similarly, Milton's "art" is not "nice" but profuse yet patterned so that the writing and the reader are not over-managed (as in Bentley's and Dryden's redactions), yet everything is complexly connected to everything else.

---

32   Davies, *The Feminine Reclaimed*, 246–7.

33   Hutchinson, *Order and Disorder*, Canto 2, ll. 251, 268, 279.

34   Campbell, "Paradisal Appetite and Cusan Food in *Paradise Lost*," 244, 248.

35   Evans, *Milton's Imperial Epic*, 49–51. Compare Gardner Campbell's contrasting discussion of the provocations, pleasures, and opportunities of desire and abundance in "Paradisal Appetite and and Cusan Food."

36   Evan Eisenberg, *The Ecology of Eden*, 171.

Why, as in no other representation of unfallen life, do Adam and Eve work at all? Taking care of the Garden is a calling, Adam says, that distinguishes human beings from other species:

> Man hath his daily work of body or mind
> Appointed, which declares his dignity,
> And the regard of Heav'n on all his ways;
> While other animals unactive range,
> And of their doings God takes no account. [4.618–20]

Adam overstates this distinction—he cannot know that after he lets Death in God will take account of the fall of the sparrow, but will learn from Michael later that God is immanent in all that lives. His point here is that mankind is accountable. The plants of Paradise behave in ways familiar to us and need familiar care. Though Adam and Eve clear paths for their bare feet, add borders and plantations, prune fruit trees, and wind vines, their tending aims to encourage plants' intrinsic abilities "gently" by attention to their responses. Eve is especially the planter and tender of flowers and their fruits. Her daily attention to her nursery calls her perilously away from Adam on the morning of the Fall, but is in itself exemplary.[37] While Adam asks Raphael speculative questions about astronomy, Milton reminds us that other creatures respond to us as Eve goes forth

> among her fruits and flow'rs,
> To visit how they prospered, bud and bloom,
> Her nursery; they at her coming sprung
> And touched by her fair tendance gladlier grew. [8.44-47]

Eve departs neither incapable of, nor undelighted with, astronomical discourse, which she prefers to hear from Adam; but in fact, Raphael's teaching is filled with egalitarian and monistic imagery and ends with an exhortation to do as Eve does, dreaming not of other worlds but attending to the Paradise at hand. A whole unlapsed global population devoted to gardening could eventually tame the "wilderness of sweets" if they chose, but the gardening itself teaches temperance and diversity. Pruning and supporting respond to the nature of the plants, which are also mirrors of the natures of humankind, so that gardening is a subtle commentary on the balance of liberty and law in government and creativity and discipline in citizenship or art.

Like the poet, Eve is an artist. Satan approaches "Among thick-woven arborets and flow'rs / Embordered on each bank, the hand of Eve" (9.437–8). At the expulsion, she bids her flowers goodbye with grief:

> O flowr's,
> That never will in other climate grow,
> My early visitation, and my last
> At ev'n, which I bred up with tender hand
> From the first op'ning bud, and gave ye names,

---

37 I have discussed her motives in *Milton's Eve*, Chapter 5.

Who now shall rear ye to the sun, or rank
Your tribes, and water from th'ambrosial fount?   [11.273–9]

Like the catalogers, she names and orders her particular garden, as a lover, not a marketer. Who will take care of you now? she asks, and leaves the answer for us to supply. After the Judgment, Adam's need to earn bread "by the sweat of his brow" is not just a punishment, but a restoration of responsibility, made onerous by the degradation of nature that will result from the Earth-wounding break with God and nature called "The Fall." Their work is a pattern for the remedy of *nocence* and a pleasure that polluters and clear-cutters lack. When Satan fells his victims, they still have the rudiments with which to make repairs.

Neither the "incomparable Monarch" of whom Evelyn hoped so much in *Fumifugium* nor the members of parliament whom he addressed acted on his recommendations. But Milton, whether or not he knew Evelyn's tract, incorporates them into his epic. His imagery of Hell, including the Apples of Sodom, resembles Evelyn's of London; his Garden of Eden and its gardeners are patterns for the restoration, even during the unsatisfactory Restoration, of a polluted earth. If Eve had chosen not to fall, or Adam had sought grace rather than falling also, their care of the natural world might have preserved and enhanced it. Instead, after Satanic pollution enters human history, everything in their unfallen experience becomes applicable to an ethic of reparation.

Meet conversation: Language as habitat

Adam and Eve are also gardeners of speech, and their job is to name things according to their natures. Adam does so in a troubling passage. When God brings the animals to "pay thee fealty / With low subjection" and receive their names, Adam narrates, the beasts come "cow'ring low / With blandishment" and "each bird stooped on his wing."

I named them, as they passed, and understood
Their nature, with such knowledge God endued
My sudden apprehension; but in these
I found not what methought I wanted still.   [8.352–5]

If Milton had written "and understood their natures" it would be clear that in the Ur-language, names express inner truths. But by "Their nature" he might mean only that they are beasts and he is not.[38] In either case, Adam's language is not a set of reductive labels, like "bipedal viviparous omnivore"; once Adam has passed the test of knowing his own nature, he has much to learn by experience about the nature of other beings. In the passage that follows, God lightly reprimands Adam's

---

38   Hugh McCallum discusses this point in *Milton and the Sons of God*, 140, and John Leonard discusses the names of animals in *Naming in Paradise*, "Each Beast of the Field," 261–74. On Eve's naming of the flowers see Leonard, 46–7.

underestimation of animal intelligence and what Gilbert White calls "sociality,"[39] but praises Adam's knowledge of his own nature as he pleads for an equal mate "fit to participate / All rational delight, wherein the brute / Cannot be human consort; they rejoice / Each with their kind, lion with lioness; / So fitly them in pairs thou hast combined" (8.390–94). The rejoicing animals are Adam's pattern for felicity and also help him know that what he wants is "rational delight," a human being with whom he can "converse," turn toward, on all levels of being.

Adam and Eve, the archangels Raphael and Michael, and the Son speak a language that is creative and gestural. Critics challenge Milton's assumption that he can compose unfallen speeches, being part of the "fallen" world himself, but they forget how strongly Milton believed that God will, in the present life, restore the freedom of a regenerate person *"In all the faculties of his mind"*[40] He also reports the operations of the celestial muse, and I see no reason to doubt him. A narrator or bard[41] may err, admit contradictions, or, like a Greek chorus, utter conventional responses that other passages perplex. But to doubt his bardic veracity—however Socratic or challenging or evolving—is to crumble the poem.

Adam and Eve before the Fall fulfill Arne Naess's description of the ecocentric self. Their morning prayer (5.145–208) is an epitome of reciprocal perception and responsive form. They speak or sing spontaneously, as speakers of authentic language do according to Merleau-Ponty, "In various style" and "fit strains pronounced or sung / Unmeditated;" (5.146, 148–9). They are aware the responsiveness and joy of not only animals but also trees and flowers and address angels, stars, air, mists, clouds, rain, winds, and streams. Their hymn contains the whole circle of life within the circling cosmos, with much circular imagery, and its rhythms fit the beings spoken of: varying for the "yonder starry sphere / of planets and of fixed in all her wheels" that dances in "mazes intricate, / Eccentric, intervolved, yet regular / Then most, when most irregular they seem" (5.620–24), shifting to a triplet for the Trinity, and giving three strong beats in other lines about God. The motion of the sun, from an earthly viewpoint, climbs, spreads its noontime light, and falls in mimetic syntax:

> sound His praise
> In thy eternal course, both when thou climb'st,
> And when high noon hast gained, and when thou fall'st.

The mists and exhalations onomatopoetically "wet the thirsty earth with falling showers," the "winds, that from four quarters blow" are invoked to "Breathe soft or loud" in open vowels. "Wave your tops, ye pines, / With every plant" is pricklier with plosive consonants, while "Fountains and ye, that warble as ye flow, / Melodious murmurs, warbling tune His praise" imitates the layered sound of moving water. The birds that "singing, up to heaven gate ascend" and the animals, "Ye that in

---

39 White, *The Natural History of Selbourne*, Letters XXIV (177–8) and XXXIV (194–5).

40 Milton, *Christian Doctrine* I, 15.367, in *Complete Prose Works*, vol. 6.

41 Barbara Kiefer Lewalski's use of "bard" makes the narrator a persona of the poet.

waters glide, and ye that walk / The earth, and stately tread, or lowly creep" are all acknowledged in imitative flights and gaits of prosody.[42]

Adam and Eve invoke all creatures to join their praise by doing what they naturally do, the vocal ones to "Join voices," and all to "Witness if I be silent, morn or even, / To hill, or valley, fountain, or fresh shade / Made vocal by my song, and taught his praise" (5.197–204). "Witness if I be silent" means not only "Notice that I am not silent" but also "testify should human voices fail," and all nature is "taught his praise" by human song. As Stephen Fallon says, "The landscape here is called upon to echo human song, not passively, but rather as one voice responding to another. In this hymn and elsewhere in the poem Milton turns the pathetic fallacy on its head; it is no illusion to speak of nature sharing thoughts and emotions."[43] "Witness" implies that the creatures consciously respond not only to good care but to the quality of presence Adam and Eve supply. The creatures are both conscious witnesses of what Adam and Eve do and fellow witnesses of what God does. They express vitality in active verbs—the elements run, mix, let, nourish, vary, birds and animals ascend, glide, walk, tread, creep—giving a sense of self-directing propulsion, not the collision of externally moved inert atoms envisioned by Hobbes.[44] (Wilkins's universal language, Stillman points out, "dispenses with verbs by affording marks to describe the modes of action appropriate to substantives."[45]) Adam tells Raphael that the sun will delay to hear his story, or the stars and moon will be his audience, and the attentive universe is more than a courtly hyperbole since creation depends on all things, even Chaos, responding to God's voice. When the Son repairs the war-torn heavens, mountains hear his voice. Plants respond to Eve's presence. The language of nature is the singing of this reciprocal experience, and its sensuous surface bears gestural meaning irreducible to conventional objectifications.

The morning hymn's cultural resonance also makes complex connections. It elaborates Psalm 147 and the Benedicite, a morning canticle in the English and Latin liturgies, sung in the fiery furnace of their Babylonian conquerors by the Hebrew friends of Daniel.[46] Shadrach, Meshach, and Abednego raise their song of praise in a crucible of oppression, and the volatile king Nebuchadnezzar responds to the miracle of their survival by praising their God who "delivered his servants that trusted in him, . . . and yielded their bodies, that they might not serve nor worship any god, except

---

42 I discuss this passage more fully in *A Gust for Paradise*, 140–44. On Edenic language, see also John Leonard, *Naming in Paradise*, Cheryl Thrash, "'How cam'st thou speakable of mute . . . ?' " and Beverley Sherry, "Speech in *Paradise Lost*." On Milton's choices particular plants, see James Patrick McHenry, *A Milton Herbal*; for animals, see Karen Edwards, "Milton's Reformed Animals: An Early Modern Bestiary ."

43 Fallon, *Milton among the Philosophers*, 200–201. (That whales respond to Bach, music that links us, too, to cosmic numbers, is now established.)

44 Of Hobbes's materialism Raymond B. Waddington comments "[If] Milton could imagine bodies of spirit, Thomas Hobbes went in the opposite direction. In *Leviathan* (1651), he restored the suspect translation of anima, "Eate not the Bloud, for the Bloud is the Soule, that is, the Life" (Deut. 12.23), using it to maintain that soul cannot be "Substance Incorporeall" [*Leviathan*, ed. Tuck, 425.]: "Blood, Soul, and Mortalism," 80 and 90, n. 35.

45 Stillman, *The New Philosophy and Universal Language*, 252, 48.

46 From an apocryphal section of the Book of Daniel.

their own God." The passage summons a history of subjection utterly opposed to the primal freedom of Adam and Eve. Yet they too are under trial, having just had their first taste of evil in Eve's dream imposed by the volatile oppressor Satan. Milton, in exile under a restored monarch whom he may have connected with the persecuting and luxury-loving Belshazzar, had spent his life battling the subjection of conscience and expression. These connections give poignancy to the end of the hymn,

> Hail universal Lord, be bounteous still
> To give us only good; and if the night
> Have gathered aught of evil, or concealed,
> Disperse it, as now light dispels the dark.

The accuracy of the hymn, from a scientific point of view, may be questioned. Its astronomy is perceptual, hence earth-centered. Its ecological accuracy inheres in its comprehensiveness and its weft of verbal music, an aspect of the wovenness of the nature, and fluid meanings may be truer than Wilkins's verbless categories. Karen Edwards states that "the value of God's other book lies not in its provision of conclusive answers but in its openness to constant rereading and reviewing," and that in this hymn Adam no longer demands" as in his first moments of consciousness "that the sun tell him how to know and praise. He has read the sun's declaration of the Creator in its rising and falling; he knows that declaring and praising the Creator are one; and he has learned that by articulating the sun's praise, he himself praises the Creator." Milton's poem "makes it clear that while the creatures have meaning, they do not have *a* meaning." In Book 8, Raphael will address Adam's astronomical questions without subscribing to any orthodoxy; as Edwards observes, "His reading of heaven is at one with his reading of creeping things; it is open-ended and richly indeterminate." But "When Eve determines to know absolutely, to fix interpretation, she indeed reaches for death."[47]

The effort to "reduce" nature to order by categorical terminology, as in Sturtevant or Wilkins, made it possible to talk about minerals, plants, and animals as abstractions, not dynamic processes, individuals, or self-activating beings. Hobbes and later mechanists sought abstract certainty. Poets replenish the vital and dynamic particulars. Even when Adam and Eve sing generically of elements and species, they do so with varied music and beauty of form that respond to the varied beauty of these creations. Eve sings a love song to Adam in a circular form, like the diurnal cycle she sings of, and like the turns and returns of the round dance of the universe and the angels, and draws all of nature into the song:

> Sweet is the breath of morn, her rising sweet,
> With charm of earliest birds; pleasant the sun
> When first on this delightful land he spreads
> His orient beams, on herb, tree, fruit, and flow'r,
> Glist'ring with dew; fragrant the fertile earth
> After soft showers; and sweet the coming on
> Of grateful ev'ning mild, then silent night,

---

47 Edwards, *Milton and the Natural World*, 66 and 69.

> With this her solemn bird and this fair moon,
> And these the gems of heav'n, her starry train . . . . [4.641–9][48]

The rest of the song returns this imagery to make human love the crowning joy; none of these "without thee is sweet." Though Adam, and also Eve's critics, would have liked her to leave it at that, this expression of human love as the source of all love nevertheless places that love in a circle of life, and when it appears to her that their union could become forgetful of all else, as she may have heard Adam confess to Raphael, she departs to right the balance. When instead she trades these loves for a false hope of transcendence, "Earth felt the wound."

Milton's own poignant declaration of his love of visual beauty is expressed in poetry of much aural beauty as he laments his blindness but feeds on thoughts

>   that voluntary move
> Harmonious numbers; as the wakeful bird
> Sings darkling, and in shadiest covert hid
> Tunes her nocturnal note. Thus with the year
> Seasons return, but not to me returns
> Day, or the sweet approach of ev'n or morn,
> Or sight of vernal bloom, or summer's rose,
> Or flocks, or herds, or human face divine;
> But cloud in stead, and ever-during dark
> Surrounds me, from the cheerful ways of men
> Cut off, and for the Book of Knowledge fair
> Presented with Universal blank
> Of Nature's works to me expunged and razed,
> And wisdom at one entrance quite shut out.
> So much the rather thou celestial Light
> Shine inward, and the mind through all her powers
> Irradiate, there plant eyes, all mist from thence
> Purge and dispense, that I may see and tell
> Of things invisible to mortal sight.   [3.37–55]

Things visible to mortal sight, even so, are not forgotten.

In comparison, Dryden's imitative *The State of Innocence* lacks the irriguous quality of Milton's flexible lines and the stage set is a static, symmetrical garden:

> *Paradise. Trees cut out on each side, with several Fruits upon them: a Fountain in the midst: at the far end, the Prospect terminates in Walks.*

Dryden does pick up the theme of nature's gaze while attributing Adam's first question in *Paradise Lost* to Eve, but in a tragicomically human-centered way.

---

48 David-Everett Blythe in "Milton's Bird Charm" suggests that Eve's phrase "the charm of earliest birds" (4.642) originates in "*chirm* (or *churm*). . . . the dawn's onset of chirps, cries, twitters, flutters, and shakings, and such varied types of calls (*including* song) as commonly signal breath of morn" and balances the "silent night" of line 637.

Tell me ye Hills and Dales, and thou fair Sun,
Who shin's above, what am I? whence begun?
Like my self, I see nothing: from each Tree
The feather'd kind peep down, to look on me;
And Beasts, with up-cast eyes, forsake their shade,
And gaze, as if I were to be obey'd.
Sure I am somewhat which they wish to be,
And cannot: I myself am proud of me.

Dryden also incorporates Milton's view that the Fall brought violence into the natural world as well as the human heart, but ends with farewells not only to a particular garden but to earthly joys and responsibilities, and with a vision of a transcendent Heaven. Dryden's Raphael then speaks the final lines:

The rising winds urge the tempestuous Ayr;
And on their wings, deformed Winter bear:
The beasts already feel the change; and hence,
They fly, to deeper coverts, for defence:
The feebler herd, before the stronger run;
For now the war of nature is begun:
But, part you hence in peace, and having mourn'd your sin,
For outward *Eden* lost, find *Paradise* within.[49]

This pat conclusion says nothing, as Milton's Adam does, about preserving "all the creatures" (11.873). Dryden's dualism, like Bentley's, makes it possible for him to read Milton's epic reductively and evade its message of responsibility for the natural world.

In *Paradise Lost*, the paradise of language briefly becomes impoverished of radiance and empathy as Adam and Eve temporarily lose interest in God and other creatures. But part of their recovery is the recovery of natural eloquence, and the epic's wealth of unfallen and regenerate speeches shows how those entwined processes, nature and language, can be restored.

Animal intelligence and the problem of predation

In "Milton and the Reasoning of Animals" Bruce Boehrer reports a debate in Cambridge in 1615, with James I in attendance, on "whether dogs could make syllogisms," which the affirmative debater won by quoting Plutarch. Boehrer points out that in Prolusion 7 Milton professes ". . . we will offer Ignorance Circe's cup, and bid her throw off her human shape, and walk no longer erect, and betake her to the beasts. To the beasts, did I say? They will surely refuse to receive so infamous a guest, at any rate if they are . . . endowed with some kind of inferior reasoning power, as many maintain . . . . For Plutarch tells us that in the pursuit of game, dogs show some knowledge of dialectic, and if they chance to come to cross-roads, they obviously make use of a disjunctive syllogism." Boehrer takes this statement

---

49 Dryden, *The State of Innocence*, in *Works* 12:110–111 and 146.

seriously, as I agree is right even in a playful genre, and considers its implications, remarking that "Milton's prose distinguishes canine reason from an ignorance that loses its personhood through a variety of Circean transformation" and argues that Milton's Plutarchian view of rationality in animals also bears on the acceptance of different ways of knowing and so on the acceptance of differently gendered intelligence.[50] One might add "differently genred" as another way in which justice to animals and justice to human differences are connected.

In the epic, Adam, Eve, and God express differing views of animal intelligence. Adam thinks that "other animals unactive range, / And of their doings God takes no account" (4.621–2). But when he complains (chronologically earlier) of his loneliness, the Creator replies

> What call'st thou solitude, is not the earth
> With various living creatures, and the air
> Replenisht, and all these at thy command
> To come and play before thee? Know'st thou not
> Their language and thir ways? They also know,
> And reason not contemptibly.   [8.369–74]

The Creator is teasing out Adam's self-knowledge and need for a mate of his own kind, but at the same time teaching him not to underestimate the beings in his domain. "Play" implies free movement as well as performance and pleasurable exercise, and plays fitfully against "command"—Adam's is a dominion that asks the animals only to "come and play." Nevertheless, Milton puts into the mouth of God a direct refutation of Descartes's supposition that animals are automata, which is, with Bacon's imperialism over nature, at the root of unethical uses of animals. To supplement Harvey's account of the movements of the heart, Descartes explains that "If you slice off the pointed end of the heart of a live dog, and insert a finger into into one of the cavities," you can feel its contractions, and recommends that the reader "unversed in anatomy" should "have the heart of some large animal with lungs dissected before him." Though he cannot entirely claim that animals are not sentient, Descartes argues that they are certainly not intelligent. Like the human body, a machine similar to those men devise but that only God can make, animals are automata; but, unlike the human body, they are not coupled to a rational soul. To demonstrate that animals lack reason, he argues that if a manmade machine

> had the organs and outward shape of a monkey or of some other animal that lacks reason, we should have no means of knowing that they did not possess entirely the same nature as these animals; whereas if any such machines bore a resemblance to our bodies and imitated our actions as closely as possible . . . we should still have two very certain means of recognizing that they were not real men.

The first of these is that although a machine could be constructed that utters words in response to stimuli, it could never "give an appropriately meaningful answer to whatever is said in its presence, as the dullest of men can do." The second is that

---

50 Boehrer, "Milton and the Reasoning of Animals," 52 and *passim*.

"whereas reason is a universal instrument which can be used in all kinds of situations, these organs need some particular disposition for each particular action," and no machine could have "enough different organs to make it act in all the contingencies of life in the way in which our reason makes us act." Descartes supposes he has thus proven "the difference between man and beast":

> For it is quite remarkable that there are no men so dull-witted or stupid—and this includes even madmen—that they are incapable of arranging various words together and forming an utterance from them in order to make their thoughts understood; whereas there is no other animal, however perfect and well-endowed it may be, that can do the like.

Parrots and magpies can form words, but "cannot show that they are thinking what they are saying," and men born unable to hear and speak can communicate their thoughts by inventing their own signs. "This shows not merely that animals have less reason than men, but that they have no reason at all."[51]

The words of Milton's God cast doubt on Descartes's two proofs for an absolute difference between men and animals, that they lack language and reason. But God makes a more important, and perhaps disturbing, distinction: Adam's lively argument for a mate of his own kind shows that he knows himself, "Expressing well the spirit within thee free, / My image, not imparted to the brute" (8.440–41). This is the distinction that gives Adam and Eve right of "dominion." But the image of God in them, then, would include the kind of respectful open-mindedness about animal intelligence that God teaches Adam; that lesson mitigates the Baconian and Cartesian idea of dominion. The divine image is also endued with "sanctity of reason" and fit to "govern the rest, self-knowing, and from thence / Magnanimous to correspond with Heav'n, / But grateful to acknowledge whence his good / Descends" (7.508, 510–13). As Montaigne says, even if we fail to abate our presumption of "imaginary sovereignty."[52]

Descartes's absolutism betrays itself in his circular reasoning at "some other animal that lacks reason." By questioning it in the voice of God, in the first decade of the Royal Society, Milton challenges such assumptions. Descartes won out in experimental science, though philosophers and poets continued to question his principles, and Darwin and numerous ethologists have confirmed their intuitions that animals as Milton writes "reason not contemptibly." As to the many benefits of experiments on animals to suffering human beings, the more "humanely" the experiments are carried out the more accurate the results are likely to be.[53]

The question of animals' ability to think or speak returns when Eve is surprised that the Serpent speaks to her.

> What may this mean? Language of man pronounced
> By tongue of brute, and human sense expressed?

---

51 Descartes, *Philosophical Writings* I: *Description of the Human Body*, 317, and *Discourse on Method*, 134, 139–40.

52 Montaigne, "Of Crueltie," in *Essays*, trans. Florio, 2:126.

53 I owe this point to Sherwood Parker, a high-energy physicist whose research on protein crystallography includes medical applications.

The first at least of these I thought denied
To beasts, whom God on their Creation-Day
Created mute to all articulate sound;
The latter I demur, for in thir looks
Much reason, and in their actions oft appears.   [9.553–9]

Adam gives the animals too little credit, and Eve gives the Serpent's claim that the Forbidden Fruit gave him speech too much credence; both are still in the process of learning about the creatures for whose well-being they are responsible. Their differing views invited readers to consider and debate the capacities of animals at a time when their intelligence and sense experience were often disregarded.[54] Edenic animals supply, not meat, pulling power, or advantage in war, but otherness. Adam and Eve delight in them, and their beneficent regard for beings unlike themselves is an example to Milton's and subsequent generations.

After the Fall, the amicable animals would become "wild, and of all chase / In wood or wilderness, forest or den" (4.341–2). In Eden they are spontaneously responsive to the moral governance ("dominion") of Adam and Eve, which presumably combines justice with minimal interference as good government does in *Areopagitica*. The image of God in Adam and Eve makes them capable not of equality but of generosity.[55] The animals are not as wild as lovers of wilderness might like, because in Eden there is no death, but they are wild enough to offer Adam and Eve true otherness. When they lose their self-governance, the animals turn savage. Nevertheless the status Milton's God gives Edenic animals as possibly reasoning and certainly expressive beings coincides with the findings of later natural historians and argues against human savagery towards them.

After the Fall, among the changes Adam fearfully observes in the natural world—mirroring his own—is discord among the animals.

Beast now with beast gan war, and fowl with fowl,
And fish with fish; to graze the herb all leaving,
Devoured each other; nor stood much in awe
Of man, but fled him, or with count'nance grim
Glared on him passing.   [10.710–14]

The predation of animals upon each other that dismays Milton's fallen Adam presents a theological problem of justifying God's ways. How could a good God impose on the innocent a system based on pain? This question, oddly enough, produced non-anthropocentric ideas about animal's rights to their own lives and well-being. Henry More in *Antidote against Atheism* (1655), as we have seen, responds to objections that predation is "inconsistent with . . . Eternal Goodness" by asserting

---

54   See Thomas Aquinas, *Summa Theologica* II, Question 64, and René Descartes, Letter to the Marquess of Newcastle, 23 November, 1646, in *Philosophical Letters*. Bacon's *New Atlantis*, in *Francis Bacon*, provides no ethic for mitigating the suffering of experimental animals.

55   Andrew Linzey discusses the "Equality Paradigm" and the "Generosity Paradigm" in *Animal Theology*, chapter 2.

that God provides for all creatures' enjoyment of their diverse capacities and that we should not assume they were made for us alone.[56]

Milton does not make excuses for predation. Satan gloats (naively) that God has given up "Both his beloved man and all his world, / To Sin and Death a prey" (10.488–90), and Adam counts it among his "growing miseries" (10.715). The suffering of animals is the fault of Adam's and Eve's moral abdication, and Adam renews his vocation in that over-confident but exemplary exclamation after his regenerative vision of the animals emerging from the Ark (11.871–3) that "man shall live / With all the creatures, and their seed preserve."

Earth's wound and Nimrod's dominion

The Fall, in Milton's rendition, is an ecological disaster. "Earth felt the wound, and Nature from her seat / Sighing through all her works gave signs of woe / That all was lost" (9.782–4). When Adam falls, "Earth trembl'd from her entrails, as again / in pangs, and Nature gave a second groan" (9.1000–1001). Adam and Eve, desiring the transcendence that Satan fraudulently persuades them they need, have become consumers of the one sacred reminder of their responsibility to all creation, and *Earth* felt the wound; *all*—not just human probity—was lost. In one of Milton's many inversions of gender stereotypes, the male's sin is excessive compliance and the female's a desire for transcendence and sovereignty. Ambition for transcendence, which separates dualists from their fellow creatures, has wounded earth's very womb.[57]

Before the Fall, Adam and Eve have "dominion" over their domain, in which plants are nurtured and animals are free and "obedient"—responsive to a relation that develops the best capacities of all concerned. They forsake their calling when they consume the one taboo—an arbitrary restraint, hence one that does not bind their powers but exercises their wills and gives them, too, an opportunity to obey— etymologically, to hear and respond. It is in a sense God's signature on his creation, which he gives to his creatures with one reservation, that they remember their Maker and temper their consumption.

In the judgment, the pleasant task of dressing and keeping the earth becomes the necessity of tilling the soil by the sweat of one's brow; original responsibility now becomes regenerative necessity. The beginning of repentance follows when Adam witnesses the animals' violence and carnivorousness and recognizes what he has brought upon his children. When Eve approaches, he utters the most fallen of speeches, but she perseveres in language that has regained its empathetic music.

As with issues of gender and power, Milton addresses human dominion over nature in multiple ways, not shunning the conflicts, but inviting debate. The Son

---

56 More, *Antidote against Anthiesm*, 124–5.

57 See also Richard DuRocher, "The Wounded Earth in *Paradise Lost*" and Ken Hiltner, "The Portrayal of Eve in *Paradise Lost*: Genius at Work." John Tanner writes that sin "render[s] the objective world more polar than before" and "causes humans to perceive the natural world differently . . . . [T]he Fall cracks nature and dis-integrates the way we know it" (*Anxiety in Eden*, 90).

as "Omnific Word" (7.217)[58] and God's "Omnipresence" in "every kind that lives" (11.336–7) oppose dualist instrumentalism, but this point is perplexed by Adam's only partially regenerate response to Michael's account of Nimrod.

Francis Bacon's three "grades of ambition in mankind" were to extend personal power, national power, and "the power and dominion of the human race itself over the universe." Milton brings these kinds of ambition together in the story of Nimrod, the "mighty Hunter" and the type of all tyrants (12.33; Gen. 10.9). The story of Nimrod appears warningly next after the story of his ancestor Noah:

>   one shall rise
> Of proud ambitious heart, who not content
> With fair equality, fraternal state,
> Will arrogate dominion undeserved
> Over his brethren, and quite dispossess
> Concord and law of Nature from the Earth.   [12.24–32]

Adam heatedly responds,

>   O execrable son so to aspire
> Above his brethren, to himself assuming
> Authority usurpt, from God not giv'n:
> He gave us only over beast, fish, fowl
> Dominion absolute; that right we hold
> By his donation; but man over men
> He made not lord: such title to himself
> Reserving, human left from human free.   [12.64–71]

As a political statement this passage shows Adam reviving, but he forgets that he has already lost his beneficent "Dominion absolute" and released Death when

> Beast now with beast gan war, and fowl with fowl,
> And fish with fish; to graze the herb all leaving,
> Devoured each other; nor stood much in awe
> Of man . . . .   [10.710–13]

In the contexts of a restored monarchy, the scientific conquest of nature, and the European conquest of the Americas, the vision of Nimrod opens the concept of dominion for debate and suggests wary scrutiny of any assumption of a divine right to it, at the time when science set out to subdue nature systematically, Europe set out to conquer the American wilderness, and monarchy reasserted its "divine right" to rule. Adam's words should be weighed in the contexts of the kind of dominion he has practiced until the Fall and of the human servitude to passions and hence to tyrants that Michael's reply foretells.

Michael does not imply, as Ovid does in Golding's passionate and gory translation, that animal slavery and bloodshed were precursors of war and tyranny, and Adam's

---

58 The Son's identity as creative Word comes from John 1.1–3, "In the beginning was the Word, and the Word was with God . . . All things were made by him", and John 1.14, "And the Word was made flesh and dwelt among us."

response makes a sharp distinction between dominion over animals and dominion over human beings. Yet many of Milton's readers would have been aware of the two philosophical traditions that link tyranny over animals to tyranny over human beings in opposite ways: Aristotle and the Peripatetics, who thought it natural that animals, women, and slaves should devote their lives to the sustenance of those more capable of the philosophical life, and the Pythagoreans, who opposed violence to any sentient beings. Adam's idea of dominion has nothing to do with eating or enslaving. He recognizes that human government of other species comes only by God's "donation" and must now be concerned with preserving their seed in a world turned predatory as a result of his own dereliction of moral responsibility. Adam and Eve and their progeny, including Milton's readers, have before them the choice of tyranny and depredation, represented by Nimrod, or of rich biotic communities, represented by Noah's ark.

We have seen again and again the importance of place in Milton's poems.[59] When Michael announces the expulsion from the Garden, repentant Adam laments the loss of this best of earthy places (11.315–29):

> This most afflicts me, that departing hence,
> As from [God's] face I shall be hid, deprived
> His blessèd count'nance; here I could frequent
> With worship, place by place where he vouchsafed
> Presence divine . . . .

He associates divinity with particular places, trees, and fountains he would like to show his sons, where he would build altars and "Offer sweet smelling gums and fruits and flow'rs." But In yonder nether world where shall I seek / His bright appearances, or footstep trace?"

Adam's grief is a hopeful though inadequate contrast to unrepentant Satan's insistence that "The mind is its own place" (1.254). But Michael assures Adam that God's "Omnipresence fills / Land, sea, and air, and every kind that lives . . . as here, and will be found alike / Present . . . his face / Express, and of his steps the track Divine" (11.336–54).

Michael's view of divine immanence both retains the significance of place and figuratively fells two pillars of violence: he rejects the absolute division between immortal man and other species that has allowed the devastation of both species and places; and he rejects the divisiveness of place-based religions, because all places and whatever lives in them are sacred.

Politics of nature: *Paradise Regained*

Paradise Regained picks up ecological strands from both the *Mask* and *Paradise Lost* as the Son of God in the wilderness confronts temptations that infringe on political and ecological justice. The simple style in which the young Christ replies refutes the

---

59 Ken Hiltner's *Milton and Ecology* provides a rich history of the concept of place from Job to Paul to Luther to Heidegger, Wittgenstein, and Derrida.

poetry that glorifies animal, vegetable, and mineral servitude and the conquest of land and people. He rejects Satan's clever enticements to display miracles, conquer kingdoms, exploit the earth, or pursue wealth, power, and worldly knowledge—even for apparently good causes. He systematically rejects pursuits that lead to suffering and corruption, which are also costly to nature: war, imperial power, wealth used for personal advancement and display, luxurious consumption. His refutations show awareness of the limitations of easy (for him) temporary solutions to poverty such as turning stones to bread. He will not be a bountiful lord over a weak populace at the devil's behest, or a deus ex machina, winning admiration without transforming hearts. These renunciations reject ambitions and ways of life that devastate people and nature and invite inner transformations by which the young Messiah through trial understands his vocation to renew what Adam and Eve lost: "Recover'd Paradise to all mankind" (1.3).

Satan masks the first temptation, to turn bread to stone, as a request to use his power to help the hungry. But Jesus will not feed the poor at the devil's instigation using means that circumvent nature. Charity begins, as the Lady of the *Mask* understands, with the just and personally responsible use of nature's provisions. In the long run, Jesus's simplicity of life, though not of mind, and his spiritual readiness will be the source of plenitude, figured in the banquet with which the poem concludes; and he will later employ a small amount bread and fish to feed thousands both physically and spiritually.

Milton interpolates a scene not found in the Gospel accounts,[60] in which Satan offers a banquet to Jesus, long fasted and hungry. When Jesus refuses gifts from such a giver, Satan asks, "Has thou not right to all Created things, / Owe not all Creatures by just right to thee / Duty and Service, nor to stay till bid, but tender all their power?" That is, he tempts Jesus to assume the right to the "empire over nature" that Bacon sought and that civilization since has made its driving quest.

In the menagerie of Charles II, as described in Waller's *To St. James's Park*,

> All that can, living, feed the greedy eye,
> Or dead, the palate, here you may descry;
> The choicest things that furnished Noah's ark,
> Or Peter's sheet, inhabiting this park.

In the illusory banquet Satan offers Jesus

> A table richly spread, in regal mode,
> With dishes piled, and meats of noblest sort
> And savour, beasts of chase, or fowl of game,
> In pastry built, or from the spit, or boiled,
> Grisamber-steamed; all fish from sea or shore,
> Freshet, or purling brook, or shell or fin,
> And exquisitest name, for which was drained
> Pontus and Lucine bay, and Afric coast.
> Alas how simple, to these cates compared,

---

60   Matthew 4 and Luke 4. Ken Hiltner shows how *Paradise Regained* works "to deconstruct the idea of human dominion over the Earth" (94) in *Milton and Ecology*, chapter 6.

Was that crude apple that diverted Eve!   [2.340–49]

In rejecting this earth-and-sea-scouring array, the Son objects not to nourishment or pleasure but death, primarily the death of the human body-and-spirit lurking in luxury. He could, if he wished,

> call swift flights of angels ministrant
> Arrayed in glory on my cup to attend
> Why shouldst thou then obtrude this diligence,
> In vain, where no acceptance it can find,
> And with my hunger what hast thou to do?
> Thy pompous delicacies I contemn,
> And count thy specious gifts no gifts but guiles.   [2:385–91]

The Lady in *A Mask* similarly holds that "none / But such as are good men may give good things" (702–703). Both dislike their tempters' motives and invite us to scrutinize the sources and effects of our consumption.

The Son also rejects temptations to gain wealth, power, and glory, to go out like Alexander and gain an empire. What do conquerors do

> But rob and spoil, burn, slaughter, and enslave
> Peaceable Nations, neighbouring, or remote,
> Made captive, yet deserving freedom more
> Than those their conquerors, who leave behind
> Nothing but ruin wheresoe'er they rove . . .   [?]3.75–80]

Satan then oils the temptations to power with the motive of liberating his people, as the prophets have said the Messiah would do: he has a duty, Satan says, "to free / Thy country from her Heathen servitude . . . by conquest or by league" (3.175–6, 370). Jesus rejects both war and "politic maxims" (3.400); captivity and liberty begin within, the "captive Tribes . . . wrought their own captivity, fell off / From God" to adopt "all the Idolatries of Heathen round" (3.413–15); Israel will not be restored by conquest, but God "at length, time to himself best known, / May bring them back repentant and sincere" (3.435).

In his sonnet to Henry Vane, Milton speaks of war's "two main nerves, iron and gold." In *Paradise Regained* metallurgy, the exploitation of animals, and the abuse of the land are effects of "military pride"(3.320–36) and deflated with prosodic ridicule: steel armor and steel bows that "shot / Sharp sleet of arrowy showers"—an onomatopoeic tongue-twister—horses clad in mail, "the field all iron"—animals and vegetables mineralized—bearing the human "flower" of provinces; elephants punningly "endorsed with towers," "mules, camels, and dromedaries," and the "pioneers . . . with spades and axes armed / To lay hills plain, fell woods, or valleys fill, / Or where plain was raise hill"—the chiasmic reversal and internal rhyme mimicking the reengineering of the land. Rivers are bridged "as with a yoke"; mules, camels, and dromedaries, are also presumably yoked: nature throughout raided and enslaved by raiders and enslavers of nations. Satan tells Jesus that only by such military power can he expect to save his people and regain the throne of David; Jesus replies that the "cumbersome / Luggage of war" is "argument of human weakness rather than of strength" (3.400–401).

Jesus refuses even philosophy and the arts when they become separated from the people and the land. God's word and "Zion's songs" suffice. But when the trial is over, angels carry the victor to a "green bank" and offer "A table of celestial food" of quite a different kind: "divine, / Ambrosial, fruits fetched from the Tree of Life, / And from the Fount of Life ambrosial drink" (4.587–90). And they perform a work of angelic art, a celebratory anthem recognizing the now incarnate Son—whose elevation as vicegerent over them has been the first step in his increasing alliance with the creatures created by his agency as Omnific Word, and who by "vanquishing / Temptation, hast regained lost Paradise" (2.607–8). Because he renounces imperial power, wealth, the authoritarian misuse of spiritual power, the philosophy that elevated human reason above all else, and bodily luxury acquired at the cost of spiritual blessing, he is "by merit" able to redeem mankind and all the creatures that groan "under the bondage of corruption" waiting for "the glorious liberty of the children of God" (Romans 8.19). By accepting creaturehood (which Satan commits the first sin by refusing to do), and by refusing empire, the Son has become worthy of the scepter when, as Michael has prophesied to Adam (12.463–4), "the earth / Shall be all Paradise."

Bibliography

Primary Works

Alain of Lille. *Complaint of Nature*, trans. Douglas M. Moffat. New York, 1908.

Alciati, *Emblemata*, Lyons, 1550. Trans. and annot. John Manning. Scolar Press, Aldershot, UK. Burlington, Vermont: Ashgate, 1996.

Anderson, Lorraine, Scott Slovic, and John P. O'Grady. *Literature and the Environment: A Reader on Nature and Culture*. New York: Longman, 1998.

Aquinas, Thomas. *The "Summa theologica" of St. Thomas Aquinas*, trans. Fathers of the English Dominican province. London : Burns, Oates, and Washbourne; New York, 1920–1935.

Aristotle. *Aristotles Politiques, or Discourses of Government*, French translation by Loys Le Roy, Englished by J. Dickenson. London, 1598.

Aristotle. *Historia Animalium*. 3 vols: vol. 1 and 2 trans. A.L. Peck. Cambridge, Mass.; London: William Heinemann 1965 and 1970; vol. 3, ed. and trans. D.M. Balme. Cambridge, Mass. and London, England: Harvard University Press, 1991.

Austen, Ralph. *The Spiritual Use of an Orchard*. Oxford, 1597.

Austen, Ralph. *A Treatise of Fruit-Trees*. Oxford, 1653.

Bacon, Francis. *Francis Bacon: A Critical Edition of the Major Works*, ed. Brian Vickers. Oxford: Oxford University Press, 1996.

Bacon, Francis. *New Organon*, in *The New Organon and Related Writings*, ed. Fulton H. Anderson, trans. James Spedding, Robert Leslie Ellis, and Douglas Denon Heath. Indianapolis: Bobbs Merrill, 1960.

Bacon, Francis. *Sylva Sylvarum, or A Natural History in Ten Centuries*. London, 1664.

Bacon, Francis. *The Works of Francis Bacon*, ed. James Spedding, Robert Leslie Ellis, and Douglas Denon Heath. 14 vols. London: Longman and Co., 1857–.

B[eale], I[ohn]. *Herefordshire-Orchards*. Epistolary Address to Samuel Hartlib Esq. London, 1730.

Behn, Aphra. "On a Juniper Tree, Cut Down to Make Busks," in Rudrum, et al., *The Broadview Anthology*.

Bentley, Richard. *Milton's Paradise Lost. A New Edition*. London Jacob Tonson et al., 1732.

Bentley, Richard. Sermons preached "In the First Year," 1692, in *A Defense of Natural and Revealed Religion: Being a Collection of the Sermons Preached at the Lecture found be the Honourable Robert Boyle, Esq. (From the Year 1691 to the Year 1732)*. 3 vols. Ed. Sampson Letsome. London: D. Midwinter et al., 1739. Vol. 1: Sermons preached "In the First Year," 1692.

Berners, Dame Juliana. *A Treatyse of Fysshynge wyth an Angle*. Westminster: Wynkyn de Worde, 1496. Facsimile, intro. M.G. Watkins. London, 1880.

[Berners, paraphrased.] *A Iewell for Gentrie*. Intro. T.S. London: John Helme, 1614.

Berry, Wendell. *Home Economics: Fourteen Essays*. San Francisco: North Point Press, 1987.

Berry, Wendell. *Life Is a Miracle: An Essay Against Modern Superstition*. New York: Counterpoint, 2001.

Berry, Wendell. *Standing by Words. Essays by Wendell Berry*. New York: North Point Press. 1983.

Beza, Theodore. *Job expounded by Theodore Beza*. Cambridge, UK, 1589.

Blith, Walter. *The English Improver Improved*. London, 1649 and 1653.

Blount, Sir Thomas Pope. *Natural History*. London, 1693.

Blount, Sir Thomas Pope. *De Re Poetica*. London, 1694.

Boate, Gerard. *Ireland's Naturall History*. London, 1657.

Bockskay, Georg, see Hoefnagel, Joris.

Boyle, Robert. *The General History of the Air*. London: Awnsham and John Churchill, 1692.

Boyle, Robert. *Works*. 6 vols. London, 1772.

Boyle, Robert. Royal Society manuscript draft of a letter to a friend, described, and quoted by Alan Rudrum in an Appendix to "Ethical Vegetarianism."

Brady, Nicholas. *Ode on St. Cecilia's Day*, see Purcell, Henry.

Brieger, Peter H., trans., *The Trinity Apocalypse*. London, 1967.

Britten, Benjamin. "Our Hunting Fathers." Op. 8: Symphonic cycle for voice and orchestra. EMI CDN 7 69522 (1988).

Brooks, Paul. *Speaking for Nature*. San Francisco: Sierra Club Books, 1980.

Browne, Sir Thomas. *Works*, ed. Geoffrey Keynes. 4 vols. University of Chicago Press, 1964.

Burnet, Thomas. *The Sacred Theory of the Earth*. London, 1684.

Bushell, Thomas. *Mr. Bushell's Abridgment of the Lord Chancellor Bacon's Philosophical Theory in Mineral Prosecutions* [pamphlets, letters, patents, petitions, et al., with separate pagination for each section]. London, 1659.

Bushell, Thomas. *The Severall Speeches and Songs, at the presentment of Mr. Bushells Rock to the Queenes Most Excellent Majesty*. 23 August 1636. Oxford: Leonard Lichfield, 1636.

Byrd, William. *Gradualia: The Marian Masses*, vol. 1. William Byrd Choir, dir. Gavin Turner. Hyperion CDA66451, London, 1990.

Calendar of State Papers, Domestic Series, ed. Mary Anne Everett Green.Nendeln/ Liechtenstein: Kraus Reprint Ltd., 1968.

Calendar of the Clarendon State Papers Preserved in the Bodleian Library, ed. O. Ogle and W. H. Bliss. Oxford: Clarendon Press, 1872. Vol. 1: To January 1649.

Calvin, John. *Sermons of Master Iohn Caluin, vpon the Booke of Iob*, trans. Arthur Golding. London, 1574.

Carew, Thomas. *Select Psalmes of a New Translation, to be sung in Verse and Chorus of five Parts, with Symphonies of Violins, organ, and other instruments* (22 November 1655). From the Bridgewater collection, Huntington Library shelfmark RB131907. For description see Nixon, Scott. For setting on CD see Lawes, Henry.

Caryl, Joseph. *An Exposition . . . of the Book of Job*. London, 1649.

Catesby, Mark. *The Natural History of Carolina, Florida, and the Bahama Islands*. London, 1731–1743.

Cavendish, Margaret. *CCXI Sociable Letters*. London: William Wilson, 1664.

Cavendish, Margaret. *The Life of the Thrice noble, high, and puissant Prince, William Cavendish. . . by. . . Margaret, Duchess of Newcastle, his Wife*. London: A. Maxwell, 1667.

Cavendish, Margaret. *The Life of William Cavendish, Duke of Newcastle, to which is added the true relation of my birth*, ed. C.H. Firth. New York: Scribner and Welford, 1886.

Cavendish, Margaret. *The Philosophical and Physical Opinions*. London, 1655.

Cavendish, Margaret. *Poems and Fancies*. London: Printed by T.R. for F. Martin and F. Allestrye, 1653.

Clusius, Carolus. *Exoticorum Libri Decem*. Antwerp: Plantin Press, 1605.

Coleridge, Samuel Taylor. *Bibliographia literaria*. London: Rest Fenner, 1817.

Colet, John. *An Exposition of St. Paul's Epistle to the Romans*, trans. J.H. Lupton. London: Bell and Daldy, 1873. [Includes Latin text.]

Combes, Thomas. *The Theater of Fine Devices* (Adapted from *Le Théâtre de bons engins*, Guillaume de la Perrière.) Facsimile, The Huntington Library, 1983.

Commonwealth. London, 1881. Krause Reprint Ltd. Vaduz, 1965.

Conway, Anne. *The Principles of the Most Ancient and Modern Philosophy*, trans. and ed. Allison P. Coudert and Taylor Corse. Cambridge, UK: Cambridge University Press, 1996.

Corns, Thomas. *The Development of Milton's Prose Style*. Oxford: Clarendon Press, 1982.

Corns, Thomas. *Milton's Language*. Blackwell's Language Library. Oxford: Blackwell, 1990.

Cowley, Abraham. *Complete Works*, ed. Alexander B. Grosart. 2 vols. Edinburgh University Press, 1881. Rpt. New York: AMS Press, 1967.

Cowley, *Abrahami Couleij Angli, Poemata Latina*. London, 1668.

Cudworth, Ralph. *The True Intellectual System of the Universe*. 3 vols. London: Thomas Tegg, 1845.

Dante Alighieri. Letter to Can Grande. P. Toynbee, *Dantis Alagherii Epistolae: The Letters of Dante*. Oxford, 1966.

D'Avenant, Sir William. *Gondibert*, ed. David F. Gladish. Oxford: Clarendon Press, 1971.

Denham, John. *The Poetical Works*, ed. Theodore Howard Banks. Archon Books, 1969.

Denham, John. "Coopers Hill," in Brendan O Hehir, ed., *Expans'd Hieroglyphicks*. Berkeley and Los Angeles: University of California Press, 1969.

D'Ewes, Simonds. *The Journal of Sir Simonds D'Ewes from the beginning of the long parliament to the opening of the trial of the Earl of Strafford*, ed. Wallace Notestein. New Haven: Yale University Press, 1923.

Descartes, René. *Discours de la Méthode*, ed. André Robinet. Paris: Librarie Larousse, 1969.

Descartes, René. *Philosophical Letters*, trans. and ed. Anthony Kenny. Oxford: Clarendon Press, 1970.

Descartes, René. *The Philosophical Writings*, trans. John Cottingham, Robert Stoothof, and Dugald Murdoch. 2 vols. Cambridge, UK: Cambridge University Press, 1985.

Donne, John. *The Complete Poetry*, ed. John T. Shawcross. Garden City, New York:

Anchor Books, Doubleday, 1967.

Donne, John. *Essayes in Divinity*, ed. Evelyn M. Simpson. Oxford: Clarendon Press,1952.

Drayton, Michael. *Poly-Olbion*. London, 1622.

Drayton, Michael. *Works*, vol. 4: *Poly-Olbion.*, ed. J. William Hebel. Oxford: Basil Blackwell, 1933.

Dryden, John. *The Works of John Dryden*, vol. 5: *The Works of Virgil in English*, 1697. Berkeley, Los Angeles, London: University of California Press, 1987.

Dryden, John. *The Works of Virgil: Containing His Pastorals, Georgics, and Aeneis*. London: Jacob Tonson, 1697.

Dryden, John. *The Poetical Works*, rev. George Noyes. Boston: Houghton Mifflin, 1950.

Du Bartas. Guillaume de Salust, seigneur du Bartas. *Oevvres*. Paris, 1614. Huntington Library copy with bookplate of the Bridgewater Library.

Eliot, George (Mary Ann Evans). *Silas Marner* (1861), ed. Q.D. Leavis. Harmondsworth: Penguin Books, 1967.

Emerson, Ralph Waldo. In *Nature/Walking*, intro. John Elder. Boston: Beacon Press, 1991.

Evelyn, John. *Aceteria: Or, a Discourse of Sallets*, in *Silva, or a Discourse of Forest—Trees*. 4th edition, 1706.

Evelyn, John. "An abstract of a Letter from the worshipful John Evelyn Esq." In *Philsophical Transactions of the Royal Society of London*, vol. 14 #158: 559–63. Dated from Says Court Deptford, 14 April 1684.

Evelyn, John. The Diary of John Evelyn. Introduction and notes by Austin Dobson. 3 vols. London and New York: Macmillan, 1906.

Evelyn, John. *Fumifugium: Or the Inconvenience of the Aer and Smoake of London Dissipated*. 1661.

Evelyn, John. *Sylva, or A Discourse of Forest-Trees, and the Propagation of Timber In his Majesties Dominions*. By J.E. Esq. As it was Deliver'd to the Royal Society the xvth of October, 1664. London: Jo. Martyn and Ja. Allestrye, Printers to the Royal Society, 1664.

Falisci, Gratius. *Cynegeticon, or, A Poem of Hunting*, trans. and illus. Christopher Wase. London, 1654. Ded. William Herbert. Huntington Library copy with bookplate of the Bridgewater Library.

Ficino, Marsilio. *Iamblichus de mysteriis*. Lyons, 1570.

Finch, Anne. *The Poems of Anne Countess of Winchilsea,* ed. Myra Reynolds. Chicago: University of Chicago Press, 1903.

Fludd, Robert. *Mosaicall philosophy: grounded upon the essentiall truth or eternal sapience*. Written first in Latin, and afterwards thus rendred into English. By Robert Fludd, Esq; & Doctor of Physick. London: Printed for Humphrey Moseley, at the Prince's Armes in St. Paul's Church-yard, 1659.

Gassendi, Pierre. *Opera Omnia*. 6 vols. Lyons, 1558.

Gassendi, Pierre. *Selected Works*, ed. and trans. Craig B. Brush, New York: Johnson Reprint Corp., 1972.

Gassendi, Pierre. *Animadversiones*, London, 1649.

Geneva Bible, The. Facsimile of the 1560 edition, intro. Lloyd E. Berry. Madison, Milwaukee and London: University of Wisconsin Press, 1969.

Gesner, Konrad. *Historiae Animalium Liber II: qui est de Quadrupedibus Ouiparis*.

Frankfurt, Johanis Wecheli, 1586. Bound with vol. 5 on serpents, in Frankfurt Latin edition of 1586.

Goodman, Godfrey. *The Creatures Praysing God*. Kingston, 1622.

Greer, Germaine, Susan Hastings, Jeslyn Medoff, Melinda Sansone, eds, *Kissing the Rod: An Anthology of Seventeenth-Century Women's Verse*. London: Virago, 1988.

Grew, Nehemiah. *The Anatomy of Plants*. London: W. Rawlins, 1682. Huntington Library shellfmark D Folio G 1945, 14186 with bookplate of the Bridgewater Library.

Grew, Nehemiah. *The Anatomy of Vegetables Begun*. London: Printed for Spencer Hickman, Printer to the R. Society. London, 1672.

Grew, Nehemiah. *Musaeum Regalis Societatis: Or, A Catalogue and Description of the Natural and Artificial Rarities Belonging to the Royal Society, And preserved at Gresham Colledge*. London: Thomas Malthus, 1685.

ap Gwilym, Daffyd. *Poems*, trans. Richard Morgan Loomis. Binghamton: MRTS, 1982.

Hakluyt, Richard. *The principal nauigations, voyages, traffiques and discoueries of the English nation . . . deuided into three seuerall volumes*[.] London: George Bishop, Ralph Newberie, and Robert Barker, 1599–1600.

Hakluyt, Richard. *Voyages and Discoveries: The Principal Navigations, Voyages, Traffiques and Discoveries of the English Nation* [abridged]. Ed. Jack Beeching. London: Penguin Books, 1972.

Harriot, Thomas. *A briefe and true report of the new found land of Virginia. The Complete 1590 Theodore de Bry edition*, intro. Paul Hulton. New York: Dover, 1972.

Hartlib, Samuel, publisher. *The Reformed Virginian Silk-Worm*. London, 1655.

Harvey, William. *The anatomical exercises of Dr. William Harvey: De motu cordis 1628: De circulatione sanguinis 1649: the first English text of 1653 now newly edited by Geoffrey Keynes*. London: The Nonesuch Press, 1928.

Herbert, George. *The English Poems*, ed. C.A. Patrides. London: Dent, 1974.

Herodotus. *The Histories*, trans. Aubrey de Sélincourt. Baltimore: Penguin Books, 1954.

Herrick, Robert. *The Complete Poems*, ed. Alexander B. Grosart. 3 vols. London: Chatto and Windus, Piccadilly, 1876.

Heyrick, Thomas. *Miscellany Poems*. London, 1691.

Hobbes, Thomas. *Leviathan*, ed. Richard Tuck. Cambridge, UK: Cambridge University Press, 1996.

Hoefnagel, Joris, illus. to Georg Bocskay's *Mira calligraphiae monumenta*, reprod. J. Paul Getty Museum and Thames and Hudson, 1992; selections in Lee Hendrix and Thea Vignau-Wilberg, *Nature Illuminated: Flora and Fauna from the Court of the Emperor Rudolph II* (Los Angeles: The J. Paul Getty Museum, 1997).

Hooke, Robert. *Micrographia*. London, 1665.

Hutchinson, Lucy. *Order and Disorder*, ed. David Norbrook. Oxford: Blackwell, 2001.

Jonson, Ben. *The Complete Poems*, ed. George Parfitt. New Haven and London: Yale University Press, 1982.

Juvenal. *The Satires of Juvenal*, trans. Rolphe Humphries. Bloomington: University of Indiana Press, 1970.

Knightley, Chris, and Steve Madge. *Pocket Guide to the Birds of Britain*. New Haven and London: Yale University Press, 1998.

Lawes, Henry. *Henry Lawes: Sitting by the Streams*. The Consort of Musicke, dir. Anthony Rooley. Hyperion CDA66135. London, 1984.

L., J. *A Discourse Concerning the Great Benefit of Drayning and imbanking. Presented to the High Court of Parliament by [J].L*. Printed by G.M., 1641.

Lilburne, John. *The Case of the Tenants of the Mannor of Epworth In the Isle of Axholm in the County of Lincoln*. London, 1651.

Lister, Martin. "A further Account concerning . . . some Acts in Plants resembling those of Sense. . . Letter of Januar 8. 1672/73. and exhibited to the R. Society." *Philosophical Transactions* 7–8. 90: 5131–7.

Locke, John. *A Paraphrase and Notes on the Epistles of St. Paul*, ed. Arthur W. Wainwrith. 2 vols. Oxford: Clarendon Press, 1987.

Locke, John. *An Essay Concerning the Understanding*, ed. Benjamine Rand. Cambridge, Mass.: Harvard University Press, 1931.

Locke, John. *An Essay Concerning Human Understanding*, ed. Alexander Campbell Fraser. 2 vols. Oxford: Clarendon Press, 1894.

Lucretius (Titus Lucretius Carus). *De rerum natura*, trans. W.H.D. Rouse. London: W. Heinemann; New York: G.P. Putnam's Sons, 1924.

Lucretius. *"The Way Things Are: The "De Rerum Natura" of Titus Lucretius Carus*, trans. Rolfe Humphries. London and Bloomington: Indiana University Press. 1972.

Manwood, John. *A Treatise of the Laws of the Forest*. London: Company of Stationers, 1665 [a revised and enlarged edition of *Treatise and Discourse of the Laws of the Forest*, 1598].

Marvell, Andrew. *The Complete Poems*, ed. Elizabeth Story Donno. Harmondsworth: Penguin Books, 1978.

Marvell. *The Poems of Andrew Marvell*, ed. Nigel Smith. London, New York, and worldwide: Pearson Longman, 2003.

Marx, Karl. *The Communist Manifesto*, ed. Frederic L. Bender. New York and London: W.W. Norton, 1988.

Merleau-Ponty, Maurice. *Phenomenology of Perception*, trans. Colin Smith. London and New York: Routledge, 1996.

Mersenne, Marin. *Traité de L'harmonie universell*. Paris, 1627.

Milton, John. *Complete Poems and Major Prose*, ed. Merritt Y. Hughes. Indianapolis: The Odyssey Press, 1980.

Milton, John. *The Complete Poems*, ed. John Leonard. London: Penguin Books, 1998.

Milton, John. *The Complete Prose Works of John Milton*, gen. ed. Don M. Wolfe. Vol 2, ed. Ernest Sirluck, 1959; vol. 6, ed. Maurice Kelley, 1973. New Haven: Yale University Press, 1973.

Milton, John. *John Milton's Complete Poetical Works reproduced in Photographic Facsimile*, ed. Harris Francis Fletcher. Urbana: University of Illinois Press, 1943–1948.

Milton, John. Poems of Mr. John Milton, Both English and Latin, Compos'd at

Several Times. London: Humphrey Moseley, 1645.

Milton, John. *The Riverside Milton*, ed. Roy Flannagan. Boston and New York: Houghton Mifflin Company, 1998.

Milton, John. *Paradise Lost*, ed. John Leonard. London, Penguin Books, 2000.

Montaigne, Michel de. *The Essays of Montaigne. Done into English by John Florio* (1603). London: David Nutt, 1893.

More, Henry. *Antidote against Atheism*. 2nd ed. London: J. Flesher, 1655.

More, Henry. *Conjectura Cabbalistica*. London: J. Flesher, 1653.

More, Sir Thomas. *Utopia*. Trans. Raphe Robinson. London, 1551.

Mouffet, Thomas. *The Theater of Insects* (1658), bound and consecutively paginated with Topsell, 1658.

Muir, John. *The Eight Wilderness Discovery Books*, intro. Terry Gifford. London: Diadem Books; Seattle: The Mountaineers, 1992.

Muir, John. *The Mountains of California*, ed. Robert C. Baron. Golden, Colorado: Fulcrum, 1988.

Naess, Arne. "Self-Realization: An Ecological Approach to Being in the World," and "The Place of Joy in a World of Fact," in Sessions, ed., *Deep Ecology*.

Ortiz, Simon J. "Our Homeland: A National Sacrifice Area," in *Woven Stone*. Tucson and London: University of Arizona Press, 1992.

Ovid. *Ex P. Ovidii Nasonis Metamorphoseon Libris XV*, trans. Jacobus Pontanus. Antwerp, 1618. Facsimile, New York and London: Garland, 1976.

Ovid *(Publius Ovidius Naso). Ovid's Metamorphosis Englished, Mythologiz'd, and Represented in Figures*, trans. G[eorge] S[andys]. Oxford, 1632. Facsimile. New York and London: Garland, 1976.

Ovid. *The. xv. Bookes of P. Ouidius Naso, entytuled Metamorphosis*, trans. Arthyr Golding. London: Willyam Seres, 1567.

Ovid. *The Metamorphoses*. trans. Horace Gregory. New York and Toronto, New American Library, 1958.

Paracelsus. (Theophrastus . . . von Hohenheim). *The Hermetic and Alchemical Writings*, ed. A.E. White. London, 1896.

Parliament of England. An Ordinance of the Lords and Commons . . . For the cutting and felling of Wood within threescore miles of London. London: Printed for Iohn Wright in the Old-baily, 3 October 1643.

Plattes, Gabriel. *A Discovery of Subterraneall Treasure*. London: I. Oakes, 1639.

Pliny (Gaius Plinius Secundus). *The Historie of the World: Commonly called, The Natural Historie*, trans. Philémon Holland (1601). Rpt. with corrections. 2 vols. London: Adam Islip, 1634.

Plutarch. *The Philosophie, commonlie called, The Morals*, trans. Philémon Holland. London: Arnold Hatfield, 1603.

Porphyry. *Select Works . . . on Abstinence from Animal Food*, trans. Thomas Taylor. London, 1823.

Power, Henry. *Experimental Philosophy. . . Microscopical, Mercurial, and Magnetical*. London, 1664.

Purcell, Henry, and Nicholas Brady. *Ode on St. Cecilia's Day* (1692), ed. Michael Tippett and Walter Bergmann. London: Schott, 1995.

Purchas, Samuel. *Pvrchas his Pilgrimage, or Relations of the World and the religions*

. . . from the Creation vnto this Present. 2nd ed. London, 1614.

Ralegh, Sir Walter. *The discovery of . . . Guiana* (1595). In *Selected Writings*, ed. Gerald Hammond. Fyfield Books, Carconet Press, 1984.

Ravenscroft, Thomas. "Hawking for the Partridge," for four voices, in *A Briefe Discovrse, Of the true (but neglected) vse of Charact'ring the Degrees. . . in the Harmony of 4. Voyces, Concerning the Pleasure of 5 usuall Recreations: Hunting, Hawking, Dauncing, Drinking, Enamouring*. London: Edw. Allde for Tho. Adams. 1614.

Ray, John. *The Ornithology of Francis Willughby*, trans. and enlarged by John Ray. London: John Martyn, 1678. (Ray incorporates the work of his deceased young colleague Francis Willughby.)

Ray, John. *Philosophical Letters*. London: William and John Innys, 1718.

Ray, John. *Three Physico-Theological Discourses, concerning I. The Primitive CHAOS, and Creation of the World. II. The General Deluge, its Causes, and Effects. III. The Dissolution of the World, and Future Conflagration*. 2nd ed. London: Sam. Smith, 1693.

Ray, John. *The Wisdom of God Manifested in the Works of the Creation*. London: S. Smith, 1692.

Ray, John. *The wisdom of God manifested in the works of the creation in two parts, ... With answers to some objections*. By John Ray. The fifth edition corrected, and very much enlarged. London: printed by J.B. for Benj. Walford, 1709.

Reisner, Marc. *Cadillac Desert: The American West and Its Disappearing Water*. New York: Penguin Books, 1993.

Romney Marsh. *The Charter of Romney Marsh*. London: S.R. for Samuel Keble, 1686.

Rudrum, Alan, Joseph Black, and Holly Faith Nelson. *The Broadview Anthology of Seventeenth Century Verse & Prose*. Ontario, Canada: Broadview Press, 2000.

Ruskin, John. *Modern Painters*, vol. 3, in *The Works of John Ruskin*, vol. 5, ed. E.T. Cook and Alexander Wedderburn. London: George Allen, 1904.

Sandys, George. *A Paraphrase vpon Iob*, in *A Paraphrase vpon the Divine Poems*. London, 1638.

Sandys, George. *Ovids Metamorphosis Englished, Mythologiz'd, and Represented in Figures*. Oxford, 1632. Rprt. New York and London: Garland Publishing, 1976.

Scheuchzer, Johanne Jakob. *Physica Sacra*. 8 vols. Augsburg and Ulm, 1731–1735.

Shakespeare, William. *The Complete Works*, ed. G.B. Harrison. New York, 1952.

Shakespeare. *The Tempest*, ed. Robert Langbaum. Signet Classic edition, New York, 1963.

Shelley, Percy Bysshe. *Shelley's Poetry and Prose*, ed. Donald H. Reiman and Sharon B. Powers. New York: W.W. Norton, 1977.

Silko, Leslie Marmon. *Ceremony*. New York: Penguin Books, 1977.

Smart, Christopher. *Jubilated Agno*, ed. W.H. Bond. London: R. Hart-Davis, 1954.

Snyder, Gary. *A Place in Space: Ethics, Aesthetics, and Watersheds*. Washington, DC: Counterpoint, 1995.

Sprat, Thomas. *The History of the Royal-Society of London*. London, 1667. Rpt. with critical apparatus by Jackson I. Cope and Harold Whitmore Jones. London: Routledge & Kegan Paul, 1959.

Stegner, Wallace. *Angle of Repose*. Garden City, New York: Doubleday, 1971.

Streater, John. *Observation Historical, Political, and Philosophical, upon Aristotles first Book of Political Government*. London, 1654.

[Stringer, Moses.] *Opera Mineralis Explicata: or, the Mineral Kingdom, within the Dominions of Great Britain, Display'd*. By M.S., M.D. London, 1713.

Sturrock, June. "Cock-crowing." *Scintilla* 5: 152–8.

Sturrock, June. "Like Swallows." Unpublished poem.

Sturtevant, Simon. *Metallica*. London, 1612.

Taylor, John. *Works of John Taylor The Water Poet*. First Collection. John Haviland, London, 1632. Printed for the Spenser Society, 1870.

Topsell, Edward. *The fowles of heaven; or history of birdes*, ed. Thomas P. Harrison and F. David Hoeniger. Austin: University of Texas, 1972.

Topsell, Edward. *The Historie of foure-footed Beastes*. London: William Iaggard, 1607.

Tradescants, see Allan, Mea.

Traherne, Thomas. *Centuries, Poems, and Thanksgivings*, ed. H.M. Margoliouth. 2 vols. Oxford: Clarendon Press, 1958.

Traherne. *Selected Poems and Prose*, ed. Alan Bradford. London: Penguin Books, 1991.

Traherne. *Meditations on the Six Days of Creation*. London, 1717. Rpt. with intro. by George Herbert Guffey. Los Angeles: William Andrews Clark Memorial Library, 1966.

Tryon, Thomas. *Wisdom's Dictates, or, Aphorisms . . . to which is added a bill of fair of seventy fine noble dishes*. London, 1691.

Vaughan, Henry. *The Complete Poems*, ed. Alan Rudrum. New Haven: Yale University Press, 1981.

Vaughan, Thomas. *The Works of Thomas Vaughan*, ed. Alan Rudrum. Oxford: Clarendon Press, 1984.

Vergil (Publius Vergilius Maro). trans. Dryden, see Dryden, *The Works of Virgil*.

Vergil. *The Georgics*, trans. L.P. Wilkinson. (1982). Rpt. Harmondsworth: Penguin Books, 1984.

Voltaire, François Marie Arouet de. *Candide, Zadig and Selected Stories*, trans. Donald M. Frame. New York: New American Library, 1961.

Waller, Edmund. *A Poem on St. James's Park As lately improved by his Maiesty*. London, 1661.

White, Gilbert. *The Natural History of Selborne*, ed. Richard Mabey. New York: Penguin Books, 1997.

Wilkins, John. *An Essay towards a Real Character and a Philosophical Language*. London, 1668.

Willet, Andrew. *Hexapla: That is, A Six-Fold Commentarie vpon . . . S. Paul to the Romanes*. Cambridge, UK: Cantrell Legge, 1620.

Willughby, Francis, see Ray, John.

Wilson, Alexander. *American Ornithology*. 9 vols. Philadelphia: Bradford and Inskeep, 1808–1814. Quoted in *The Norton Book of Nature Writing*, eds. Robert Finch and John Elder. New York: W.W. Norton, 1990.

Winstanley, Gerrard. *Works*. Ithaca: Cornell University Press, 1941. See also the new edition by David Loewenstein.

Xenophon. *Oeconomicus*, trans. Sarah B. Pomeroy. Oxford: Clarendon Press, 1994.

Xenophon. *Xenophons treatise of Householde*, trans. Gentian Hervet. London: John Allde, 1573.

Secondary Works

Abram, David. *The Spell of the Sensuous: Perception and Language in a More-Than-Human World*. New York: Vintage Books, 1997.

Allan, Mea. *The Tradescants: Their Plants, Gardens and Museum, 1570–1662*. London: Michael Joseph, 1964.

Alter, Robert. *The Art of Biblical Poetry*. New York: Basic Books,1985.

Arndt, William F., and F. Wilbur Gingrich. *Greek-English Lexicon of the New Testament and Other Early Christian Literature* [translated and adapted from the German].

Aune, M. G. "Elephants, Englishmen and India: Early Modern Travel Writing and the Pre-Colonial Movement." *Early Modern Literary Studies* 11.1 (May 2005) 2:1–35. <URL:http://purl.oclc.org/emls/11-1/auneelep.htm>.

Barker, Arthur E. *Milton and the Puritan Dilemma, 1641–1660*. Toronto: University of Toronto Press, 42; rpt. 1971.

Bennett, Joan S. "Virgin Nature in Comus." *Milton Studies* 23 (1987): 21–32.

Blythe, David-Everett. "Milton's Bird Charm." *Milton Quarterly* 30 (1996): 170–71.

Blythe, Joan. "Cain and Abel in 'Paradise Regained': Fratricide, Regicide, and Cultural Equity," in Pruitt and Durham, eds, *Milton's Legacy*. Selingsgrove: Susquehanna University Press, 2005, 70–82.

Boehrer, Bruce. "Milton and the Reasoning of Animals: Variations on a Theme by Plutarch." *Milton Studies* 39 (2000): 50–73.

Brink, Jean R. *Michael Drayton Revisited*. Boston: Twayne Publisher, 1990.

Buell, Lawrence. *Writing for an Endangered World*. Cambridge, Mass., and London: The Belknap Press of Harvard University Press, 2001.

Bynum, Caroline Walker. *Holy Feast and Holy Fast: The Religious Significance of Food to Medieval Women*. Berkeley, Los Angeles, and London: University of California Press, 1987.

Campbell, W. Gardner. "Paradisal Appetite and and Cusan Food in Paradise Lost," in McColgan and Durham, eds, *Arenas of Conflict*, 239–50.

Cassirer, Ernst. *The Platonic Renaissance in England*, trans. James Pettegrove. Edinburgh,1953.

Chambers, Douglas. "'Wild Pastorall Encounter': John Evelyn, John Beale and the Renegotiation of Pastoral in the Mid-Seventeenth Century," in Leslie and Raylor, eds, *Culture and Cultivation*, 173–94.

Cohen, Jeremy. *'Be fertile and increase, fill the earth and master it': The Ancient and Medieval Career of a Biblical Text*. Ithaca: Cornell University Press, 1989.

Cohen, Murray. *Sensible Words: Linguistic Practice in England, 1640–1785*. Baltimore and London: Johns Hopkins University Press, 1977.

Colie, Rosalie L. *"My Ecchoing Song": Andrew Marvell's Poetry of Criticism*. Princeton University Press, 1970.

Creaser, John. "Prosodic Style and Conceptions of Liberty in Milton and Marvell." *Milton Quarterly* 34 (March 2000): 1–13.

Creaser. "Prosody and Liberty in Milton and Marvell," in Graham Parry and Joad

Raymond, eds, *Milton and the Terms of Liberty*. Cambridge, UK: D.S. Brewer, 2002, 37–55.

Cummins, Juliet Lucy. "Milton's Gods and the Matter of Creation," *Milton Studies* 40 (2002): 81–105.

Davies, Stevie. *The Feminine Reclaimed*. Lexington: The University Press of Kentucky, 1986.

Demaray, John G. *Milton and the Masque Tradition: The Early Poems, "Arcades," and Comus*. Cambridge, Mass.: Harvard University Press, 1968.

Dickson, Donald R., and Holly Faith Nelson, eds. *Of Paradise and Light: Essays on Henry Vaughan and John Milton in Honor of Alan Rudrum*. Newark, Delaware: University of Delaware Press, 2004.

Dictionary of National Biography [The]: from the earliest times to 1900. Founded in 1882 by George Smith, eds. Leslie Stephen and Sidney Lee. London: Oxford University Press, 1921–1922.

Dijksterhuis, D.J. *The Mechanization of the World Picture*, trans. C.D. Dikshoorn. Oxford: Clarendon Press, 1961.

Donnelly, Phillip J. "'Matter' versus Body: The Character of Milton's Monism." *Milton Quarterly* 33 (1999): 79–83.

Donno, Elizabeth Story, ed. *Andrew Marvell: The Complete Poems*. Harmondsworth: Penguin Books, 1972; rpt. 1978.

DuRocher, Richard J. "Careful Plowing: Culture and Agriculture in *Paradise Lost*." *Milton Studies* 31 (1994): 91–107.

DuRocher, Richard J. *Milton Among the Romans*. Pittsburgh: Duquesne University Press, 2001.

DuRocher, Richard J. "The Wounded Earth in Paradise Lost." *Studies in Philology* 93 (1996): 93–115.

Edwards, Karen L. *Milton and the Natural World: Science and Poetry in "Paradise Lost."* Cambridge, UK: Cambridge University Press, 1999.

Edwards, Karen L. "Milton's Reformed Animals: An Early Modern Bestiary." *Milton Quarterly*: Introduction, October 2005; Part 1 (Beasts A–C) December 2006; Part 2 (Beasts D–F) May 2006; others forthcoming.

Eisenberg, Evan. *The Ecology of Eden*. New York: Alfred A. Knopf, 1998.

Evans, J. Martin. *Milton's Imperial Epic: Paradise Lost and the Discourse of Colonialism*. Ithaca and London: Cornell University Press, 1996.

Fallon, Stephen M. *Milton among the Philosophers*. Ithaca and London: Cornell University Press, 1991.

Fitter, Christopher. *Poetry, Space, Landscape: Toward a New Theory*. Cambridge, UK:Cambridge University Press, 1995.

Forsyth, Neil. *The Old Enemy: Satan and the Combat Myth*. Princeton University Press, 1987.

Fowler, Alastair. "The Beginnings of English Georgic," in Lewalski, ed., *Renaissance Genres*, 105–25.

Fowler, Alastair. "Country House Poems: The Politics of a Genre," in *The Seventeenth Century*, vol. 1 (1986): 1–14.

Fowler, Alastair. *The Country House Poem: A Cabinet of Seventeenth-Century Estate Poems and Related Items*. Edinburgh: Edinburgh University Press, 1994.

Fowler, Alistair, ed. *The New Oxford Book of Seventeenth Century Verse*. Oxford and New York: Oxford University Press, 1992.

Francaviglia, Richard V. *Hard Places: reading the landscape of America's historic mining districts*. Iowa City: University of Iowa Press, 1991.

Friedman, Donald M. "Andrew Marvell," in Thomas N. Corns, ed., *The Cambridge Companion to English Poetry: Donne to Marvell*. Cambridge, UK: Cambridge University Press, 1993, 275–303.

Friedman, Donald M. "The Lady in the Garden: On the Literary Genetics of Milton's Eve," *Milton Studies* 35 (1997): 114–33.

Furman-Adams, Wendy, and Virginia James Tuft. "Saying it with Flowers: Jane Gerauds Eco-Feminist Paradise Lost, 1848," in Charles W. Durham and Kristin A. Pruitt, eds, *Reassembling Truth: Twenty-First Century Milton* (Susquehanna University Press, 2003).

Furman-Adams, Wendy, and Virginia James Tuft. "'Earth Felt the Wound': Gendering Ecological Consciousness in Nineteenth-Century Illustrations of Paradise Lost." Paper given at the Seventh International Milton Symposium, University of South Carolina, Beaufort, June 2002.

Glacken, Clarence J. *Traces on the Rhodian Shore: Nature and Culture in Western Thought*. Berkeley, Los Angeles, and London: University of California Press, 1967.

Glotfelty, Cheryll, and Harold Fromm, eds. *The Ecocriticism Reader*. Athens, Georgia, and London: The University of Georgia Press, 1996.

Gould, Stephen Jay. *Eight Little Piggies: Reflections in Natural History*. New York and London: W.W. Norton, 1993.

Gould, Stephen Jay. *The Hedgehog, the Fox, and Magister's Pox: Mending the Gap Between Science and the Humanities*. New York: Harmony Books, 2003.

Griffiths, Asheley. "The Instructive Creatures of Appleton House." Paper presented at the convention of the Modern Language Association, Chicago, 1995.

Grove, Richard H. *Green Imperialism: Colonial expansion, Tropical Island Edens, and the Origins of Environmentalism, 1600–1860*. Cambridge, UK: Cambridge University Press, 1995.

Gulden, Ann Torday. "Is Art 'nice'? Art and Artifact at the Outset of Temptation in *Paradise Lost*." *Milton Quarterly* 34 (March 2000): 17–24.

Harrison, Robert Pogue. *Forests: The Shadow of Civilization*. Chicago and London: University of Chicago Press, 1992.

Hart, D. Bentley. "Matter, Monism, and Narrative: An Essay on the Metaphysics of *Paradise Lost*." *Milton Quarterly* 30 (1996), 16–27.

Helgerson, Richard. *Forms of Nationhood: The Elizabethan Writing of England*. University of Chicago Press, 1992.

Herendeen, Wyman H. *From Landscape to Literature: The River and the Myth of Geography*. Pittsburgh: Duquesne University Press, 1986.

Hiltner, Ken. *Milton and Ecology*. Cambridge, UK: Cambridge University Press, 2003.

Hiltner, Ken. "Place, Body, and Spirit Joined: The Earth-Human Wound in Paradise Lost." *Milton Quarterly* 35 (2001): 113–17.

Hiltner, Ken. "The Portrayal of Eve in Paradise Lost: Genius at Work." *Milton Studies* 40 (2001), 61–80.

Hodgkins, Christopher. *Authority, Church, and Society in George Herbert: Return to the Middle Way*. Columbia and London: University of Missouri Press, 1993.

Hodgkins, Christopher. *Reforming Empire: Protestant Colonialism and Conscience in British Literature*. Columbia and London: University of Missouri Press, 2002.

Hoskins, W.G. *The Making of the English Landscape*. London: Book Club Associates, 1955.

Hunt, John Dixon. "Gard'ning Can Speak Proper English," in Leslie and Raylor, eds, *Culture and Cultivation*, 195–222.

Hunt, John Dixon, and Peter Willis, eds. *The Genius of the Place: The English Landscape Garden 1620–1820*. Cambridge, Mass, and London, England: MIT Press, 1988.

Hunter, William B. "The Provenance of the Christian Doctrine," *Studies in English Literature* 32 (1992): 129–42.

Hunter, William B., Barbara Lewalski, and John T. Shawcross. "Forum: Milton's Christian Doctrine." *Studies in English Literature* 32 (1992): 143–66.

Landy, Francis. "The Song of Songs," in Robert Alter and Frank Kermode, eds, *The Literary Guide to the Bible* (Cambridge, Mass.: The Belknap Press of Harvard University Press 1987), 1990: 306 and 319.

Landy, Stephen D. "Mapping the Universe," in *Scientific American*, June 1999.

Leiss, William. *The Domination of Nature*. New York: George Braziller, 1972.

Leonard, John. *Naming in Paradise: Milton and the Language of Adam and Eve*. Oxford: Clarendon Press, 1990.

Leslie, Michael, and Timothy Raylor, eds. *Culture and Cultivation in Early Modern England*. Leicester and London: Leicester University Press, 1992.

Leslie, Michael. "The Spiritual Husbandry of John Beale," in Leslie and Raylor, eds, *Culture and Cultivation*, 15–72.

Lewalski, Barbara Kiefer. *The Life of John Milton: A Critical Biography*. Oxford: Blackwell, 2000.

Lewalski, Barbara Kiefer. "Milton and the Hartlib Circle: Educational Projects and Epic Paideia," in Diana Treviño Benet and Michael Lieb, eds, *Literary Milton: Text, Pretext, Context*. (Pittsburgh: Duquesne University Press, 1994) 202–19.

Lewalski, Barbara Kiefer. *Protestant Poetics and the Seventeenth-Century Religious Lyric*. Princeton: Princeton University Press, 1979.

Lewalski, Barbara Kiefer, ed. *Renaissance Genres: Essays on Theory, History, and Interpretation*. Cambridge, Mass., and London: Harvard University Press, 1986.

Lewis, C.S. *The Discarded Image: An Introduction to Medieval and Renaissance Literature*. Cambridge, UK: Cambridge University Press, 1964.

Liddell, Henry George, Robert Scott, et al. *A Greek-English Lexicon*. Oxford: Clarendon Press ; New York: Oxford University Press, 1996.

Lieb, Michael. "De Doctrina Christiana and the Question of Authorship." *Milton Studies* 41 (2002): 172–230.

Lindenbaum, Peter. *Changing Landscapes: Anti-Pastoral Sentiment in the English Renaissance*. Athens: University of Georgia Press, 1986.

Lindley, Keith. *Fenland Riots and the English Revolution*. London: Heineman, 1982.

Linzey, Andrew. *Animal Theology*. Urbana and Chicago: University of Illinois Press, 1995.

Lovejoy, Arthur O. *The Great Chain of Being*. Cambridge, Mass.: Harvard University Press, 1936.

Low, Anthony. *The Georgic Revolution*. Princeton University Press, 1985.

Martin, Catherine Gimelli. "The Ahistoricism of the New Historicism: Knowledge as Power versus Power as Knowledge in Bacon's New Atlantis," in Claude Summers and Ted-Larry Pebworth, eds, *Faultlines in the Field*. Columbia: University of Missouri Press, 2002.

MacCallum, Hugh. *Milton and the Sons of God: The Divine Image in Milton's Epic Poetry*. Toronto: University of Toronto Press, 1986.

Martin, Catherine Gimelli. "The Enclosed Garden and the Apocalypse: Immanent versus Transcendent Time in Milton and Marvell," in Juliet Cummins, ed., *Milton and the Ends of Time: Essays on the Apocalypse and the Millennium*, Juliet Cummins, ed. (Cambridge, UK: Cambridge University Press, 2002).

Martin, Catherine Gimelli. *The Ruins of Allegory: "Paradise Lost" and the Metamorphosis of the Epic Convention*. Durham: Duke University Press, 1998.

Marcus, Leah. "Justice for Margery Evans: A 'Local' reading of Comus," in Walker, ed., *Milton and the Idea of Woman*, 66–85.

Marjara, Harinder Singh. *Contemplation of Created Things: Science in "Paradise Lost."* Toronto, Buffalo, and London: Cornell University Press, 1996.

McColley, Diane Kelsey. *A Gust for Paradise: Milton's Eden and the Visual Arts*. Urbana: University of Illinois Press, 1993.

McColley, Diane Kelsey. "Milton and Nature: Greener Readings." *Huntington Library Quarterly* 62.3–4 (2001): 423–44.

McColley, Diane Kelsey. *Milton's Eve*. Urbana: University of Illinois Press, 1983.

McColley, Grant, ed. *Literature and Science*. Chicago: Packard, 1940.

McColley, Grant. *Paradise Lost: An Account of its Growth and Major Origins*. Chicago: Packard, 1940.

McColgan, Kristin Pruitt, and Charles W. Durham, eds. *Arenas of Conflict: Milton and the Unfettered Mind*. Selinsgrove: Susquehanna University Press, and London: Associated University Presses, 1997.

McHenry, James Patrick. "A Milton Herbal." *Milton Quarterly* 30.2 (May 1996): 45–115.

McKibben, Bill. *The End of Nature*. New York: Random House, 1989; rpt. Anchor Books, Doubleday, 1990.

McRae, Andrew. "Husbandry Manuals and the Language of Agrarian Improvement," in Leslie and Raylor, eds, *Culture and Cultivation*, 34–62.

Merchant, Carolyn. *Radical Ecology*. New York and London: Routledge, 1992.

Metzger, Bruce M., and Michael D. Coogan, eds. *The Oxford Companion to the Bible*. New York and Oxford: Oxford University Press, 1993.

Murray, David. *Museum : Their History & their Use*. Glasgow: MacLehose, 1904.

Nardo, Anna K. *The Ludic Self in Seventeenth-Century English Literature*. Albany: State University of New York Press, 1991.

Nicholl, Charles. *The Chemical Theatre*. London, Boston, and Henley: Routledge & Kegan Paul, 1980.

Nixon, Scott. "Henry Lawes's Hand in the Bridgewater Collection." *Huntington Library Quarterly* 62 (2001): 233–72.

Norbrook, David. *Writing the English Republic: Poetry, Rhetoric, and Politics, 1627–1660*. Cambridge, UK: Cambridge University Press, 1999.

Norton, Mary Fenton. "'The Rising World of Waters Dark and Deep': Chaos Theory and Paradise Lost." *Milton Studies* 32 (1995): 91–110.

Oxford English Dictionary. 2nd ed. Prepared by J.A. Simpson and E.S.C. Weiner. Oxford: Clarendon Press, 1989.

Oxford English Dictionary on Historical Principles, The New Shorter, ed. Lesley Brown. 2 vols. Oxford: Clarendon Press, 1993.

Parfitt, George. *English Poetry of the Seventeenth Century*. New York: Longman, 1985.

Parry, Graham. *Seventeenth-Century Poetry: The Social Context*. London: Hutchinson, 1985.

Parry, Graham, and Joad Raymond, eds. *Milton and the Terms of Liberty*. Cambridge, UK: D.S. Brewer, 2002.

Patterson, Annabel M., ed. *John Milton*. London and New York: Longman, 1992.

Patterson, Annabel M., ed. *Pastoral and Ideology: Virgil to Valéry*. Berkeley and Los Angeles: University of California Press, 1987.

Post, Jonathan, ed. *Green Thoughts, Green Shades: Contemporary Poets on the Early Modern Lyric*. Berkeley: University of California Press, 2002.

Pruitt, Kristin A. *Gender and the Power of Relationship: "United as one individual Soul" in "Paradise Lost."* Pittsburgh: Duquesne University Press, 2003.

Pruitt, Kristin A., and Charles W. Durham. *Living Texts: Interpreting Milton*. Selinsgrove: Susquehanna University Press, and London: Associated Presses, 2000.

Radzinowicz, Mary Ann. "The Politics of Paradise Lost," in Patterson, ed., *John Milton*.

Rajan, Balachandra, and Elizabeth Sauer, eds. *Milton and the Imperial Vision*. Pittsburgh: Duquesne University Press, 1999.

Raven, Charles E. *John Ray, Naturalist: His Life and Works*. Cambridge, UK: Cambridge University Press, 1942.

Revard, Stella P. *Milton and the Tangles of Neaera's Hair: the Making of the 1645 Poems*. Columbia: University of Missouri Press, 1997.

Robbins, Emmet. "Famous Orpheus," in *Orpheus: The Metamorphosis of a Myth*, ed. John Warden. Toronto: University of Toronto Press, 1982.

Rogers, John. *The Matter of Revolution: Science, Poetry, and Politics in the Age of Milton*. Ithaca and London: Cornell University Press, 1998.

Rudrum, Alan. "An Aspect of Vaughan's Hermeticism: The Doctrine of Cosmic Sympathy." *Studies in English Literature* 14 (1974): 129–38.

Rudrum, Alan. "Ethical Vegetarianism in Seventeenth-Century Britain." *The Seventeenth Century* 18.1 (Spring 2003): 76–92.

Rudrum, Alan. "For then the Earth shall be all Paradise: Milton, Vaughan, and the neo-Calvinists on the Ecology of the Hereafter." *Scintilla* 4 (2000): 39–52.

Rudrum, Alan. *Henry Vaughan for the series Writers of Wales*. University of Wales Press, 1981.

Rudrum, Alan. "Henry Vaughan's 'The Book'; A Hermetic Poem." *Journal of the Australasian Universities Language and Literature Association* 16 (1961): 161–5.

Rudrum, Alan. "Henry Vaughan, the Liberation of the Creatures, and Seventeenth-Century English Calvinism." *The Seventeenth Century* 4 (1989): 33–54.

Rudrum, Alan. "Henry Vaughan and the Theme of Transformation." *Southern Review* (Adelaide) 1 (1963): 54–68.

Rudrum, Alan. "The Influence of Alchemy in the Poems of Henry Vaughan." *Philological Quarterly* 49 (1970): 469–80.

Rudrum, Alan. "The Problem of Sexual Reference in George Herbert's Verse," *GeorgeHerbert Journal* 21.1–2 (Fall 1997/ Spring 1998): 19–32.

Rumrich, John. *Matter of Glory: A New Preface to "Paradise Lost."* Pittsburgh: University of Pittsburgh Press, 1987.

Rumrich. "Milton"s God and the Matter of Chaos," *Publications of the Modern Language Association* 110 (1995): 1035–46.

Ryan, Robert M. *The Romantic Reformation.* Cambridge, UK: Cambridge University Press, 1997.

Sarasohn, Lisa T. "Motion and Morality: Pierre Gassendi, Thomas Hobbes, and the Mechanical World-View." *Journal of the History of Ideas* 46 (1985).

Schwartz, Louis. "'Conscious Terrors' and 'the Promised Seed:' Seventeenth-Century Obstetrics and the Allegory of Sin and Death in *Paradise Lost.*" *Milton Studies* 32, ed. Albert C. Labriola. Pittsburgh: University of Pittsburgh Press, 1995.

Schwartz, Louis. "'Scarce-well-lighted Flame': Milton's 'Epitaph on the Marchioness of Winchester' and the Representation of Maternal Mortality in the Seventeenth-Century Epitaph," in Charles Durham and Kristin Priutt, eds, *'All in All': Unity, Diversity, and the Miltonic Perspective* (Selinsgrove: Susquehanna University Press, 1999).

Schwartz, Regina M. *The Curse of Cain: The Violent Legacy of Monotheism.* Chicago: University of Chicago Press, 1997.

Schwartz, Regina M. *Remembering and Repeating.* Cambridge, UK: Cambridge University Press, 1988.

Sessions, George, ed. *Deep Ecology for the Twenty-First Century.* Boston and London: Shambala, 1995.

Sessions, George. "Ecocentrism and the Anthropocentric Detour," in Sessions, ed., *Deep Ecology*, 156–83.

Shelldrake, Rupert. *The Rebirth of Nature: The Greening of Science and God.* Rochester, Vermont: Park Street Press, 1991, 1994.

Sherry, Beverley. "Speech in Paradise Lost." *Milton Studies* 8 (1975): 47–266.

Shullenberger, William. "Sorting the Seeds," in Wendy Furman, Christopher Gross, and William Schullenberger, eds, *Riven Unities*, *Milton Studies* 28. Pittsburgh: University of Pittsburgh Press, 1992.

Skulsky, Howard. *Milton and the Death of Man: Humanism on Trial in "Paradise Lost."* Newark, Delaware: University of Delaware Press; London: Associated University Presses, 2000.

Steadman, John M. *The Lamb and the Elephant: The Context of Renaissance Allegory.* San Marino: The Huntington Library, 1974.

Steadman, John M. *Milton and the Renaissance Hero.* Oxford: Clarendon Press, 1967.

Stillman, Robert E. *The New Philosophy and Universal Languages in Seventeenth-Century England: Bacon, Hobbes, and Wilkins.* Lewisburgh: Bucknell University Press, 1995.

Tanner, John S. *Anxiety in Eden: A Kierkegaardian Reading of "Paradise Lost."*

New York: Oxford University Press, 1992.

Teskey, Gordon. *Allegory and Violence*. Ithaca and London: Cornell University Press, 1996.

Theis, Jeffrey S. "The Environmental Ethics of Paradise Lost: Milton's Exegesis of Genesis I–III." *Milton Studies* 34 (1996): 61–81.

Theis, Jeffrey S. "Milton's Principles of Architecture," *English Literary Renaissance* 35.1: 102–22.

Theis, Jeffrey S. "'The purlieus of heaven': Milton's Eden as a Pastoral Forest," in Hiltner, ed., *Renaissance Ecology: Imagining Eden in Milton's England*. Forthcoming from Duquesne UP, 2008.

Thirsk, Joan, ed. *The Agrarian History of England and Wales, 1500–1640*. Cambridge, UK: Cambridge University Press, 1967.

Thirsk, Joan. "Enclosing and Engrossing," in Thirsk, ed., *The Agrarian History of England and Wales, 1500–1640*.

Thirsk. "Making a Fresh Start: Sixteenth-Century Agriculture and the Classical Inspiration," in Leslie and Raylor, eds, *Culture and Cultivation*, 27.

Thomas, Keith. *Man and the Natural World*. New York: Pantheon Books, 1983.

Thomas, Peter. "Henry Vaughan, Orpheus, and the Empowerment of Poetry," in Dickson and Nelson, *Of Paradise and Light*, 218–49.

Thrash, Cheryl. "'How cam'st thou speakable of mute . . . ?': Learning Words in Milton's Paradise." *Milton Quarterly* 31 (May1997): 42–61.

Tillyard, E.M.W. *The Elizabethan World Picture*. London: Chatto and Windus, 1943.

Treip, Mindele Anne. *Allegorical Poetics and the Epic: The Renaissance Tradition to Paradise Lost*. Lexington: University Press of Kentucky, 1994.

Waddington, Raymond B. "Blood, Soul, and Mortalism in *Paradise Lost*." *Milton Studies* 41 (2002): 76–93.

Walker, Julia M., ed. *Milton and the Idea of Woman*. University of Illinois Press, 1988.

Watson, Robert N. *Back to Nature: The Green and the Real in the Late Renaissance*. Philadelphia: University of Pennsylvania Press, 2006.

White, Lynn, Jr. "The Historical Roots of Our Ecological Crisis." *Science* 155.3767 (March 1967): 1203–7. Rpt. in Glotfelty and Fromm, eds, *The Ecocriticism Reader*, (Athens and London: University of Georgia Press, 1996), 3–14.

Wilson, E.O. *Consilience: The Unity of Knowledge*. New York: Alfred A. Knopf, 1998.

Index